문제로 **마**스터하는 **중**학 영문법

문마중

LEVEL
1

Believe you can

and you're halfway there.

할 수 있다고 믿으면

반은 이미 이룬 것이다.

- Theodore Roosevelt

Structure & Features

Chapter 내용 미리보기

Chapter에서 배울 주요 문법 내용을 가볍게 짚고 넘어갈 수 있도록 구성했습니다.

자세하게 나뉜 문법 POINT

최신 개정 교육과정을 바탕으로 중학교 필수 문법 항목을 세분화하여 POINT별로 제시했습니다. 단계적 학습으로 큰 문법 항목을 보다 쉽게 이해할 수 있습니다.

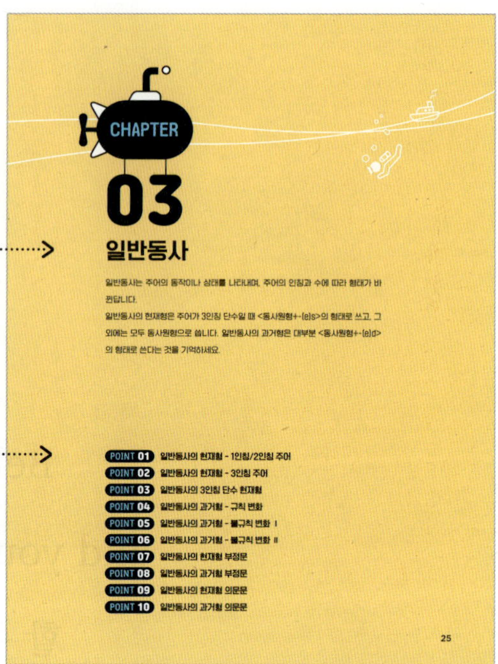

핵심만 담은 문법 설명

필수적으로 알아야 할 문법 사항을 쉽고 명확하게 설명했습니다.

(+ Plus) : POINT에서 제시한 핵심 문법과 관련된 추가 정보를 담았습니다.

내신만점 Tip : 내신 빈출 출제 포인트를 중심으로, 헷갈리기 쉬운 문법 요소나 유사 개념을 비교·대조하여 설명합니다.

다양한 유형의 연습문제

고르기·채우기와 같은 선택형 유형부터, 문장과 단어를 직접 써 보는 쓰기형 유형까지, 다양한 유형을 통해 문법 개념을 확실히 점검할 수 있습니다.

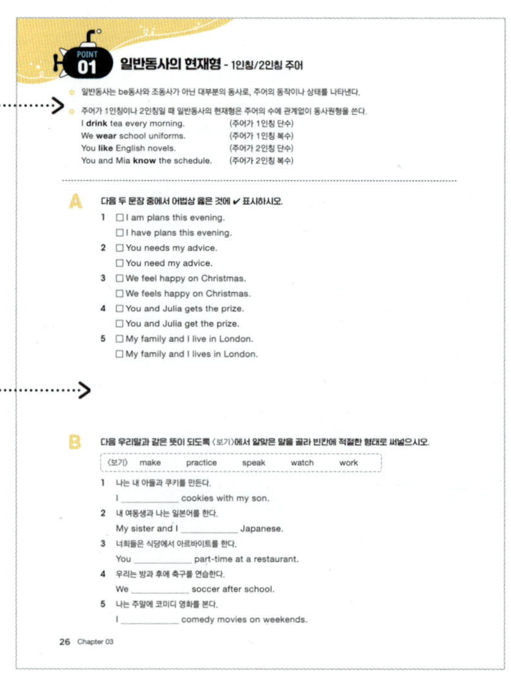

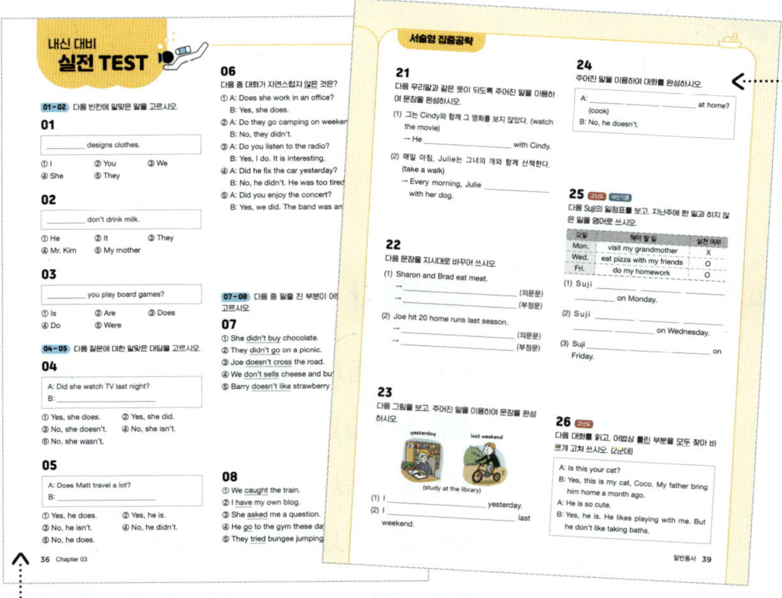

서술형 집중공략

다양한 서술형 문제를 통해 응용력과 문제 해결력을 키우고, 서술형 평가에 효과적으로 대비할 수 있습니다.

내신 대비 실전 TEST

Chapter에서 학습한 내용을 내신 유형의 문제를 통해 종합적으로 확인할 수 있도록 구성했습니다.

고난도 문제와 내신기출 유형으로 실제 학교 시험에 효과적으로 대비할 수 있습니다.

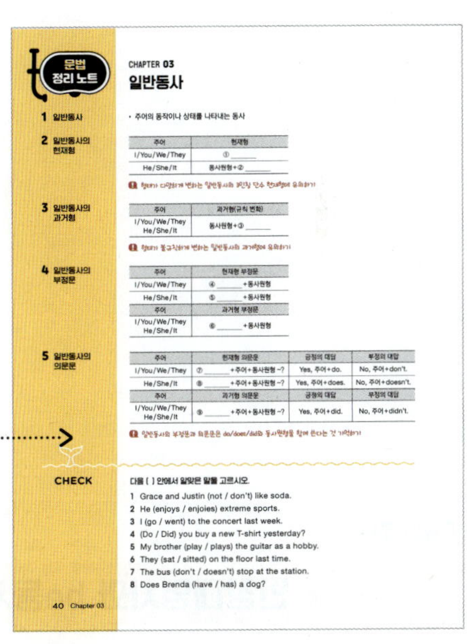

문법 정리 노트

Chapter에서 배운 문법 사항을 스스로 정리하고, CHECK 문제를 통해 최종 점검을 할 수 있습니다.

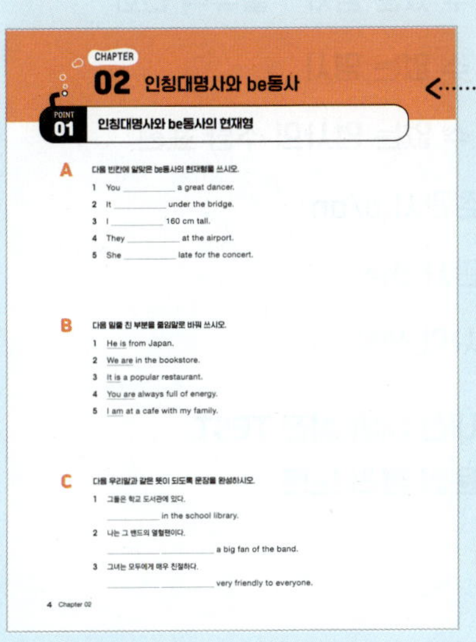

Workbook

다양한 유형으로 구성된 Point별 연습 문제를 풀어보며 각 문법 사항에 대해 충분한 반복 학습을 할 수 있습니다.

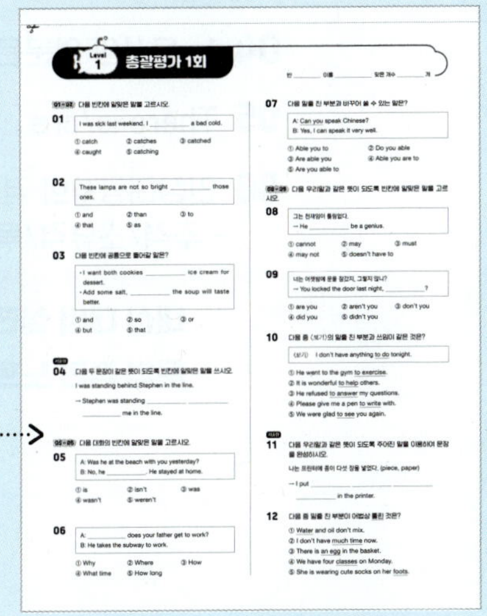

총괄평가

별도 제공된 2회분의 총괄평가를 통해 학습을 총 정리할 수 있습니다.

Contents

01

기초 문법

영어 문장을 만들고 이해하려면 문법의 기본 규칙을 아는 것이 중요합니다. 특히, 단어를 역할과 기능에 따라 분류한 8품사, 문장을 이루는 필수 요소인 문장 성분, 그리고 두 단어 이상의 말이 모여 의미를 나타내는 말 덩어리인 구와 절에 대해 정확히 이해해야 합니다. 이러한 개념을 익히면 문장의 구조를 쉽게 파악할 수 있으며, 문장의 의미를 더 분명하고 정확하게 이해할 수 있습니다. 기초부터 차근차근 익혀봅시다!

POINT 01 영어의 8품사
POINT 02 문장 성분
POINT 03 구와 절

영어의 8품사

○ 품사란 단어를 의미와 기능에 따라 분류한 것이며, 영어에는 8가지의 품사가 있다.

명사	사람, 동물, 사물, 장소, 상태 등의 이름을 나타내는 말 – Emily, cat, computer, school, peace ...
대명사	반복을 피하기 위해 명사를 대신하는 말 – I, you, she, they, this, it, one ...
동사	동작이나 상태를 나타내는 말 – go, eat, have, run, be, happen ...
형용사	형태, 성질, 상태 등을 나타내며, 명사나 대명사를 꾸미는 말 – happy, big, smart, good, many ...
부사	정도, 방법 등을 나타내며, 동사, 형용사, 부사, 문장 전체를 꾸며주는 말 – always, quickly, very, early, now ...
전치사	명사나 대명사 앞에서 시간, 장소, 방향 등을 나타내는 말 – in, on, at, after, for, with ...
접속사	단어와 단어, 구와 구, 절과 절을 연결해주는 말 – and, but, or, because, when ...
감탄사	기쁨, 슬픔, 놀람 등 감정을 나타내는 말 – Wow, Oh, Oops ...

A 다음 단어의 품사가 무엇인지 〈보기〉에서 골라 알맞은 기호를 쓰시오.

> 〈보기〉　ⓐ 명사　ⓑ 대명사　ⓒ 동사　ⓓ 형용사　ⓔ 부사　ⓕ 전치사　ⓖ 접속사　ⓗ 감탄사

1 arrive　→ (　　　) **2** friend　→ (　　　)

3 delicious　→ (　　　) **4** he　→ (　　　)

5 when　→ (　　　) **6** ouch　→ (　　　)

7 luckily　→ (　　　) **8** without　→ (　　　)

B 다음 문장에서 [ ] 안의 품사에 해당하는 단어를 찾아 쓰시오.

1 I have a cute puppy. (명사)　→ _______________

2 The weather is very cold today. (형용사)　→ _______________

3 She answered the question carefully. (부사)　→ _______________

4 We met at the park last week. (전치사)　→ _______________

5 He wanted to go outside, but it was raining. (접속사)　→ _______________

6 They have many interesting stories. (대명사)　→ _______________

7 Oh no! I lost my phone. (감탄사)　→ _______________

8 My family cleans the house every Saturday. (동사)　→ _______________

문장 성분이란 문장을 이루는 구성 요소를 말한다. 문장 속에서 단어나 여러 단어가 맡은 역할에 따라 주어, 동사, 목적어, 보어, 수식어로 나누어진다.

주어	주로 문장 맨 앞에서 동작이나 상태의 주체가 되는 말로, '~은[는/이/가]'로 해석한다. **The sun** shines brightly.
동사	주로 주어 뒤에서 주어의 움직임이나 상태를 나타내는 말로, '~이다, ~하다'로 해석한다. My dad **cooks**.
목적어	동사의 대상이 되는 말로, '~을[를]'로 해석한다. She writes **books**.
보어	주어나 목적어의 의미를 보충 설명하는 말로 '~한, ~하게'로 해석한다. The teacher is **kind**. / She painted the wall **white**.
수식어	문장의 필수 요소는 아니지만, 다른 말을 꾸며 문장에 더 자세한 의미를 더해주는 말이다. He lives **in a small town**.

+Plus 같은 품사라도 문장에서 하는 역할에 따라 다른 문장 성분이 될 수 있다.

This book is **thick**. → 형용사 thick이 주어를 보충 설명하는 보어 역할을 한다.

It is a **thick** book. → 형용사 thick이 명사를 꾸미는 수식어 역할을 한다.

A 다음 밑줄 친 부분의 문장 성분으로 알맞은 것을 〈보기〉에서 골라 기호를 쓰시오.

〈보기〉 ⓐ 주어 ⓑ 동사 ⓒ 목적어 ⓓ 보어 ⓔ 수식어

1 Tom plays soccer <u>every Sunday</u>. (   )

2 She <u>bought</u> a new book. (   )

3 They are <u>happy</u> today. (   )

4 I put <u>my keys</u> on the table. (   )

5 <u>Kate</u> fixes computers. (   )

B 다음 문장을 밑줄 친 부분에 유의하여 우리말로 해석하시오.

1 Steve drinks <u>hot coffee</u>.

→ ____

2 I listened to music and danced <u>at the concert</u>.

→ ____

3 Birds sing <u>very beautifully</u>.

→ ____

4 The test looks <u>difficult</u>.

→ ____

○ 구는 〈주어+동사〉를 포함하지 않는 두 개 이상의 단어 덩어리이다.

We eat dinner **at the table**. (at+the+table)
I go home **after class**. (after+class)
Eating an apple is healthy. (Eating+an+apple)

○ 절은 〈주어+동사〉를 포함하는 여러 단어가 모인 단어 덩어리이다.

Many people think **that you are smart**.
주어 동사

When the bell rings, we sit down.
주어 동사

Please wash the dishes **after you eat**.
주어 동사

+ Plus **절 vs. 문장** 절과 문장 모두 〈주어+동사〉를 포함한다는 점에서 같지만, 절 중에서도 아래의 조건을 갖추어 완전한 의미를 가진 것을 '문장'이라고 한다.

① 문장은 〈주어+동사〉를 포함하며, 의미가 완전해야 한다. ➡ When I go to school. (의미가 완전하지 않음, 문장이 아님)

② 문장의 첫 글자는 대문자로 시작해야 한다. ➡ he is a doctor. (대문자로 시작하지 않음, 문장이 아님)

③ 문장의 끝은 마침표(.), 물음표(?), 느낌표(!) 등 적절한 문장 부호로 끝나야 한다. ➡ Is this your bag (물음표가 없음, 문장이 아님

A 다음 단어 덩어리가 구인지 절인지 고르시오.

1 before sunrise ☐ 구 ☐ 절
2 because he was late ☐ 구 ☐ 절
3 with a big smile ☐ 구 ☐ 절
4 that she passed the test ☐ 구 ☐ 절
5 sitting under the tree ☐ 구 ☐ 절

B 다음 문장의 밑줄 친 부분이 구인지 절인지 쓰시오.

1 I know <u>that she is honest</u>. → ______________
2 We eat a snack <u>when class is over</u>. → ______________
3 My parents waited <u>in front of the school</u>. → ______________
4 She told me <u>how she solved the problem</u>. → ______________
5 <u>The bag on the piano</u> is mine. → ______________
6 He said <u>that he was tired</u>. → ______________
7 I like cake <u>because it is sweet</u>. → ______________
8 They are cheerleaders <u>for our baseball team</u>. → ______________

CHAPTER 01

기초 문법

1 영어의 8품사

명사	사람, 동물, 사물 등의 이름을 나타내는 말
① __________	명사를 대신하는 말
동사	동작이나 상태를 나타내는 말
형용사	명사나 대명사를 꾸미는 말
부사	동사, 형용사, 부사, 문장 전체를 꾸며주는 말
② __________	명사나 대명사 앞에서 시간, 장소, 방향 등을 나타내는 말
접속사	단어, 구, 절, 문장을 각각 연결하는 말
감탄사	감정을 표현하는 말

2 문장 성분

주어	동작이나 상태의 주체가 되는 말로, '~은[는/이/가]'로 해석
③ __________	주어의 움직임이나 상태를 나타내며, '~이다, ~하다'로 해석
목적어	동사의 대상을 나타내며, '~을[를]'로 해석
보어	④ __________ 나 목적어를 보충 설명하며, '~한, ~하게'로 해석
수식어	문장의 필수 요소는 아니지만, 더 자세한 의미를 더해주는 말

3 구와 절

- 구: 〈주어＋동사〉를 포함하지 않는 두 개 이상의 단어 덩어리
- 절: ⑥ 〈__________〉를 포함하는 단어 덩어리

 문장이 되려면 의미가 완전하며, 첫 단어는 대문자로, 문장의 끝은 문장 부호로 끝나야 한다는 것 기억하기

CHECK

설명이 맞으면 ○, 틀리면 X 표시하고 바르게 고치시오.

1 명사는 동작이나 상태를 나타내는 말이다.
2 부사는 동사나 형용사를 수식하여 꾸며주는 말이다.
3 대명사는 명사를 대신하는 말이며, 문장에서 주어로 쓰일 수 있다.
4 문장에서 주어와 동사가 없는 경우도 있다.
5 목적어는 주어를 보충 설명하며, '~을[를]'로 해석한다.
6 He is a doctor.에서 a doctor는 목적어이다.
7 The rabbit runs fast.에서 fast는 부사이며, 동사를 수식하는 역할을 한다.
8 The book on the table is mine.에서 on the table은 수식어 역할을 하는 구이다.

02

인칭대명사와 be동사

인칭대명사는 사람, 동물, 사물을 대신하는 말로, 1인칭(I, we), 2인칭(you), 3인칭 (he, she, it, they)으로 나눌 수 있어요. 인칭대명사는 문장 안에서 어떤 역할을 하는지에 따라 주격, 소유격, 목적격으로 쓰인답니다.

be동사는 우리말 '~이다', '(~에) 있다'에 해당하는 동사입니다. be동사는 주어에 따라 am, are, is로, 또 과거의 일을 나타낼 때는 was, were로 형태가 바뀐답니다.

POINT 01 인칭대명사와 be동사의 현재형

- 인칭대명사는 사람, 동물, 사물을 대신하는 말이다.
  Emma is a middle school student. **She** is smart.
- be동사는 주어 뒤에 쓰여 '~이다', '(~에) 있다'라는 뜻을 나타낸다.
- be동사의 현재형은 주어에 따라 형태가 달라지며, 〈인칭대명사＋be동사〉는 줄여서 쓸 수 있다.

<table>
<tr><td rowspan="5">단수</td><td colspan="2">인칭대명사</td><td>be동사의
현재형</td><td>줄임말</td></tr>
<tr><td>1인칭</td><td>I</td><td>am</td><td>I'm</td></tr>
<tr><td>2인칭</td><td>You</td><td>are</td><td>You're</td></tr>
<tr><td rowspan="3">3인칭</td><td>He</td><td rowspan="3">is</td><td>He's</td></tr>
<tr><td>She</td><td>She's</td></tr>
<tr><td>It</td><td>It's</td></tr>
</table>

<table>
<tr><td rowspan="4">복수</td><td colspan="2">인칭대명사</td><td>be동사의
현재형</td><td>줄임말</td></tr>
<tr><td>1인칭</td><td>We</td><td rowspan="3">are</td><td>We're</td></tr>
<tr><td>2인칭</td><td>You</td><td>You're</td></tr>
<tr><td>3인칭</td><td>They</td><td>They're</td></tr>
</table>

It is[It's] a beautiful flower.　　　**We are[We're]** in the kitchen.

＋Plus 줄임말에 사용하는 문장 부호 '는 아포스트로피(apostrophe)라고 한다.

A 다음 빈칸에 알맞은 be동사의 현재형을 쓰시오.

1 We ＿＿＿＿＿＿ at the library.

2 He ＿＿＿＿＿＿ in Tokyo.

3 You ＿＿＿＿＿＿ a great cook.

4 I ＿＿＿＿＿＿ from Korea.

5 Jake and Maggie are my friends. They ＿＿＿＿＿＿ kind.

B 다음 밑줄 친 부분을 줄임말로 바꿔 쓰시오.

1 <u>She is</u> a new teacher.

2 <u>It is</u> next to the bakery.

3 <u>They are</u> always busy.

4 <u>I am</u> a guitarist in the school band.

5 <u>You are</u> in a gallery. Please be quiet.

C 다음 우리말과 같은 뜻이 되도록 문장을 완성하시오.

1 그것은 매우 좋은 영화이다.

　　＿＿＿＿＿＿ a very good movie.

2 너는 수학에 재능이 있다.

　　＿＿＿＿＿＿ ＿＿＿＿＿＿ talented in math.

3 나는 조부모님 댁에 있다.

　　＿＿＿＿＿＿ ＿＿＿＿＿＿ at my grandparents' house.

be동사의 과거형

○ be동사의 과거형은 '~이었다', '(~에) 있었다'라는 뜻으로 과거의 일을 나타낸다.

	be동사의 현재형	be동사의 과거형
단수	I am	I **was**
	You are	You **were**
	He is	He **was**
	She is	She **was**
	It is	It **was**

	be동사의 현재형	be동사의 과거형
복수	We are	We **were**
	You are	You **were**
	They are	They **were**

I **was** twelve years old last year.　　　They **were** in Busan yesterday.

A　다음 빈칸에 알맞은 be동사의 과거형을 쓰시오.

1　I ＿＿＿＿＿＿＿ tired yesterday.

2　It ＿＿＿＿＿＿＿ a difficult test.

3　We ＿＿＿＿＿＿＿ happy with the gift.

4　They ＿＿＿＿＿＿＿ at the movie theater last night.

5　The singer ＿＿＿＿＿＿＿ popular all around the world.

B　다음 [ ] 안에서 알맞은 말을 고르시오.

1　My parents (are / were) home now.

2　You (are / were) great in the concert yesterday.

3　Nancy (is / was) my classmate last year.

4　He (is / was) in Hong Kong right now.

5　They (are / were) elementary school students three years ago.

C　다음 우리말과 같은 뜻이 되도록 문장을 완성하시오.

1　그것은 큰 실수였다.

　　It ＿＿＿＿＿＿＿ a big mistake.

2　Jennie는 지금 체육관에 있다.

　　Jennie ＿＿＿＿＿＿＿ at the gym now.

3　그 학생들은 매우 용감했다.

　　The students ＿＿＿＿＿＿＿ very brave.

4　우리는 작년에 운이 좋았다.

　　＿＿＿＿＿＿＿ ＿＿＿＿＿＿＿ lucky last year.

5　그는 오늘 아침 시청 앞에 있었다.

　　＿＿＿＿＿＿＿ ＿＿＿＿＿＿＿ in front of City Hall this morning.

be동사의 부정문

- be동사 뒤에 not을 써서 '~가 아니다', '(~에) 있지 않다'라는 뜻을 나타낸다.

주어		be동사+not	줄임말	
단수	I	**am not**	**I'm not**	
	You	**are not**	You**'re not**	You **aren't**
	He		He**'s not**	He **isn't**
	She	**is not**	She**'s not**	She **isn't**
	It		It**'s not**	It **isn't**
복수	We		We**'re not**	We **aren't**
	You	**are not**	You**'re not**	You **aren't**
	They		They**'re not**	They **aren't**

I **am not** a child.　　　　　　　They **aren't** in the pool.

> (+Plus) be동사 과거형의 부정문은 was not[wasn't] 또는 were not[weren't]을 쓴다.
> She **was not[wasn't]** thirsty. / We **were not[weren't]** at the library.

A　다음 [ ] 안에서 알맞은 말을 고르시오.

1　He (not is / is not) an actor.

2　You (isn't / aren't) alone.

3　It (wasn't / weren't) my fault.

4　Kate and I (am not / are not) in the same class.

B　다음 밑줄 친 부분을 줄임말로 바꿔 쓰시오.

1　I am not a baseball player.

2　They were not in New York last month.

3　We are not busy now.

4　She is not thirteen years old.

C　다음 문장을 부정문으로 바꿀 때, 빈칸에 알맞은 말을 쓰시오.

1　I am good at math.

→ ___________ ___________ ___________ good at math.

2　Mark was there at that time.

→ ___________ ___________ ___________ there at that time.

3　Some people are afraid of ghosts.

→ ___________ ___________ ___________ afraid of ghosts.

4　My mother is in the office.

→ ___________ ___________ ___________ ___________ in the office.

be동사의 의문문

○ be동사를 주어 앞에 써서 '~입니까?', '(~에) 있습니까?'라는 뜻을 나타낸다.

	be동사+주어 ~?	긍정의 대답	부정의 대답
단수	**Am** I ~?	Yes, you are.	No, you aren't[you're not].
	Are you ~?	Yes, I am.	No, I'm not.
	Is he ~?	Yes, he is.	No, he isn't[he's not].
	Is she ~?	Yes, she is.	No, she isn't[she's not].
	Is it ~?	Yes, it is.	No, it isn't[it's not].
복수	**Are** we ~?	Yes, we / you are.	No, we / you aren't[you're not].
	Are you ~?	Yes, we are.	No, we aren't[we're not].
	Are they ~?	Yes, they are.	No, they aren't[they're not].

A: **Are** you free this evening? – B: Yes, I am. / No, I'm not.

A 다음 우리말과 같은 뜻이 되도록 문장을 완성하시오.

1 우리는 여기에서 안전한가요?

_______________ _______________ safe here?

2 그것은 당신이 가장 좋아하는 노래인가요?

_______________ _______________ your favorite song?

3 그녀는 어제 병원에 있었나요?

_______________ _______________ in the hospital yesterday?

4 너는 작년에 독서 동아리에 있었어?

_______________ _______________ in the book club last year?

5 그들이 우리 팀의 치어리더들인가요?

_______________ _______________ cheerleaders for our team?

B 다음 빈칸에 알맞은 말을 넣어 대화를 완성하시오.

1 A: _______________ _______________ a student at this school?

B: No, I'm not.

2 A: Is the museum open today?

B: Yes, _______________ _______________.

3 A: _______________ _______________ ready for the show?

B: No, he wasn't.

4 A: Were you and your friend at the supermarket yesterday?

B: Yes, _______________ _______________.

There is/are ~

- 〈There is/are ~〉는 '~가 있다'라는 뜻을 나타내며, 이때 There는 '거기에'로 해석하지 않는다.

- 〈There is＋단수명사〉, 〈There are＋복수명사〉의 형태로 쓴다.
  There is an apple in the basket. / **There are apples** in the basket.

- 부정문은 〈There is/are＋not ~〉, 의문문은 〈Is/Are there ~?〉의 형태로 쓴다.
  There is not[isn't] a cat in the room.
  A: **Is there** a ball in the box? - B: Yes, there is. / No, there isn't.

- 과거형은 〈There was/were ~〉의 형태로 쓴다.
  There was a pencil on the desk. / **There were** lions at the zoo.

> **내신만점 Tip** 〈There is/are ~〉 구문에서는 be동사 뒤에 오는 명사를 주어로 본다는 것을 기억하자.
> **There is** *a cat* on the sofa. 소파 위에 한 마리의 고양이가 있다.

A 다음 [ ] 안에서 알맞은 말을 고르시오.

1   There (is / are) famous singers on the stage.

2   There (was / were) an old tree in the park.

3   (There were not / There not were) any caps in the shop.

4   A: (Is / Are) there a computer in the room? – B: Yes, (there is / is there).

B 다음 문장을 지시대로 바꿀 때, 빈칸에 알맞은 말을 쓰시오.

1   There is a car on the street. (부정문)
    → ________________ ________________ a car in the street.

2   There is a big sports event. (과거형)
    → ________________ ________________ a big sports event.

3   There are hamburgers on the table. (의문문)
    → ________________ ________________ ________________ on the table?

C 다음 우리말과 같은 뜻이 되도록 [ ] 안의 말을 알맞게 배열하여 문장을 완성하시오.

1   그녀의 지갑에는 동전이 하나도 없다. (in her purse, there, any coins, aren't)
    ____

2   이 근처에 식당이 있나요? (there, near here, is, a restaurant)
    ____

3   지붕 위에 두 마리의 새가 있었다. (two birds, were, on the roof, there)
    ____

POINT 06 인칭대명사의 격 – 주격/소유격/목적격/소유대명사

- 주격은 문장에서 주어 역할을 하는 말로 '~은[는/이/가]'라는 뜻이다.
- 소유격은 명사 앞에 쓰여 소유 관계를 나타내는 말로 '~의'라는 뜻이다.
- 목적격은 문장에서 목적어 역할을 하는 말로 '~을[를]'이라는 뜻이다.
- 소유대명사는 '~의 것'이라는 뜻으로 〈소유격＋명사〉를 대신한다.

	주격	소유격	목적격	소유대명사
단수	I	my	me	mine
	you	your	you	yours
	he	his	him	his
	she	her	her	hers
	it	its	it	–

	주격	소유격	목적격	소유대명사
복수	we	our	us	ours
	you	your	you	yours
	they	their	them	theirs

You are a nice person.
Eric calls **me** every day.

Their products are special.
The round tent is **ours**.

+Plus 사람의 이름을 나타내는 고유명사의 소유격과 소유대명사는 명사에 's를 붙여서 쓴다.
Tom - Tom**'s** (Tom의, Tom의 것) / Betty - Betty**'s** (Betty의, Betty의 것)

A 다음 밑줄 친 부분을 어법에 맞게 고쳐 쓰시오.

1 I love he hair style.

2 Its is Hanna's notebook.

3 Green is I favorite color.

4 They visit she every weekend.

5 We photos are always fantastic.

6 Please take his to the hospital.

7 The bookcases are them.

B 다음 우리말과 같은 뜻이 되도록 문장을 완성하시오.

1 그들의 부모님은 우리에게 매우 친절하시다.

_____________ parents are very kind to _____________.

2 내 전화기는 검은색이고, 그녀의 것은 흰색이다.

_____________ phone is black, and _____________ is white.

3 그는 Laura의 이메일 주소를 안다.

_____________ knows _____________ email address.

4 이 장화들은 나의 것이다. 나는 그것들을 좋아한다.

These rain boots are _____________. I like _____________.

5 이 케이크는 너를 위한 것이다. 그것은 너의 것이다.

This cake is for _____________. It is _____________.

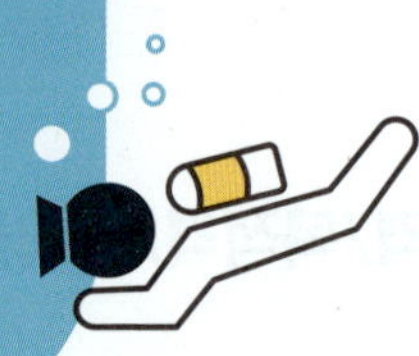

01 - 02 다음 빈칸에 알맞은 말을 고르시오.

01

Nora and Kevin __________ at school now.

① am　　　② are　　　③ is

④ was　　　⑤ were

02

__________ she in France last year?

① Am　　　② Are　　　③ Is

④ Was　　　⑤ Were

03　내신기출

다음 중 밑줄 친 부분의 의미가 나머지와 <u>다른</u> 것은?

① Jane <u>is</u> my cousin.

② We <u>are</u> best friends.

③ The box <u>is</u> very heavy.

④ They <u>are</u> good dancers.

⑤ My parents <u>are</u> in the living room.

04 - 05 다음 질문에 대한 알맞은 대답을 고르시오.

04

A: Are you and your sister twins?
B: __________________________

① Yes, she is.　　　② Yes, you are.

③ Yes, we are.　　　④ No, you aren't.

⑤ No, they aren't.

05

A: Is there a bus stop near your house?
B: __________________________

① Yes, there are.　　　② Yes, there was.

③ No, there isn't.　　　④ No, there wasn't.

⑤ No, it isn't.

06 - 08 다음 빈칸에 알맞은 말이 바르게 짝지어진 것을 고르시오.

06

A: Is that boy your son?
B: No, __________ is not. __________ son is
　　not here.

① she – My　　　② he – Your

③ she – His　　　④ he – My

⑤ she – Her

07

A: Is it Peter's smartphone?
B: No, it __________. It's not __________.

① is – hers　　　② are – yours

③ isn't – his　　　④ aren't – his

⑤ isn't – theirs

08

There __________ cookies on the table. They
are for __________.

① are – you　　　② are – your

③ is – yours　　　④ was – you

⑤ were – your

09

다음 중 대화가 자연스럽지 <u>않은</u> 것은?

① A: Am I right?
  B: Yes, you are.
② A: Are you his fans?
  B: Yes, we are.
③ A: Is Anna free today?
  B: No, she isn't.
④ A: Are they your classmates?
  B: Yes, they are.
⑤ A: Is Mr. Andrew in the teachers' room?
  B: Yes, he was.

10-11 다음 우리말을 영어로 바르게 옮긴 것을 고르시오.

10

그 가방들은 우리의 것이 아니었다.

① The bags were not us.
② The bags not were our.
③ The bags was not yours.
④ The bags were not ours.
⑤ The bags were not yours.

11

그녀의 정원에는 소나무 한 그루가 있다.

① There are a pine tree in her garden.
② There is a pine tree in her garden.
③ There is a pine tree in his garden.
④ There is a pine tree in our garden.
⑤ There are a pine tree in hers garden.

12-13 다음 중 어법상 <u>틀린</u> 것을 고르시오.

12

① They weren't from Taiwan.
② Lincoln wasn't a musician.
③ She wasn't absent from school.
④ You wasn't at the museum.
⑤ We weren't busy at that time.

13

① The baseball glove is Harry's.
② The books on the desk are their.
③ Were you in Italy last year?
④ Is the girl a new student?
⑤ Your birthday present is in my bag.

내신기출

14-15 다음 중 밑줄 친 부분의 쓰임이 나머지와 <u>다른</u> 것을 고르시오.

14

① I meet <u>her</u> every day.
② Ms. Kim loves <u>her</u> job.
③ We know <u>her</u> very well.
④ George misses <u>her</u> a lot.
⑤ He took <u>her</u> to the hospital.

15

① <u>His</u> favorite subject is English.
② John is worried about <u>his</u> future.
③ Cooking is one of <u>his</u> hobbies.
④ The socks under the chair are <u>his</u>.
⑤ He is happy with <u>his</u> new shoes.

16

다음 빈칸에 공통으로 들어갈 말은?

> • A: ___________ Ms. Jones?
> B: Yes, I am.
> • A: ___________ ready to go?
> B: No, we aren't. Please wait.

① Am I
② Are you
③ Is she
④ Are we
⑤ Are they

17

다음 중 빈칸에 들어갈 말이 나머지와 <u>다른</u> 것은?

① ___________ it your guitar?
② The story ___________ not funny.
③ ___________ there clouds in the sky?
④ Jack ___________ not a firefighter.
⑤ There ___________ a dog in the yard.

18

다음 중 문장을 지시대로 바르게 바꾸지 <u>않은</u> 것은?

① I'm nervous about the interview. (과거형)
　→ I was nervous about the interview.
② The classrooms were large. (부정문)
　→ The classrooms not were large.
③ There was a concert at the stadium. (현재형)
　→ There is a concert at the stadium.
④ She is their science teacher this year. (의문문)
　→ Is she their science teacher this year?
⑤ They are interested in the event. (부정문)
　→ They aren't interested in the event.

19

[A], [B], [C]의 괄호 안에서 알맞은 것끼리 바르게 짝지어진 것은?

> (A) [Was / Were] you late for the movie?
> (B) Mr. Kim helps [their / them] all the time.
> (C) Jason and his brother [is / are] at the park now.

	(A)	(B)	(C)
①	Was	their	is
②	Was	them	are
③	Were	them	is
④	Were	them	are
⑤	Were	their	is

20

다음 중 어법상 옳은 것끼리 짝지어진 것은?

> (a) You aren't rude at all.
> (b) The hairpins are hers.
> (c) Dan and I am good friends.
> (d) Was he popular in yours country?
> (e) Were you sad about the news?

① (a), (b), (c)
② (a), (b), (e)
③ (b), (c), (e)
④ (b), (d), (e)
⑤ (c), (d), (e)

21

주어진 말을 문맥에 맞게 알맞은 형태로 바꾸어 쓰시오.

(1) There ___________(be) many animals in the zoo. I like ___________(they) all.

(2) The letters in the box are not ___________ (she). They are ___________(Teddy).

22

다음 우리말과 같은 뜻이 되도록 문장을 완성하시오.

(1) 그는 어제 퇴근 후에 피곤하지 않았다.
___________ ___________ ___________ tired after work yesterday.

(2) 나는 고양이가 한 마리 있다. 그것은 내 방에 있다. 그것의 털은 흰색이다.
I have a cat. ___________ ___________ in my room. ___________ fur is white.

23

어법상 <u>틀린</u> 부분을 찾아 바르게 고쳐 문장을 다시 쓰시오.

(1) Was Julie and David in the same class?
(1군데)
→ ___________________________________

(2) There are a jacket on the bench. It is me.
(2군데)
→ ___________________________________

24

다음 그림을 보고, 대화를 완성하시오.

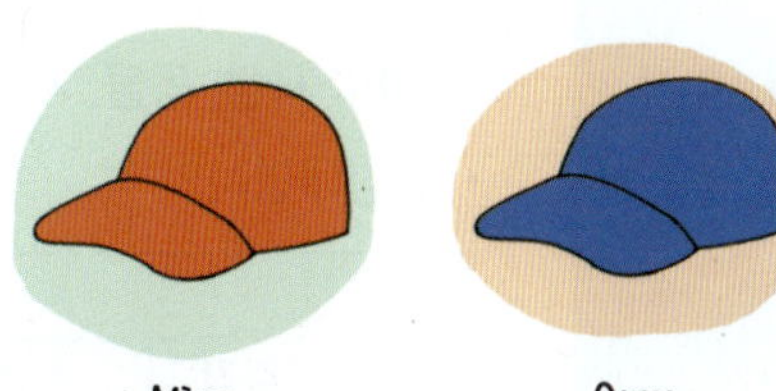

Sam: Is this red cap ___________?
Amy: No, it ___________. ___________ is blue.

25 내신기출

다음 표를 보고, 빈칸에 알맞은 말을 쓰시오.

Name	Age	Nationality	Nickname
Nick	14	Canada	Little Einstein
Junho	13	Korea	Sports Boy
Alice	13	England	Lucky

(1) Nick ___________ 14 years old. ___________ nickname is Little Einstein.

(2) Junho and Alice ___________ the same age. ___________ ___________ 13 years old.

(3) Junho: ___________ you from Canada?
Alice: No, ___________ ___________.
___________ from England.

26 고난도 내신기출

다음 〈조건〉과 주어진 말을 이용하여 우리말을 영어로 옮겨 쓰시오.

〈조건〉 1. be동사를 이용할 것
2. 적절한 인칭대명사를 이용할 것

(1) 그 담요는 그의 것이 아니다. (the blanket)
____

(2) 당신의 아들은 축구 선수였나요? (son, a soccer player)
____

CHAPTER 02

인칭대명사와 be동사

1 인칭대명사

- 의미: 사람, 동물, 사물을 대신하는 말
- 인칭대명사의 격

	단수				복수			
	주격	소유격	목적격	소유대명사	주격	소유격	목적격	소유대명사
1인칭	I	my	me	① ______	we	our	⑤ ______	ours
2인칭	you	your	you	② ______	you	your	you	yours
3인칭	he	③ ______	him	his	they	their	them	⑥ ______
	she	her	④ ______	hers				
	it	its	it	–				

! 인칭과 역할에 따라 달라지는 인칭대명사의 형태 익히기

2 be동사

- 의미: '~이다', '(~에) 있다'
- be동사의 현재형과 과거형

	주어	현재형	과거형		주어	현재형	과거형
단수	I	am	was	복수	We		
	You	are	were		You	are	⑧ ______
	He/She/It	is	⑦ ______		They		

- be동사의 부정문: 〈주어+⑨ ____________ + ____________ ~〉 '~가 아니다', '(~에) 있지 않다'
- be동사의 의문문: 〈be동사+주어 ~?〉 '~입니까?', '(~에) 있습니까?'
! be동사의 형태는 주어의 수와 시제에 따라 달라진다는 것 기억하기

3 There is/are ~

- 의미: '~가 있다'
- 형태: 〈There is/was+단수명사〉 / 〈There are/were+복수명사〉
- 부정문: 〈There is/are+not ~〉
- 의문문: 〈⑩ ______________ ~?〉

CHECK

밑줄 친 부분이 어법상 맞으면 ○, 틀리면 X 표시하고 바르게 고치시오.

1 I like milk. <u>It's</u> tasty.
2 A: <u>Am</u> he your neighbor? – B: No, he isn't.
3 <u>We not are</u> high school students.
4 This is an old piano. I like <u>it</u>.
5 A: Are Cindy and Ellie American? - B: Yes, <u>she is</u>.
6 <u>There is</u> a tall building in our town.

CHAPTER 03

일반동사

일반동사는 주어의 동작이나 상태를 나타내며, 주어의 인칭과 수에 따라 형태가 바뀐답니다.

일반동사의 현재형은 주어가 3인칭 단수일 때 <동사원형+-(e)s>의 형태로 쓰고, 그 외에는 모두 동사원형으로 씁니다. 일반동사의 과거형은 대부분 <동사원형+-(e)d>의 형태로 쓴다는 것을 기억하세요.

POINT 01 일반동사의 현재형 - 1인칭/2인칭 주어

- 일반동사는 be동사와 조동사가 아닌 대부분의 동사로, 주어의 동작이나 상태를 나타낸다.

- 주어가 1인칭이나 2인칭일 때 일반동사의 현재형은 주어의 수에 관계없이 동사원형을 쓴다.

I **drink** tea every morning.	(주어가 1인칭 단수)
We **wear** school uniforms.	(주어가 1인칭 복수)
You **like** English novels.	(주어가 2인칭 단수)
You and Mia **know** the schedule.	(주어가 2인칭 복수)

A 다음 두 문장 중에서 어법상 옳은 것에 ✔ 표시하시오.

1 ☐ I am plans this evening.
☐ I have plans this evening.

2 ☐ You needs my advice.
☐ You need my advice.

3 ☐ We feel happy on Christmas.
☐ We feels happy on Christmas.

4 ☐ You and Julia gets the prize.
☐ You and Julia get the prize.

5 ☐ My family and I live in London.
☐ My family and I lives in London.

B 다음 우리말과 같은 뜻이 되도록 〈보기〉에서 알맞은 말을 골라 빈칸에 적절한 형태로 써넣으시오.

〈보기〉	make	practice	speak	watch	work

1 나는 내 아들과 쿠키를 만든다.

I ______________ cookies with my son.

2 내 여동생과 나는 일본어를 한다.

My sister and I ______________ Japanese.

3 너희들은 식당에서 아르바이트를 한다.

You ______________ part-time at a restaurant.

4 우리는 방과 후에 축구를 연습한다.

We ______________ soccer after school.

5 나는 주말에 코미디 영화를 본다.

I ______________ comedy movies on weekends.

일반동사의 현재형 - 3인칭 주어

○ 주어가 3인칭 단수일 때 일반동사의 현재형은 보통 〈동사원형＋-s〉의 형태로 쓴다.

He **dances** well.　　　　　(dance＋s)
She **works** in a hospital.　　(work＋s)
It **grows** fast.　　　　　　(grow＋s)

○ 주어가 3인칭 복수일 때 일반동사의 현재형은 동사원형을 쓴다.

They **eat** cereal with milk.
My brothers **play** tennis every day.

A 다음 밑줄 친 부분이 어법상 맞으면 O, 틀리면 X 표시하고 바르게 고치시오. (단, 현재형으로 쓸 것)

1 My cat <u>eat</u> too much.

2 She <u>likes</u> K-pop music.

3 My friends <u>calls</u> me "Dr. No."

4 Kate <u>know</u> a lot of funny stories.

5 They <u>walk</u> to school every morning.

6 Mr. Johnson <u>works</u> late every Thursday.

7 His parents <u>gets</u> up at five o'clock in the morning.

B 다음 우리말과 같은 뜻이 되도록 [ ] 안의 말을 이용하여 문장을 완성하시오.

1 그는 오늘 슬퍼 보인다. (look)

He ＿＿＿＿＿＿ sad today.

2 이 수업은 오후 2시 30분에 시작한다. (begin)

This class ＿＿＿＿＿＿ at 2:30 p.m.

3 그 아이들은 초콜릿을 원한다. (want)

The kids ＿＿＿＿＿＿ some chocolate.

4 그 카페는 밤 11시에 문을 닫는다. (close)

The cafe ＿＿＿＿＿＿ at 11:00 p.m.

5 Benny와 June은 일요일마다 자전거를 탄다. (ride)

Benny and June ＿＿＿＿＿＿ bicycles on Sundays.

6 Olivia는 매년 나에게 카드를 보낸다. (send)

Olivia ＿＿＿＿＿＿ a card to me every year.

7 그들은 한 달에 한 번 등산한다. (climb)

They ＿＿＿＿＿＿ a mountain once a month.

일반동사의 3인칭 단수 현재형

 주어가 3인칭 단수일 때 일반동사의 현재형은 대부분 〈동사원형+-s〉의 형태로 쓰지만, 불규칙하게 변하는 동사도 있다.

대부분의 동사	동사원형+-s	eat**s**, meet**s**, buy**s**, like**s**, read**s**, want**s**
〈-o, -s, -ch, -sh, -x〉로 끝나는 동사	동사원형+-es	goe**s**, pass**es**, watch**es**, wash**es**, fix**es**
〈자음+y〉로 끝나는 동사	y를 i로 바꾸고+-es	cry → cr**ies**, study → stud**ies**, try → tr**ies**
불규칙하게 변하는 동사		have → **has**

He **wants** a new jacket.   She **watches** baseball every evening.
My sister **studies** at the library.   The computer **has** a large screen.

A 다음 밑줄 친 부분을 어법에 맞게 고쳐 쓰시오. [단, 현재형으로 쓸 것]

1 Time <u>fly</u>.

2 Ms. Miller <u>teach</u> math.

3 James <u>have</u> a guitar.

4 She <u>enjoy</u> a challenge.

5 The child <u>cry</u> a lot.

6 Monica <u>use</u> honey instead of sugar.

7 He <u>play</u> badminton once a week.

8 The student <u>do</u> his homework at night.

9 Ross <u>wash</u> the dishes after meals.

10 My mother <u>read</u> magazines in the morning.

B 다음 우리말과 같은 뜻이 되도록 〈보기〉에서 알맞은 말을 골라 빈칸에 적절한 형태로 써넣으시오.

〈보기〉	brush	envy	fix	go	make

1 그녀는 매주 일요일 교회에 간다.

   She ＿＿＿＿＿＿ to church on Sundays.

2 그는 잠자기 전에 머리를 빗는다.

   He ＿＿＿＿＿＿ his hair before bed.

3 Smith 씨는 그 가게에서 차를 수리한다.

   Mr. Smith ＿＿＿＿＿＿ cars at the shop.

4 Sophia는 그녀의 제일 친한 친구를 부러워한다.

   Sophia ＿＿＿＿＿＿ her best friend.

5 할머니는 우리에게 애플파이를 자주 만들어 주신다.

   My grandmother often ＿＿＿＿＿＿ apple pies for us.

일반동사의 과거형 - 규칙 변화

○ 일반동사의 과거형은 주어의 인칭과 수에 관계없이 보통 〈동사원형＋-(e)d〉의 형태로 쓴다.

대부분의 동사	동사원형＋-ed	work**ed**, visit**ed**, learn**ed**, show**ed**
〈자음＋e〉로 끝나는 동사	동사원형＋-d	live**d**, like**d**, move**d**, love**d**
〈자음＋y〉로 끝나는 동사	y를 i로 바꾸고＋-ed	cry → cr**ied**, study → stud**ied**, try → tr**ied**
〈단모음＋단자음〉으로 끝나는 동사	자음을 한 번 더 쓰고＋-ed	stop → stop**ped**, drop → drop**ped**, plan → plan**ned**

I **worked** at a bank last year.
The baby **cried** all night.

They **lived** in Italy in 2020.
We **planned** the event together.

A 다음 밑줄 친 부분을 어법에 맞게 고쳐 쓰시오.

1 It <u>snow</u> here yesterday.

2 We <u>study</u> very hard last week.

3 I <u>open</u> a coffee shop last month.

4 A police officer <u>stop</u> me last night.

5 You <u>ask</u> her a lot of questions last time.

6 My best friend <u>move</u> to Jeju two years ago.

7 They <u>visit</u> their grandparents last winter.

B 다음 우리말과 같은 뜻이 되도록 [ ] 안의 말을 이용하여 문장을 완성하시오.

1 그는 유리잔을 떨어뜨렸다. (drop)

He ______________ the glass.

2 그녀는 자신의 친구들을 믿었다. (trust)

She ______________ her friends.

3 우리는 어제 서울에 도착했다. (arrive)

We ______________ in Seoul yesterday.

4 나는 온종일 그 호텔에 머물렀다. (stay)

I ______________ at the hotel all day long.

5 그들은 인도로의 여행을 계획했다. (plan)

They ______________ a trip to India.

6 Janet은 그 시험에서 최선을 다했다. (try)

Janet ______________ her best on the test.

7 Ben은 그의 그림들을 나에게 보여 주었다. (show)

Ben ______________ his drawings to me.

일반동사의 과거형 - 불규칙 변화 I

○ 일반동사의 과거형이 -(e)d가 붙지 않고, 형태가 불규칙하게 변하는 동사가 있다.

go → **went**	eat → **ate**	find → **found**	see → **saw**
sit → **sat**	do → **did**	give → **gave**	feel → **felt**
get → **got**	come → **came**	have → **had**	hear → **heard**
lose → **lost**	make → **made**	meet → **met**	build → **built**
say → **said**	pay → **paid**	send → **sent**	leave → **left**
tell → **told**	take → **took**	write → **wrote**	know → **knew**
think → **thought**	catch → **caught**	buy → **bought**	bring → **brought**

I **got** up late yesterday.　　　　　　　　She **bought** a dress online.

A 다음 [ ] 안의 말을 빈칸에 적절한 형태로 써넣으시오.

1 I ____________ Tom for lunch yesterday. (meet)

2 Rachel ____________ home late last night. (come)

3 The dog ____________ too much yesterday. (eat)

4 They ____________ to Myeong-dong last weekend. (go)

5 You ____________ nothing at yesterday's meeting. (say)

6 He ____________ a ticket in his pocket this morning. (find)

7 Owen ____________ flowers to Jenny last Saturday. (give)

8 We were at the museum. We ____________ an actress there. (see)

9 Eva's cat died last year. I ____________ sorry for her. (feel)

B 다음 우리말과 같은 뜻이 되도록 〈보기〉에서 알맞은 말을 골라 빈칸에 적절한 형태로 써넣으시오.

〈보기〉	build	catch	leave	hear	think

1 Peter는 심한 감기에 걸렸다.

Peter ____________ a bad cold.

2 우리는 라디오에서 그 소식을 들었다.

We ____________ the news on the radio.

3 Miranda는 그 문제에 대해 생각해 보았다.

Miranda ____________ about the problem.

4 그들의 친구들은 아침 일찍 떠났다.

Their friends ____________ early in the morning.

5 우리 할아버지께서 20년 전에 이 집을 지으셨다.

My grandfather ____________ this house 20 years ago.

일반동사의 과거형 - 불규칙 변화 II

 과거형이 현재형과 같은 일반동사도 있다.

put → **put**	cut → **cut**	hit → **hit**	set → **set**
read → **read**	hurt → **hurt**	cost → **cost**	shut → **shut**

I always **put** my bag on the chair.   (현재형)
I **put** my bag on the chair last night.   (과거형)

> **+Plus**   read는 현재형과 과거형의 형태가 같지만 발음이 다르다.
> read [riːd] (현재형) – read [red] (과거형)

A 다음 밑줄 친 부분이 어법상 맞으면 O, 틀리면 X 표시하고 바르게 고치시오.

1 He <u>hit</u> 55 home runs last year.

2 They <u>readed</u> the email yesterday.

3 She <u>hurted</u> her back last Sunday.

4 Last year, the tickets <u>cost</u> $60.

5 We <u>shuted</u> the store early this evening.

6 I <u>put</u> the milk in the fridge last night.

7 Amber <u>cut</u> the cake at her birthday party.

8 My brother and I <u>setted</u> the table for dinner yesterday.

B 다음 우리말과 같은 뜻이 되도록 〈보기〉에서 알맞은 말을 골라 빈칸에 적절한 형태로 써넣으시오.

〈보기〉	cost	cut	hit	put	read

1 그녀는 망치로 벽을 쳤다.

She ______________ the wall with a hammer.

2 그 콘서트 티켓은 25달러였다.

The concert ticket ______________ 25 dollars.

3 Jimmy는 사과를 반으로 잘랐다.

Jimmy ______________ the apple in half.

4 나는 선물 상자에 쿠키 몇 개를 넣었다.

I ______________ some cookies in the gift box.

5 그 학생들은 지난 겨울 방학에 많은 책을 읽었다.

The students ______________ many books last winter vacation.

일반동사의 현재형 부정문

○ 현재형 부정문은 주어에 따라 동사원형 앞에 don't나 doesn't를 써서 만든다.

주어	현재형 부정문
I / You / We / They	**don't**+동사원형
He / She / It	**doesn't**+동사원형

You **don't need** my help.　　　　They **don't like** sweets.
She **doesn't wear** glasses.　　　It **doesn't smell** good.

A 다음 ( ) 안에서 알맞은 말을 고르시오.

1　I (eat not / don't eat) chocolate cake.

2　It (don't / doesn't) sound interesting.

3　You (don't / doesn't) keep a diary.

4　My father doesn't (get / gets) enough sleep at night.

5　Ellie and Chris (don't / doesn't) know him very well.

B 다음 문장을 부정문으로 바꿀 때, 빈칸에 알맞은 말을 쓰시오.

1　Alex likes action movies.

　→ Alex ______________ ______________ action movies.

2　I practice the violin in the morning.

　→ I ______________ ______________ the violin in the morning.

3　My dog looks healthy.

　→ My dog ______________ ______________ healthy.

4　Nick and Lily have lunch together at school.

　→ Nick and Lily ______________ ______________ lunch together at school.

C 다음 우리말과 같은 뜻이 되도록 ( ) 안의 말을 이용하여 문장을 완성하시오.

1　그것은 내 컴퓨터에서 작동하지 않는다. (work)

　______________ ______________ ______________ on my computer.

2　우리는 패스트푸드점에 가지 않는다. (go)

　______________ ______________ ______________ to fast-food restaurants.

3　그녀는 옷에 많은 돈을 쓰지 않는다. (spend)

　______________ ______________ ______________ much money on clothes.

일반동사의 과거형 부정문

○ 과거형 부정문은 주어의 인칭과 수에 관계없이 동사원형 앞에 didn't를 써서 만든다.

주어	과거형 부정문
I / You / We / They He / She / It	**didn't**＋동사원형

I **didn't call** you last night.

He **didn't watch** the show last Saturday.

It **didn't rain** yesterday.

They **didn't eat** dinner yesterday.

＋Plus 일반동사의 부정문에서 부정의 의미를 강조할 때 do/does/did not의 형태로 쓰기도 하지만, 일상적으로 줄임말 don't/doesn't/didn't가 주로 쓰인다.

A 다음 [ ] 안에서 알맞은 말을 고르시오.

1 She (passed not / didn't pass) the exam.

2 It didn't (move / moves) from the table.

3 We (don't / didn't) meet Tim yesterday.

4 I didn't (understand / understood) the questions.

B 다음 문장을 부정문으로 바꿀 때, 빈칸에 알맞은 말을 쓰시오.

1 Jake told me about the rumor.

→ Jake ＿＿＿＿＿＿＿ ＿＿＿＿＿＿＿ me about the rumor.

2 You wanted a skateboard for a gift.

→ You ＿＿＿＿＿＿＿ ＿＿＿＿＿＿＿ a skateboard for a gift.

3 They finished their meal quickly.

→ They ＿＿＿＿＿＿＿ ＿＿＿＿＿＿＿ their meal quickly.

C 다음 우리말과 같은 뜻이 되도록 [ ] 안의 말을 이용하여 문장을 완성하시오.

1 나는 불을 끄지 않았다. (turn)

＿＿＿＿＿＿＿ ＿＿＿＿＿＿＿ ＿＿＿＿＿＿＿ off the light.

2 Ross는 그녀에게 이메일을 쓰지 않았다. (write)

＿＿＿＿＿＿＿ ＿＿＿＿＿＿＿ ＿＿＿＿＿＿＿ an email to her.

3 그들은 집을 청소할 시간이 없었다. (have)

＿＿＿＿＿＿＿ ＿＿＿＿＿＿＿ ＿＿＿＿＿＿＿ time to clean the house.

4 그녀는 슬펐지만 울지 않았다. (feel, cry)

＿＿＿＿＿＿＿ ＿＿＿＿＿＿＿ sad, but ＿＿＿＿＿＿＿ ＿＿＿＿＿＿＿ ＿＿＿＿＿＿＿.

POINT 09 일반동사의 현재형 의문문

○ 현재형 의문문은 주어 앞에 Do나 Does를 쓰고 주어 뒤에 동사원형을 써서 만든다.

주어	현재형 의문문	긍정의 대답	부정의 대답
I / you / we / they	**Do**＋주어＋동사원형 ~?	Yes, 주어＋do.	No, 주어＋don't.
he / she / it	**Does**＋주어＋동사원형 ~?	Yes, 주어＋does.	No, 주어＋doesn't.

A: **Do** they **play** rock music?
B: Yes, they do. / No, they don't.

A: **Does** he **read** soccer magazines?
B: Yes, he does. / No, he doesn't.

A 다음 밑줄 친 부분을 어법에 맞게 고쳐 쓰시오.

1 Do look I smart?

2 Does he eats garlic?

3 Does you live in Beijing now?

4 A: Does she study French?

 B: No, she does.

B 다음 문장을 의문문으로 바꿀 때, 빈칸에 알맞은 말을 쓰시오.

1 You need glasses.

 → ＿＿＿＿＿＿ ＿＿＿＿＿＿ ＿＿＿＿＿＿ glasses?

2 Kate has three brothers.

 → ＿＿＿＿＿＿ ＿＿＿＿＿＿ ＿＿＿＿＿＿ three brothers?

3 We take a test every month.

 → ＿＿＿＿＿＿ ＿＿＿＿＿＿ ＿＿＿＿＿＿ a test every month?

C 다음 [ ] 안의 말을 이용하여 대화를 완성하시오.

1 A: ＿＿＿＿＿＿ ＿＿＿＿＿＿ ＿＿＿＿＿＿ Indian food? (love)

 B: Yes, he does.

2 A: ＿＿＿＿＿＿ ＿＿＿＿＿＿ ＿＿＿＿＿＿ your address? (know)

 B: Yes, they do.

3 A: Does ＿＿＿＿＿＿ ＿＿＿＿＿＿ the piano? (play)

 B: No, she ＿＿＿＿＿＿.

4 A: ＿＿＿＿＿＿ ＿＿＿＿＿＿ ＿＿＿＿＿＿ to school? (walk)

 B: No, ＿＿＿＿＿＿ ＿＿＿＿＿＿. I ride my bike to school.

5 A: ＿＿＿＿＿＿ this bus ＿＿＿＿＿＿ to City Hall? (go)

 B: Yes, ＿＿＿＿＿＿ ＿＿＿＿＿＿. It stops right in front of the building.

일반동사의 과거형 의문문

○ 과거형 의문문은 주어의 인칭과 수에 관계없이 주어 앞에 Did를 쓰고 주어 뒤에 동사원형을 써서 만든다.

주어	과거형 의문문	긍정의 대답	부정의 대답
I / you / we / they he / she / it	**Did**＋주어＋동사원형 ~?	Yes, 주어＋did.	No, 주어＋didn't.

A: **Did** you **go** to the museum yesterday?
B: Yes, I did. / No, I didn't.

> **내신만점 Tip** 일반동사의 부정문과 의문문에서는 주어의 인칭과 시제에 따라 do/does/did를 이용하고, 뒤에 동사원형을 쓴다는 것을 기억하자.

A 다음 ( ) 안에서 알맞은 말을 고르시오.

1 (Do / Did) we have enough time now?

2 (Do / Did) you enjoy your trip last weekend?

3 (Does / Did) your sister learn yoga these days?

4 (Does / Did) he go to bed before ten last night?

B 다음 문장을 의문문으로 바꿀 때, 빈칸에 알맞은 말을 쓰시오.

1 He caught the ball.

　→ ＿＿＿＿＿ ＿＿＿＿＿ ＿＿＿＿＿ the ball?

2 They helped the old man.

　→ ＿＿＿＿＿ ＿＿＿＿＿ ＿＿＿＿＿ the old man?

3 You lost the game.

　→ ＿＿＿＿＿ ＿＿＿＿＿ ＿＿＿＿＿ the game?

C 다음 ( ) 안의 말을 이용하여 대화를 완성하시오.

1 A: ＿＿＿＿＿ he ＿＿＿＿＿ Busan yesterday? (leave)

　B: No, he ＿＿＿＿＿.

2 A: ＿＿＿＿＿ Ben and Kelly ＿＿＿＿＿ my present? (like)

　B: Yes, ＿＿＿＿＿ ＿＿＿＿＿. They thanked you.

3 A: ＿＿＿＿＿ ＿＿＿＿＿ ＿＿＿＿＿ fun with Damon? (have)

　B: Yes, we ＿＿＿＿＿. We had great fun.

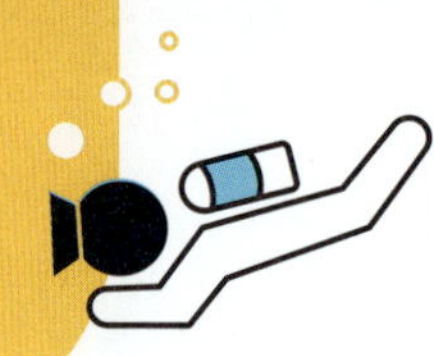

01-02 다음 빈칸에 알맞은 말을 고르시오.

01

> __________ designs clothes.

① I   ② You   ③ We
④ She   ⑤ They

02

> __________ don't drink milk.

① He   ② It   ③ They
④ Mr. Kim   ⑤ My mother

03

> __________ you play board games?

① Is   ② Are   ③ Does
④ Do   ⑤ Were

04-05 다음 질문에 대한 알맞은 대답을 고르시오.

04

> A: Did she watch TV last night?
> B: __________

① Yes, she does.   ② Yes, she did.
③ No, she doesn't.   ④ No, she isn't.
⑤ No, she wasn't.

05

> A: Does Matt travel a lot?
> B: __________

① Yes, he does.   ② Yes, he is.
③ No, he isn't.   ④ No, he didn't.
⑤ No, he does.

06

다음 중 대화가 자연스럽지 <u>않은</u> 것은?

① A: Does she work in an office?
   B: Yes, she does.
② A: Do they go camping on weekends?
   B: No, they didn't.
③ A: Do you listen to the radio?
   B: Yes, I do. It is interesting.
④ A: Did he fix the car yesterday?
   B: No, he didn't. He was too tired.
⑤ A: Did you enjoy the concert?
   B: Yes, we did. The band was amazing.

07-08 다음 중 밑줄 친 부분이 어법상 <u>틀린</u> 것을 고르시오.

07

① She <u>didn't buy</u> chocolate.
② They <u>didn't go</u> on a picnic.
③ Joe <u>doesn't cross</u> the road.
④ We <u>don't sells</u> cheese and butter.
⑤ Barry <u>doesn't like</u> strawberry jam.

08

① We <u>caught</u> the train.
② I <u>have</u> my own blog.
③ She <u>asked</u> me a question.
④ He <u>go</u> to the gym these days.
⑤ They <u>tried</u> bungee jumping yesterday.

09-10 다음 빈칸에 공통으로 들어갈 말을 고르시오.

09

- _________ Frank live in New York?
- She _________ not want to meet him again.

① Is[is]
② Are[are]
③ Was[was]
④ Do[do]
⑤ Does[does]

10

- I was there yesterday, but I _________ stay for long.
- A: Did they swim at the lake?
  B: No, they _________.

① wasn't
② weren't
③ didn't
④ don't
⑤ aren't

11

다음 우리말을 영어로 바르게 옮긴 것은?

그는 충고를 원하지 않는다.

① He wants not advice.
② He don't want advice.
③ He didn't want advice.
④ He doesn't want advice.
⑤ He doesn't wants advice.

12

다음 밑줄 친 부분을 바르게 고친 것을 모두 고르면? [2개]

Yesterday, we ① look for a cake at the bakery. We ② buy one. It ③ cost 25 dollars and I ④ pay for it. We ⑤ give it to my friend Kelly.

① lookd
② bought
③ costted
④ payed
⑤ gave

13-14 다음 빈칸에 알맞은 말이 바르게 짝지어진 것을 고르시오.

13

A: Does Victoria study English hard?
B: Yes, she _________. She _________ it almost every day.

① do – study
② do – studies
③ does – study
④ does – studies
⑤ did – studies

14

A: _________ they _________ the window?
B: No, they didn't.

① Do – open
② Do – opened
③ Did – open
④ Did – opened
⑤ Does – open

15-16 다음 중 어법상 **틀린** 것을 고르시오.

15

① Did you talk to Rick?
② Does Cindy get up early?
③ Does your baby sleep well?
④ Did David call you last night?
⑤ Does your parents like Italian food?

16

① He looks very nice.
② I tried my best during the game.
③ She stoped the car at the red light.
④ Minho read comic books yesterday.
⑤ They sent a letter to their grandparents.

17 [내신기출]

다음 중 밑줄 친 부분의 쓰임이 나머지와 **다른** 것은?

① <u>Does</u> he like his job?
② My mom <u>does</u> not buy flowers.
③ The watch <u>does</u> not work.
④ He <u>does</u> not eat junk food.
⑤ She <u>does</u> her homework after school.

18 [고난도]

다음 중 빈칸에 들어갈 말이 나머지와 **다른** 것은?

① We __________ not have a meeting last Friday.
② He __________ not wear his jacket yesterday.
③ __________ you go on a vacation last week?
④ __________ Amy take a shower an hour ago?
⑤ I __________ not remember his name right now.

19 [고난도] [내신기출]

다음 중 어법상 옳은 문장의 개수는?

(a) Do he speak Korean?
(b) We doesn't like rock music.
(c) Colin went to the library with his friend.
(d) Lily didn't make noise in the classroom.

① 0개　② 1개　③ 2개　④ 3개　⑤ 4개

20

다음 중 문장을 지시대로 바르게 바꾸지 **않은** 것은?

① She really likes the singer. (과거형)
　→ She really liked the singer.
② He finished the report. (부정문)
　→ He didn't finished the report.
③ Ted and Lisa worry about the final test. (과거형)
　→ Ted and Lisa worried about the final test.
④ They clean their office every day. (부정문)
　→ They don't clean their office every day.
⑤ You and your sister woke the baby. (의문문)
　→ Did you and your sister wake the baby?

21

다음 우리말과 같은 뜻이 되도록 주어진 말을 이용하여 문장을 완성하시오.

(1) 그는 Cindy와 함께 그 영화를 보지 않았다. (watch the movie)

→ He ________________________ with Cindy.

(2) 매일 아침, Julie는 그녀의 개와 함께 산책한다. (take a walk)

→ Every morning, Julie ________________ with her dog.

22

다음 문장을 지시대로 바꾸어 쓰시오.

(1) Sharon and Brad eat meat.

→ ________________________________ (의문문)

→ ________________________________ (부정문)

(2) Joe hit 20 home runs last season.

→ ________________________________ (의문문)

→ ________________________________ (부정문)

23

다음 그림을 보고, 주어진 말을 이용하여 문장을 완성하시오.

(study at the library)

(1) I ____________________________ yesterday.

(2) I ________________________________ last weekend.

24

주어진 말을 이용하여 대화를 완성하시오.

A: __________ __________ __________ at home?
(cook)

B: No, he doesn't.

25 [고난도] [내신기출]

다음 Suji의 일정표를 보고, 지난주에 한 일과 하지 않은 일을 영어로 쓰시오.

요일	해야 할 일	실천 여부
Mon.	visit my grandmother	X
Wed.	eat pizza with my friends	O
Fri.	do my homework	O

(1) Suji __________ __________ __________ __________ on Monday.

(2) Suji __________ __________ __________ __________ __________ on Wednesday.

(3) Suji __________ __________ __________ on Friday.

26 [고난도]

다음 대화를 읽고, 어법상 틀린 부분을 모두 찾아 바르게 고쳐 쓰시오. (2군데)

A: Is this your cat?

B: Yes, this is my cat, Coco. My father bring him home a month ago.

A: He is so cute.

B: Yes, he is. He likes playing with me. But he don't like taking baths.

일반동사

1 일반동사

2 일반동사의
현재형

3 일반동사의
과거형

4 일반동사의
부정문

5 일반동사의
의문문

• 주어의 동작이나 상태를 나타내는 동사

주어	현재형
I / You / We / They	① ________
He / She / It	동사원형+② ________

❗ 형태가 다양하게 변하는 일반동사의 3인칭 단수 현재형에 유의하기

주어	과거형(규칙 변화)
I / You / We / They He / She / It	동사원형+③ ________

❗ 형태가 불규칙하게 변하는 일반동사의 과거형에 유의하기

주어	현재형 부정문
I / You / We / They	④ ________ +동사원형
He / She / It	⑤ ________ +동사원형
주어	과거형 부정문
I / You / We / They He / She / It	⑥ ________ +동사원형

주어	현재형 의문문	긍정의 대답	부정의 대답
I / You / We / They	⑦ ________ +주어+동사원형 ~?	Yes, 주어+do.	No, 주어+don't.
He / She / It	⑧ ________ +주어+동사원형 ~?	Yes, 주어+does.	No, 주어+doesn't.
주어	과거형 의문문	긍정의 대답	부정의 대답
I / You / We / They He / She / It	⑨ ________ +주어+동사원형 ~?	Yes, 주어+did.	No, 주어+didn't.

❗ 일반동사의 부정문과 의문문은 do/does/did와 동사원형을 함께 쓴다는 것 기억하기

CHECK

다음 [ ] 안에서 알맞은 말을 고르시오.

1 Grace and Justin (not / don't) like soda.

2 He (enjoys / enjoies) extreme sports.

3 I (go / went) to the concert last week.

4 (Do / Did) you buy a new T-shirt yesterday?

5 My brother (play / plays) the guitar as a hobby.

6 They (sat / sitted) on the floor last time.

7 The bus (don't / doesn't) stop at the station.

8 Does Brenda (have / has) a dog?

04

명사와 관사

명사는 사람, 사물, 장소 등을 나타내는 말로, 셀 수 있는 명사와 셀 수 없는 명사로 나뉩니다.

관사는 명사 앞에 쓰여 명사의 의미나 성격에 대한 정보를 나타내는 말로, 부정관사 a/an과 정관사 the가 있습니다.

셀 수 있는 명사 – 규칙 변화 I

- 명사는 사람, 사물, 장소 등을 나타내는 말로, 셀 수 있는 명사와 셀 수 없는 명사로 나뉜다.
- 셀 수 있는 명사가 둘 이상일 때는 보통 명사 뒤에 -(e)s를 붙여 복수형으로 쓴다.

대부분의 명사	명사+-s	cup → cup**s** book → book**s**	dog → dog**s** bottle → bottle**s**
〈-s, -sh, -ch, -x, -o〉로 끝나는 명사	명사+-es	bus → bus**es** church → church**es** potato → potato**es** 〈예외〉 piano → piano**s**	dish → dish**es** box → box**es** photo → photo**s**

He has three **dogs**.
I ate **potatoes** for lunch.

There are five empty **dishes**.
The **photos** show happy memories.

A 다음 명사의 복수형을 쓰시오.

1 cat ____________________   2 tomato ____________________

3 fox ____________________   4 flower ____________________

5 star ____________________   6 present ____________________

7 piano ____________________   8 watch ____________________

9 friend ____________________   10 card ____________________

11 bus ____________________   12 brush ____________________

13 photo ____________________   14 computer ____________________

15 ship ____________________   16 bench ____________________

17 address ____________________   18 hero ____________________

B 다음 밑줄 친 부분을 어법에 맞게 고쳐 쓰시오.

1 An octopus has eight <u>arm</u>.

2 All the <u>dish</u> are clean.

3 Nancy made four <u>sandwich</u>.

4 These two <u>house</u> look the same.

5 We have three <u>class</u> today.

6 Albert always asks me many <u>question</u>.

7 The island has two beautiful <u>beach</u>.

8 There are many <u>bananaes</u> in the basket.

9 They found four old <u>boxs</u> in the garage.

10 I need an <u>eggs</u> and five <u>potato</u>.

11 He put two <u>shirt</u> and three <u>sweater</u> in his bag.

셀 수 있는 명사 - 규칙 변화 II

〈모음+y〉로 끝나는 명사	명사+-**s**	boy → boy**s** day → day**s**	toy → toy**s** monkey → monkey**s**
〈자음+y〉로 끝나는 명사	**y**를 i로 바꾸고+-**es**	city → cit**ies** baby → bab**ies**	lady → lad**ies** cherry → cher**ries**
〈-f, -fe〉로 끝나는 명사	**f, fe**를 **v**로 바꾸고+-**es**	leaf → lea**ves** wife → wi**ves** 〈예외〉 roof → roof**s**	thief → thie**ves** knife → kni**ves** chef → chef**s**

The **boys** ride bikes.

Thieves took the jewelry.

Cherries are my favorite fruit.

The **chefs** cleaned the kitchen.

A 다음 명사의 복수형을 쓰시오.

1 country __________		**2** key __________
3 factory __________		**4** shelf __________
5 donkey __________		**6** body __________
7 army __________		**8** fly __________
9 hobby __________		**10** half __________
11 way __________		**12** party __________
13 roof __________		**14** puppy __________
15 diary __________		**16** life __________
17 wolf __________		**18** family __________

B 다음 밑줄 친 부분을 어법에 맞게 고쳐 쓰시오.

1 The <u>leafs</u> change color in the fall.

2 <u>Monkeies</u> jump from tree to tree.

3 Their <u>lifes</u> are full of adventure.

4 My aunt has two <u>babyes</u>. They are twins!

5 The birds are on the <u>roofes</u> of the houses.

6 The boy got a lot of <u>toyes</u> for his birthday.

7 Be careful with those <u>knifes</u> and forks.

8 My grandfather tells me many interesting <u>story</u>.

9 The <u>lady</u> are my brothers' <u>wifes</u>.

10 A lot of <u>citys</u> have many tall <u>building</u>.

11 New Year's Day and Chuseok are two big <u>holiday</u> in Korea.

POINT 03 셀 수 있는 명사 - 불규칙 변화

 셀 수 있는 명사 중에 복수형이 불규칙하게 변하는 것들이 있다. 단수형과 복수형이 같은 명사들도 있다.

불규칙하게 변하는 명사	man → **men** foot → **feet**	woman → **women** mouse → **mice**	child → **children** goose → **geese**	tooth → **teeth** ox → **oxen**
단수형 = 복수형 명사	fish → **fish**	deer → **deer**	sheep → **sheep**	

The **children** have fun together.   The **fish** are colorful.

A 다음 밑줄 친 부분을 어법에 맞게 고쳐 쓰시오.

1 She has white <u>tooth</u>.

2 I talked to a group of young <u>mans</u>.

3 The <u>fishes</u> eat small plants.

4 Two <u>deers</u> suddenly appeared.

5 My <u>foots</u> are very cold.

6 There are three <u>ox</u> on the farm.

7 <u>Mouse</u> make nests in the walls.

8 The boy takes care of four <u>sheeps</u>.

9 The <u>womans</u> don't know each other.

10 Her <u>childs</u> are middle school students.

B 다음 우리말과 같은 뜻이 되도록 [ ] 안의 말을 이용하여 문장을 완성하시오.

1 쥐들은 정말 치즈를 좋아하나요? (mouse)

Do ______________ really love cheese?

2 Beth는 하루에 두 번 이를 닦는다. (tooth)

Beth brushes her ______________ twice a day.

3 많은 큰 물고기들이 강에 산다. (fish)

Many large ______________ live in the river.

4 그 노래는 여자들에게 인기가 있다. (woman)

The song is popular with ______________.

5 아이들은 매일 새로운 것들을 배운다. (child)

______________ learn new things every day.

6 그 농부는 많은 닭들과 거위들을 가지고 있다. (goose)

The farmer has many chickens and ______________.

POINT 04 · 셀 수 없는 명사

○ 하나, 둘, 셋처럼 개수를 셀 수 없는 명사는 항상 단수형으로 쓰고, 앞에 관사 a/an을 쓰지 않는다.

추상명사	형체가 없는 추상적인 개념을 나타내는 명사 love, luck, beauty, truth, peace, hope 등
고유명사	사람의 이름, 지명, 월 등 고유한 것을 나타내는 명사 Alex, Ms. Dale, Han River, London, August 등
물질명사	재료, 음식, 입자 등 형태가 일정하지 않고 셀 수 없는 물질을 나타내는 명사 water, snow, salt, rice, sand, bread, money 등

Love makes life beautiful.　　　　　　**Russia** is a big country.

> **내신만점 Tip**　셀 수 없는 명사 중 advice(충고), news(소식/뉴스), information(정보), furniture(가구)는 셀 수 있는 명사로 혼동하기 쉬운데, 항상 단수형으로 쓴다는 것을 기억하자.

A  다음 [ ] 안에서 알맞은 말을 고르시오.

1　(A sugar / Sugar) tastes sweet.

2　Beauty (is / are) all around us.

3　The printer is out of (ink / inks).

4　She came from (a France / France).

5　People need more (information / informations).

B　다음 밑줄 친 부분을 어법에 맞게 고쳐 쓰시오.

1　Cheese <u>are</u> my favorite food.

2　They listened to the <u>musics</u>.

3　Pancakes are great with <u>honeys</u>.

4　He wished me <u>a luck</u> on the test.

5　I need some <u>advices</u> about this project.

C　다음 〈보기〉에서 알맞은 말을 골라 빈칸에 적절한 형태로 써넣으시오. [단, 한 번씩만 사용할 것]

〈보기〉	America	health	money	news	water

1　The ______________ gives us information.

2　I'm thirsty. Please give me some ____________.

3　Tom is rich. He makes a lot of ____________.

4　Parents care about their children's ____________.

5　In ____________, people eat turkey on Thanksgiving Day.

POINT 05 — 셀 수 없는 명사의 수량 표현

● 셀 수 없는 명사의 수량은 물질의 양을 측정하는 단위나 물질을 담는 용기를 나타내는 말인 단위 명사를 이용해서 표현한다. 복수형을 나타낼 때는 단위 명사에 -(e)s를 붙인다.

〈수량+단위 명사+of+셀 수 없는 명사〉	
a glass of water / milk / juice **a bowl of** rice / soup **a loaf of** bread **a slice of** bread / pizza / cheese	**two cups of** tea / coffee **three bottles of** water / juice / cola **four loaves of** bread **five pieces of** paper / cake / bread / pizza / cheese

I drink **a glass of milk** every day.　　　There are **two pieces of cake** on the plate.

> **+Plus**　glasses(안경), scissors(가위), pants(바지) 등은 항상 복수형으로 쓰며, pair를 이용해 수량을 나타낸다.
> **a pair of** glasses / **two pairs of** pants

A 다음 밑줄 친 부분을 어법에 맞게 고쳐 쓰시오.

1　You had a <u>pieces</u> of cheese this morning.

2　Mary brought three <u>bottle</u> of water.

3　Give me two glasses of <u>apple juices</u>, please.

4　I was hungry, so I ate two <u>bowl of rices</u>.

5　Tim bought a <u>pairs of pant</u> and a shirt.

B 다음 우리말과 같은 뜻이 되도록 〈보기〉와 [ ] 안의 말을 이용하여 문장을 완성하시오. [단, 한 번씩만 사용할 것]

〈보기〉	bottle	bowl	cup	pair	piece	slice

1　우리 어머니는 하루에 차 네 잔을 마신다. (tea)

　　My mother drinks four ________________________ a day.

2　나는 어제 선글라스를 하나 샀다. (sunglass)

　　I bought a ________________________ yesterday.

3　그들은 콜라 두 병을 주문했다. (cola)

　　They ordered two ________________________.

4　David는 한 장의 종이 위에 자신의 이름을 썼다. (paper)

　　David wrote his name on ________________________.

5　우리는 저녁으로 수프 두 그릇을 나눠 먹었다. (soup)

　　We shared ________________________ for dinner.

6　그는 빵 두 조각과 달걀 한 개로 샌드위치를 만들었다. (bread)

　　She made a sandwich with ________________________ and an egg.

부정관사 a/an

○ 관사는 명사 앞에서 명사의 의미나 성격에 대한 정보를 나타내는 말로, 부정관사 a/an과 정관사 the가 있다.
○ 부정관사 a나 an은 셀 수 있는 명사의 단수형 앞에 쓴다.

– 막연한 하나를 나타낼 때	She is **a** doctor.
– 개수가 하나(one)임을 나타낼 때	I have **an** orange and two apples.
– '~마다(= per)'를 나타낼 때	He plays basketball twice **a** week.

> **+Plus** 발음이 자음으로 시작하는 명사 앞에 a를 쓰고, 발음이 모음으로 시작하는 명사 앞에는 an을 쓴다.
> **a** house, **a** student, **a** uniform / **an** egg, **an** airplane, **an** hour

---

A 다음 빈칸에 a와 an 중 알맞은 말을 쓰시오. (불필요하면 X 표시할 것)

1 I had ____________ cookie for dessert.

2 Lilly sent me ____________ invitation.

3 Ms. Harris is full of ____________ love.

4 He doesn't wear ____________ uniform.

5 Vincent is ____________ actor in this movie.

6 We stayed in Sokcho for ____________ month.

7 They have ____________ exam on Friday.

8 There is ____________ woman at the door.

9 I always carry ____________ umbrella in my bag.

10 He visits his grandparents four times ____________ year.

B 다음 우리말과 같은 뜻이 되도록 부정관사와 ( ) 안의 말을 이용하여 문장을 완성하시오.

1 나는 내 질문에 대한 답을 받았다. (answer)

I received ____________ ____________ to my question.

2 우리는 어제 잡지 한 권을 샀다. (magazine)

We bought ____________ ____________ yesterday.

3 그들은 버스 정류장에서 한 시간 동안 기다렸다. (hour)

They waited for ____________ ____________ at the bus stop.

4 우리 언니는 대학생이다. (university student)

My sister is ____________ ____________ ____________.

5 그는 하루에 한 번 나에게 전화를 한다. (once, day)

He calls me ____________ ____________ ____________.

정관사 the

- 정관사 the는 특정한 것이나 명확한 것을 가리킬 때 사용하며, 셀 수 있는 명사와 셀 수 없는 명사 앞에 모두 쓸 수 있다.
  - 앞에 언급된 명사를 가리킬 때   He sang a song. **The** song was great.
  - 서로 알고 있는 것을 가리킬 때   Close **the** window, please.
  - 수식어가 뒤에서 꾸며주고 있을 때   **The** books on the desk are yours.
  - 세상에 하나밖에 없는 것을 말할 때   **the** sun, **the** sky, **the** moon, **the** earth
  - 악기 이름, 일부 매체를 말할 때   **the** flute, **the** violin, **the** Internet, **the** radio

> **내신만점 Tip**   부정관사 a/an과 정관사 the를 사용하는 경우를 잘 구분하자.
>
> a/an+불특정한 하나   the+특정한 것(들)

A   다음 [ ] 안에서 알맞은 말을 고르시오.

1. Can you pass (a / the) salt for me, please?
2. He goes to the dentist twice (a / the) year.
3. Sophia practices (a / the) violin every day.
4. I found a box. There was a photo in (a / the) box.
5. George was (an / the) hour late for the meeting.
6. Did you walk around in (a / the) sun yesterday?
7. A girl said hello to me. But I didn't know (a / the) girl.
8. (A / The) stars filled in (a / the) sky last night.
9. There was (a / the) rose in the vase. (A / The) rose smelled amazing.

B   다음 우리말과 같은 뜻이 되도록 관사와 [ ] 안의 말을 이용하여 문장을 완성하시오.

1. 나는 인터넷에서 뉴스를 읽는다. (Internet)

   I read the news on ＿＿＿＿＿ ＿＿＿＿＿.

2. 그들은 보고서를 위해 책을 한 권 빌렸다. (book)

   They borrowed ＿＿＿＿＿ ＿＿＿＿＿ for the report.

3. 그 테이블 옆에 있는 병들은 비어 있다. (bottle)

   ＿＿＿＿＿ ＿＿＿＿＿ next to the table are empty.

4. 달은 지구 주위를 돈다. (moon, earth)

   ＿＿＿＿＿ ＿＿＿＿＿ moves around ＿＿＿＿＿ ＿＿＿＿＿.

5. 우리는 거리에서 고양이 한 마리를 봤다. 그 고양이는 배고파 보였다. (cat)

   We saw ＿＿＿＿＿ ＿＿＿＿＿ in the street. ＿＿＿＿＿ ＿＿＿＿＿

   looked hungry.

POINT 08 관사의 생략

- 부정관사 a/an, 정관사 the 중 어느 것도 쓰지 않는 경우가 있다.
  - 식사 이름을 나타내는 명사 앞   I already had **lunch**.
  - 운동 경기 이름을 나타내는 명사 앞   They play **soccer** after school.
  - 〈by＋교통/통신수단〉의 형태로 쓸 때   We came here by **taxi**.
  - 건물/장소가 본래의 용도로 사용될 때   She usually goes to **school** at 8:30.

> **＋Plus**   식사 이름 앞에 수식하는 말이 올 때는 관사를 쓴다. I had **a** *great* breakfast.

- 문맥에 따라 관사를 쓰기도 하고 생략하기도 하므로, 문장에서 사용되는 명사의 뜻에 유의한다.

Alison wants **a cello**. (막연한 악기 하나)   He went to **bed** a minute ago. (잠을 자다)

Alison plays **the cello**. (악기를 연주하다)   He went to **the bed** and sat down. (가구 '침대')

> **내신만점 Tip**   관사를 생략하는 대표적인 관용 표현인 go to bed(자다), go to school/work/church(~에 다니다), have breakfast/lunch/dinner(~ 식사를 하다), watch TV(TV를 보다) 등을 잘 기억하자.

A   다음 빈칸에 알맞은 관사를 쓰시오. (불필요하면 X 표시할 것)

1   Did you play ____________ tennis with Eddie?

2   The dog is under ____________ bed.

3   He sent the file by ____________ email.

4   What time do you go to ____________ work?

5   They play ____________ drums together.

6   We always have ____________ breakfast at six o'clock.

7   Mia goes to Daejeon by ____________ train.

8   My family has ____________ expensive dinner once ____________ month.

9   Students go to ____________ school five days a week.

10   I went to ____________ bed late last night. I felt tired this morning.

B   다음 우리말과 같은 뜻이 되도록 관사와 [ ] 안의 말을 이용하여 문장을 완성하시오. (관사가 불필요하면 생략할 것)

1   (school)   Lisa는 그때 수업 중이었다.   Lisa was at ____________ then.

               그녀는 그 학교에서 일한다.   She works at ____________.

2   (bus)   우리는 버스를 타고 집에 왔다.   We came home by ____________.

               그 버스는 사람들로 가득했다.   ____________ was full of people.

3   (guitar)   그는 가게에서 기타 하나를 봤다.   He saw ____________ in the shop.

               나는 매일 기타를 연주한다.   I play ____________ every day.

4   (bed)   우리 아기는 지금 자고 있다.   My baby is in ____________ now.

               Jim은 오늘 그 침대를 정돈했다.   Jim made ____________ today.

실전 TEST

01

다음 중 명사의 단수형과 복수형이 잘못 연결된 것은?

① bus – buses ② beach – beachs
③ tooth – teeth ④ sheep – sheep
⑤ holiday – holidays

02-03 다음 빈칸에 들어갈 수 없는 말을 고르시오.

02

> There was a ___________ under the chair.

① toy ② note
③ coin ④ water
⑤ mouse

03

> We need ___________ every day.

① air ② love
③ book ④ food
⑤ sleep

04-05 다음 빈칸에 알맞은 말이 바르게 짝지어진 것을 고르시오.

04

> • Dave bought a ___________ of scissors.
> • Please give me two ___________ of juice.

① pair – cup ② bottle – pair
③ slices – cups ④ pair – glasses
⑤ pieces – glasses

05

> • I ordered a book on ___________ Internet.
> • Sean runs four kilometers ___________ day.

① a – a ② the – a
③ an – a ④ a – the
⑤ an – the

06-07 다음 중 밑줄 친 부분이 어법상 틀린 것을 고르시오.

06

① Their <u>wives</u> talked together.
② We caught three <u>fish</u> in the river.
③ I visited different <u>cities</u> in England.
④ Those <u>childs</u> have fun at the park.
⑤ There are two grand <u>pianos</u> in the shop.

07

① She gives great <u>advice</u>.
② I need some <u>luck</u> today.
③ We shared a bowl of <u>salad</u>.
④ The <u>news</u> was on TV at 9:00 p.m.
⑤ They used <u>butters</u> for the toast.

08-09 다음 중 빈칸에 a나 an이 들어갈 수 없는 문장을 고르시오.

08

① People need __________ air.
② She is __________ fashion model.
③ Jamie is __________ English actor.
④ There is __________ bank near here.
⑤ I saw __________ accident this morning.

09

① I was __________ teacher.
② Jena lives in __________ apartment.
③ My mother loves __________ coffee.
④ He had __________ apple in the morning.
⑤ We have two dogs and __________ cat.

10

다음 우리말을 영어로 바르게 옮긴 것은?

나는 샌드위치에 치즈 두 조각을 넣었다.

① I put two cheese on the sandwich.
② I put two slice of cheese on the sandwich.
③ I put two slice of cheeses on the sandwich.
④ I put two slices of cheese on the sandwich.
⑤ I put two slices of cheeses on the sandwich.

11-12 다음 빈칸에 공통으로 들어갈 말을 고르시오.

11

- __________ sun rises in the east.
- __________ woman on your left is our new homeroom teacher.

① A
② An
③ The
④ Its
⑤ Two

12

- There is a __________ of paper on the desk.
- Jessica had a __________ of cake for dessert.

① cup
② pair
③ piece
④ loaf
⑤ bottle

13

다음 중 밑줄 친 명사의 성격이 나머지와 다른 것은?

① There is snow on the street.
② My feet were wet from the rain.
③ We received good information.
④ Do you have enough money?
⑤ Her beauty comes from her kindness.

14 내신기출

다음 우리말과 같은 뜻이 되도록 주어진 말을 배열할
때 네 번째에 올 단어는?

> 우리는 가구 두 점을 샀다.
> (bought, furniture, two, of, we, pieces)

① bought　　② two　　③ furniture
④ of　　⑤ pieces

15-17 다음 중 어법상 틀린 것을 고르시오.

15

① Tim went to bed early.
② She wears a uniform at work.
③ We had a wonderful lunch.
④ I took a walk for an hour.
⑤ Dorothy wore a pairs of glasses.

16

① Maggie loves cookies.
② There is sand on the beach.
③ We work eight hour a day.
④ Please turn off the light.
⑤ They sat down on a bench.

17

① He drank a cup of juice.
② I baked two loaves of bread.
③ She put salt in the hot soup.
④ He usually travels by the subway.
⑤ Jack spent three weeks in London.

18 고난도

다음 중 〈보기〉의 밑줄 친 부분과 쓰임이 같은 것은?

> 〈보기〉 Let's take a taxi.

① I drink tea twice a day.
② She cried for an hour.
③ Chris is a computer programmer.
④ We need a piece of paper.
⑤ Ann has a son and two daughters.

19

다음 중 밑줄 친 부분의 쓰임이 잘못된 것은?

① Look at the sky. It's so blue.
② I saw a man. The man looked very tired.
③ The girls were talking in front of the church.
④ She played the harp at the wedding.
⑤ Do you have the breakfast with your brother
　 every day?

20 고난도　내신기출

다음 중 어법상 옳은 것끼리 짝지어진 것은?

> (a) Paris is a capital of France.
> (b) The children drink milk every day.
> (c) I'm waiting for three womans.
> (d) Joy plays basketball really well.
> (e) I added sugar to the lemonade.

① (a), (b), (d)　　② (a), (c), (d)
③ (b), (c), (e)　　④ (b), (d), (e)
⑤ (c), (d), (e)

21

주어진 두 문장을 한 문장으로 바꾸어 쓸 때, 빈칸에 알맞은 말을 쓰시오.

He found a mouse in the kitchen.
He found three more in the bathroom.

→ He found four ____________ in the house.

22 내신기출

어법상 **틀린** 부분을 모두 찾아 바르게 고쳐 쓰시오.

(1)
Mom bought me a violin. Now I play a violin every day. (1군데)

(2)
There were cute baby at the event. I took some photoes with them. (2군데)

23

다음 그림을 보고, 문장을 완성하시오.

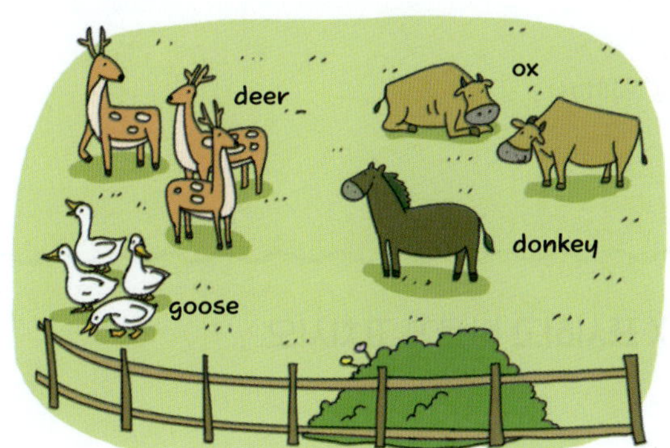

There is a big farm in my town. It has four ____________ and two ____________. It also has three ____________. Yesterday, a ____________ joined the other animals at the farm.

24

주어진 말을 알맞게 배열하여 대화를 완성하시오.

A: Did Gary eat rice?
B: Yes, he did. He ____________________.
   (bowls, ate, of, rice, two)

25 내신기출

다음 Paul과 Jane이 점심으로 먹은 것을 보고, 주어진 말을 이용하여 문장을 완성하시오.

(pizza, milk, slice, glass)   (cake, juice, piece, bottle)

(1) Paul had ________ ________ ________ ________ and ________ ________ ________ ________ for lunch.

(2) Jane had ________ ________ ________ ________ and ________ ________ ________ ________ for lunch.

26 고난도

다음 Willy의 일기를 읽고, 빈칸에 알맞은 관사를 쓰시오. (불필요하면 X 표시할 것)

Last night, my brother hid my smartphone. I looked for it for ____________ hour. So I went to ____________ bed late. Today, I was very sleepy at ____________ school.

CHAPTER 04
명사와 관사

1 명사

- 의미: 사람, 사물, 장소 등을 나타내는 말
- 종류: 셀 수 있는 명사, 셀 수 없는 명사(추상명사, 고유명사, 물질명사)
- 셀 수 있는 명사의 복수형

대부분의 명사	명사+-s book → ① _______	〈-f, -fe〉로 끝나는 명사	f, fe를 v로 바꾸고+-es leaf → ④ _______
〈-s, -sh, -ch, -x, -o〉로 끝나는 명사	명사+-es potato → ② _______	단수형 = 복수형 명사	deer → ⑤ _______ fish → fish
〈자음+y〉로 끝나는 명사	y를 i로 바꾸고+-es city → ③ _______	불규칙하게 변하는 명사	man → ⑥ _______ tooth → teeth

- 셀 수 없는 명사의 수량 표현

〈수량+단위 명사+of+셀 수 없는 명사〉	
– a glass of water / milk / juice – a bowl of rice / soup – a slice of bread / pizza / cheese	– two cups of tea / coffee – three bottles of water / juice / cola – four ⑦ _______ of paper / cake / bread / pizza / cheese

❗ 명사는 셀 수 있는지, 없는지에 따라 쓰임과 형태가 달라진다는 것 기억하기

2 관사

- 의미: 명사의 의미나 성격에 대한 정보를 나타내는 말
- 종류: 부정관사(a/an), 정관사(the)
- a/an: 셀 수 있는 명사의 단수형 앞에 사용

  a doctor (막연한 하나) / ⑧ _______ orange (개수가 하나) / once ⑨ _______ week
  (~마다)

- the: 특정한 것이나 명확한 것을 가리킬 때 사용

  the book on the desk (꾸밈을 받는 대상) / ⑩ _______ sun (세상에 하나뿐인 것) / the
  flute (악기)

❗ 관사의 사용에 따라 달라지는 의미를 예문으로 익히기

CHECK

밑줄 친 부분이 어법상 맞으면 ○, 틀리면 X 표시하고 바르게 고치시오.

1 We saw two <u>sheeps</u> on the hill.
2 There are a lot of clouds in <u>the</u> sky.
3 I ate three <u>piece of cakes</u>.
4 She plays the piano once <u>a week</u>.
5 <u>A</u> sun heats the water in the lake.
6 We talked on the phone for <u>a</u> hour.

05

대명사

대명사는 명사를 대신해서 쓰는 말로, 주로 명사의 반복을 피하기 위해 사용합니다.
특정한 사람이나 사물을 가리키는 지시대명사, 정해지지 않은 사람이나 사물을 가리
키는 부정대명사, '~ 자신'이나 '직접'이라는 의미의 재귀대명사가 있답니다.

지시대명사

○ 지시대명사는 특정한 사람이나 사물을 가리키는 말로, 대상과의 거리와 대상의 수에 따라 다르게 쓴다.

	단수 / 복수	의미
가까이 있는 대상	**this / these**	이것(들), 이 사람(들)
멀리 있는 대상	**that / those**	저것(들), 저 사람(들)

This is Luna.　　　　　　　**These** are my friends.
Is **that** your car?　　　　　　**Those** are oranges.

> **(+Plus)** this/these와 that/those는 명사 앞에서 '이 ~', '저 ~'라는 뜻의 지시형용사로도 쓰인다.
> I like **this** *picture*. / **Those** *T-shirts* are on sale.

A　다음 [ ] 안에서 알맞은 말을 고르시오.

1　What's (this / that) right here?

2　Is (that / those) Steve's sister?

3　I got (this / these) flowers from Jim.

4　(That / Those) aren't the right keys.

5　(This / That) bag over there isn't mine.

6　She put her phone on (this / these) shelf.

B　다음 우리말과 같은 뜻이 되도록 빈칸에 알맞은 지시대명사를 쓰시오.

1　이것들은 여성들을 위한 재킷이다.

　　_____________ are jackets for women.

2　그가 오늘 아침에 저것을 망가뜨렸다.

　　He broke _____________ this morning.

3　이거 네 영어 숙제야?

　　Is _____________ your English homework?

4　저기 있는 저것들이 보이니?

　　Do you see _____________ over there?

C　다음 밑줄 친 부분을 어법에 맞게 고쳐 쓰시오.

1　Are <u>this</u> your dogs near my leg?

2　<u>Those</u> looks expensive for me.

3　Julie brought <u>these</u> for you. You should read it.

4　Do you know <u>that</u> children across the street?

5　<u>That</u> is my cousin, Shawn. Please say hello!

부정대명사 one

- 부정대명사는 정해지지 않은 사람이나 사물을 가리키는 말이다.
- 부정대명사 one은 앞에서 언급된 명사와 같은 종류의 불특정한 대상을 가리킬 때 쓰며, 복수형은 ones이다.
  I need a blue pen. Can you lend **one** to me?   (one = a blue pen)
  She has pretty earrings. I want the same **ones**.   (ones = earrings)

> **+Plus** 앞에서 언급된 특정한 대상 그대로를 가리킬 때는 인칭대명사 it(단수) 또는 them(복수)을 쓴다.
> This coat is too small. I can't wear **it**. (it = this coat)

- one은 일반적인 '사람'을 가리킬 때도 사용된다.
  One should be honest.   (one = a person)

A   다음 [ ] 안에서 알맞은 말을 고르시오.

1   Her bike is old. She needs a new (it / one).

2   Did you see my wallet? I lost (it / one).

3   Roy doesn't like cold drinks. He likes hot (one / ones).

4   This game is boring. Do you have a fun (it / one)?

5   A: Do you have any red pins? – B: No, but I have green (one / ones).

B   다음 우리말과 같은 뜻이 되도록 빈칸에 알맞은 부정대명사를 쓰시오.

1   사람은 경험에서 배운다.

    ______________ learns from experience.

2   나는 빨간색 컵 두 개와 파란색 컵 두 개를 샀다. 나는 빨간 것들이 더 좋다.

    I bought two red cups and two blue cups. I like the red ____________ better.

3   Katie는 작은 식물들을 모은다. 그래서 나는 그녀에게 하나를 사 주었다.

    Katie collects tiny plants. So I bought ____________ for her.

C   다음 빈칸에 one, ones, it, them 중 알맞은 말을 쓰시오.

1   Those towels are wet. Please bring dry ____________.

2   ____________ should respect one's parents.

3   I read these comics yesterday. You'll love ____________.

4   His keyboard doesn't work. He wants a new ____________.

5   Let's have the seafood pizza at Mama's. ____________ is my favorite.

6   There are three dresses in her closet: a white ____________ and two black

    ____________.

부정대명사 some/any

- some은 주로 긍정문과 권유문에서 쓰이며, '조금', '약간'이라는 뜻이다.
  We invited ten friends. **Some** came early. (긍정문)
  There is orange juice in the fridge. Would you like **some**? (권유문)

- any는 주로 부정문과 의문문에서 쓰이며, '조금', '어떤', '아무'의 뜻이다.
  Ella took a lot of photos, but she didn't show me **any**. (부정문)
  I'm out of money. Do you have **any**? (의문문)

> **+ Plus** some/any는 셀 수 있는 명사 또는 셀 수 없는 명사 앞에서 '조금의', '약간의', '어떤'이라는 뜻의 형용사로도 쓰인다.
> There are **some** *biscuits* on the table. / I don't have **any** *questions*.
> I need **some** *water*. / Did you bring **any** *food*?

A 다음 빈칸에 some과 any 중 알맞은 말을 쓰시오.

1 I made lemonade. Would you like ___________?

2 He looked for pencils, but he didn't find ___________.

3 I'm thirsty. I want ___________ water.

4 Are there ___________ giraffes in the zoo?

5 Joe gave these books to us. ___________ are in French.

6 Don't put ___________ sugar in your tea.

7 We picked apples this morning. Will you have ___________?

8 I got ___________ snacks from Oliver. Did you get ___________?

9 I don't have ___________ toys, but my brother has ___________.

10 I had to buy ___________ coffee because we didn't have ___________ at home.

B 다음 우리말과 같은 뜻이 되도록 〈보기〉에서 알맞은 말을 골라 문장을 완성하시오.

〈보기〉	any	one	ones	some

1 우리는 신선한 빵을 사고 싶었지만, 가게에 아무것도 없었다.
   We wanted to buy some fresh bread, but the store didn't have ___________.

2 그 접시들은 너무 더럽다. 깨끗한 것들을 사용해라.
   These plates are too dirty. Use the clean ___________.

3 나는 우산이 없다. 하나를 빌려야 한다.
   I don't have an umbrella. I need to borrow ___________.

4 그 미술관은 많은 새로운 그림을 가지고 있다. 몇 점은 정말 아름답다.
   The gallery has a lot of new paintings. ___________ are really beautiful.

비인칭 주어 it

시간, 날씨, 요일, 계절, 거리, 명암 등을 나타낼 때 문장의 주어로 대명사 it을 쓴다. 이때는 앞에 가리키는 대상이 없기 때문에 it을 비인칭 주어라고 하며 '그것'이라고 해석하지 않는다.

What time is **it**?　　　(시간)
It is very cold now.　　(날씨)
It's Monday today.　　(요일)

> **내신만점 Tip**　특정 대상을 가리키는 인칭대명사 it과는 분명한 쓰임의 차이가 있음을 기억하자.
> **It** rained all day. (비인칭 주어) / *This pen* is very good. **It**'s for you. (인칭대명사)

A　다음 두 문장 중에서 밑줄 친 It[it]이 비인칭 주어인 것에 ✔ 표시하시오.

1　☐ It is spring now.
　　☐ It is a warm blanket.

2　☐ It is not my phone.
　　☐ It is about five kilometers.

3　☐ It was cloudy yesterday.
　　☐ It was important to her.

4　☐ Does it start at 7:00 p.m.?
　　☐ What day is it today?

5　☐ It takes half an hour.
　　☐ They found it in the park.

B　다음 우리말과 같은 뜻이 되도록 [ ] 안의 말을 이용하여 문장을 완성하시오.

1　밖이 어둡다. (dark)
　　_____________ _____________ _____________ outside.

2　오늘은 내 생일이다. (birthday)
　　_____________ _____________ _____________ _____________ today.

3　기차로 세 시간 걸린다. (take, hour)
　　_____________ _____________ _____________ by train.

4　6시 10분 전이다. 나는 늦었다. (ten to six)
　　_____________ _____________. I'm late.

5　여기서 시청까지는 500미터이다. (meter)
　　_____________ _____________ _____________ from here to City Hall.

6　오늘 아침에는 비가 왔는데, 지금은 화창하다. (rainy, sunny)
　　_____________ _____________ this morning, but _____________
　　_____________ now.

POINT 05 재귀대명사

- 주어가 자신에게 행위를 할 때 혹은 주어의 행위를 강조할 때 '~ 자신'이라는 뜻의 재귀대명사를 쓴다.
- 재귀대명사의 단수형은 인칭대명사의 소유격이나 목적격에 -self를, 복수형은 -selves를 붙인다.

인칭	단수	복수
1인칭	myself	ourselves
2인칭	yourself	yourselves
3인칭	himself / herself / itself	themselves

Henry sometimes draws **himself**.　　　　　*We* found the answer **ourselves**.

A　다음 빈칸에 알맞은 재귀대명사를 쓰시오.

1　Rachel ____________ made dinner.

2　My cat cleans ____________.

3　The children dressed ____________.

4　He made ____________ a sandwich.

5　I don't think about ____________ much.

6　You guys don't love ____________.

7　William and I enjoyed ____________ at the party.

B　다음 우리말과 같은 뜻이 되도록 문장을 완성하시오.

1　나는 나 자신을 잘 표현한다.

I express ____________ well.

2　당신 자신에 관한 에세이를 쓰세요.

Write an essay about ____________.

3　Betty는 그녀 자신의 사진을 찍었다.

Betty took a picture of ____________.

4　그들은 그들의 방을 직접 청소했다.

They cleaned their rooms ____________.

5　그 도구 자체가 매우 유용하다.

The tool ____________ is very useful.

6　우리는 우리 자신에 대해 배우려고 노력했다.

We tried to learn about ____________.

7　Ben은 그 자신에 대해 이야기하는 것을 좋아하지 않는다.

Ben doesn't like to talk about ____________.

재귀대명사의 용법

- 재귀 용법: 주어와 목적어가 같을 때 동사나 전치사의 목적어로 재귀대명사를 쓴다.
  Emily loves **herself**. (동사 love의 목적어)
  We felt proud of **ourselves**. (전치사 of의 목적어)

- 강조 용법: 주어나 목적어를 강조할 때 강조하는 말 바로 뒤나 문장의 맨 끝에 재귀대명사를 쓴다. '직접', '스스로'라는 뜻을 나타내며 생략할 수 있다.
  My dad **himself** made the spaghetti. (주어 강조)
  They enjoyed the music **itself**. (목적어 강조)

(**+ Plus**) 재귀 용법으로 쓰인 재귀대명사는 문장에서 반드시 필요한 요소로, 생략할 수 없다는 것을 기억하자.
You should trust yourself. (O) / You should trust. (X)

A 다음 밑줄 친 재귀대명사를 생략할 수 있으면 ○, 없으면 X 표시하시오.

1 I cut myself by mistake.

2 We wrote these songs ourselves.

3 She taught herself Spanish.

4 I looked at myself in the mirror.

5 He himself painted this room.

6 They thought of themselves as heroes.

7 The food itself was great. But the service was terrible.

B 다음 우리말과 같은 뜻이 되도록 재귀대명사와 [ ] 안의 말을 이용하여 문장을 완성하시오.

1 Sophia가 직접 이 케이크를 만들었다. (bake)
  Sophia ______________ ______________ this cake.

2 나는 솔직히 내 자신에게 화가 났다. (angry at)
  I was ______________ ______________ ______________, honestly.

3 우리는 그 책 자체에 관심이 없다. (book)
  We're not interested in the ______________ ______________.

4 내 남동생은 자주 혼잣말을 한다. (talk to)
  My brother often ______________ ______________ ______________.

5 그 예술가들은 직접 그 그림들에 대해 설명했다. (artist)
  The ______________ explained the paintings ______________.

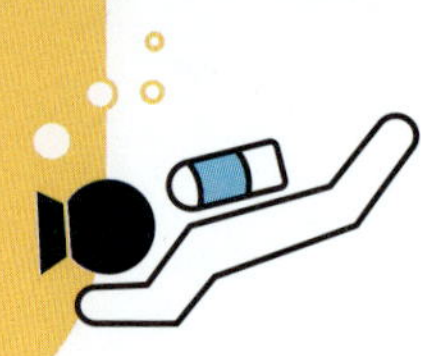

01 – 03 다음 빈칸에 알맞은 말을 고르시오.

01

His computer is too slow. He needs a new __________.

① it
② them
③ one
④ ones
⑤ some

02

You have a lot of comic books! I want __________.

① it
② any
③ some
④ itself
⑤ themselves

03

Did you like the movie? I saw __________ several times.

① it
② them
③ one
④ ones
⑤ some

04 `내신기출`

다음 중 밑줄 친 <u>this</u>의 쓰임이 나머지와 <u>다른</u> 것은?

① Will you buy <u>this</u> necklace?
② I didn't find the book in <u>this</u> library.
③ My son visited <u>this</u> toy store before.
④ Is <u>this</u> a present for your brother?
⑤ <u>This</u> room is my favorite place in my house.

05

A: Do you have __________ good ideas for our team project?
B: Yes, I have __________.

① a – some
② any – it
③ some – it
④ any – some
⑤ some – any

06

A: My sister gave me this purse. She got a new __________.
B: __________ looks nice.

① one – One
② one – Ones
③ one – It
④ it – One
⑤ it – They

07

A: There are __________ muffins on the table.
B: I baked them for you __________.

① a – me
② some – myself
③ any – myself
④ some – themselves
⑤ any – yourself

08

다음 중 대화가 자연스럽지 <u>않은</u> 것은?

① A: That is a beautiful dress!
  B: Molly made it herself.
② A: I brought some snacks. Would you like some?
  B: Yes, please.
③ A: Do you have any pens?
  B: Sorry, I don't have some.
④ A: When is your birthday?
  B: It's August 2.
⑤ A: I need a charger. Can I borrow one?
  B: Sure, here you go.

09 - 10 다음 중 〈보기〉의 밑줄 친 부분과 쓰임이 <u>다른</u> 것을 고르시오.

09

〈보기〉 <u>It</u> is 10:00 a.m.

① <u>It</u> is a gift for you.
② <u>It</u> is summer now.
③ <u>It</u> is a lovely day.
④ <u>It</u> is September 14.
⑤ <u>It</u> is about 3 kilometers from here to the mall.

10

〈보기〉 You did all the work <u>yourself</u>!

① Joe wrote the book <u>himself</u>.
② Holly calls <u>herself</u> a princess.
③ I <u>myself</u> made this website.
④ We grow the tomatoes <u>ourselves</u>.
⑤ They came up with the idea <u>themselves</u>.

11 고난도 내신기출

다음 밑줄 친 부분을 바르게 고친 것끼리 짝지어진 것은?

(a) Are <u>this</u> shoes his?
  → these
(b) There aren't <u>some</u> books on the desk.
  → any
(c) Your tie is very nice. I want the same <u>it</u>.
  → ones
(d) <u>That's</u> going to be dark soon.
  → It's
(e) They don't take care of <u>themself</u>.
  → itself

① (a), (b), (d) 　② (a), (b), (e)
③ (b), (c), (d) 　④ (b), (c), (e)
⑤ (c), (d), (e)

12

다음 우리말을 영어로 바르게 옮긴 것은?

우리는 우리 자신을 자랑스러워한다.

① We are proud of ourself.
② We are proud of ours.
③ We are proud of us.
④ We are proud of ourselves.
⑤ We are proud of ourselfs.

13

다음 중 밑줄 친 부분이 어법상 <u>틀린</u> 것은?

① I can't find <u>any</u> boxes here.
② Will you have <u>some</u> orange juice?
③ Did you use <u>any</u> of these coupons?
④ He read <u>some</u> of those books.
⑤ There aren't <u>some</u> people in the theater.

14 - 16 다음 빈칸에 공통으로 들어갈 말을 고르시오.

14

A: Wow! ___________ is snowing.
B: Yes! ___________ is a white Christmas!

① This   ② That
③ There   ④ It
⑤ One

15

- The children enjoyed ___________ on the swings.
- Many people don't know ___________ very well.

① itself   ② myself
③ himself   ④ yourselves
⑤ themselves

16

- I didn't read ___________.
- Are there ___________ pigeons in the park?

① one   ② some
③ any   ④ ones
⑤ it

17

다음 중 밑줄 친 부분을 생략할 수 있는 것은?

① I blamed myself.
② We believe in ourselves.
③ He had lunch by himself.
④ She learned things about herself.
⑤ They did their homework themselves.

18 - 19 다음 중 어법상 틀린 것을 고르시오.

18

① Those don't look safe.
② It was very cold last winter.
③ There are any elephants here.
④ I paid for the ticket myself.
⑤ Would you like a sandwich? I bought one for you.

19

① She fixed the television herself.
② This over there is my friend's house.
③ Help yourself to the apple pies.
④ He didn't get any gifts on his birthday.
⑤ I made a lot of bread. Please have some.

20

[A], [B], [C]의 괄호 안에서 알맞은 것끼리 바르게 짝지어진 것은?

(A) [One / It] is ten o' clock now.
(B) Leo sent us postcards. [Any / Some] were from Italy.
(C) The [child / children] talks to herself.

	(A)	(B)	(C)
①	One	Any	children
②	It	Any	child
③	One	Some	child
④	It	Some	child
⑤	It	Some	children

21

다음 문장을 지시대로 바꾸어 쓰시오.

(1) Is that your pet? (pet을 pets로)

→ ___________ ___________ ___________

___________ ?

(2) This is my new tablet PC. I sold the old one yesterday. (tablet PC를 tablet PCs로)

→ ___________ ___________ my new ___________

___________. I sold ___________ ___________

___________ yesterday.

22

다음 〈보기〉에서 알맞은 말을 골라 빈칸을 완성하시오.

〈보기〉	it	them	one	ones

(1) ___________ should always keep promises.

(2) That is a nice bag. ___________ is Tony's.

23

다음 그림을 보고, 빈칸에 적절한 대명사를 쓰시오.

(1) ___________ was rainy. I was going to wear my black jacket, but I couldn't find (2) ___________. So I wore my blue (3) ___________ instead.

24

다음 우리말과 같은 뜻이 되도록 대명사와 주어진 말을 이용하여 문장을 완성하시오.

(1) 그는 그 자신에 대해서 신경 쓴다. (care about)

→ He ___________ ___________ ___________.

(2) 이 바지가 너무 꽉 낀다. 나는 헐렁한 것을 입어야겠다. (pant, loose)

→ These ___________ are too tight. I'll wear the ___________ ___________.

25 고난도 내신기출

다음 〈조건〉에 맞게 우리말을 영어로 옮겨 쓰시오.

〈조건〉 1. 재귀대명사를 이용할 것
　　　 2. 표현 move the box, look at, in the mirror를 이용할 것

(1) Mike가 그 상자를 직접 옮겼니?

→ ___________________________________

(2) 그들은 거울 속의 자기 자신들을 봤다.

→ ___________________________________

26 고난도 내신기출

다음 대화의 밑줄 친 부분을 어법에 맞게 고쳐 쓰시오.

A: Do you have (1) <u>some</u> raincoats?
B: Yes, we have (2) <u>any</u>.
A: (3) <u>Those</u> pink one looks good.
B: We are out of pink ones in your size, but we have the same design in a different color.

대명사

1 지시대명사

- 의미: 특정한 사람이나 사물을 가리키는 말
- 형태

	단수	복수
대상이 가까울 때	① __________	these
대상이 멀 때	that	② __________

2 부정대명사

- 의미: 정해지지 않은 사람이나 사물을 가리키는 말
- 형태
  - one (복수형: ③ __________)
  - ④ __________ (긍정문, 권유문에 사용)
  - ⑤ __________ (부정문, 의문문에 사용)

❗ 부정대명사 one, some, any의 쓰임 구분하기

3 비인칭 주어 it

- 시간, 날씨, 요일, 계절, 거리, 명암 등을 나타낼 때 사용 ('그것'이라고 해석하지 않음)

❗ 비인칭 주어 it과 인칭대명사 it의 쓰임 바로 알기

4 재귀대명사

- 재귀 용법: 주어와 목적어가 같을 때 동사나 전치사의 목적어로 사용
- 강조 용법: 주어나 목적어를 강조할 때 문장의 맨 끝이나 강조하는 말 바로 뒤에 사용

인칭	단수	복수
1인칭	myself	⑥ __________
2인칭	⑦ __________	yourselves
3인칭	himself / herself / itself	⑧ __________

CHECK

밑줄 친 부분이 어법상 맞으면 O, 틀리면 X 표시하고 바르게 고치시오.

1 Put <u>those</u> away. You don't need it now.
2 <u>It</u>'s getting cold outside.
3 The children enjoyed <u>yourselves</u> at the show.
4 Logan <u>himself</u> made a plan for a field trip.
5 There are three skirts in the drawer: a red one and two black <u>some</u>.
6 A: Did Kelly buy apples at the market? – B: No. She didn't buy <u>any</u>.

06

시제

시제는 동작이나 사건이 언제 일어나는지 보여 주는 것을 말합니다. 동사의 형태를 변화시켜서 현재('~한다'), 과거('~했다'), 진행형('~하는 중이다', '~하는 중이었다') 등과 같이 시제를 나타낸답니다.

현재시제

현재시제는 현재의 상태나 지속적인 성질, 일상적인 행동이나 습관, 과학적 사실이나 불변의 진리를 나타낼 때 쓴다.

I **am** hungry now.	(현재의 상태)
My brother **walks** to school.	(일상적인 행동)
Water **freezes** at 0℃.	(과학적 사실)

A 다음 [ ] 안의 말을 빈칸에 적절한 형태로 써넣으시오.

1 Whales ______________ mammals. (be)

2 I ______________ up early these days. (get)

3 The sun ______________ in the east. (rise)

4 Look! My father ______________ on TV now! (be)

5 Jessica ______________ two little sisters. They are always together. (have)

B 다음 밑줄 친 부분을 어법에 맞게 고쳐 쓰시오.

1 Big Ben <u>was</u> in London.

2 There <u>were</u> 12 months in a year.

3 Brian is 14 years old. He <u>went</u> to middle school now.

4 The garbage truck <u>came</u> today. Let's take out the trash.

5 The shop <u>opened</u> at 9:00 a.m. and closes at 6:00 p.m. every day.

C 다음 우리말과 같은 뜻이 되도록 〈보기〉에서 알맞은 말을 골라 빈칸에 적절한 형태로 써넣으시오.

〈보기〉 be boil eat practice study

1 물은 섭씨 100도에서 끓는다.

Water ______________ at 100℃.

2 Alice는 시험 전에 열심히 공부한다.

Alice ______________ hard before her exams.

3 한국에는 사계절이 있다.

There ______________ four seasons in Korea.

4 그 밴드의 멤버들은 수요일마다 연습을 한다.

The members of the band ______________ on Wednesdays.

5 우리 부모님은 매일 아침 7시에 아침 식사를 하신다.

My parents ______________ breakfast at seven o'clock every morning.

POINT 02 과거시제

- 과거시제는 과거의 동작이나 상태, 역사적 사실을 나타낼 때 쓴다.
- yesterday, last ~, in＋연도, ~ ago 등과 같이 과거를 나타내는 표현과 주로 함께 쓰인다.

They **went** to the concert **yesterday**.　　　(과거의 동작)
He **was** sick **last week**.　　　(과거의 상태)
World War I **broke** out **in 1914**.　　　(역사적 사실)

> **＋Plus**　시제를 판단할 때는 현재시제 또는 과거시제와 함께 쓰이는 부사(구)가 있는지 확인하자.
> She **looks** so tired *now*. / She **looked** so tired *last night*.

A 다음 [ ] 안의 말을 빈칸에 적절한 형태로 써넣으시오.

1 It ＿＿＿＿＿＿＿＿ yesterday. (snow)

2 She ＿＿＿＿＿＿＿＿ back to school last week. (come)

3 Anne Frank ＿＿＿＿＿＿＿＿ her diary in the 1940s. (write)

4 He ＿＿＿＿＿＿＿＿ *The Little Prince* last month. (read)

5 Vincent van Gogh ＿＿＿＿＿＿＿＿ sunflowers several times. (paint)

B 다음 [ ] 안에서 알맞은 말을 고르시오.

1 I was happy because Laura (sits / sat) next to me.

2 Paul (puts / put) his towel on the bench, but it disappeared.

3 I (am / was) slim now, but I (am / was) much heavier last year.

4 It (is / was) Jane's birthday yesterday, so we (give / gave) her a gift.

5 He usually (drives / drove) slowly, but he (drives / drove) fast yesterday.

C 다음 우리말과 같은 뜻이 되도록 [ ] 안의 말을 이용하여 문장을 완성하시오.

1 Donald는 어젯밤 악몽을 꿨다. (have)

Donald ＿＿＿＿＿＿＿＿ a nightmare last night.

2 우리는 그 배우에게 많은 팬레터를 보냈다. (send)

We ＿＿＿＿＿＿＿＿ a lot of fan letters to the actor.

3 나는 3일 전에 쇼핑몰에서 Sue를 만났다. (meet)

I ＿＿＿＿＿＿＿＿ Sue at the mall three days ago.

4 그녀의 어머니는 지난 주말에 빵을 구웠다. (bake)

Her mother ＿＿＿＿＿＿＿＿ bread last weekend.

POINT 03 진행형 만드는 방법

- 진행형은 〈be동사+v-ing〉의 형태로 특정 시점에 진행 중인 일을 나타낼 때 쓴다.
- be동사는 주어의 인칭과 수를 따르며, v-ing는 동사원형에 -ing를 붙여서 만든다.

대부분의 동사	동사원형+-ing	go → go**ing** play → play**ing**	eat → eat**ing** study → study**ing**
-e로 끝나는 동사	e를 빼고+-ing	come → com**ing**	make → mak**ing**
-ie로 끝나는 동사	ie를 y로 고치고+-ing	lie → l**ying**	die → d**ying**
〈단모음+단자음〉으로 끝나는 동사	자음을 한 번 더 쓰고+-ing	cut → cut**ting** stop → stop**ping**	get → get**ting** run → run**ning**

We **are playing** in the yard.   She **is making** sandwiches.

> (+Plus) 소유, 상태, 감정을 나타내는 동사(have, know, understand, want, need, like 등)는 진행형으로 쓰지 않는다.
> 단, have가 '먹다'라는 뜻일 때는 진행형으로 쓸 수 있다.
> **I know** the answer. (O) / I'm knowing the answer. (X)

A 다음 동사를 <v-ing>의 형태로 바꾸어 쓰시오.

1 sleep __________   2 write __________
3 tie __________   4 sit __________
5 ride __________   6 meet __________
7 run __________   8 die __________
9 drive __________   10 swim __________

B 다음 두 문장 중에서 어법상 옳은 것에 ✔ 표시하시오.

1 ☐ I'm wanting a cat.   ☐ I'm looking for my student ID.
2 ☐ He is sending a text message.   ☐ He is knowing my phone number.
3 ☐ They are liking spicy food.   ☐ They are having lunch together.

C 다음 〈보기〉에서 알맞은 말을 골라 빈칸에 적절한 형태로 써넣으시오.

〈보기〉	arrive	drink	lie	put	rain	smile

1 It is __________ very hard.
2 I'm __________ on my shoes.
3 Billy is __________ a glass of milk.
4 They are __________ happily at the baby.
5 The lions are __________ down on the grass.
6 The train is __________ at the station.

현재진행형과 과거진행형

- 〈be동사의 현재형+v-ing〉는 '~하는 중이다', '~하고 있다'라는 뜻으로 현재 진행 중인 일을 나타낸다.
  Charlie **is sleeping** now.　　　　　　We **are drawing** flowers.

- 〈be동사의 과거형+v-ing〉는 '~하는 중이었다', '~하고 있었다'라는 뜻으로 과거의 특정 시점에 진행 중이던 일을 나타낸다.
  I **was swimming** at that time.　　　　They **were studying** in the library.

A 다음 문장을 진행형으로 바꿀 때, 빈칸에 알맞은 말을 쓰시오.

1 I learn French.
→ I _______________ _______________ French.

2 Peter flew to Hawaii.
→ Peter _______________ _______________ to Hawaii.

3 We make Christmas cards.
→ We _______________ _______________ Christmas cards.

4 They talked on the phone.
→ They _______________ _______________ on the phone.

5 The monkey climbs the tree.
→ The monkey _______________ _______________ the tree.

B 다음 우리말과 같은 뜻이 되도록 [ ] 안의 말을 이용하여 문장을 완성하시오.

1 나는 보고서를 쓰는 중이다. (write)
_______________ _______________ the report.

2 Cathy는 그때 울고 있었다. (cry)
_______________ _______________ _______________ at the time.

3 우리는 액세서리를 고르고 있었다. (choose)
_______________ _______________ _______________ accessories.

4 그는 지금 수학 문제를 푸는 중이다. (solve)
_______________ _______________ _______________ math problems now.

5 나의 남동생들은 낮잠을 자는 중이다. (brothers, take)
_______________ _______________ _______________ a nap.

6 그 아이들은 소파 위에서 뛰고 있었다. (children, jump)
_______________ _______________ _______________ on the sofa.

진행형의 부정문

- 진행형의 부정문은 〈be동사+not+v-ing〉의 형태로 쓴다.
  I'm not taking a bath.　　　(현재진행형의 부정문)
  He **wasn't looking** at you.　　(과거진행형의 부정문)

A　다음 [ ] 안에서 알맞은 말을 고르시오.

1　I (do / am) not going shopping.

2　She (was not / not was) reading your diary.

3　We are not (visit / visiting) London.

4　Andrew (is / does) not driving his car.

5　They (wasn't / weren't) wearing uniforms.

B　다음 문장을 지시대로 바꿀 때, 빈칸에 알맞은 말을 쓰시오.

1　I'm waiting for her speech. (현재진행형 부정문)

　→ I'm _____________ _____________ for her speech.

2　Kate and Alex weren't lying to each other. (과거진행형 긍정문)

　→ Kate and Alex _____________ _____________ to each other.

3　The dog wasn't playing with a ball. (현재진행형 부정문)

　→ The dog _____________ _____________ with a ball.

4　You aren't wasting my time. (과거진행형 부정문)

　→ You _____________ _____________ my time.

C　다음 우리말과 같은 뜻이 되도록 [ ] 안의 말을 이용하여 문장을 완성하시오.

1　나는 그것에 대해 생각하고 있지 않다. (think)

　_____________ _____________ _____________ about it.

2　그는 최선을 다하고 있지 않았다. (do)

　_____________ _____________ _____________ his best.

3　Tina는 가방을 싸고 있지 않다. (pack)

　_____________ _____________ _____________ her bag.

4　그들은 영화를 보고 있지 않았다. (watch)

　_____________ _____________ _____________ a movie.

5　Kevin과 나는 아무것도 숨기고 있지 않다. (hide)

　Kevin and _____________ _____________ _____________ anything.

진행형의 의문문

- 진행형의 의문문은 〈be동사+주어+v-ing ~?〉의 형태로 쓴다.
  A: **Are** you **making** pancakes?　　　　　(현재진행형의 의문문)
  B: Yes, I am. / No, I'm not.

  A: **Were** they **dancing** to the music?　　　(과거진행형의 의문문)
  B: Yes, they were. / No, they weren't.

A　다음 [ ] 안에서 알맞은 말을 고르시오.

1　Is she (exercise / exercising) now?

2　Am (I talking / talking I) too much?

3　(Was / Were) Tony fixing his computer?

4　(Is / Are) they running at the playground?

5　Were you (slept / sleeping) at the library?

B　다음 빈칸에 알맞은 말을 넣어 대화를 완성하시오.

1　A: ________________ ______________ writing a new novel?

　　B: Yes, I am.

2　A: Was Patrick drinking coffee?

　　B: ___________, ____________ ___________. He was drinking grape juice.

3　A: Are Dan and Sarah speaking Chinese?

　　B: ___________, ____________ ___________. They're getting ready for a trip to
　　China.

4　A: ___________ you swimming in the pool?

　　B: No, ______________ _____________. We were playing outside.

C　다음 우리말과 같은 뜻이 되도록 [ ] 안의 말을 이용하여 문장을 완성하시오.

1　Vicky는 손을 씻고 있니? (wash)

　　________________ ________________ ___________ her hands?

2　너는 이 반지를 찾고 있었니? (look for)

　　________________ ________________ ___________ ___________ this ring?

3　그들은 케이크를 자르고 있나요? (cut)

　　________________ ________________ ___________ the cake?

4　그는 땅 위에 누워 있었나요? (lie)

　　________________ ________________ ___________ on the ground?

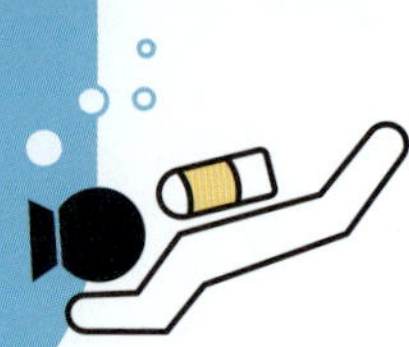

01-03 다음 빈칸에 알맞은 말을 고르시오.

01

Steven __________ a blue shirt yesterday.

① wear ② wears
③ wore ④ wearing
⑤ is wearing

02

Your phone __________ now. Answer it, please.

① is ringing ② rang
③ ring ④ was ringing
⑤ are ringing

03

We __________ about ghosts last night.

① talk ② talks
③ are talking ④ were talking
⑤ was talking

04

다음 중 밑줄 친 동사의 형태가 <u>잘못된</u> 것은?

① I was <u>tying</u> my scarf.
② He is <u>drinking</u> a cup of tea.
③ She is <u>moveing</u> to a new house.
④ Is your son <u>holding</u> a trophy in his hand?
⑤ We were <u>making</u> dinner for our family.

05-06 다음 빈칸에 들어갈 수 <u>없는</u> 말을 고르시오.

05

She was __________ Jerry.

① visiting ② knowing
③ helping ④ talking to
⑤ looking for

06

They __________ advice from him.

① need ② needed
③ are needing ④ don't need
⑤ didn't need

07-08 다음 질문에 대한 알맞은 대답을 고르시오.

07

A: Are you checking your email?
B: __________ I'm playing computer games.

① Yes, I am. ② Yes, I was.
③ No, I'm not. ④ No, I wasn't.
⑤ No, you weren't.

08

A: Was it raining at this time yesterday?
B: __________ It was raining very hard.

① Yes, it is. ② Yes, it was.
③ No, it isn't. ④ No, it wasn't.
⑤ No, it rained.

09 내신기출

다음 빈칸에 공통으로 들어갈 말은?

- Where ___________ you sitting in the theater this afternoon?
- They ___________ sleeping at ten o'clock last night.

① was
② do
③ did
④ are
⑤ were

10-11 다음 빈칸에 알맞은 말이 바르게 짝지어진 것을 고르시오.

10

A: What are you ___________ right now?
B: I'm ___________ a travel show.

① do – watch
② do – watching
③ doing – watches
④ did – watching
⑤ doing – watching

11

A: ___________ they talking to the teacher?
B: No, they aren't. They ___________ to her 10 minutes ago.

① Are – talk
② Are – talks
③ Are – talked
④ Were – talk
⑤ Were – talked

12

다음 우리말과 같은 뜻이 되도록 주어진 말을 배열할 때 네 번째에 올 단어는?

그들은 우리에게 손을 흔들고 있지 않았다.
(us, at, were, waving, they, not)

① at
② waving
③ us
④ were
⑤ not

13

다음 중 대화가 자연스럽지 <u>않은</u> 것은?

① A: Did you study last night?
   B: Yes, I did. I studied English.
② A: Was she absent from school?
   B: Yes, she was. She was sick.
③ A: What do you do after school?
   B: I take piano lessons every day.
④ A: Do they close their store on Sundays?
   B: No, they didn't. They were open every day.
⑤ A: What were you doing at that time?
   B: I was having lunch.

14 고난도 내신기출

다음 중 어법상 옳은 것을 <u>모두</u> 고르면? (2개)

① Was you reading a book at the library?
② The dance club meets at 3:00 p.m. on Mondays.
③ I buy a pair of shoes last month.
④ She not was using the laptop then.
⑤ We're looking for new members these days.

15-17 다음 중 어법상 <u>틀린</u> 것을 고르시오.

15

① I watch the news at 9:00 a.m.
② Madrid is the capital of Spain.
③ Daniel has a talent for music.
④ The earth moves around the sun.
⑤ The Korean War breaks out in 1950.

16

① Everybody was running.
② We were looking at you then.
③ Larry loves action movies.
④ I'm having a lot of nicknames.
⑤ He read the magazine last night.

17

① I'm not listening to music.
② They went to the zoo yesterday.
③ The sun sets in the west.
④ Did they working at that time?
⑤ We were looking after the baby.

18

다음 우리말을 영어로 바르게 옮긴 것은?

> Ian과 Sue는 전화로 수다를 떨고 있지 않았다.

① Ian and Sue don't chat on the phone.
② Ian and Sue aren't chatting on the phone.
③ Ian and Sue weren't chatting on the phone.
④ Ian and Sue not was chatting on the phone.
⑤ Ian and Sue were chatting not on the phone.

19 내신기출

다음 중 어법상 옳은 것끼리 짝지어진 것은?

> (a) I met my old friend yesterday.
> (b) Are you lying to me?
> (c) She take a walk every morning.
> (d) I was recording with guests right now.

① (a), (b) ② (a), (d) ③ (b), (c)
④ (b), (d) ⑤ (c), (d)

20 고난도 내신기출

[A], [B], [C]의 괄호 안에서 알맞은 것끼리 바르게 짝지어진 것은?

> (a) Hangeul [is / was] the Korean alphabet.
> (B) I [am finding / found] the keys last night.
> (C) They [had / were having] a nice house then.

	(A)	(B)	(C)
①	is	am finding	had
②	is	found	were having
③	is	found	had
④	was	found	had
⑤	was	am finding	were having

21

다음 〈보기〉에서 알맞은 말을 골라 빈칸에 적절한 형태로 써넣으시오.

〈보기〉	clean	be	bring

(1) It __________ very cold tonight.

(2) Max __________ his brother to the concert yesterday.

(3) Rose __________ her room every day these days.

22

다음 우리말과 같은 뜻이 되도록 주어진 말을 알맞게 배열하여 문장을 완성하시오.

> 내 친구들은 무대에서 춤을 추고 있지 않았다.
> (not, on stage, were, dancing, friends, my)

→ ___________________________________

23

다음 문장을 지시대로 바꾸어 쓰시오.

(1) He stays at his cousin's house.

→ ___________________________________
(현재진행형 평서문)

→ ___________________________________
(과거진행형 의문문)

(2) They ate strawberries for dessert.

→ ___________________________________
(현재진행형 의문문)

→ ___________________________________
(과거진행형 부정문)

24

다음 그림을 보고, 주어진 말을 이용하여 문장을 완성하시오.

(lie, sit, run)

(1) A woman __________ __________ on the bench now.

(2) A man __________ __________ on the grass now.

(3) The children __________ __________ along the river now.

25 내신기출

다음 표를 보고, 물음에 답하시오.

Name	An Hour Ago	Now
Amy	draw a picture	listen to music
Fred	exercise at the gym	make some food

(1) Q: Was Amy listening to music an hour ago?

A: __________, __________ __________. She __________ __________ __________ __________.

(2) Q: Is Fred exercising at the gym right now?

A: __________, __________ __________. He __________ __________ __________ __________.

26 고난도 내신기출

대화를 읽고, [ ] 안의 동사를 적절한 형태로 써넣으시오.

> A: Where __________ (be) you yesterday? I __________ (call) you many times.
> B: Sorry, I __________ __________ (go out) to go shopping in the afternoon.

시제

1 현재시제

- 현재의 상태나 지속적인 성질을 나타낼 때
- 일상적인 행동이나 습관을 나타낼 때
- 과학적 사실이나 불변의 진리를 나타낼 때

2 과거시제

- 과거의 동작을 나타낼 때
- 과거의 상태를 나타낼 때
- 역사적 사실을 나타낼 때

 현재시제 또는 과거시제와 함께 쓰이는 부사(구) 알아두기

3 진행형

- 특정 시점에 진행 중인 일을 나타낼 때
- 현재진행형: 〈① ____________의 현재형+② ____________〉
- 과거진행형: 〈③ ____________+v-ing〉
- 진행형의 부정문: ④ 〈____________+____________+____________〉
- 진행형의 의문문: Q: ⑤ 〈____________+주어+____________ ~?〉
  A: 〈Yes, 주어+be동사.〉 / 〈No, 주어+be동사+⑥ ____________.〉

진행형의 형태 기억하기

CHECK

다음 [ ] 안에서 알맞은 말을 고르시오.

1 Miri usually (goes / went) to bed at 10:00 p.m. these days.
2 Our team (loses / lost) the game last night.
3 King Sejong (invents / invented) Hangeul in 1443.
4 Henry (is / was) cooking in the kitchen right now.
5 My sister (wants / is wanting) a robot for her birthday.
6 We (not were / were not) hiring new staff at the time.
7 (Did / Were) you watching TV this morning?

07

조동사

조동사는 동사의 앞에 쓰여 동사에 미래, 가능, 허가, 추측, 의무 등의 의미를 더해 주
는 말입니다. 조동사의 형태는 주어의 인칭이나 수에 따라 변하지 않으며, 조동사 뒤
에는 항상 동사원형이 쓰인답니다.

will

- 조동사는 동사에 미래, 가능, 허가, 추측, 의무 등의 의미를 더해 주는 말이다. 주어의 인칭이나 수에 따라 형태가 변하지 않으며, 조동사 뒤에는 항상 동사원형을 쓴다.

- will은 '~할 것이다', '~하겠다'라는 의미로 미래의 일이나 주어의 의지를 나타낸다.
  He **will** be fifteen next year.　　(미래의 일)
  I **will** find a way.　　(주어의 의지)

- will의 의문문은 〈Will + 주어 + 동사원형 ~?〉, 부정형은 won't[will not]로 쓴다. 〈Will you ~?〉는 '~해 주시겠어요?'라는 요청의 의미를 나타내기도 한다.
  A: **Will** you come to the party? (요청) – B: Yes, I **will**. / No, I **won't**.
  I **won't[will not]** do it again.

> **+ Plus**　〈주어 + will〉은 '(아포스트로피)를 사용해서 I'll, We'll 등과 같이 줄여 쓸 수 있다.

A 　다음 [ ] 안에서 알맞은 말을 고르시오.

1 　They (joined / will join) us tomorrow.

2 　Will the store (open / opens) next week?

3 　I (will not / not will) wear this dress.

4 　You don't need an umbrella. It (will / won't) rain today.

B 　다음 밑줄 친 부분을 어법에 맞게 고쳐 쓰시오.

1 　I <u>will am</u> a high school student next year.

2 　Tony won't <u>not give</u> the report to us.

3 　Will she <u>comes</u> back in the afternoon?

4 　They will <u>ask not</u> me that question.

C 　다음 우리말과 같은 뜻이 되도록 [ ] 안의 말을 이용하여 문장을 완성하시오.

1 　그 뮤지컬은 6시에 시작할 것이다. (begin)
　　The musical ＿＿＿＿＿＿＿ ＿＿＿＿＿＿＿ at six o'clock.

2 　이번 주 토요일에 저에게 전화해 주시겠어요? (call)
　　＿＿＿＿＿＿＿ you ＿＿＿＿＿＿＿ me this Saturday?

3 　오늘 밤 Lucy는 노래를 부르지 않을 것이다. (sing)
　　Lucy ＿＿＿＿＿＿＿ ＿＿＿＿＿＿＿ a song tonight.

4 　A: 내년 이맘때 당신은 여기에 있을 건가요? (be)
　　＿＿＿＿＿＿＿ you ＿＿＿＿＿＿＿ here this time next year?
　　B: 아니요, 저는 아프리카에 있을 거예요.
　　No, ＿＿＿＿＿＿＿ ＿＿＿＿＿＿＿ in Africa.

be going to

- be going to는 '~할 것이다', '~할 예정이다'라는 의미로 가까운 미래에 대한 예측이나 이미 정해진 계획을 나타낸다.
I **am going to** clean my room.

- be going to의 의문문은 〈be동사+주어+going to+동사원형 ~?〉, 부정문은 〈주어+be동사+not+going to+동사원형〉으로 쓴다.
A: **Are** you **going to** call him? – B: Yes, I am. / No, I'm not.
He **isn't going to** meet her. (= He**'s not going to** meet her.)

A 다음 [ ] 안에서 알맞은 말을 고르시오.

1 We (are / will) going to play basketball this Sunday.

2 (Be / Is) Dad going to make lunch for us?

3 I'm (going not / not going) to buy a new TV.

4 Is the train (goes / going) to arrive at Seoul Station soon?

B 다음 우리말과 같은 뜻이 되도록 be going to와 [ ] 안의 말을 이용하여 문장을 완성하시오.

1 나는 설거지를 할 것이다. (wash)

I ____________________ the dishes.

2 너는 다음 달에 요가를 배울 예정이니? (learn)

____________________ yoga next month?

3 오늘 오후에는 날씨가 좋을 겁니다. (be nice)

The weather ____________________ this afternoon.

4 Helen과 Dave는 그 영화를 보지 않을 것이다. (watch)

Helen and Dave ____________________ the movie.

C 다음 우리말과 같은 뜻이 되도록 [ ] 안의 말을 알맞게 배열하여 문장을 완성하시오.

1 너는 나를 도와줄 거니? (are, me, going, help, you, to)

____

2 그는 헤어스타일을 바꾸지 않을 것이다. (going, he, change, to, his hairstyle, isn't)

____

3 나는 일본에 있는 내 친구를 만날 것이다. (my friend, I'm, meet, going, in Japan, to)

____

- can은 '~할 수 있다'라는 의미로 주어의 능력이나 가능을 나타낸다.
  Jake **can** drive a car.

- can의 의문문은 〈Can＋주어＋동사원형 ~?〉, 부정형은 can't[cannot]로 쓴다.
  A: **Can** you speak Spanish? – B: Yes, I **can**. / No, I **can't**.
  Penguins **can't[cannot]** fly.

- can은 '~해도 좋다'라는 허가의 의미를 나타내기도 한다.
  Can I use your phone?
  You **can't** swim in this river.

(**＋Plus**) can의 과거형은 could, 부정형은 couldn't[could not]이다.
  I **couldn't** hear you because of the loud music.

A 다음 ( ) 안에서 알맞은 말을 고르시오.

1 He can (play / plays) the guitar.

2 Can (turn you / you turn) off the light?

3 I (cannot find / can find not) my wallet.

4 They could (see / saw) the stars last night.

B 다음 빈칸에 알맞은 말을 넣어 대화를 완성하시오.

1 A: _____________ _____________ play outside?

  B: No, you can't. It's too late.

2 A: _____________ _____________ ride a bicycle?

  B: Yes, I can. I ride one every weekend.

3 A: Can your brother play the guitar?

  B: No, _____________ _____________.

C 다음 우리말과 같은 뜻이 되도록 can과 ( ) 안의 말을 이용하여 문장을 완성하시오.

1 제가 지금 선물을 열어 봐도 될까요? (open)

  _____________ _____________ _____________ the present now?

2 Dorothy는 수화를 할 수 있다. (use)

  _____________ _____________ _____________ sign language.

3 너는 수업 중에 휴대폰을 사용해서는 안 된다. (use)

  _____________ _____________ _____________ your phone during class.

4 너는 한 손으로 문자 메시지를 보낼 수 있어? (send)

  _____________ _____________ _____________ a text message with one hand?

can과 be able to

- 능력/가능(~할 수 있다)을 나타내는 can은 be able to로 바꾸어 쓸 수 있다.

- be able to의 be동사는 주어의 인칭과 수, 문장의 시제에 알맞은 형태로 바꾸어 쓴다.
  Danny **can** read Chinese.   → Danny **is able to** read Chinese.
  Can you finish it on time?   → **Are** you **able to** finish it on time?
  I **couldn't** sleep last night. → I **wasn't able to** sleep last night.

A 다음 밑줄 친 부분을 어법에 맞게 고쳐 쓰시오.

1 She <u>be</u> able to pay for it now.

2 <u>Were</u> you able to help me today?

3 Sadly, they <u>wasn't</u> able to find the dog yesterday.

4 <u>I'm</u> able to see the parade last weekend.

B 다음 〈보기〉와 같이 be able to를 이용한 문장으로 바꾸어 쓰시오.

> 〈보기〉   Stella can do magic. → Stella is able to do magic.

1 I can make egg tarts.   → I ________________________ egg tarts.

2 Can you do this job?   → ________________________ this job?

3 They could hear my voice.   → They ________________________ my voice.

4 He couldn't use the machine.   → He ________________________ the machine.

5 We can deliver it for you.   → We ________________________ it for you.

C 다음 우리말과 같은 뜻이 되도록 [ ] 안의 말을 이용하여 문장을 완성하시오.

1 나는 그 이야기를 영어로 말할 수 있다. (tell)
   ________________ ________________ ________________ ________________ the story in English.

2 Joe는 빨리 달릴 수 있나요? (run)
   ________________ ________________ ________________ ________________ ________________ fast?

3 우리는 그 상자를 들어 올릴 수 없었다. (lift)
   ____ the box.

4 Peter는 비 때문에 골프를 칠 수 없다. (play)
   ________________ ________________ ________________ ________________ golf due
   to the rain.

5 그녀는 오늘 아침에 기차를 탈 수 있었나요? (catch)
   ________________ ________________ ________________ ________________ the train
   this morning?

POINT 05 may

- may는 '~해도 좋다'라는 의미로 허가를 나타낸다. can과 바꾸어 쓸 수 있지만, may가 좀 더 정중한 표현이다.
  You **may** come to my office.
  May I see your passport?

- may는 '~일지도 모른다'라는 추측의 의미를 나타내기도 한다.
  He **may** win the game.
  She **may** not be here in time.

+ Plus 〈May/Can I ~?〉에 대한 부정의 대답은 No, you may not.이나 No, you can't.와 같이 직설적인 표현 대신 I'm afraid you may not.이나 I'm sorry you can't. 등을 쓰는 것이 좋다.

A 다음 〈보기〉에서 알맞은 말을 골라 대화를 완성하시오.

| 〈보기〉 | may be sick | may not be true | may I use | may I have |

1 A: Dad, ___________________ some ice cream?
   B: Sure. Vanilla or chocolate?

2 A: Nora, ___________________ your laptop?
   B: I'm sorry, but I left it at home.

3 A: Brad is going to leave this town soon.
   B: That ___________________. He likes this town.

4 A: I can't find Grace in the classroom.
   B: She's absent today. She ___________________.

B 다음 우리말과 같은 뜻이 되도록 may와 [ ] 안의 말을 이용하여 문장을 완성하시오.

1 당신은 여기 앉으시면 안 됩니다. (sit)
   You ___________ ___________ ___________ here.

2 제가 이 모자를 써 봐도 되나요? (try)
   ___________ ___________ on this hat?

3 내일 날씨가 안 좋을 수도 있다. (be bad)
   The weather ___________ ___________ ___________ tomorrow.

4 제가 당신과 함께 사진을 찍어도 될까요? (take)
   ___________ ___________ ___________ a picture with you?

5 그는 네 전화번호를 모르고 있을지도 모른다. (know)
   ___________ ___________ ___________ your phone number.

must

- must는 '~해야 한다'라는 의미로 의무를 나타낸다. 부정형 must not은 '~하면 안 된다'라는 금지의 의미를 나타낸다.
  You **must** wear a swimsuit here. (의무)
  You **must not** make any noise. (금지)

- must는 '~임이 틀림없다'라는 강한 추측의 의미를 나타내기도 한다.
  He didn't eat lunch. He **must** be hungry. (강한 추측)

> **+Plus** '~일 리가 없다'라는 강한 부정적 추측의 의미는 must not이 아니라 can't[cannot]로 나타낸다.
> It can't[cannot] be true. (그것은 사실일 리가 없다.)

A 다음 [ ] 안에서 알맞은 말을 고르시오.

1 She must (come / comes) home by nine o'clock.

2 We must (waste not / not waste) water.

3 You (must / must not) run here. The floor is slippery.

4 Alan won the prize. His parents (must / can't) be proud of him.

B 다음 밑줄 친 부분의 의미를 〈보기〉에서 골라 그 기호를 쓰시오.

> 〈보기〉 ⓐ ~해야 한다 ⓑ ~하면 안 된다 ⓒ ~임이 틀림없다 ⓓ ~일 리가 없다

1 That restaurant <u>must</u> be great. People love to eat there. ( )

2 We don't have much time. We <u>must</u> leave here now. ( )

3 You <u>must not</u> touch this machine. It is very dangerous. ( )

4 I just saw him at school. He <u>can't</u> be at the hospital now. ( )

C 다음 우리말과 같은 뜻이 되도록 must와 〈보기〉의 말을 이용하여 문장을 완성하시오.

> 〈보기〉 be talk enter follow

1 저 영화는 틀림없이 재미있을 것이다.
  That film ______________ ______________ interesting.

2 그녀는 그 방에 들어가서는 안 된다.
  ______________ ______________ ______________ ______________ the room.

3 우리는 교통 법규를 따라야 한다.
  ______________ ______________ ______________ the traffic rules.

4 너는 시험 중에 말하면 안 된다.
  ______________ ______________ ______________ during the test.

have to

- have to는 must와 같이 '~해야 한다'라는 의미로 의무를 나타낸다.
  They **have to** wear uniforms.　→ They **must** wear uniforms.

- have 동사는 주어의 인칭과 수, 문장의 시제에 알맞은 형태로 바꾸어 쓴다.
  Arthur **has to** save money.
  We **had to** get up early yesterday.

- have to의 의문문은 〈Do / Does / Did + 주어 + have to ~?〉로 쓴다. 부정형은 don't / doesn't / didn't have to 로 '~할 필요가 없다'라는 의미를 나타낸다.
  A: **Does** she **have to** take the test? – B: Yes, she does. / No, she doesn't.
  You **don't have to** study tonight.

> **내신만점 Tip**　must not(금지)과 don't have to(불필요)의 의미를 구분하자.
> You **must not** do it again. (너는 그것을 다시 하면 안 된다.)
> You **don't have to** do it again. (너는 그것을 다시 할 필요가 없다.)

A　다음 [ ] 안에서 알맞은 말을 고르시오.

1　We (must / have) to clean the classroom.

2　He (has / have) to go to the dentist.

3　Jane (don't / doesn't) have to buy this book.

4　I (had / have) to call my parents yesterday.

5　You (must not / don't have to) be late for the exam.

B　다음 우리말과 같은 뜻이 되도록 [ ] 안의 말을 이용하여 문장을 완성하시오.

1　그는 9시부터 6시까지 일해야 한다. (work)
　He ＿＿＿＿＿＿ ＿＿＿＿＿＿ ＿＿＿＿＿＿ from nine to six.

2　Karen이 해외에 가야 하나요? (go)
　＿＿＿＿＿＿ Karen ＿＿＿＿＿＿ ＿＿＿＿＿＿ ＿＿＿＿＿＿ abroad?

3　너는 Tom을 만나서 이야기해야 한다. (meet)
　＿＿＿＿＿＿ ＿＿＿＿＿＿ ＿＿＿＿＿＿ ＿＿＿＿＿＿ Tom and talk to him.

4　Jacob은 안경을 쓸 필요가 없었다. (wear)
　Jacob ＿＿＿＿＿＿ ＿＿＿＿＿＿ ＿＿＿＿＿＿ ＿＿＿＿＿＿ glasses.

5　저희가 이것을 오늘 끝내야 하나요? (finish)
　＿＿＿＿＿＿ we ＿＿＿＿＿＿ ＿＿＿＿＿＿ ＿＿＿＿＿＿ this today?

6　나는 지갑을 잃어버려서 어제 집에 걸어와야 했다. (walk)
　I lost my wallet, so ＿＿＿＿＿＿ ＿＿＿＿＿＿ ＿＿＿＿＿＿ ＿＿＿＿＿＿ home yesterday.

should

- should는 '~해야 한다', '~하는 것이 좋겠다'라는 의미로 의무나 충고, 제안 등을 나타낸다. must나 have to보다 약한 의무를 나타낸다.
  You **should** wash your hands.

- should의 의문문은 〈Should+주어+동사원형 ~?〉, 부정형은 shouldn't[should not]로 쓴다.
  Should I pay the bill now?
  You **shouldn't[should not]** run in this building.

A 다음 〈보기〉에서 알맞은 말을 골라 should나 shouldn't를 이용하여 대화를 완성하시오.

〈보기〉	apologize	believe	take	use	wear

1 A: It's snowing a lot. Driving may be dangerous.

B: Oh, ______________ I ______________ the subway instead?

2 A: I lied to Rachel. She is angry with me.

B: You ______________ ______________ to her.

3 A: I heard some bad news about a singer.

B: You ______________ ______________ rumors.

4 A: I'm going to ride a motorcycle.

B: Okay, but you ______________ ______________ a helmet.

5 A: My eyes hurt. I looked at a screen all day.

B: You ______________ ______________ your smartphone too much.

B 다음 우리말과 같은 뜻이 되도록 〈보기〉와 [ ] 안의 말을 이용하여 문장을 완성하시오.

〈보기〉	should	shouldn't	don't have to	can't

1 우리는 아침을 거르지 않는 것이 좋다. (skip)

______________ ______________ ______________ breakfast.

2 너는 이 노래를 들어 봐야 한다. (listen)

______________ ______________ ______________ to this song.

3 그는 어제 일찍 자서, 지금 피곤할 리가 없다. (be tired)

He went to bed early yesterday, so ______________ ______________

______________ now.

4 그들은 모든 질문에 답할 필요가 없다. (answer)

______________ ______________ ______________ ______________ every question.

실전 TEST

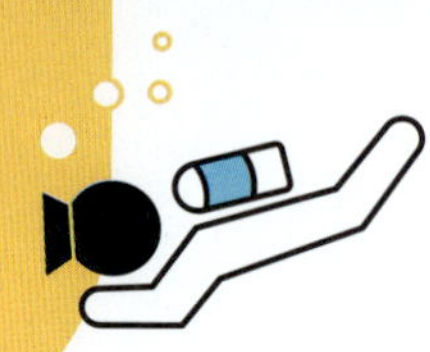

01-03 다음 빈칸에 알맞은 말을 고르시오.

01

> You ___________ play with fire. It is not safe.

① can
② must
③ have to
④ must not
⑤ not able to

02

> It ___________ rain this afternoon. Bring an umbrella with you.

① will
② have to
③ must not
④ may not
⑤ doesn't have to

03

> Eric ___________ be tired. He played sports all day yesterday.

① must not
② must
③ may not
④ cannot
⑤ doesn't have to

04-05 다음 밑줄 친 부분과 바꾸어 쓸 수 있는 말을 고르시오.

04

> <u>Can</u> I have a cookie?

① Should
② Must
③ May
④ Will
⑤ Do

05

> John <u>is going to</u> enter college.

① will
② must
③ can
④ may
⑤ should

06-07 다음 우리말을 영어로 바르게 옮긴 것을 고르시오.

06

> 당신은 대전에서 기차를 갈아타야 한다.

① You can change trains in Daejeon.
② You may change trains in Daejeon.
③ You will change trains in Daejeon.
④ You should change trains in Daejeon.
⑤ You're going to change trains in Daejeon.

07

> 그는 게으른 학생임이 틀림없다.

① He can be a lazy student.
② He must be a lazy student.
③ He will be a lazy student.
④ He can't be a lazy student.
⑤ He doesn't have to be a lazy student.

08-09 다음 질문에 대한 알맞은 대답을 고르시오.

08

> A: Will you tell me the secret?
> B: No, ___________.

① I will
② I won't
③ I don't
④ you will
⑤ you won't

09

> A: Can I see you tomorrow?
> B: _________________ How about next Saturday?

① Sure.　　　　② No, you will not.
③ Why not?　　　④ Yes, you can.
⑤ I'm afraid not.

10

다음 중 대화가 자연스럽지 <u>않은</u> 것은?

① A: Will you go to the party?
　B: No, I won't.
② A: Can I use your phone?
　B: Yes, you can.
③ A: May I go out now?
　B: I'm afraid you may not.
④ A: Must I read this book now?
　B: No, you don't have to.
⑤ A: Should we go and see him?
　B: Yes, we had to.

11 　내신기출

다음 중 밑줄 친 must의 의미가 나머지와 <u>다른</u> 것은?

① Kids like this song. It <u>must</u> be funny.
② You <u>must</u> take the school bus.
③ You <u>must</u> put your trash in the trash can.
④ The pot is very hot. We <u>must</u> be careful.
⑤ They <u>must</u> do their homework themselves.

12

다음 중 우리말을 영어로 옮긴 것이 <u>잘못된</u> 것은?

① 제가 놀이공원에 가도 되나요?
　Can I go to the amusement park?
② 그 둘은 자매일 리가 없다.
　Those two can't be sisters.
③ 나는 차 한 잔을 마셔야 했다.
　I had to drink a cup of tea.
④ 그녀는 그를 초대하지 않을지도 모른다.
　She may not invite him.
⑤ 그는 한국에서 유명한 피아니스트임이 틀림없다.
　He can be a famous pianist in Korea.

　고난도

13 - 14 다음 빈칸에 알맞은 말이 바르게 짝지어진 것을 고르시오.

13

> A: Does your mother _________ to wake you up every morning?
> B: No, she _________. I have an alarm clock.

① has – doesn't　　② has – must not
③ have – doesn't　　④ have – not
⑤ have – can't

14

> Chris got up late, so he _________ able to be there on time. He _________ apologize to everyone.

① was – could　　② is – should
③ wasn't – had to　④ could – couldn't
⑤ couldn't – has to

15 내신기출

다음 빈칸에 공통으로 들어갈 말은?

> • You __________ talk loudly in the library.
> • I'm afraid you __________ borrow this book.
> • You are 14 years old, so you __________ drive a car.

① can't ② may
③ must ④ can
⑤ don't have to

16 내신기출

다음 짝지어진 두 문장의 의미가 같지 <u>않은</u> 것은?

① She can ride a horse.
→ She is able to ride a horse.
② We will have a piece of cake.
→ We are going to have a piece of cake.
③ May I borrow your pencil?
→ Can I borrow your pencil?
④ You must not waste your money.
→ You don't have to waste your money.
⑤ All students should be seated when the bell rings.
→ All students have to be seated when the bell rings.

17-18 다음 중 어법상 <u>틀린</u> 것을 고르시오.

17

① Tim must be busy now.
② Can you speak English?
③ Do we have to wait for him?
④ Lucy mays go to Scotland.
⑤ She should leave tomorrow.

18

① May I try on this T-shirt?
② Sam has to meet her right now.
③ We can able to finish the project on time.
④ Students must follow the school rules.
⑤ Are you going to go to church this Sunday?

19

다음 대화의 순서로 알맞은 것은?

> (a) You have to go to the service center.
> (b) No, I'm not able to.
> (c) Can you fix this camera?
> (d) Then what should I do?

① (a) – (c) – (b) – (d)
② (a) – (d) – (c) – (b)
③ (c) – (a) – (d) – (b)
④ (c) – (b) – (d) – (a)
⑤ (d) – (a) – (c) – (b)

20 고난도 내신기출

다음 중 어법상 옳은 것끼리 짝지어진 것은?

> (a) We can won the game.
> (b) She won't change her mind.
> (c) You must cleaned your room yesterday.
> (d) They must stay inside today.
> (e) He was able to download the music file yesterday.

① (a), (b), (c) ② (a), (d), (e)
③ (b), (c), (d) ④ (b), (d), (e)
⑤ (c), (d), (e)

21

주어진 말을 이용하여 대화를 완성하시오.

(1)
A: I wasn't able to have anything for lunch.
B: Oh, you ________ ________ ________.
I'll prepare some food now. (hungry)

(2)
A: Look at that boy. Isn't that Luke?
B: That ________ ________ Luke. He is in China right now. (be)

22

다음 문장을 지시대로 바꾸어 쓰시오. [단, 줄임말로 쓸 것]

(1) He is going to say hello to her.

→ _________________________________
(부정문)

→ _________________________________
(의문문)

(2) She had to come back home by ten.

→ _________________________________
(부정문)

→ _________________________________
(의문문)

23

다음 우리말과 같은 뜻이 되도록 주어진 말을 알맞게 배열하여 문장을 완성하시오.

너는 좋은 자리를 잡을 수 있었어?
(able, a good seat, were, get, to, you)

→ _________________________________

24

다음 표를 보고, 공연장에서 지켜야 할 규칙을 〈보기〉와 같이 must를 이용하여 쓰시오.

Do	Don't
Turn off your phone	Eat any food
(1) Stay silent during the show	(2) Take pictures during the show

〈보기〉 You must turn off your phone.

(1) You _________________________________.

(2) You _________________________________.

25 내신기출

다음 그림을 보고, 주어진 말을 이용하여 Yuna가 할 수 있는 일과 할 수 없는 일을 쓰시오.

(1) Yuna ________ ________ a car. (drive)

(2) Yuna ________ ________ ________ ________ the guitar. (play)

26 고난도 내신기출

주어진 말과, 상자 안에 제시된 표현을 한 번씩 사용하여 〈보기〉와 같이 문장을 완성하시오. [단, 필요하면 부정형으로 쓸 것]

go out and play / go to school / be kind

〈보기〉 He already finished his homework.
So he can go out and play. (can)

(1) She always helps her classmates.

She _________________________. (must)

(2) It's Sunday. He _________________________.
(have to)

조동사

1 조동사

- 의미: 동사에 미래, 가능, 허가, 추측, 의무 등의 의미를 더해 주는 말
- 형태: 조동사+① ____________
  *주어의 인칭이나 수에 따라 변하지 않음 (be going to, be able to, have to 제외)

2 조동사의 종류

will	– 미래의 일: ② ____________ – 주어의 의지: ~하겠다
be going to	– 가까운 미래에 대한 예측이나 이미 정해진 계획: ~할 것이다, ~할 예정이다
can	– 주어의 능력이나 가능: ~할 수 있다 (= ③ ____________) – 허가: ~해도 좋다
④ ____________	– 허가: ~해도 좋다 – 추측: ~일지도 모른다
must	– 의무: ~해야 한다 – 금지 ⑤ ____________ : ~하면 안 된다 – 강한 추측: ~임이 틀림없다 / *강한 부정적 추측 can't[cannot]: ~일 리가 없다
⑥ ____________	– 의무: ~해야 한다 (= must) – 불필요 don't have to: ⑦ ____________
should	– 의무, 충고, 제안: ~해야 한다, ~하는 것이 좋겠다

 같은 의미로 서로 바꿔 쓸 수 있는 표현 기억하기

must not과 don't have to 의미 구분하기

CHECK

1 다음 우리말과 같은 뜻이 되도록 [ ] 안에서 알맞은 말을 고르시오.

(1) 너의 남동생은 축구를 좋아하는 게 틀림없다.
　　Your brother (can / must) like soccer.

(2) 너는 아직 떠날 필요가 없다.
　　You (must not / don't have to) leave yet.

(3) 그녀는 어제 회의에 올 수 없었다.
　　She wasn't (able to / going to) come to the meeting yesterday.

2 밑줄 친 부분이 어법상 맞으면 O, 틀리면 X 표시하고 바르게 고치시오.

(1) May I introduces you to Ms. Gwen?

(2) Can I use the fax machine?

(3) James should is nicer to his mother.

(4) It's really sunny. Have I to stay inside?

(5) I'm getting better. So I not will go to see a doctor.

08

형용사, 부사, 비교

형용사는 명사나 대명사를 수식하거나, 주어나 목적어를 보충 설명하는 말입니다.

부사는 동사, 형용사, 다른 부사 또는 문장 전체를 수식하는 말입니다.

형용사나 부사의 원급, 비교급, 최상급 표현을 사용하여 둘 이상의 대상을 비교할 수 있습니다.

형용사의 역할

● 형용사는 명사나 대명사를 수식하는 역할을 하며, 보통 명사 앞에 쓰인다.
He has a **new** *smartphone*.

> **+ Plus** -thing, -body, -one으로 끝나는 대명사는 형용사가 뒤에서 수식한다.
> I want *something* **cold** to drink.

● 형용사는 주격 보어나 find, make, keep, leave 등의 동사의 목적격 보어로 쓰여 주어나 목적어의 상태·성질을 보충 설명해 준다.
She is **kind** and **friendly**.　　　(주격 보어)
I found *this book* **difficult**.　　　(목적격 보어)

A 　다음 문장에서 형용사가 수식하는 말을 찾아 밑줄로 표시하시오.

1　Amelia has long hair.

2　I left the window open.

3　They were hard questions.

4　Her dress is really beautiful.

5　There was nothing useful in this magazine.

B 　다음 밑줄 친 부분을 어법에 맞게 고쳐 쓰시오.

1　This road is very <u>danger</u>.

2　I found him <u>nicely</u>.

3　He is a <u>photographer famous</u>.

4　The soup smells <u>deliciously</u>.

5　I want to be <u>important someone</u>.

C 　다음 우리말과 같은 뜻이 되도록 〈보기〉와 [ ] 안의 말을 이용하여 문장을 완성하시오.

> 〈보기〉　wet　　　angry　　　necessary　　　simple

1　그것은 아이들을 위한 간단한 게임이다. (game)
It is a ＿＿＿＿＿＿ ＿＿＿＿＿＿ for kids.

2　그의 실수는 나를 화나게 만들었다. (me)
His mistake made ＿＿＿＿＿＿ ＿＿＿＿＿＿.

3　바닥에 있는 옷들이 젖어 있었다. (clothes)
The ＿＿＿＿＿＿ on the floor were ＿＿＿＿＿＿.

4　당신은 저녁 식사에 필요한 모든 것을 샀나요? (everything)
Did you buy ＿＿＿＿＿＿ ＿＿＿＿＿＿ for dinner?

수량 형용사

- 수량 형용사는 명사 앞에 쓰여 정해지지 않은 수나 양을 대략적으로 나타낸다.

많은	조금 있는, 약간의	거의 없는	명사
many	a few	few	+ 셀 수 있는 명사의 복수형
much	a little	little	+ 셀 수 없는 명사
a lot of (= lots of)	–	–	+ 셀 수 있는 명사의 복수형 셀 수 없는 명사

Peter took **many** *pictures*.
I have **a few** *problems*.
A lot of *fans* joined the club.

Joan didn't do **much** *work*.
They showed **little** *interest*.
There is **lots of** *water* in the bottle.

내신만점 Tip 셀 수 있는 명사나 셀 수 없는 명사와 함께 사용되는 각각의 수량 형용사를 확실히 구분하여 기억하자.

A 다음 [ ] 안에서 알맞은 말을 고르시오.

1 I met (many / much) people on my trip.

2 Robert has (a few / a little) money now.

3 (Few / Little) shops are open today.

4 (A few / A lot of) noise came from the street.

B 다음 빈칸에 들어갈 수 <u>없는</u> 것에 ✔ 표시하시오.

1 This soup needs a little __________. ☐ carrot ☐ salt ☐ milk

2 I saw __________ animals yesterday. ☐ many ☐ much ☐ lots of

3 We found few __________ in the book. ☐ errors ☐ mistakes ☐ information

4 They have __________ things to do. ☐ a few ☐ a little ☐ a lot of

C 다음 우리말과 같은 뜻이 되도록 [ ] 안의 말을 이용하여 문장을 완성하시오.

1 그는 주스를 너무 많이 마셨다. (juice)

He drank too ______________ ____________.

2 내 주머니 안에 열쇠 몇 개가 있다. (key)

There are ______________ ______________ ____________ in my pocket.

3 Sue는 시험 후에 힘이 거의 없었다. (energy)

Sue had ______________ ____________ after the exam.

4 그들은 후식으로 많은 쿠키를 가져왔다. (cookie)

They brought ______________ ______________ ____________ ____________ for dessert.

부사의 역할과 형태

○ 부사는 동사, 형용사, 다른 부사 또는 문장 전체를 수식하는 역할을 한다.

Thomas *appeared* **suddenly**.　　　　　　　　　　　　　　(동사 수식)

Strangely, *we met at the same place several times*.　　　(문장 전체 수식)

○ 대부분의 부사는 형용사에 -ly를 붙인 형태이지만, 예외적인 경우도 있다.

대부분의 부사	형용사+-ly	real – real**ly**	serious – serious**ly**
-y로 끝나는 형용사의 부사	y를 i로 바꾸고+-ly	happy – happ**ily**	lucky – luck**ily**
-le로 끝나는 형용사의 부사	e를 빼고+-y	gentle – gentl**y**	simple – simpl**y**
형용사와 형태가 같은 부사	**fast**(빠르게)　**hard**(열심히)　**late**(늦게)　**early**(일찍)　**high**(높게)		
예외	good - **well**		

+Plus　-ly가 붙어 형용사와 전혀 다른 뜻을 가지는 부사로 hardly(거의 ~않다), lately(최근에), highly(매우) 등이 있다.

A  다음 [ ] 안에서 알맞은 말을 고르시오.

1　She opened the bottle (easy / easily).

2　I have a (simple / simply) question.

3　They lived (happy / happily) together.

4　The train arrived a little (late / lately).

5　(Lucky / Luckily), I found a cheap apartment.

6　Your drawing looks (great / greatly).

7　Kate (hard / hardly) slept last weekend.

8　The man entered the room (quiet / quietly).

9　We did very (good / well) on the math test.

10　He hit the ball (high / highly) in the air.

B 다음 [ ] 안의 말을 빈칸에 적절한 형태로 써넣으시오.

1　(kind)　She is very ___________.

　　　　　He spoke ___________.

2　(heavy)　It rained ___________ all night.

　　　　　The backpack was ___________.

3　(terrible)　The food tasted ___________.

　　　　　They played ___________ today.

4　(fast)　Don't drive so ___________.

　　　　　George is a ___________ runner.

5　(good)　Sally explained the topic ___________.

　　　　　His cooking skills are really ___________.

● 빈도부사는 어떤 일이 얼마나 자주 일어나는지를 나타내며, be동사나 조동사의 뒤, 일반동사의 앞에 쓴다.

never(결코 ~않다) < seldom(거의 ~않다) < sometimes(가끔) < often(자주) < usually(대개, 보통) < always(항상)

0% ◀——————————————————————————————▶ 100%
(빈도)

Sarah *is* **usually** very cheerful.　　　(be동사 뒤)
I *will* **always** miss you.　　　(조동사 뒤)
Nick **never** *tells* a lie.　　　(일반동사 앞)

내신만점 Tip　빈도부사는 be동사나 조동사 뒤, 일반동사 앞에 온다는 것을 기억하자.

A　다음 [ ] 안의 빈도부사가 들어갈 알맞은 위치를 고르시오.

1　(usually)　　　She ① wears ② a ③ skirt.

2　(sometimes)　　I ① am ② hungry at ③ night.

3　(never)　　　　I ① can ② forget ③ that moment.

B　다음 우리말과 같은 뜻이 되도록 빈칸에 알맞은 빈도부사를 쓰시오.

1　Paul은 항상 안경을 쓴다.

　　Paul ＿＿＿＿＿＿＿＿ wears glasses.

2　그녀는 수업에 자주 늦는다.

　　She is ＿＿＿＿＿＿＿＿ late for classes.

3　3월에 가끔 눈이 온다.

　　It ＿＿＿＿＿＿＿＿ snows in March.

4　그는 결코 일을 그만두지 않을 것이다.

　　He will ＿＿＿＿＿＿＿＿ quit his job.

5　나는 보통 방과 후에 수영을 하러 간다.

　　I ＿＿＿＿＿＿＿＿ go swimming after school.

C　다음 우리말과 같은 뜻이 되도록 [ ] 안의 말을 알맞게 배열하여 문장을 완성하시오.

1　그녀는 거의 버스를 타고 등교하지 않는다. (goes, school, seldom, to)

　　She ＿＿＿＿＿＿＿＿＿＿＿＿＿＿ by bus.

2　너는 길을 건널 때 항상 조심해야 한다. (should, be careful, always)

　　You ＿＿＿＿＿＿＿＿＿＿＿＿＿＿ when you cross the street.

3　Mike는 그의 할머니에게 전화를 자주 한다. (his, calls, grandmother, often)

　　Mike ＿＿＿＿＿＿＿＿＿＿＿＿＿＿.

- 〈as+형용사/부사의 원급+as〉는 '…만큼 ~한/하게'라는 뜻을 나타내는 비교 표현이다.
  I am **as tall as** my brother.
  Ben studies **as hard as** Tim does.

- 〈not+as[so]+형용사/부사의 원급+as〉는 '…만큼 ~하지 않은/않게'라는 뜻을 나타낸다.
  This model is **not as[so] popular as** other models.
  I don't work out **as[so] often as** Laura.

A　다음 우리말과 같은 뜻이 되도록 〈보기〉에서 알맞은 말을 골라 빈칸에 적절한 형태로 써넣으시오.

> 〈보기〉　comfortable　　expensive　　interesting　　light　　slowly　　well

1　내 코트는 티셔츠만큼 가볍다.
　My coat is ______________________ a T-shirt.

2　그 시계는 보이는 것만큼 비싸지 않다.
　The watch is ______________________ it looks.

3　Betty의 아버지는 어머니만큼 느리게 말한다.
　Betty's father speaks ______________________ her mother.

4　이 소파는 내 것만큼 편하다.
　This sofa is ______________________ mine.

5　이번 회는 지난 회만큼 재미있지 않다.
　This episode is ______________________ the last one.

6　Josh는 선생님만큼 기타를 잘 연주할 수 있다.
　Josh can play the guitar ______________________ his teacher.

B　다음 〈보기〉와 같이 'as ~ as'를 이용하여 두 문장을 한 문장으로 만드시오.

> 〈보기〉　I'm 17 years old. Paul is 17 years old, too.
> 　　　　→ Paul is as old as me.

1　This picture frame is 1 meter wide. That one is 1 meter wide, too.
　→ This picture frame is ______________________ that one.

2　Your book is 13 centimeters thick. Mine is 20 centimeters thick.
　→ Your book is ______________________ mine.

3　She runs 100 meters in 12 seconds. He runs 100 meters in 12 seconds, too.
　They run fast.
　→ He runs ______________________ she does.

POINT 06 비교급과 최상급 만드는 방법

● 형용사나 부사의 비교급은 -(e)r 또는 more를 붙이고, 최상급은 -(e)st 또는 most를 붙인다.

대부분의 단어	+-er / -est	fast – fast**er** – fast**est**	slow – slow**er** – slow**est**
-e로 끝나는 단어	+-r / -st	large – larg**er** – larg**est**	close – clos**er** – clos**est**
〈단모음+단자음〉으로 끝나는 단어	자음을 한 번 더 쓰고 +-er / -est	hot – hot**ter** – hot**test** big – big**ger** – big**gest**	
〈자음+-y〉로 끝나는 단어	y를 i로 바꾸고 +-er / -est	happy – happ**ier** – happ**iest** easy – eas**ier** – eas**iest**	
-ful/-ous/-less/-ing/-ive로 끝나는 단어	형용사/부사 앞에 more / most	beautiful – **more** beautiful – **most** beautiful important – **more** important – **most** important	
3음절 이상의 단어			
예외	many/much – **more** – **most** good/well – **better** – **best**	little – **less** – **least** bad – **worse** – **worst**	

Her baby ate **faster** than she did.　　　　Jeju is the **largest** island in Korea.

 **A**　다음 단어의 비교급과 최상급을 쓰시오.

	비교급	최상급
1 loud	_________	_________
2 cute	_________	_________
3 thin	_________	_________
4 pretty	_________	_________
5 famous	_________	_________
6 bad	_________	_________
7 small	_________	_________
8 careful	_________	_________
9 heavy	_________	_________
10 nice	_________	_________
11 little	_________	_________
12 interesting	_________	_________

B　다음 [ ] 안에서 알맞은 말을 고르시오.

1 I feel (gooder / better) now.

2 Elephants are the (bigest / biggest) land animals.

3 This test is (badder / worse) than the last one.

4 This exam was (easier / easyer) than the last one.

5 It is the (expensivest / most expensive) necklace in the world.

6 His score was the (highest / most high) in the class.

- 〈비교급＋than〉은 '…보다 더 ~한/하게'라는 뜻을 나타내는 비교 표현이다.
  Your idea is **better than** mine.
  He drives **more carefully than** she does.

- 비교급 앞에 much, even, still, a lot, far 등을 써서 '훨씬 더 ~한/하게'라는 뜻으로 비교급을 강조할 수 있다.
  The white shoes look **much nicer than** the brown ones.

> **내신만점 Tip** '매우'라는 뜻으로 형용사나 부사를 강조할 때 자주 쓰이는 very는 비교급을 강조할 수 없다는 것을 기억하자.

A 다음 [ ] 안의 말을 이용하여 비교급 문장을 완성하시오.

1 You look _______________________ before. (healthy)

2 He ate _______________________ I did. (little)

3 Tom studies _______________________ Michael. (hard)

4 Happiness is _______________________ money. (important)

5 She jumped even _______________________ I did. (high)

6 My new backpack was _______________________ my old one. (cheap)

7 A close neighbor is _______________________ a distant cousin. (good)

8 For me, math is _______________________ English. (difficult)

9 Most fish can swim much _______________________ humans. (fast)

10 The horror movie was _______________________ the action movie. (exciting)

B 다음 우리말과 같은 뜻이 되도록 [ ] 안의 말을 이용하여 문장을 완성하시오.

1 Olivia는 전보다 더 천천히 걷는다. (slowly)

   Olivia walks _______________ _______________ than before.

2 그는 평소보다 더 일찍 잠자리에 들었다. (early)

   He went to bed _______________ _______________ usual.

3 이 고양이가 저 고양이보다 더 활발하다. (active)

   This cat is _______________ _______________ _______________ that one.

4 이 노트북은 다른 것보다 훨씬 더 무겁다. (much, heavy)

   This laptop is _______________ _______________ _______________ the other one.

5 그녀의 문제가 네 것보다 더 심각해 보인다. (serious)

   Her problem seems _______________ _______________ _______________ yours.

6 저 기타는 이것보다 훨씬 더 비싸다. (a lot, expensive)

   That guitar is _______________ _______________ _______________ _______________

   this one.

최상급 비교

- 〈the+최상급〉은 '가장 ~한/하게'라는 뜻으로 셋 이상의 대상을 비교할 때 쓰는 표현이다. 최상급 뒤에는 주로 of(~ 중에서)나 in(~ 안에서)을 써서 비교 범위를 나타내는 경우가 많다.
  Robin is **the tallest** boy *in* his class.

- 〈one of the+최상급+복수명사〉는 '가장 ~한 … 중의 하나'라는 뜻이다.
  She is **one of the most famous designers** in the world.

> **내신만점 Tip** 〈one of the+최상급〉 뒤에 단수가 아닌 복수명사가 오는지 반드시 확인하자.

A 다음 ( ) 안에서 알맞은 말을 고르시오.

1 It's the (smaller / smallest) shop on the street.

2 Brenda is (youngest / the youngest) girl in her family.

3 Tess ran the (fastest / most fastest) of all the players.

4 That is (much / the most) comfortable chair in my house.

5 It was one of the most exciting (game / games) of the season.

B 다음 ( ) 안의 말을 이용하여 최상급 문장을 완성하시오.

1 Today is _________________ day of the year. (hot)

2 This is _________________ room in our hotel. (good)

3 It was _________________ moment of my life. (happy)

4 She is one of _________________ people in this town. (rich)

5 What is _________________ animal in the world? (dangerous)

C 다음 우리말과 같은 뜻이 되도록 ( ) 안의 말을 이용하여 문장을 완성하시오.

1 Noah는 회사에서 가장 열심히 일한다. (hard)

   Noah works ___________ ___________ in the company.

2 그것은 내 인생 최악의 실수였다. (bad, mistake)

   It was ___________ ___________ ___________ of my life.

3 미국에서 가장 인기 있는 운동 경기는 무엇인가요? (popular)

   What is ___________ ___________ ___________ sport in America?

4 그녀의 책은 모든 것들 중에서 가장 인상 깊었다. (impressive)

   Her book was ___________ ___________ ___________ of all.

5 이것은 부산에서 가장 오래된 집들 중의 하나이다. (old, house)

   This is ___________ ___________ ___________ ___________ ___________ in
   Busan.

01-03 다음 빈칸에 알맞은 말을 고르시오.

01

She looked ___________ yesterday.

① happily ② sadly ③ lovely
④ strangely ⑤ angrily

05

My jacket is ___________ cheaper than his.

① much ② even ③ a lot
④ very ⑤ far

02

He is as ___________ as David.

① brave ② braver ③ bravest
④ more brave ⑤ most brave

06

I bought ___________ apples at the market.

① ten ② a few ③ a little
④ many ⑤ a lot of

03

Today is ___________ than yesterday.

① cold ② colder ③ coldest
④ more cold ⑤ coldly

07

Helen is more ___________ than Jennifer.

① patient ② wiser ③ famous
④ confident ⑤ intelligent

04 `내신기출`

다음 중 짝지어진 두 단어의 관계가 나머지와 <u>다른</u> 것
은?

① usual – usually
② loud – loudly
③ special – specially
④ friend – friendly
⑤ lucky – luckily

08

다음 중 원급, 비교급, 최상급이 <u>잘못</u> 연결된 것은?

① many – more – most
② ugly – uglyer – uglyest
③ true – truer – truest
④ light – lighter – lightest
⑤ useful – more useful – most useful

09-10 다음 빈칸에 알맞은 말이 바르게 짝지어진 것을 고르시오.

09

> • Russia is the ___________ country in the world.
> • Mount Everest is ___________ than Mount Kilimanjaro.

① large – high
② larger – higher
③ larger – highest
④ largest – highest
⑤ largest – higher

10

> • I'm cold. I need ___________ to drink.
> • They found the museum very ___________.

① hot something – impressive
② hot something – impressively
③ something hot – impressive
④ something hot – impressively
⑤ hot thing – impressively

11-12 다음 우리말을 영어로 바르게 옮긴 것을 고르시오.

11

> 꽃병 안의 꽃은 약간의 물이 필요하다.

① The flower in the vase needs few water.
② The flower in the vase needs a few water.
③ The flower in the vase needs little waters.
④ The flower in the vase needs a little water.
⑤ The flower in the vase needs a little waters.

12

> 오늘은 내 인생에서 가장 기쁜 날들 중 하루이다.

① Today is the happiest day of my life.
② Today is the most happy day of my life.
③ Today is one of the happiest day of my life.
④ Today is one of the happier days of my life.
⑤ Today is one of the happiest days of my life.

13 내신기출

다음 중 빈칸에 들어갈 말이 나머지와 <u>다른</u> 것은?
① This is cheaper ___________ that.
② I like rice better ___________ bread.
③ Bob sleeps less ___________ seven hours a day.
④ The robot is as small ___________ a finger.
⑤ I think the book was more interesting ___________ the movie.

14

다음 문장과 의미가 같은 것은?

> I don't speak German as well as Joe.

① I speak German as well as Joe.
② I speak German better than Joe.
③ Joe speaks German better than me.
④ Joe speaks German worse than me.
⑤ Joe doesn't speak German as well as me.

15

① She is much busier than you.
② The news made my father happily.
③ My aunt put a little salt in the hot soup.
④ They usually go shopping on Saturdays.
⑤ Sally comes to school much earlier than I do.

16

① Linda eats as less as I do.
② A lot of students joined the club.
③ It is the oldest building in this city.
④ There is something sharp in the bag.
⑤ Look at that bird. It is flying really high.

17

다음 중 우리말을 영어로 옮긴 것이 잘못된 것은?
① 나는 방과 후에 자주 테니스를 친다.
   I often play tennis after school.
② 그는 전보다 훨씬 더 크게 노래를 불렀다.
   He sang a lot louder than before.
③ 그 어려운 시험을 통과한 학생은 거의 없었다.
   Little students passed the difficult test.
④ 이 방이 이 건물에서 가장 어둡다.
   This room is the darkest in this building.
⑤ 너는 정보를 더 쉽게 검색할 수 있다.
   You can search for information more easily.

18

다음 중 밑줄 친 부분의 쓰임이 잘못된 것은?
① We didn't wait long for the bus.
② The cake smells wonderful.
③ Some people drive too fast.
④ He finished the work lately at night.
⑤ Everything is boring. There is nothing new!

19 고난도 내신기출

[A], [B], [C]의 괄호 안에서 알맞은 것끼리 바르게 짝 지어진 것은?

> (A) I found the food [horrible / horribly].
> (B) He didn't drink [many / much] juice.
> (C) Alex fixes things as [good / well] as Ian.

	(A)	(B)	(C)
①	horrible	many	good
②	horrible	many	well
③	horrible	much	well
④	horribly	much	well
⑤	horribly	much	good

20 고난도 내신기출

다음 중 어법상 옳은 것끼리 짝지어진 것은?

> (a) Listen carefully. It's important.
> (b) It can sometimes happen.
> (c) I had a little sandwiches this morning.
> (d) She is much more energetic than Lynne.
> (e) The theater is so near as the post office.

① (a), (b), (d) ② (a), (c), (e)
③ (b), (c), (d) ④ (b), (c), (e)
⑤ (c), (d), (e)

21

다음 표를 보고, 주어진 말을 이용하여 비교하는 문장을 완성하시오.

Jack	170 cm
Jenny	162 cm
Phillip	165 cm

(1) Jenny is ___________ __________ Phillip.
     (short)

(2) Jack is ___________ __________ of the three students. (tall)

22

다음 Mark가 한가한 시간에 하는 일을 나타낸 그래프를 보고, 주어진 말을 이용하여 문장을 완성하시오.

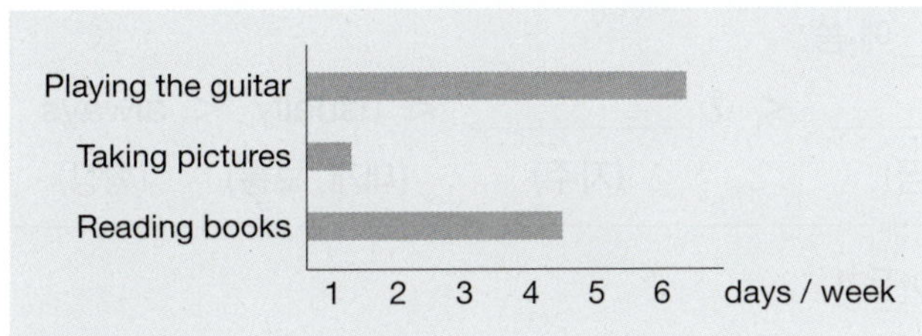

(1) Mark ___________ __________ __________ __________. (usually)

(2) Mark ___________ __________ __________. (sometimes)

(3) Mark ___________ __________ __________. (often)

23

다음 두 문장이 같은 뜻이 되도록 빈칸에 알맞은 말을 쓰시오.

(1) Seoul is not as big as New York.
     → New York is __________ __________ Seoul.

(2) Tony is more diligent than all the other boys in his class.
     → Tony is __________ __________ __________ boy in his class.

24

다음 우리말과 같은 뜻이 되도록 주어진 말을 알맞게 배열하여 문장을 완성하시오.

(1) 나는 절대 너를 잊지 않을 것이다.
     (forget, never, you, will, I)
     → _________________________________

(2) 그녀는 그 학교에서 가장 똑똑한 학생들 중 한 명이다.
     (is, of, one, students, smartest, the, she)
     → _________________________________
     in the school.

25 내신기출

다음 반려견 콘테스트 심사표를 보고, 주어진 말을 이용하여 비교하는 문장을 완성하시오.

	Cooper	Max	Luis	Becky
Age	5	3	8	2
Weight	5.7 kg	4.1 kg	7.5 kg	3.0 kg
Speed	★★★	★★★	★	★★

(1) Luis is __________ __________ Becky. (old)

(2) Cooper is __________ __________ __________ Max. (fast)

(3) Becky is __________ __________ of the four dogs. (light)

26 고난도 내신기출

주어진 말을 문맥에 맞게 알맞은 형태로 바꾸어 쓰시오.

I saw Matthew today. I could __________ (hard) believe my eyes. He looked much __________ (thin) than before. He told me about his terrible summer vacation. He said he was sick the whole time. It was one of __________ (bad) vacations of his life.

CHAPTER 08

형용사, 부사, 비교

1 형용사

- 역할: 명사·대명사를 수식하거나, 주격·목적격 보어로 쓰여 주어나 목적어의 상태·성질을 보충 설명

*수량 형용사: 명사 앞에 쓰여 정해지지 않은 수나 양을 대략적으로 나타냄			
많은	조금 있는, 약간의	거의 없는	명사
many	① _______	few	+ 셀 수 있는 명사의 복수형
② _______	a little	little	+ 셀 수 없는 명사
a lot of (= lots of)	–	–	+ 셀 수 있는 명사의 복수형 셀 수 없는 명사

❗ -thing, -body, -one으로 끝나는 대명사는 형용사가 뒤에서 수식한다는 것 기억하기

2 부사

- 역할: 동사, 형용사, 다른 부사 또는 문장 전체를 수식
- 형태: 대부분 ③ ___________의 형태이지만, 예외적인 경우도 있음

*빈도부사: 어떤 일이 얼마나 자주 일어나는지를 나타내며, be동사나 조동사의 ④ ___________, 　　　　　 일반동사의 ⑤ ___________에 씀
never　<　seldom　<　⑥ _______　<　⑦ _______　<　usually　<　always (결코 ~않다) (거의 ~않다)　　　(가끔)　　　　　　(자주)　　　(대개, 보통)　　(항상)

❗ 문장 내 빈도부사가 올 수 있는 위치 알아두기

3 비교

원급 비교	〈⑧ _______ +형용사/부사의 원급+as〉 〈not+as[so]+형용사/부사의 원급+as〉	…만큼 ~한/하게 …만큼 ~하지 않은/않게
비교급 비교	〈비교급+⑨ _______〉	…보다 더 ~한/하게
최상급 비교	〈the+최상급〉 〈one of the+최상급+⑩ _______〉	가장 ~한/하게 　가장 ~한 … 중의 하나

❗ 형용사/부사의 비교급, 최상급 형태 알아두기(특히, 불규칙 변화인 경우)
　〈one of the + 최상급〉 뒤에 복수명사가 오는지 확인하기

CHECK

밑줄 친 부분이 어법상 맞으면 O, 틀리면 X 표시하고 바르게 고치시오.

1 Serena bought a nice apartment last month.
2 Why do you eat so fastly?
3 They sometimes had meetings together.
4 Seoul is the bigger than Ulsan.
5 My father always is in his study.
6 He is one of the oldest member of our book club.
7 Rabbits are the most cutest animals in the world.
8 Kate is as polite as her sister.

CHAPTER
09

의문문, 명령문, 감탄문

의문문은 상대방에게 질문을 하여 대답을 요구하는 문장입니다. '누가, 무엇을, 언제, 어디서, 왜, 어떻게'와 같은 특정 정보에 대해 묻거나, 평서문에 덧붙여 '그럴지?'라고 동의를 구하거나, '~이지 않니?'라고 부정의 형태로 물을 때도 사용됩니다.

명령문은 상대방에게 어떤 행동을 하거나 하지 말라고 지시하거나, 어떤 행동을 권유하는 문장입니다.

감탄문은 '정말 ~하구나!'라고 기쁨, 슬픔, 놀라움 등의 감정을 표현하는 문장입니다.

POINT 01 who, what, which

- '누가, 무엇을, 언제, 어디서, 왜, 어떻게'와 같은 특정 정보에 대해 물을 때, 의문사 who, what, which, when, where, why, how 등을 사용한다. 의문사가 있는 의문문은 〈의문사+동사[be동사/do동사/조동사]+주어 ~?〉, 진행형일 경우 〈의문사+be동사+주어+v-ing ~?〉의 형태로 쓰며, Yes나 No로 대답하지 않는다.

- who는 '누구'라는 뜻으로 사람에 대해 물을 때 쓴다.
  Who is that boy?　　　　　**Who** gave you the money? (의문사가 주어 역할을 하는 경우)

- what은 '무엇'이라는 뜻으로 사물에 대해 물을 때 쓰며, 명사 앞에 오는 경우 '무슨'이라는 뜻을 나타낸다.
  What is your favorite color?　　　　　**What color** do you like most?

- which는 '어느 것'이라는 뜻으로 정해진 범위 안의 대상에 대해 물을 때 쓰며, 명사 앞에 오는 경우 '어느'라는 뜻을 나타낸다.
  Which do you like better, comedies or dramas?　　**Which brand** does she prefer?

> **+ Plus** 의문사가 주어 역할을 하는 경우 3인칭 단수로 취급한다.
> **Who** *lives* here?/ **What** *is* in your pocket?

A 다음 [ ] 안에서 알맞은 말을 고르시오.

1　A: (Who / What) did you eat for lunch?　– B: I ate a tuna sandwich.
2　A: (Who / What) played the guitar at the concert?　– B: Julian did.
3　A: (What / Which) do you like better, cats or dogs?　– B: I like cats better.
4　A: (What / Which) movie should we watch tonight?
　　B: Let's watch that new action movie.

B 다음 [ ] 안의 말을 알맞게 배열하여 의문문을 완성하시오.

1　_________________ here? (coming, is, who)
2　_________________ for dinner? (make, did, what, you)
3　_________________ on the wall? (this picture, who, drew)
4　_________________, the window seat or the aisle seat? (seat, you, do, want, which)

C 다음 우리말과 같은 뜻이 되도록 [ ] 안의 말을 이용하여 문장을 완성하시오.

1　너희 수학 선생님은 누구시니? (be)
　　_________ _________ your math teacher?
2　너는 주로 아침으로 무엇을 먹니? (eat)
　　_________ _________ you usually _________ for breakfast?
3　그녀는 그중의 어느 팀을 응원하고 있니? (cheer)
　　_________ of the teams _________ _________ _________ for?
4　그는 대학에서 무슨 과목을 공부하나요? (study)
　　_________ subject _________ _________ _________ at the university?

POINT 02 — when, where

- when은 '언제'라는 뜻으로 시간, 날짜 등을 물을 때 쓴다.
  When is your birthday?
  When will they start the game?

> (+Plus) 구체적인 시각을 묻는 when은 what time으로 바꿔 쓸 수 있다. → **What time** will they start the game?

- where는 '어디서', '어디에'라는 뜻으로 장소, 위치 등을 물을 때 쓴다.
  Where is the subway station?   **Where** can I charge my phone?

A 다음 대화의 빈칸에 알맞은 의문사를 쓰시오.

1   A: ______________ are you from? – B: I'm from Australia.
2   A: ______________ is the Summer Festival? – B: It's this weekend.
3   A: ______________ did you go with Steve? – B: We went to Green Park.
4   A: ______________ are you going to see Diana again? – B: Next Sunday.

B 다음 〈보기〉와 같이 밑줄 친 부분을 묻는 의문문을 완성하시오.

> 〈보기〉   I went to Myeongdong. → Where did you go?

1   They're going to the bookstore.   → ______________________ going?
2   I bought the cake yesterday.   → ______________________ the cake?
3   He saw Lisa at the bus stop.   → ______________________ Lisa?
4   The movie starts at 5:30.   → ______________________ start?

C 다음 우리말과 같은 뜻이 되도록 [ ] 안의 말을 이용하여 문장을 완성하시오.

1   그녀는 점심시간에 어디에 있었나요? (be)

______________ ______________ ______________ at lunch time?

2   Mark가 저에게 언제 전화했나요? (call)

______________ ______________ ______________ me?

3   그들은 한국에서 어디에 사나요? (live)

______________ ______________ ______________ in Korea?

4   너는 내일 몇 시에 Julia를 만날 거니? (meet)

______________ ______________ ______________ ______________ Julia

tomorrow?

5   그는 어디에서 음악 파일들을 다운로드하나요? (download)

______________ ______________ ______________ music files?

POINT 03 — why

why는 '왜'라는 뜻으로 원인이나 이유를 물을 때 쓴다. 대답에는 '왜냐하면'이라는 뜻의 because가 자주 쓰인다.
A: **Why** are you smiling?
B: **Because** I got a present from Brian.

> **+ Plus**
> 〈Why don't you ~?〉는 '너는 ~하는 것이 어때?'라는 뜻으로 상대방에게 권유할 때 쓰는 표현이다.
> A: **Why don't you** invite her to dinner? – B: That's a good idea.
> 〈Why don't we ~?〉는 '우리 ~하지 않을래?'라는 뜻으로 무엇을 하자고 제안할 때 쓰는 표현이며, 〈How[What] about v-ing ~?〉 또는 〈Let's+동사원형 ~〉로 바꿔 쓸 수 있다.
> A: **Why don't we** go for a walk? – B: That sounds great.

A 다음 ( ) 안에서 알맞은 말을 고르시오.

1 A: (When / Why) were you angry with Jeremy? – B: Because he was late again.
2 A: (Where / Why) did she get those earrings? – B: She got them at the mall.
3 A: Why (do / don't) you need a new phone? – B: Because my old one is broken.
4 A: (Why / What time) does the train leave? – B: It leaves at 9:30 a.m.
5 A: (Why / Why don't) you save some money? – B: That's a good idea. I'll try.

B 다음 질문에 대한 알맞은 대답을 찾아 연결하시오.

1 Why did he change his mind? •   • ⓐ Our teacher took it.
2 When did you arrive? •   • ⓑ That sounds great.
3 Why don't we take a break? •   • ⓒ Because he didn't like the plan.
4 Who took this picture of us? •   • ⓓ I got here about an hour ago.
5 Why do you like the singer? •   • ⓔ Because she has a beautiful voice.

C 다음 〈보기〉와 같이 밑줄 친 부분을 묻는 의문문을 완성하시오.

> 〈보기〉 I stayed home <u>because I was sick</u>. → Why did you stay home?

1 They ran <u>because it started to rain</u>. → ________________________ run?
2 He is studying hard <u>for a final test</u>. → ________________________ hard?
3 Her sister was born <u>in 2020</u>. → ________________________ born?
4 I came to work early <u>for a meeting</u>. → ________________________ early?
5 I will travel <u>to Italy</u> this summer. → ________________________ this summer?
6 Luna reads mystery books <u>for fun</u>. → ________________________ mystery books?

how

- how는 '어떻게', '어떤'이라는 뜻으로 수단, 방법, 상태 등을 물을 때 쓴다.
  A: **How** did you come here? (수단·방법) – B: By bus.
  A: **How** are you? (상태) – B: I'm good.

- how는 형용사나 부사와 함께 쓰여 '얼마나 ~한/하게'라는 뜻을 나타낸다.

〈how＋형용사/부사〉		
how old 몇 살의 [나이] how often 얼마나 자주 [빈도]	how tall 얼마나 큰/높은 [키·높이] how far 얼마나 먼/멀리 [거리]	how long 얼마나 긴/오래 [길이·기간] how many/much 얼마(의) [양/수·가격]

How old are you? **How long** is the program?

How often does he go to the movies? **How far** is the airport from the hotel?

> **내신만점 Tip** How many 뒤에는 셀 수 있는 명사의 복수형, How much 뒤에는 셀 수 없는 명사가 온다는 것을 알아두자.
> **How many** *people* were there at the event? / **How much** *money* do you have now?

A 다음 대화의 빈칸에 알맞은 말을 쓰시오.

1 A: _______________ is your mother? – B: She's great. Thanks.

2 A: _______________ is our holiday? – B: Ten days.

3 A: _______________ does he get to work? – B: By subway.

4 A: _______________ do they eat out? – B: Twice a month.

B 다음 〈보기〉에서 알맞은 말을 골라 대화를 완성하시오.

〈보기〉 How How tall How old How many How much

1 A: _______________ is your sister? – B: She is twenty years old.

2 A: _______________ are the black jeans? – B: They are 55,000 won.

3 A: _______________ did Ann know my name? – B: She heard it from a friend.

4 A: _______________ is that basketball player? – B: He's about 2 meters tall.

5 A: _______________ years did you live in Japan? – B: I lived there for ten years.

C 다음 〈보기〉와 같이 밑줄 친 부분을 묻는 의문문을 완성하시오.

〈보기〉 My trip to Europe was great. → How was your trip to Europe?

1 I talked to her <u>by phone</u>. → _______________ to her?

2 The store is <u>2 km away</u> from here. → _______________ the store from here?

3 My first day at school was <u>not bad</u>. → _______________ at school?

4 They go to the library <u>once a week</u>. → _______________ to the library?

부가 의문문

○ 상대방에게 동의를 구하거나 확인을 하기 위해, 평서문 뒤에 〈동사+주어?〉 형태의 의문문을 덧붙여 '그렇지?', '그렇지 않니?'의 뜻을 나타낸다.

She is a lucky person, **isn't she**?　　　　　　He didn't wash his face, **did he**?

○ 부가 의문문 만드는 방법: 앞 문장이 긍정문일 때는 부정 의문문을, 부정문일 때는 긍정 의문문을 쓴다. 시제는 앞 문장과 일치시키고, 부정 의문문은 줄임말로 쓴다.

문장의 주어 → 대명사	*Jennifer* likes milk tea, doesn't **she**?
be동사 → be동사 조동사 → 조동사 일반동사 → do동사	Henry *is* cool, **isn't** he? You *won't* come back, **will** you? This steak *smells* fantastic, **doesn't** it?

○ 부가 의문문이 긍정인지 부정인지에 상관없이, 대답의 내용이 긍정이면 Yes, 부정이면 No로 대답한다.
A: They are at home now, **aren't they**?
B: **Yes, they are.** (집에 있음) / **No, they aren't.** (집에 없음)

A　다음 밑줄 친 부분을 어법에 맞게 고쳐 쓰시오.

1　You don't eat meat, <u>don't</u> you?

2　He talks a lot, <u>don't</u> he?

3　They can drive, <u>do you</u>?

4　Grace didn't pass the test, <u>does Grace</u>?

5　You were very tired, <u>didn't we</u>?

B　다음 빈칸에 알맞은 부가 의문문을 쓰시오.

1　He doesn't know you, _____________________?

2　Emily can teach drawing, _____________________?

3　You won first prize, _____________________?

4　She didn't finish her work yesterday, _____________________?

5　Susan and Mike will join our club, _____________________?

C　다음 빈칸에 알맞은 말을 넣어 대화를 완성하시오.

1　A: The coffee isn't very hot, _____________ _____________?
　　B: No, _____________ _____________. It's just warm.

2　A: Her sister can play hockey, _____________ _____________?
　　B: Yes, _____________ _____________. She's really good.

3　A: You didn't tell him my secret, _____________ _____________?
　　B: No, _____________ _____________. I promise.

4　A: Tim lives near the school, _____________ _____________?
　　B: Yes, _____________ _____________. He can walk to school.

부정 의문문

- 의문문의 맨 앞에 동사의 부정형을 써서 '~이지 않니?'라는 뜻을 나타낸다. 이때 동사의 부정형은 모두 줄임말로 쓴다.

  Aren't you angry?　　　　　(be동사)
  Can't she try again?　　　　(조동사)
  Didn't he catch the train?　　(일반동사)

- 부정 의문문에 대한 대답의 내용이 긍정이면 Yes, 부정이면 No로 대답한다.

  A: **Don't** you like pasta? – B: **Yes, I do.** (파스타를 좋아함) / **No, I don't.** (파스타를 좋아하지 않음)

A 다음 문장을 〈보기〉와 같이 부정 의문문으로 바꾸어 쓰시오.

> 〈보기〉　　It is cold. → Isn't it cold?

1 This is yours.　　　　　　　→ ______________________________

2 It was expensive.　　　　　→ ______________________________

3 You feel thirsty.　　　　　　→ ______________________________

4 They can deliver it.　　　　→ ______________________________

5 He took notes.　　　　　　　→ ______________________________

6 They are designers.　　　　→ ______________________________

7 He plays tennis well.　　　　→ ______________________________

8 She will move to New York.　→ ______________________________

9 You were interested in animals.　→ ______________________________

B [ ] 안의 우리말과 같은 뜻이 되도록 대화를 완성하시오.

1 A: ______________ she your cousin? (그녀가 너의 사촌 아니야?)

　　B: Yes, ______________ ______________. How did you know?

2 A: ______________ ______________ join us for dinner tonight? (오늘 밤에 우리랑 저녁 먹지 않겠니?)

　　B: ______________, ______________ won't. I have to finish a report.

3 A: ______________ ______________ like rock music? (그는 록 음악을 좋아하지 않나요?)

　　B: Yes, ______________ ______________. He listens every day.

4 A: ______________ ______________ come home today? (그들은 오늘 집에 올 수 없니?)

　　B: No, ______________. They have a lot of work.

5 A: ______________ ______________ close the window? (그녀가 창문을 닫지 않았나요?)

　　B: Yes, ______________.

명령문은 상대방에게 어떤 행동을 지시하거나 권유하는 문장으로, 주어(you)를 생략하고 동사로 시작한다. '~해라'라는 뜻의 긍정 명령문은 〈동사원형 ~〉, '~하지 마라'라는 뜻의 부정 명령문은 〈Don't[Do not]+동사원형 ~〉으로 쓴다.

Go to bed early.　　　　　　　　　　**Don't wear** my clothes.

> **+ Plus**　부탁이나 요청을 공손하게 나타내는 경우에는 문장의 앞이나 뒤에 please를 쓴다.
>
> **Call** me back later, *please*.

〈명령문+and/or ~〉는 '…해라, 그러면/그러지 않으면 ~할 것이다'라는 뜻이다.

Do it now, **and** you will finish by six. (→ If you do it now, you will finish by six.)

Do it now, **or** you won't finish by six. (→ If you don't do it now, you won't finish by six.)

권유의 명령문 〈Let's+동사원형 ~〉은 '~하자', 〈Let's not+동사원형 ~〉은 '~하지 말자'라는 뜻이다.

Let's go to the concert.　　　　　　　**Let's not go** outside.

A　다음 [ ] 안에서 알맞은 말을 고르시오.

1　(Are / Be) nice to people.

2　(Not / Do not) tell him the truth.

3　Let's (had / have) lunch together.

4　(Let's not / Not let's) swim in the lake.

5　(Don't / Let's) touch that! It's dangerous.

6　Eat something, (and / or) you will be hungry later.

7　Ask Sally, (and / or) she'll lend you her notebook.

B　다음 〈보기〉에서 알맞은 말을 골라 명령문을 완성하시오.

〈보기〉	go	study	take	visit
	get up	go out	listen to	turn on

1　I am tired! ______________ ______________ a rest.

2　______________ ______________ ______________ alone late at night.

3　______________ hard, ______________ you won't pass the exam.

4　It's getting dark. Please ______________ ______________ the light.

5　______________ the website, ______________ you will get a coupon.

6　______________ ______________ ______________ loud music. It's not good for your ears.

7　______________ ______________ early tomorrow. You have class in the morning.

8　______________ ______________ ______________ to that restaurant. We don't have
enough money.

- 감탄문은 '정말 ~하구나!'라고 기쁨, 슬픔, 놀라움 등의 감정을 표현하는 문장이다.

- what으로 시작하는 감탄문은 〈What+a/an+형용사+명사(+주어+동사)!〉의 형태로 쓴다. 명사가 복수형이거나 셀 수 없는 명사인 경우 a나 an을 쓰지 않는다.
  What a tasty doughnut (this is)!   **What** terrible news (it is)!

- how로 시작하는 감탄문은 〈How+형용사/부사+주어+동사!〉의 형태로 쓴다.
  How tall the model is!   **How** high he jumps!

> **내신만점 Tip** what으로 시작하는 감탄문과 how로 시작하는 감탄문의 어순을 구분하자.

A 다음 밑줄 친 부분을 어법에 맞게 고쳐 쓰시오.

1 <u>How a huge</u> airplane it is!
2 How interesting <u>is the story</u>!
3 <u>What peaceful</u> this village is!
4 How <u>these shoes small</u> are!
5 What <u>lovely dress</u> she is wearing!

B 다음 문장을 〈보기〉와 같이 감탄문으로 바꾸어 쓰시오.

〈보기〉	It is a very beautiful day.	→ What a beautiful day it is!
	It is very cheap.	→ How cheap it is!

1 The dog is very friendly.   → ______________________________
2 He has a nice car.   → ______________________________
3 The game was very exciting.   → ______________________________
4 She sent a very long message.   → ______________________________

C 다음 우리말과 같은 뜻이 되도록 ( ) 안의 말을 알맞게 배열하여 문장을 완성하시오.

1 그건 정말 영리한 개구나! (it, is, a, what, dog, clever)

   ____

2 이 문제가 정말 어려웠구나! (this, how, was, problem, difficult)

   ____

3 그가 경주에서 정말 빨리 달렸구나! (fast, he, in the race, how, ran)

   ____

4 그 감독이 정말 좋은 영화들을 만드는구나! (the director, great, what, makes, films)

   ____

01

> A: ____________ is my phone?
> B: It's on the desk.

① Why　　② What　　③ Who
④ Where　　⑤ When

02

> A: I will always help you.
> B: ____________ a good friend you are!

① Be　　② Do　　③ How
④ What　　⑤ Let's

03

> A: You got my email, ____________?
> B: No, I didn't. Please send it again.

① do you　　② don't you
③ didn't you　　④ aren't you
⑤ weren't you

04-05 다음 중 빈칸에 들어갈 말이 나머지와 <u>다른</u> 것을 고르시오.

04

① ____________ are you angry at me?
② ____________ did she leave so early?
③ ____________ don't you dance with him?
④ ____________ was she late for the party?
⑤ ____________ do you like better, jazz or rock?

05

① ____________ cold it is!
② ____________ smart you are!
③ ____________ deep the sea is!
④ ____________ small your hat is!
⑤ ____________ long fingers you have!

06-08 다음 질문에 대한 알맞은 대답을 고르시오.

06

> A: When did you visit London?
> B: ____________

① I went to Paris.
② About ten days.
③ I traveled by plane.
④ I went there last month.
⑤ Because I wanted to see Big Ben.

07

> A: You can speak Chinese, can't you?
> B: ____________ Do you need my help?

① Yes, I do.　　② No, you don't.
③ Yes, I can.　　④ No, you can't.
⑤ No, I won't.

08

> A: Isn't she a great actress?
> B: ____________ I love her movies.

① Yes, she is.　　② Yes, she isn't.
③ No, she is.　　④ No, she isn't.
⑤ Yes, she does.

09

다음 중 우리말을 영어로 옮긴 것이 <u>잘못된</u> 것은?

① 저 책들을 읽는 게 어때?

   Why don't you read those books?

② Frank는 여기 있을 거야, 그렇지 않니?

   Frank will stay here, won't he?

③ 정말 시끄럽군요! 조용히 해 주세요.

   How noisy you are! Be quiet, please.

④ 밤에 먹지 마, 그렇지 않으면 살이 찔 거야.

   Eat at night, or you will gain weight.

⑤ Kate는 운전 면허증이 없어, 그렇지?

   Kate doesn't have a driver's license, does she?

10-11 다음 빈칸에 공통으로 들어갈 말을 고르시오.

10

> • ___________ is the title of the book?
> • ___________ a great song it is!
> • ___________ time does the class start?

① What   ② How

③ When   ④ Which

⑤ Where

11

> • ___________ was the picnic yesterday?
> • ___________ delicious this sandwich is!
> • ___________ many people are there in your family?

① What   ② How

③ Why   ④ Which

⑤ Who

12

다음 중 밑줄 친 부분의 쓰임이 나머지와 <u>다른</u> 것은?

① <u>What</u> did Sarah do last night?

② <u>What</u> food can you cook?

③ <u>What</u> languages can you speak?

④ <u>What</u> day is it today?

⑤ <u>What</u> movie is your favorite?

13-14 다음 중 대화가 자연스럽지 <u>않은</u> 것을 고르시오.

13

① A: How do you get to work?

   B: I take the bus to work.

② A: Who gave you that chocolate?

   B: I like it.

③ A: Where is my cheesecake?

   B: I put it in the refrigerator.

④ A: Which backpack did you buy?

   B: I bought the one with frogs on it.

⑤ A: When do you usually get up?

   B: I usually get up at seven.

14

① A: Won't she go to the beach?

   B: Yes, she will.

② A: He made a mistake, didn't he?

   B: No, he didn't.

③ A: Let's go bungee jumping.

   B: Yes, let's not. It looks dangerous.

④ A: The museum is closed on Mondays, isn't it?

   B: Yes, it is. Let's go on Tuesday.

⑤ A: I didn't clean my room.

   B: Do it now, or Mom will get angry.

15

다음 대화의 빈칸에 알맞은 말이 바르게 짝지어진 것은?

> A: ___________ do you play soccer?
> B: About three times a week. I really enjoy it.
> A: ___________ do you like soccer?
> B: Because I can play with my friends and run a lot.

① When – Why
② When – Who
③ How often – Who
④ How often – Why
⑤ What – Why

16 고난도 내신기출

다음 중 밑줄 친 부분을 바르게 고치지 <u>않은</u> 것은?

① You were absent yesterday, <u>did you</u>?
    → weren't you
② <u>Cannot he</u> come to Korea?
    → Can't he
③ I bought this watch. <u>Didn't it</u> nice?
    → Doesn't it
④ Your brother is wearing glasses, <u>doesn't he</u>?
    → isn't he
⑤ Violet worked for a car company, <u>did she</u>?
    → didn't she

17 내신기출

다음 중 어느 빈칸에도 들어갈 수 <u>없는</u> 것은?

> (a) How ___________ do you go shopping?
> (b) How ___________ milk do you drink?
> (c) How ___________ copies do you need?
> (d) How ___________ is your summer vacation?
> (e) How ___________ books did you read this month?

① long
② much
③ tall
④ often
⑤ many

18

다음 중 어법상 <u>틀린</u> 것은?

① What lovely shoes they are!
② Who want some cookies now?
③ You will come back, won't you?
④ When did the accident happen?
⑤ Walk fast, and you'll get there on time.

19

[A], [B], [C]의 괄호 안에서 알맞은 것끼리 바르게 짝지어진 것은?

> (A) [What / How] well they dance!
> (B) Don't [be / are] in a hurry.
> (C) [What / Which] sport do you watch more often, baseball or basketball?

	(A)	(B)	(C)
①	What	be	What
②	What	are	Which
③	How	be	What
④	How	be	Which
⑤	How	are	Which

20 고난도 내신기출

다음 중 어법상 옳은 것끼리 짝지어진 것은?

> (a) Why is he so happy?
> (b) The story is scary, isn't it?
> (c) Where your cousin does live?
> (d) Let's don't buy the ring for Jenny.
> (e) Take this medicine, and you will feel better.

① (a), (b), (c)
② (a), (b), (e)
③ (b), (c), (d)
④ (b), (c), (e)
⑤ (c), (d), (e)

21

다음 밑줄 친 부분을 묻는 의문문을 완성하시오.

(1) My favorite actor is <u>Ryan Brooks</u>.

　→ ___________ ___________ your favorite actor?

(2) She cried yesterday <u>because she lost her doll</u>.

　→ ___________ ___________ ___________ cry yesterday?

22　내신기출

다음 두 문장이 같은 뜻이 되도록 빈칸에 알맞은 말을 쓰시오.

(1) The vegetables are very fresh.

　→ ___________ ___________ the vegetables are!

(2) Why don't we go to the movies?

　→ ___________ ___________ to the movies.

23　내신기출

다음 그림을 보고, 주어진 말을 이용하여 문장을 완성하시오.

(1) 

의문문: ___________ ___________ ___________ from? (be)

대답: He is from England.

 David, 영국

(2) 

명령문: ___________ ___________ ___________ on the street. (throw trash)

24

다음 우리말과 같은 뜻이 되도록 주어진 말을 알맞게 배열하여 문장을 완성하시오.

(1) 너는 언제 그에게 크리스마스 카드를 보냈니?

(him, did, when, send, you)

　→ ___________________________ a Christmas card?

(2) Bob은 컴퓨터 게임을 하지 않아, 그렇지?

(he, does, play, computer games, doesn't)

　→ Bob ___________________________?

25　고난도

다음 대화를 읽고, 어법상 틀린 부분을 모두 찾아 바르게 고쳐 쓰시오. (2군데)

A: What far is it to the airport?
B: It's 30 km from here. It takes about an hour by bus.
A: Really? Aren't we going to be late?
B: Oh yes, we are. Let take a taxi.

26　고난도

다음 대화를 읽고, 〈보기〉의 말을 이용하여 (A)~(D)의 빈칸에 알맞은 말을 쓰시오.

〈보기〉	did	how	what	will

A: You will go to the concert hall tomorrow, (A) ___________ you?
B: Yes, I will. My favorite band, Won V, is playing.
A: (B) ___________ they have a concert last month?
B: Yes, they did. I went to that one too.
A: (C) ___________ was it?
B: It was really great. (D) ___________ amazing musicians they are!

의문문, 명령문, 감탄문

1 의문문

	의문사가 있는 의문문	부가 의문문	부정 의문문
형태	〈① __________ (who / what / which / when / where / why / how)+동사[be동사/ do동사 / 조동사]+주어 ~?〉	〈긍정문+② __________의 부가 의문문〉 / 〈부정문+③ __________의 부가 의문문〉	〈be동사/조동사/do동사+ ④ __________의 축약형+ 주어 ~?〉
의미	'누구/무엇/어느 것/ 언제/어디서/왜/어떻게 ~?'	'그렇지 않니?/그렇지?'	'~이지 않니?'
대답	구체적인 정보로 대답	대답의 내용이 긍정이면 Yes, 부정이면 No로 대답	

❗ 의문사가 있는 의문문의 어순 기억하기 / 부가 의문문의 형태와 대답 알아두기

2 명령문

	형태	의미
긍정 명령문	〈⑤ __________ ~〉	'~해라'
부정 명령문	〈⑥ __________+동사원형 ~〉	'~하지 마라'
권유의 긍정 명령문	〈⑦ __________+동사원형 ~〉	'~하자'
권유의 부정 명령문	〈⑧ __________+동사원형 ~〉	'~하지 말자'
명령문 활용 표현	〈명령문+and/or ~〉	'…해라, 그러면/그러지 않으면 ~할 것이다'

3 감탄문

형태	의미
〈⑨ __________+a/an+형용사+명사(+주어+동사)!〉	'정말 ~하구나'
〈⑩ __________+형용사/부사+주어+동사!〉	

❗ what으로 시작하는 감탄문과 how로 시작하는 감탄문의 어순 구분하기

CHECK

밑줄 친 부분이 어법상 맞으면 O, 틀리면 X 표시하고 바르게 고치시오.

1 <u>What a nice</u> bag!
2 <u>Are</u> kind to your neighbors.
3 Let's <u>don't go</u> for a walk today. It's going to be rainy.
4 A: <u>Didn't</u> Kevin join the music club? – B: Yes, he did.
5 A: This food is delicious, <u>is it</u>? – B: Yes, it is. It's very tasty.
6 A: <u>Where</u> is she doing? – B: She's watering the plants.
7 A: <u>How many</u> money do you need? – B: I need just one dollar.
8 A: <u>When</u> were you laughing? – B: Because Dan told me a funny story.
9 A: <u>Who is</u> going to work with me?
   B: I'm not sure. Why don't you ask Jimmy?

CHAPTER

10

문장의 형식

문장은 단어들이 일정한 순서로 모여 의미를 나타내는 것으로, 이러한 단어들의 역할을 문장 성분이라고 합니다. 가장 기본적인 문장 성분은 주어와 동사이며, 동사의 종류에 따라 '누구를[무엇을]'에 해당하는 목적어가 필요하거나, 주어 또는 목적어를 보충 설명해 주는 보어가 필요할 수도 있습니다. 이처럼 문장이 어떤 성분으로 구성되는지에 따라 문장의 형식이 달라집니다.

POINT 01 1형식 / 2형식

POINT 02 2형식 – 감각동사+형용사

POINT 03 3형식 / 4형식

POINT 04 4형식 → 3형식 – 전치사 to를 쓰는 경우

POINT 05 4형식 → 3형식 – 다른 전치사를 쓰는 경우

POINT 06 5형식 – 목적격 보어가 명사/형용사인 경우

POINT 07 5형식 – 목적격 보어가 to부정사인 경우

POINT 08 5형식 – 지각동사/사역동사

1형식 / 2형식

- 문장은 주어, 동사, 보어, 목적어 등의 성분으로 구성되며, 성분의 구성 방식에 따라 5가지 형식으로 나눌 수 있다.

- 1형식 문장은 〈주어+동사〉의 구조로 이루어지며, 이때 쓰이는 동사는 자동사이다. 부사(구), 전치사구 등의 수식어가 함께 쓰이는 경우가 많다.

  The sun rises.　　　　　　　　　　**The baby cried** all night.
  　주어　　동사　　　　　　　　　　　　주어　　동사

- 2형식 문장은 〈주어+동사+주격 보어〉의 구조로 이루어지며, 이때 쓰이는 동사는 불완전 자동사이다. 주격 보어로는 명사(구)나 형용사(구)가 오며, 주어의 상태·성질을 보충 설명한다.

  Aiden is a soccer player.　　　　**Those boys are polite**.
  　주어　동사　　보어(명사구)　　　　　　주어　　　　동사　보어(형용사)

A 다음 문장에서 주어, 동사, 보어를 찾아 밑줄로 표시하고 성분을 쓰시오. (보어가 없으면 X 표시할 것)

1 He sings well.

2 Marie became a scientist.

3 The phone on the table rang.

4 The dress in the shop is pretty.

5 We were playing in the backyard.

6 This city is famous for its film festival.

B 다음 우리말과 같은 뜻이 되도록 [ ] 안의 말을 알맞게 배열하여 문장을 완성하고, 몇 형식인지 쓰시오.

1 그녀는 오후 3시에 도착할 것이다. (will, she, arrive)
　　__________________________ at 3:00 p.m.　　　　〈　　　〉형식

2 Chris는 고등학생이다. (a, student, high school, is)
　　Chris __________________________.　　　　〈　　　〉형식

3 그들은 바닷가를 따라 걷고 있다. (are, they, walking)
　　__________________________ along the beach.　　　　〈　　　〉형식

4 그 잎들은 가을에 노래진다. (yellow, the leaves, turn)
　　__________________________ in fall.　　　　〈　　　〉형식

5 나는 시험 전에 보통 긴장한다. (nervous, am, usually, I)
　　__________________________ before tests.　　　　〈　　　〉형식

6 작년에 나의 부모님은 보스턴으로 이사 가셨다. (moved, my, Boston, parents, to)
　　Last year, __________________________.　　　　〈　　　〉형식

2형식 – 감각동사+형용사

- 2형식 문장에는 감각을 표현하는 동사 look, feel, smell, sound, taste 등이 자주 쓰인다.

- 감각동사 뒤에는 주격 보어로 형용사가 온다.

You **look tired**.

The herb tea **smells nice**.

>  **내신만점 Tip** • 감각동사 뒤에 부사가 아닌 형용사가 온다는 것을 기억하자.
> That **sounds great**. (O)　　　　That **sounds** *greatly*. (X)
> • 감각동사 뒤에 〈전치사 like+명사〉를 쓰면 '~처럼 …하다'의 뜻을 나타낸다는 것을 알아두자.
> The house **looks** *like a castle*. (그 집은 성처럼 보인다.)

A   다음 ( ) 안에서 알맞은 말을 고르시오.

1 The sweater feels (soft / softness).

2 Her plan sounded (good / well) to me.

3 The men (look / look like) models.

4 This spaghetti tastes (wonderful / wonderfully).

B   다음 밑줄 친 부분을 어법에 맞게 고쳐 쓰시오.

1 The flowers smell <u>sweetly</u>.

2 That sounds <u>a good</u> idea.

3 These orange cookies taste <u>terribly</u>.

4 Harper felt <u>like sick</u> after dinner.

C   다음 우리말과 같은 뜻이 되도록 〈보기〉와 [ ] 안의 말을 이용하여 문장을 완성하시오.

〈보기〉	feel	smell	sound	taste

1 레몬은 신맛이 난다. (sour)

Lemons ＿＿＿＿＿＿＿ ＿＿＿＿＿＿＿.

2 그들은 다시 허기가 졌다. (hungry)

They ＿＿＿＿＿＿＿ ＿＿＿＿＿＿＿ again.

3 그의 억양은 영국식으로 들린다. (British)

His accent ＿＿＿＿＿＿＿ ＿＿＿＿＿＿＿.

4 그 주스는 약 같은 냄새가 났다. (medicine)

The juice ＿＿＿＿＿＿＿ ＿＿＿＿＿＿＿ ＿＿＿＿＿＿＿.

3형식 / 4형식

- 3형식 문장은 〈주어＋동사＋목적어〉로 이루어진 문장이다. 목적어는 주어가 하는 동작의 대상이 되는 말이다.

  I **have two sisters**.
  주어 동사　　목적어

  We **won the game**.
  주어　동사　　목적어

- 4형식 문장은 〈주어＋동사＋간접목적어＋직접목적어〉로 이루어진 문장이다.

- 4형식 문장에는 '~해 주다'라는 의미를 지닌 수여동사 give, buy, make, send, tell, lend, show, teach 등이 자주 쓰인다. 수여동사 뒤에는 두 개의 목적어, 즉 간접목적어(…에게)와 직접목적어(~을)가 온다.

  Tony **gave me a watch**.
  　　　　　간접목적어　직접목적어

  Alice **bought her son a toy**.
  　　　　　　　간접목적어　　직접목적어

A 다음 빈칸에 들어갈 수 <u>없는</u> 것에 ✔ 표시하시오.

1 They ___________ the project.　　☐ finished　☐ gave　☐ changed

2 I'll ___________ him the keys.　　☐ lend　☐ show　☐ watch

3 She sent ___________ text messages.　☐ the book　☐ Rachel　☐ her friends

B 다음 [ ] 안의 말을 알맞게 배열하여 문장을 완성하시오.

1 ______________________________, please. (a cheeseburger, want, I)

2 Ms. Kim ______________________________. (math, children, teaches)

3 ______________________________ for lunch. (me, lent, he, $10)

4 ______________________________ there a few days ago. (Kevin, saw, we)

5 Sarah ______________________________. (her, will show, new car, us)

C 다음 우리말과 같은 뜻이 되도록 [ ] 안의 말을 이용하여 문장을 완성하시오.

1 주방장은 그에게 파이를 만들어 주었다. (make, a pie)

  The chef ___________ ___________ ___________ ___________.

2 그는 내 컴퓨터를 쉽게 고쳤다. (fix, computer)

  ___________ ___________ ___________ ___________ easily.

3 저에게 역으로 가는 길을 말씀해 주시겠어요? (tell, the way)

  Can you ___________ ___________ ___________ ___________ to the station?

4 그녀는 유명한 사람들을 많이 알고 있다. (know, famous people)

  ___________ ___________ a lot of ___________ ___________.

5 부모님은 우리에게 크리스마스 선물을 주셨다. (give, Christmas gifts)

  My parents ___________ ___________ ___________ ___________.

POINT 04 · 4형식 → 3형식 – 전치사 to를 쓰는 경우

- 〈주어＋동사＋간접목적어＋직접목적어〉 형태의 4형식 문장은 두 목적어의 위치를 바꾸고 전치사를 써서 〈주어＋동사＋직접목적어＋전치사＋간접목적어〉 형태의 3형식 문장으로 바꿀 수 있다.

- 간접목적어 앞에 쓰는 전치사(to, for, of)는 동사에 따라 달라진다. give, send, tell, lend, show, teach, write, pass, bring 등 대부분의 수여동사는 전치사 to를 쓴다.

Richard **gave** me a ring.　　　(4형식)

Richard **gave** a ring **to** me.　　(3형식)

A 다음 3형식 문장은 4형식 문장으로, 4형식 문장은 3형식 문장으로 바꾸어 쓰시오.

1 James sent a package to her.

→ James sent ________________________.

2 Who told you the story?

→ Who told ____________________?

3 My brother gave his bicycle to me.

→ My brother ________________________.

4 I can lend David an umbrella.

→ I can lend ______________________.

5 Bring us two glasses of water, please.

→ Bring ___________________, please.

6 Sana will teach Japanese to them.

→ Sana ___________________.

B 다음 우리말과 같은 뜻이 되도록 [ ] 안의 말을 이용하여 문장을 완성하시오.

1 나는 Ruth에게 내 사진을 보여 주었다. (show, picture)

I __________ __________ __________ __________ Ruth.

2 그녀는 사촌에게 이메일을 썼다. (write, an email)

She __________ __________ __________ __________ her cousin.

3 나에게 그 만화책을 건네줘. (the comic book)

Pass __________ __________ __________.

4 Daniel이 우리에게 이 표를 주었다. (give, these tickets)

Daniel __________ __________ __________ __________ __________.

5 우리는 우리 선생님에게 보고서를 보내야 한다. (send, a report, teacher)

We should __________ __________ __________ __________ __________

__________.

POINT 05 · 4형식 → 3형식 - 다른 전치사를 쓰는 경우

- 4형식 문장을 3형식 문장으로 바꿀 때 간접목적어 앞에 전치사 for나 of를 쓰는 동사들이 있다.

- buy, make, get, cook 등의 동사는 전치사 for를 쓴다.
  She **made** me hot chocolate. (4형식)
  → She **made** hot chocolate **for** me. (3형식)

- ask는 직접목적어가 favor인 경우 전치사 of를 쓴다.
  Ben **asked** her a favor. (4형식)
  → Ben **asked** a favor **of** her. (3형식)

> **내신만점 Tip** 4형식 문장을 3형식 문장으로 바꿀 때 전치사 to, for, of를 사용하는 동사를 구분하여 알아두자.

A 다음 ( ) 안에서 알맞은 말을 고르시오.

1 I'll buy a wallet (to / for) my friend.

2 He already sent the file (to / of) you.

3 We cooked a pizza (them / for them).

4 The waiter (got / gave) a chair for me.

B 다음 문장을 3형식 문장으로 바꾸어 쓰시오.

1 Ellen made him fresh salad.

→ Ellen made ________________________.

2 Can I ask you a favor?

→ Can I ask ________________________?

3 He often buys his wife flowers.

→ He often ________________________.

C 다음 우리말과 같은 뜻이 되도록 ( ) 안의 말을 이용하여 문장을 완성하시오.

1 그녀는 개에게 집을 만들어 주었다. (make, a doghouse)
  She __________ __________ __________ __________ her dog.

2 아빠는 매일 우리에게 저녁을 요리해 주신다. (cook, dinner)
  Dad __________ __________ __________ __________ every day.

3 내가 너에게 오렌지 주스 좀 가져다줄까? (get, some orange juice)
  Can I __________ __________ __________ __________
  __________?

4 우리는 아이들에게 도넛 한 상자를 사 주었다. (buy, doughnuts, the kids)
  We __________ a box of __________ __________ __________.

POINT 06

5형식 – 목적격 보어가 명사/형용사인 경우

- 5형식 문장은 〈주어＋동사＋목적어＋목적격 보어〉로 이루어진 문장이다. 동사에 따라 목적격 보어로 명사(구), 형용사(구), to부정사(구), 동사원형 등이 오며, 목적어의 상태·성질을 보충 설명한다.

- call, make, name 등의 동사는 목적격 보어로 명사(구)를 쓴다.

  People **call** her **"Pop Princess."**
  동사 목적어　목적격 보어(명사)

- find, keep, make, leave 등의 동사는 목적격 보어로 형용사(구)를 쓴다.

  Please **keep your phone silent**.
  동사　　목적어　　목적격 보어(형용사)

A 다음 우리말과 같은 뜻이 되도록 [ ] 안에서 알맞은 말을 고르시오.

1 그의 이야기는 나를 슬프게 만들었다.

His story made me (sad / sadly).

2 그들은 Diane을 천사라고 부른다.

They call (an angel Diane / Diane an angel).

3 채소는 너를 건강하게 유지시켜 준다.

Vegetables keep you (health / healthy).

B 다음 우리말과 같은 뜻이 되도록 [ ] 안의 말을 알맞게 배열하여 문장을 완성하시오.

1 그녀는 그 책이 재미있다는 것을 알았다. (the book, she, interesting, found)

____

2 그 소식은 우리를 화나게 만들었다. (us, the news, angry, made)

____

3 그는 그의 딸을 'sweetie'라고 부른다. (calls, he, "sweetie", daughter, his)

____

C 다음 우리말과 같은 뜻이 되도록 〈보기〉와 [ ] 안의 말을 이용하여 문장을 완성하시오.

〈보기〉	make	find	keep	leave

1 나는 그 문제가 쉽다는 것을 알게 되었다. (easy)

I _____________ the problem _____________.

2 그녀는 어젯밤 그 문을 열어 두었다. (door, open)

She _____________ _____________ _____________ _____________ last night.

3 너는 네 교복을 깨끗하게 유지해야 한다. (uniform, clean)

You have to _____________ _____________ _____________ _____________.

4 그의 노력이 그를 훌륭한 선수로 만들었다. (a good player)

His hard work _____________ _____________ _____________ _____________.

5형식 – 목적격 보어가 to부정사인 경우

- 5형식 문장에서 want, ask, tell, expect, order, allow 등의 동사는 목적격 보어로 to부정사(구)를 쓴다.
  I **want** you **to come** with me.
  He **expected** her **to be** there.

> **+ Plus** 목적어와 목적격 보어인 to부정사는 주어와 서술어의 관계이다. 즉, 목적어가 to부정사의 동작을 하는 주체가 된다.
> Tina asked **me to help her**. (Tina는 내가 그녀를 도와줄 것을 부탁했다.)

A 다음 〈보기〉에서 알맞은 말을 골라 빈칸에 적절한 형태로 써넣으시오.

> 〈보기〉 be   read   stop   close   take care of

1 I want you ___________________ this book.

2 They expected Betty ___________________ late.

3 He told her ___________________ the window.

4 The police ordered me ___________________ my car.

5 She asked us ___________________ her cat for two days.

B 다음 우리말과 같은 뜻이 되도록 [ ] 안의 말을 알맞게 배열하여 문장을 완성하시오.

1 나는 그에게 떠나라고 말하지 않았다. (tell, to, him, leave)
   I didn't ___________________.

2 부모님은 내가 자신감을 갖기를 원하신다. (confident, want, to, me, be)
   My parents ___________________.

3 Luke는 그녀가 그의 노트북을 사용하는 것을 허락했다. (to, her, allowed, Luke, use)
   ___________________ his laptop.

C 다음 우리말과 같은 뜻이 되도록 [ ] 안의 말을 이용하여 문장을 완성하시오.

1 너는 지금 내가 그녀에게 전화하기를 원하니? (want, call)
   Do you _________ _________ _________ _________ her now?

2 우리는 그들이 토요일에 돌아올 거라고 예상했다. (expect, come)
   We _________ _________ _________ _________ back on Saturday.

3 그는 Helen에게 돈을 좀 빌려 달라고 부탁할 것이다. (ask, lend)
   He will _________ _________ _________ _________ him some money.

4 선생님은 우리가 교실에 머무는 것을 허락하셨다. (allow, stay)
   The teacher _________ _________ _________ _________ in the
   classroom.

POINT 08 · 5형식 - 지각동사/사역동사

○ 5형식 문장에서 see, watch, hear, feel 등과 같은 지각동사(~하는 것을 보다/듣다/느끼다)와 have, make, let과 같은 사역동사(~하도록 시키다, ~하게 하다)는 목적격 보어로 동사원형을 쓴다.
I saw him **wave** at you.
She **made** me **apologize**.

> **+ Plus** 동작이 진행 중임을 강조할 때, 지각동사의 목적격 보어로 현재분사(v-ing)를 쓰기도 한다.
> **I saw** him **delivering** a pizza. (나는 그가 피자를 배달하고 있는 것을 보았다.)

○ 준사역동사 help(~하는 것을 돕다)는 목적격 보어로 to부정사와 동사원형을 모두 쓸 수 있다.
He **helped** us **(to) move** the chairs.

> **내신만점 Tip** 5형식 문장은 동사에 따라 목적격 보어로 명사(구), 형용사(구), to부정사(구), 동사원형을 쓴다는 것을 기억하자.

A 다음 밑줄 친 부분을 어법에 맞게 고쳐 쓰시오.

1 I saw her hands to shake.

2 My parents don't let me eating too much junk food.

3 We asked them be quiet in the theater.

4 The doctor had her stayed in the hospital.

5 She heard someone to knock on the door.

B 다음 [ ] 안의 말을 알맞게 배열하여 문장을 완성하시오.

1 The teacher ______________________ our desks. (clean, us, made)

2 You can ______________________ tonight. (the stars, see, shine)

3 ______________________ the wall. (them, paint, had, she)

4 Jason will ______________________. (write, Mia, report, help, her)

5 ______________________ in the hall. (shout, heard, I, the students)

C 다음 우리말과 같은 뜻이 되도록 [ ] 안의 말을 이용하여 문장을 완성하시오.

1 나는 바람이 내 얼굴을 어루만지는 것을 느꼈다. (feel, touch)

   I ____________ the wind ____________ my face.

2 언니는 내가 그녀의 옷을 입지 못하게 한다. (let, wear)

   My sister doesn't ____________ ____________ ____________ her clothes.

3 우리는 배들이 물 위에 떠 있는 것을 지켜보았다. (watch, float)

   ____________ ____________ the boats ____________ on the water.

4 David는 Maggie가 마술사가 되는 것을 도와주었다. (help, become)

   David ____________ ____________ ____________ ____________ a magician.

01

George bought a robot ___________ his son.

① to　　　　② of　　　　③ for
④ on　　　　⑤ in

02

We watched the baby ___________.

① sleep　　　② slept　　　③ sleepy
④ to sleep　　⑤ to be sleeping

03

I expected them ___________ my house.

① visit　　　② to visit　　③ visiting
④ be visiting　⑤ to be visit

04 내신기출

다음 중 빈칸에 들어갈 말이 나머지와 <u>다른</u> 것은?
① Pass the chili sauce ___________ me.
② He gave his sunglasses ___________ her.
③ She showed her accessories ___________ us.
④ Nora told her daily plan ___________ me.
⑤ I made tomato pasta ___________ my sister.

05

His new hairstyle looks ___________.

① good　　　　② nicely　　　③ bad
④ terrible　　　⑤ strange

06

It ___________ wonderful.

① feels　　　② looks　　　③ sounds
④ tastes　　　⑤ shows

07

The movie made Kate ___________.

① happy　　　② bored　　　③ laugh
④ to cry　　　⑤ a star

08

다음 우리말을 영어로 바르게 옮긴 것은?

그들은 그가 뉴욕으로 여행하게 했다.

① They let him travel to New York.
② They let him to travel to New York.
③ They let him travelling to New York.
④ They had him travels to New York.
⑤ They had him to travel to New York.

09-11 다음 빈칸에 알맞은 말이 바르게 짝지어진 것을 고르시오.

09

> A: You should keep your kids __________.
> B: Yes, I don't want them __________ hurt.

① safe – get　　② safe – to get
③ safely – getting　　④ safely – get
⑤ safely – to get

10

> A: I'm __________.
> B: I'm sorry, but they don't let us __________ the heater in this room.

① cold – use　　② cold – to use
③ cold – using　　④ coldly – use
⑤ coldly – to use

11

> A: I saw Mike __________ with Emma yesterday.
> B: I know. He already sent a message about that __________ me.

① dance - of　　② to dance - of
③ to dance - to　　④ dance - to
⑤ dancing - for

12-13 다음 빈칸에 공통으로 들어갈 말을 고르시오.

12

> • I lent my laptop __________ Chris.
> • Linda asked him __________ turn off the TV.

① to　　② of　　③ for
④ on　　⑤ with

13

> • The song __________ the singer famous.
> • He __________ every student wear a school uniform.

① kept　　② found　　③ made
④ wanted　　⑤ taught

14 내신기출

다음 중 문장의 전환이 바르지 <u>않은</u> 것은?

① I'll bring you a thick coat.
　→ I'll bring a thick coat to you.
② I showed them my old pictures.
　→ I showed my old pictures to them.
③ They bought me a pair of skates.
　→ They bought a pair of skates to me.
④ Dad made me blueberry pancakes.
　→ Dad made blueberry pancakes for me.
⑤ They wrote their guests some letters.
　→ They wrote some letters to their guests.

 다음 중 어법상 <u>틀린</u> 것을 고르시오.

15

① You look cool today.
② He wanted me to rest.
③ I found science difficult.
④ She got me some dessert.
⑤ I can teach you to Spanish.

16

① They saw me run away.
② He told me to walk fast.
③ Pass the paper to me, please.
④ Mike helped me carry the boxes.
⑤ I heard James to play the guitar.

17

다음 중 문장의 형식이 나머지와 <u>다른</u> 것은?
① I made the taxi driver angry.
② He asked me to wait outside.
③ My friend sent me that candy.
④ People called him "Mr. President."
⑤ We let our children play on the sand.

18 내신기출

다음 중 어법상 <u>틀린</u> 것을 모두 고르면? [2개]
① The perfume smells terrible.
② Mr. Kang teaches us Chinese.
③ Emily had me to make dinner.
④ I found the travel map usefully.
⑤ We lent a ladder to our neighbor.

19 고난도

(A), (B), (C)의 괄호 안에서 알맞은 것끼리 바르게 짝지어진 것은?

(A) This bread tastes [great / greatly].
(B) He asked a small favor [for / of] me.
(C) I saw someone [to come / coming] towards me.

	(A)	(B)	(C)
①	great	of	coming
②	great	for	to come
③	greatly	for	coming
④	great	of	to come
⑤	greatly	of	coming

20 고난도 내신기출

다음 중 어법상 옳은 것끼리 짝지어진 것은?

(a) Those dolls look lions.
(b) My parents don't let me go out at night.
(c) I made a cookie my brothers.
(d) Could you give the English menu for me?
(e) She asked me to join the surfing club.

① (a), (d)　　　　② (b), (e)
③ (a), (b), (c)　　④ (b), (c), (d)
⑤ (c), (d), (e)

21

다음 3형식 문장은 4형식 문장으로, 4형식 문장은 3형식 문장으로 바꾸어 쓰시오.

(1) Peter passed the ball to Sam.

→ Peter passed ________________________.

(2) Did you get them some bread?

→ Did you get ________________________?

22 내신기출

다음 〈보기〉와 같이 두 문장을 한 문장으로 쓰시오.

> 〈보기〉 Tony swam in the river.
> Ann watched him.
> → Ann watched Tony swim in the river.

(1) The rain fell on his head.

He felt the rain.

→ He ________________________.

(2) I washed the dishes.

Joan helped me.

→ Joan ________________________.

23

다음 우리말과 같은 뜻이 되도록 [ ] 안의 말을 이용하여 문장을 완성하시오.

(1) 그는 Ned에게 조용히 있으라고 명령했다.

(order, stay silent)

→ He ________________________.

(2) 우리는 그녀가 사람들에게 소리치는 것을 들었다.

(hear, shout at people)

→ We ________________________.

24 고난도

각 상자에서 알맞은 말을 골라 문장을 완성하시오.
[단, 한 번씩만 사용할 것]

The soup	told	her happy
She	made	delicious
We	smells	us the big news

(1) The soup ________________________.

(2) She ________________________.

(3) We ________________________.

25

다음을 보고, 〈보기〉와 같이 문장을 완성하시오.

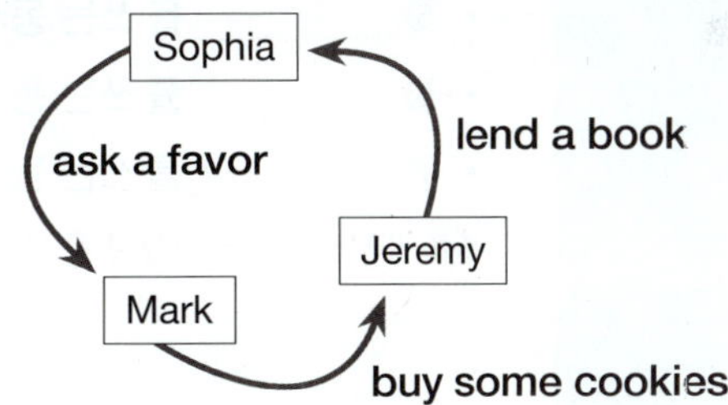

> 〈보기〉 Sophia asked a favor of Mark.

(1) Mark bought ________ ________

________ ________.

(2) Jeremy lent ________ ________

________ ________.

26

다음 메모를 보고, Julie의 엄마가 Julie에게 시킨 일에 대한 문장을 완성하시오.

> (1) read an English book
> (2) clean the bathroom
> (3) take care of her sister

(1) Julie's mom wanted her ________________.

(2) Julie's mom had her ________________.

(3) Julie's mom made her ________________.

CHAPTER 10
문장의 형식

1 문장의 5형식

1형식	주어+동사	Thomas smiled.
2형식	주어+동사+주격 보어 (주어+감각동사+① _________)	Michelle was a nurse. (The girls look happy.)
3형식	주어+동사+② _________	I love soccer.
4형식	주어+동사+간접목적어+직접목적어	She gave him a blanket.
5형식	주어+동사+목적어+③ _________	My grandmother called me darling.

2 4형식 → 3형식

- 형태: 주어+동사+<u>간접목적어</u>+<u>직접목적어</u>

  주어+동사+<u>직접목적어</u>+④ _________ +<u>간접목적어</u>
- 간접목적어 앞에 쓰는 전치사
- ⑤ _________ 를 쓰는 동사: give, send, tell, lend, show 등
- ⑥ _________ 를 쓰는 동사: buy, make, get, cook 등
- ⑦ _________ 를 쓰는 동사: ask

❗ 4형식 문장을 3형식 문장으로 바꿀 때 전치사 to/for/of를 쓰는 동사 구분하여 알아두기

3 목적격 보어

5형식 문장에서는 명사(구), 형용사(구), to부정사(구), 동사원형 등이 목적격 보어가 될 수 있음

- 목적격 보어로 ⑧ _________ 를 쓰는 동사: want, ask, tell, expect, order, allow 등
- 목적격 보어로 ⑨ _________ 을 쓰는 동사: 지각동사(see, watch, hear, feel), 사역동사(have, make, let)

❗ 5형식 문장에서 목적격 보어로 명사(구)/형용사(구)/to부정사(구)/동사원형을 쓰는 동사 구분하여 알아두기

CHECK

밑줄 친 부분이 어법상 맞으면 ○, 틀리면 X 표시하고 바르게 고치시오.

1 His idea sounded <u>greatly</u>.

2 I didn't expect you <u>to come</u> so early.

3 They gave the present <u>for</u> Fred.

4 She kept the soup <u>warmly</u> for him.

5 We bought <u>Nicole</u> a lovely skirt.

6 I saw them <u>make</u> a sandcastle.

7 Let me <u>to carry</u> it for you.

CHAPTER 11

to부정사와 동명사

to부정사와 동명사는 동사의 형태를 바꾸어 만든 말로 동사 본연의 의미와 성질을
가지면서, 문장에서 동사가 아닌 다른 품사의 역할을 할 수 있습니다.
to부정사는 <to+동사원형>의 형태로 문장에서 명사, 형용사, 부사 역할을 합니다.
동명사는 <동사원형+-ing>의 형태로 문장에서 명사 역할을 합니다.

POINT 01 to부정사의 명사적 용법 - 주어 역할
POINT 02 to부정사의 명사적 용법 - 보어/목적어 역할
POINT 03 to부정사의 명사적 용법 - 의문사+to부정사
POINT 04 to부정사의 형용사적 용법 - (대)명사 수식
POINT 05 to부정사의 부사적 용법 - 목적
POINT 06 to부정사의 부사적 용법 - 감정의 원인 / 결과
POINT 07 동명사 - 주어/보어 역할
POINT 08 동명사 - 목적어 역할

to부정사의 명사적 용법 - 주어 역할

- to부정사는 〈to+동사원형〉의 형태로 문장에서 명사, 형용사, 부사 역할을 한다.

- to부정사가 명사처럼 쓰이면 문장에서 주어, 보어, 목적어 역할을 한다.

- to부정사가 주어로 쓰인 경우 '~하는 것은'이라는 뜻을 나타낸다. 이때 보통 주어 자리에 가주어 it을 쓰고 진주어인 to부정사(구)를 뒤로 보낸다.

  To watch fireworks is amazing.
  　　　주어

  → **It** is amazing **to watch** fireworks.
  　가주어　　　　　　　　　진주어

> (+Plus) 주어로 쓰인 to부정사(구)는 3인칭 단수 취급한다.
> **To play online games** *is* fun.

A 다음 두 문장이 같은 뜻이 되도록 빈칸에 알맞은 말을 쓰시오.

1 To travel alone is dangerous.

→ It is dangerous ______________ ______________ alone.

2 To go on a picnic is exciting.

→ ______________ is exciting ______________ ______________ on a picnic.

3 It is not easy to start a blog.

→ ______________ ______________ a blog ______________ not easy.

4 It is relaxing to jog along the river.

→ ______________ ______________ ______________ ______________ ______________ is relaxing.

5 To learn a new language is not easy.

→ ______________ ______________ ______________ ______________ ______________ ______________

a new language.

B 다음 우리말과 같은 뜻이 되도록 [ ] 안의 말을 이용하여 문장을 완성하시오.

1 간호사가 되는 것은 그녀의 꿈이다. (become)

______________ ______________ a nurse is her dream.

2 약속을 지키는 것은 중요하다. (keep)

______________ is important ______________ ______________ promises.

3 TV를 매일 보는 것은 불필요하다. (watch)

______________ ______________ TV every day ______________ unnecessary.

4 도시에 가게를 여는 것이 내 목표이다. (open)

______________ ______________ my goal ______________ ______________ a shop in the city.

5 그 상황을 이해하는 것은 어려웠다. (difficult, understand)

______________ ______________ ______________ ______________ ______________ the situation.

to부정사의 명사적 용법 – 보어/목적어 역할

- to부정사가 주어의 성질, 상태 등을 보충 설명하는 보어로 쓰인 경우 '~하는 것(이다)'이라는 뜻을 나타낸다. 이때 주어와 to부정사(구)는 동격 관계이다.
  My plan is **to lose** seven kilograms. (My plan = to lose seven kilograms)

- to부정사가 동사의 목적어로 쓰인 경우 '~하는 것(을)'이라는 뜻을 나타낸다. to부정사를 목적어로 쓰는 동사에는 want, hope, need, plan, decide, expect, promise, refuse 등이 있다.
  I want **to go** to the concert.
  We decided **to help** them.

> **+ Plus** to부정사의 부정형은 to부정사 앞에 not이나 never를 써서 나타낸다.
> She decided **not to** call him. (그녀는 그에게 전화하지 않기로 결심했다.)

A 다음 〈보기〉에서 알맞은 말을 골라 빈칸에 적절한 형태로 써넣으시오.

> 〈보기〉 bake   become   come   write

1 They hope ___________ ___________ here again soon.
2 Her goal is ___________ ___________ a photographer.
3 He planned ___________ ___________ a cake for his dad.
4 Our homework is ___________ ___________ a short story.

B 다음 [ ] 안의 말을 알맞게 배열하여 문장을 완성하시오.

1 His job ___________________________. (to, repair, is, cars)
2 I ___________________________ for work. (be late, to, want, don't)
3 ___________________________ a new bicycle. (buy, she, to, needed)
4 You ___________________________ anyone. (not, promised, tell, to)

C 다음 우리말과 같은 뜻이 되도록 [ ] 안의 말을 이용하여 문장을 완성하시오.

1 그들은 그 경기를 이길 것이라고 예상한다. (expect, win)
   They ___________ ___________ ___________ the game.
2 그녀의 희망은 오케스트라에서 첼로를 연주하는 것이다. (play)
   Her hope ___________ ___________ ___________ the cello in an orchestra.
3 우리는 테니스 동아리에 들어가지 않기로 결정했다. (decide, join)
   We ___________ ___________ ___________ ___________ the tennis club.
4 내 계획은 이번 달에 영어 소설 한 권을 읽는 것이다. (plan, read)
   My ___________ ___________ ___________ ___________ an English novel this month.

to부정사의 명사적 용법 - 의문사+to부정사

〈의문사+to부정사〉는 문장에서 명사처럼 쓰여, 주로 동사의 목적어 역할을 한다.
- what+to부정사: 무엇을 ~할지
- when+to부정사: 언제 ~할지
- where+to부정사: 어디에(서) ~할지
- how+to부정사: 어떻게 ~할지, ~하는 방법
- who(m)+to부정사: 누구를 ~할지

I don't know **what to eat** for lunch.
Can you show me **how to make** waffles?

A 다음 밑줄 친 부분을 어법에 맞게 고쳐 쓰시오.

1 Dan understood <u>to do what</u>.

2 Can you tell me <u>when go</u> to the show?

3 I want to learn <u>what to drive</u> a car.

B 다음 [ ] 안의 말을 알맞게 배열하여 문장을 완성하시오.

1 You need to choose ________________________. (with, who, sit, to)

2 She taught me ________________________. (play, how, guitar, to, the)

3 Ted told us ________________________. (in, where, stay, to, London)

4 I'm not sure ________________________. (when, wake up, tomorrow, to)

5 We didn't know ________________________. (to, the, wear, party, to, what)

C 다음 우리말과 같은 뜻이 되도록 〈보기〉에서 알맞은 말을 골라 문장을 완성하시오.

〈보기〉	buy	come	go	invite	use

1 저에게 언제 다시 올지 말씀해 주세요.
   Please tell me ____________ ____________ ____________ again.

2 그는 우리에게 누구를 파티에 초대할지 물었다.
   He asked us ____________ ____________ ____________ to the party.

3 Sally는 휴가로 어디를 갈지 결정했다.
   Sally decided ____________ ____________ ____________ for her vacation.

4 나는 생일 선물로 그녀에게 무엇을 사 줄지 모르겠다.
   I don't know ____________ ____________ ____________ her for her birthday.

5 그녀는 그들에게 세탁기를 어떻게 사용하는지 보여 주었다.
   She showed them ____________ ____________ ____________ the washing machine.

POINT 04 to부정사의 형용사적 용법 - (대)명사 수식

○ to부정사는 형용사처럼 (대)명사를 수식하여 '~하는', '~할'이라는 뜻을 나타낸다. 이때 to부정사는 (대)명사 뒤에 온다.
There are a lot of books **to read**.

○ -thing, -one, -body로 끝나는 대명사를 형용사와 to부정사가 함께 수식하는 경우에는 〈-thing / -one / -body + 형용사 + to부정사〉의 순서로 쓴다.
I want something **cold to drink**.

내신만점 Tip -thing, -one, -body로 끝나는 대명사를 형용사와 to부정사가 함께 수식하는 경우의 어순에 주의하자.

A 다음 밑줄 친 부분을 어법에 맞게 고쳐 쓰시오.

1 It is time leave now.

2 We had no to spend money.

3 I'm looking for someone help me.

4 They have nothing to say important.

5 He's not going to come. He has a lot of things doing.

B 다음 〈보기〉에서 알맞은 말을 골라 빈칸에 적절한 형태로 써넣으시오.

〈보기〉	eat	talk	use	wear

1 Do you have anyone ______________ ______________ to?

2 She bought a lamp ______________ ______________ in her room.

3 I really need something sweet ______________ ______________.

4 My brother doesn't have a suit ______________ ______________.

C 다음 우리말과 같은 뜻이 되도록 [ ] 안의 말을 알맞게 배열하여 문장을 완성하시오.

1 그것은 건강을 유지하는 좋은 방법이다. (stay, a good way, to, healthy)
It is ______________________________.

2 할 만한 재미있는 일이 있나요? (to, interesting, do, anything)
Is there ______________________________?

3 Ted는 마쳐야 할 숙제가 좀 있다. (homework, to, has, finish, some)
Ted ______________________________.

4 그 도시에는 방문할 곳이 많다. (places, visit, to, many)
There are ______________________________ in the city.

POINT 05 · to부정사의 부사적 용법 - 목적

- to부정사가 부사처럼 쓰이면 동사, 형용사, 부사를 수식하는 역할을 한다.

- 부사적 용법의 to부정사는 '~하기 위해', '~하러'라는 뜻으로 목적을 나타낼 수 있다.
  I went to Peru **to see** Machu Picchu.
  They came to Korea **to teach** English.

> (+Plus) 목적을 나타내는 to부정사는 의미를 명확히 하기 위해 〈in order to+동사원형〉의 형태로 쓰기도 한다.
> He studied hard **in order to get** a perfect score. (그는 만점을 받기 위해 열심히 공부했다.)

A 다음 두 문장이 같은 뜻이 되도록 빈칸에 알맞은 말을 쓰시오.

1 I want to buy a new backpack, so I'm saving money.

→ I'm saving money _______________ _______________ a new backpack.

2 He wanted to buy some new clothes, so he went to the store.

→ He went to the store _______________ _______________ some new clothes.

3 You need to fill out this form to join the club.

→ You need to fill out this form _______________ _______________ _______________
_______________ the club.

B 다음 [ ] 안의 말을 알맞게 배열하여 문장을 완성하시오.

1 They _______________________ me. (to, early, help, came)

2 Alice _______________________ awake. (stay, coffee, to, drinks)

3 We _______________________ the bus. (order, ran, to, catch, in)

4 What should I _______________________? (be, to, successful, do)

C 다음 우리말과 같은 뜻이 되도록 [ ] 안의 말을 이용하여 문장을 완성하시오.

1 우리는 그 소식을 너에게 알려 주기 위해 이메일을 보냈다. (tell)

We sent the email _______________ _______________ _______________ the news.

2 나는 그들과 수영을 하러 해변에 갔다. (swim, with)

I went to the beach _______________ _______________ _______________ _______________.

3 그녀는 소지품을 싸려고 상자 몇 개를 가져왔다. (pack, her things)

She brought some boxes _______________ _______________ _______________ _______________.

4 Peter는 그의 아이디어를 공유하기 위해 블로그를 시작할 것이다. (share, ideas)

Peter will start a blog _______________ _______________ _______________.

to부정사의 부사적 용법 – 감정의 원인 / 결과

- 부사적 용법의 to부정사는 '~해서', '~하니'라는 뜻으로 감정의 원인을 나타낼 수 있다. 이때 to부정사는 주로 happy, glad, sad, sorry, angry 등 감정을 나타내는 형용사 뒤에 온다.
  I'm *glad* **to see** you again.

- 부사적 용법의 to부정사는 '(…해서) ~하다'라는 뜻으로 결과를 나타낼 수 있다.
  He grew up **to be** a pilot.

- 〈too+형용사/부사+to부정사〉는 '너무 ~해서 …할 수 없다' 또는 '…하기에는 너무 ~하다'라는 뜻이다.
  They are **too young to get** married.

- 〈형용사/부사+enough+to부정사〉는 '…할 만큼 충분히 ~하다'라는 뜻이다.
  The boy is **tall enough to reach** the top shelf.

A 다음 두 문장이 같은 뜻이 되도록 빈칸에 알맞은 말을 쓰시오.

1 They read the bad news, so they were upset.
  → They were upset ＿＿＿＿＿＿ ＿＿＿＿＿＿ the bad news.

2 The coffee is hot. We can't drink it.
  → The coffee is ＿＿＿＿＿ ＿＿＿＿＿＿ ＿＿＿＿＿＿ ＿＿＿＿＿.

3 Emma was tired last night. She couldn't study.
  → Emma was ＿＿＿＿＿ ＿＿＿＿＿ ＿＿＿＿＿ ＿＿＿＿＿ last night.

B 다음 [ ] 안의 말을 알맞게 배열하여 문장을 완성하시오.

1 The soup is ＿＿＿＿＿＿＿＿＿. (hot, to, too, eat)

2 My grandfather ＿＿＿＿＿＿＿＿＿ 90 years old. (be, to, lived)

3 Linda is ＿＿＿＿＿＿＿＿＿ her brother. (to, enough, lift, strong)

4 Jeff was ＿＿＿＿＿＿＿＿＿ from Eve. (a message, to, happy, get)

C 다음 우리말과 같은 뜻이 되도록 [ ] 안의 말을 이용하여 문장을 완성하시오.

1 우리는 네가 떠난다는 것을 듣고 슬펐다. (sad, hear)
  We were ＿＿＿＿＿ ＿＿＿＿＿ ＿＿＿＿＿ that you are leaving.

2 그는 너무 바빠서 점심을 먹지 못했다. (busy, have)
  He was ＿＿＿＿＿ ＿＿＿＿＿ ＿＿＿＿＿ lunch.

3 그녀는 자라서 작가가 되었다. (grow up, become)
  She ＿＿＿＿＿ ＿＿＿＿＿ ＿＿＿＿＿ ＿＿＿＿＿ a writer.

4 그들은 그 영화를 볼 만큼 충분히 나이가 들었다. (old, watch)
  They are ＿＿＿＿＿ ＿＿＿＿＿ ＿＿＿＿＿ the movie.

- 동명사는 〈동사원형+-ing〉의 형태로 명사처럼 문장에서 주어, 보어, 목적어 역할을 한다.

- 동명사가 주어로 쓰인 경우 '~하는 것(은)'이라는 뜻을 나타낸다.
  Solving this problem is impossible.
  (→ **It** is impossible **to solve** this problem.)

- 동명사가 보어로 쓰인 경우 '~하는 것(이다)'이라는 뜻을 나타낸다.
  One of my hobbies is **making** cookies.
  (→ One of my hobbies is **to make** cookies.)

+ Plus 주어로 쓰인 동명사(구)는 3인칭 단수 취급한다.
Studying math *is* not easy.

A 다음 〈보기〉에서 알맞은 말을 골라 빈칸에 동명사 형태로 써넣으시오. [단, 한 번씩만 사용할 것]

〈보기〉	drive	get	listen	meet	play	read	take

1 _____________ new people is interesting.

2 Her goal was _____________ good grades.

3 _____________ safely is important for everyone.

4 My favorite activity is _____________ to music.

5 _____________ the book made me feel better.

6 His job is _____________ care of children.

7 _____________ tennis with my cousin was fun.

B 다음 우리말과 같은 뜻이 되도록 [ ] 안의 말을 알맞게 배열하여 문장을 완성하시오.

1 영화를 만드는 것은 오랜 시간이 걸린다. (a film, takes, making)
_____________________________ a long time.

2 가장 좋았던 점은 다른 사람들을 돕는 것이었다. (others, was, helping)
The best part _____________________________.

3 롤러코스터를 타는 것은 나를 두렵게 한다. (scares, roller coasters, riding)
_____________________________ me.

4 탄산음료를 마시는 것은 건강에 좋지 않다. (is, soda, good, not, drinking)
_____________________________ for your health.

5 Brian의 나쁜 습관 중 하나는 아침에 늦게 일어나는 것이다. (in the morning, getting up, is, late)
One of Brian's bad habits _____________________________.

- 동명사가 동사의 목적어로 쓰인 경우 '~하는 것(을)'이라는 뜻을 나타낸다. 동명사를 목적어로 쓰는 동사에는 enjoy, finish, stop, keep, mind, avoid, give up, quit, consider 등이 있다.
  I *enjoy* **going** shopping every weekend.

- 동명사는 전치사의 목적어로도 쓰인다.
  The restaurant is famous *for* **serving** traditional Korean food.

> **내신만점 Tip** to부정사와 동명사를 목적어로 쓰는 동사를 구분하여 알아두자.

A 다음 밑줄 친 부분을 어법에 맞게 고쳐 쓰시오.

1 They kept <u>walk</u> for an hour.

2 He was interested in <u>drive</u> a car.

3 My grandparents wanted <u>making</u> a garden.

4 Do you mind <u>to help</u> me carry this bag?

5 Thank you for <u>to visit</u> us today!

B 다음 〈보기〉와 같이 동명사를 이용하여 두 문장을 한 문장으로 만드시오.

> 〈보기〉 I baked a cake. I enjoyed it. → I enjoyed baking a cake.

1 I used to play soccer professionally. I stopped.
   → I stopped ________________________.

2 James may miss the train. He is worried about it.
   → James is worried about ________________________.

3 Ben tried to fix the computer. But he gave up.
   → Ben gave up ________________________.

C 다음 우리말과 같은 뜻이 되도록 [ ] 안의 말을 이용하여 문장을 완성하시오.

1 그가 드디어 설거지를 끝냈다. (finish, wash)
   He finally ____________ ____________ the dishes.

2 너 자신에게 도전하는 것을 멈추지 마라. (stop, challenge)
   ____________ ____________ ____________ yourself.

3 나는 동물 그리는 것을 잘한다. (be good at, draw)
   ____________ ____________ ____________ animals.

4 우리는 비닐봉지를 사용하는 것을 피해야 한다. (should, avoid, use)
   ____________ ____________ ____________ plastic bags.

실전 TEST

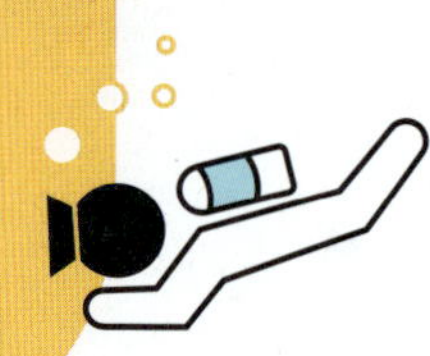

01

> ___________ is easy to use chopsticks.

① All   ② It   ③ That
④ This   ⑤ What

02

> Nick avoided ___________ too much at night.

① eat   ② ate   ③ to eat
④ eating   ⑤ to eating

03

> I don't have a cookbook. Can you show me ___________ to make mushroom soup?

① how   ② what   ③ why
④ when   ⑤ where

04 내신기출

다음 중 〈보기〉의 밑줄 친 부분과 쓰임이 같은 것은?

> 〈보기〉 She kept talking with James.

① Learning new languages is fun.
② I just finished making the bed.
③ His problem is wasting too much money.
④ Ann's hobby is collecting old coins.
⑤ We are thinking about going bowling tonight.

05-07 다음 빈칸에 알맞은 말이 바르게 짝지어진 것을 고르시오.

05

> I plan ___________ Japanese. ___________ will be exciting to read Japanese books.

① learn – It   ② to learn – It
③ learning – It   ④ to learn – That
⑤ learning – That

06

> A: Why don't you go outside and play?
> B: It's ___________ cold ___________ outside.

① enough – to play   ② not – playing
③ enough – play   ④ too – to play
⑤ too – playing

07

> I want ___________ healthy. So I gave up ___________ junk food.

① be – eating   ② being – eating
③ to be – eating   ④ to be – to eat
⑤ to be – eat

08-09 다음 대화의 빈칸에 알맞은 말을 고르시오.

08

> A: Can you tell me __________ to get to Namsan Park?
> B: Sure. Walk down that street and go up the stairs on your left.

① when   ② what   ③ whom
④ where   ⑤ how

09

> A: Would you like _____________________?
> B: Yes, please. I'm so thirsty.

① cold something drinking
② cold something to drink
③ drinking cold something
④ something cold to drink
⑤ something to drink cold

10

다음 우리말을 영어로 바르게 옮긴 것은?

> 그녀는 나를 도와줄 만큼 충분히 친절했다.

① She was too kind to help me.
② She was kind enough help me.
③ She was enough kind to help me.
④ She was kind enough to help me.
⑤ She was so kind that helped me.

11-12 다음 빈칸에 들어갈 수 <u>없는</u> 말을 고르시오.

11

> I __________ to play outside.

① expected   ② enjoyed
③ decided   ④ wanted
⑤ hoped

12

> Jessica __________ writing her essay.

① planned   ② kept
③ finished   ④ considered
⑤ avoided

13-14 다음 중 밑줄 친 부분의 용법이 나머지와 <u>다른</u> 것을 고르시오.

13

① I need someone <u>to talk</u> to.
② She has a dress <u>to wear</u> tonight.
③ He grew up <u>to be</u> a film director.
④ There are many things <u>to do</u> now.
⑤ There's no one <u>to tell</u> me the truth.

14

① We decided <u>to study</u> abroad.
② I'm sorry <u>to bother</u> you.
③ She was happy <u>to pass</u> the test.
④ He woke up <u>to find</u> himself alone.
⑤ They went to China <u>to see</u> the Great Wall.

 다음 중 밑줄 친 부분이 어법상 **틀린** 것을 고르시오.

15

① She wanted <u>to join</u> the art club.
② He was glad <u>to meet</u> his old friend.
③ The man quit <u>to smoke</u> a few years ago.
④ We went to Mt. Baekdu <u>to see</u> the lake.
⑤ My dream is <u>to become</u> a computer engineer.

16

① I have something <u>to show</u> you.
② Please tell me <u>where to go</u>.
③ He lived <u>be</u> 80 years old.
④ It is fun <u>to draw</u> people on the street.
⑤ Stella kept <u>looking</u> at him.

17 고난도

다음 중 빈칸에 to가 들어갈 수 **없는** 것은?

① He refused _________ make a speech.
② I saw them _________ play baseball.
③ She helped me _________ find the bank.
④ It is good for one's health _________ exercise.
⑤ My plan is _________ master English grammar.

18 내신기출

다음 우리말과 같은 뜻이 되도록 주어진 말을 배열할 때 네 번째에 올 단어는?

> 나는 저녁으로 무엇을 요리할지 결정할 수 없다.
> (for, what, cook, decide, to, I, dinner, can't)

① decide   ② can't   ③ to
④ cook   ⑤ what

19

(A), (B), (C)의 괄호 안에서 알맞은 것끼리 바르게 짝지어진 것은?

> (A) I don't mind [to eat / eating] alone.
> (B) [Walk / Walking] is good for the environment.
> (C) It is important [go / to go] to the dentist regularly.

	(A)	(B)	(C)
①	to eat	Walking	go
②	to eat	Walk	to go
③	eating	Walking	go
④	eating	Walk	go
⑤	eating	Walking	to go

20 고난도 내신기출

다음 중 어법상 옳은 것끼리 짝지어진 것은?

> (a) He decided to leave early.
> (b) This is difficult to lose weight.
> (c) Going camping will be a lot of fun.
> (d) I'm interested in to protect animals.
> (e) I need someone to help me.

① (a), (c), (d)   ② (a), (c), (e)
③ (b), (c), (d)   ④ (b), (d), (e)
⑤ (c), (d), (e)

21

다음 우리말과 같은 뜻이 되도록 주어진 말을 이용하여 문장을 완성하시오.

(1) 그 태블릿 PC는 사기에는 너무 비쌌다.
   (expensive, buy)
   → The tablet PC was ___________ ___________
   ___________ ___________.

(2) 높은 산을 오르는 것은 쉽지 않다.
   (climb, high mountains)
   → ___________ ___________ not easy ___________
   ___________ ___________ ___________.

22

다음 그림을 보고, 주어진 말을 이용하여 문장을 완성하시오.

play the violin

ride a bike

(1) He is good at ___________ ___________ ___________.

(2) ___________ ___________ ___________ is difficult for him.

23

다음 우리말과 같은 뜻이 되도록 주어진 말을 이용하여 문장을 완성하시오.

> A: 너는 먹을 것이 있니?
> B: 아니, 없어. 간식을 좀 사러 가게에 가자.

A: Do you have ___________ ___________
   ___________? (anything, eat)

B: No, I don't. Let's go to the store ___________
   ___________ some snacks. (buy)

24

다음 우리말과 같은 뜻이 되도록 주어진 말을 알맞게 배열하여 문장을 완성하시오.

(1) 그는 그 소리를 듣고 놀랐다.
   (the noise, surprised, he, hear, to, was)
   → ___________

(2) 창문을 열어 주시겠어요?
   (mind, do, the window, you, opening)
   → ___________

25 고난도 내신기출

다음 행사표를 보고, 주어진 말과 to부정사를 이용하여 문장을 완성하시오.

행사	준비물	참가 가능 연령
Go hiking	Sneakers	8세 이상
Take a diving class	Swimsuit	17세 이상

(1) Emma is nine years old. She is ___________
   ___________ ___________ ___________. (old)

(2) Andy is fourteen years old. He is ___________
   ___________ ___________ ___________ ___________
   ___________ ___________. (young)

26

다음 대화를 읽고, 질문에 답하시오.

> A: Did you decide (A) <u>무엇을 할지</u> in Seoul?
> B: Yes. I want to visit some palaces. But I don't know how I can get to them.
> A: Don't you speak Korean?
> B: No, I don't. So I need (B) (helpful, to, someone, guide) me.

(1) to부정사를 이용하여 (A)의 우리말을 영어로 옮겨 쓰시오.

   ____

(2) (B)를 알맞게 배열하여 문장을 완성하시오.

   ____

to부정사와 동명사

1 to부정사

- 형태: ⟨① ____________ + ____________⟩
- 용법
  - 명사적 용법 – 주어, 보어, ② ____________ 역할: '~하는 것'
  - 형용사적 용법 – (대)명사를 뒤에서 수식: '~하는', '~할'
    - *⟨-thing / -one / -body + ③ ____________ + to부정사⟩
  - 부사적 용법 – 동사, 형용사, 부사 수식
    - ④ ____________: '~하기 위해', '~하러' = ⟨in order to + 동사원형⟩
    - 감정의 원인: '~해서', '~하니'
    - 결과: '(…해서) ~하다'
      - *⟨⑤ ____________ + 형용사 / 부사 + to부정사⟩: '너무 ~해서 …할 수 없다'
      - *⟨형용사 / 부사 + ⑥ ____________ + to부정사⟩: '…할 만큼 충분히 ~하다'

❗ to부정사의 세 가지 용법 구분하기
⟨형용사/부사+enough+to부정사⟩와 ⟨too +형용사/부사+to부정사⟩의 어순과 쓰임 익히기

2 동명사

- 형태: ⟨⑦ ____________ + ____________⟩
- 역할: 주어, 보어, 목적어 – '~하는 것'

3 to부정사 vs. 동명사

- ⑧ ____________를 목적어로 쓰는 동사: want, hope, need, plan, decide, expect, promise, refuse 등
- ⑨ ____________를 목적어로 쓰는 동사: enjoy, finish, stop, keep, mind, avoid, give up, quit, consider 등

❗ to부정사와 동명사를 목적어로 쓰는 동사 구분하여 알아두기

CHECK

밑줄 친 부분이 어법상 맞으면 O, 틀리면 X 표시하고 바르게 고치시오.

1 I have someone introducing to you.
2 I was lucky to meet you here.
3 They kept ask me about the book.
4 My mother was too sick to eat anything.
5 The pool is enough deep to swim in.
6 Luna is afraid of to see a doctor.
7 He wanted dancing with Amy.

12

접속사

접속사는 단어와 단어, 구와 구, 절과 절을 연결해 주는 말로, 등위접속사와 종속접속사가 있습니다. 등위접속사에는 and, but, or, so 등이 있으며, 문법적으로 대등한 단어, 구, 절을 연결하는 역할을 합니다. 종속접속사에는 when, before, because, that 등이 있으며, 주절(문장에서 중심이 되는 절)과 종속절(주절의 내용을 보충하는 절)을 이어주는 역할을 합니다.

등위접속사 and

- 등위접속사는 문법적으로 대등한 단어, 구, 절을 연결하는 말로 and, but, or, so 등이 있다.

- and는 '그리고', '~와'라는 뜻으로 내용상 서로 비슷한 것을 연결하거나 시간의 순서, 인과관계 등을 나타낸다.
  Chris **and** Laura are my classmates.
  We went to the cinema **and** had dinner.

- 〈both A and B〉는 'A와 B 둘 다'라는 뜻이다.
  I like **both** bread **and** rice.

> **내신만점 Tip** 등위접속사로 연결되는 앞뒤의 말은 문장에서의 역할과 형태가 대등해야 한다는 점에 유의하자.
> We have *cats* **and** *dogs*. / He *likes strawberries* **but** *doesn't like strawberry milk*.

A 다음 [ ] 안에서 알맞은 말을 고르시오.

1 She is tall and (beauty / beautiful).

2 They swam in the river and (ate / eat) sandwiches.

3 Daniel will play the piano and (song / sing a song).

4 I like to walk in the park and (take / taking) pictures.

B 다음 두 문장을 한 문장으로 만들 때, 빈칸에 알맞은 말을 쓰시오.

1 The man is gentle. The man is smart, too.
  → The man is ____________ ____________ ____________.

2 I met Frank in Madrid. I met Sarah in Madrid, too.
  → I met ____________ ____________ ____________ in Madrid.

3 She has blue eyes. She has long, blond hair.
  → She has blue eyes ____________ ____________, ____________ ____________.

C 다음 우리말과 같은 뜻이 되도록 [ ] 안의 말을 알맞게 배열하여 문장을 완성하시오.

1 우리는 책을 읽고 그것에 관해 이야기했다. (about, and, them, talked)
  We read books ____________________________.

2 그는 중국어와 일본어를 둘 다 말할 수 있다. (Chinese, both, Japanese, and)
  He can speak ____________________________.

3 그녀는 노트북을 사고 호주로 여행을 가기 위해서 돈을 모았다. (and, to Australia, to buy, to travel, a laptop)
  She saved money ____________________________.

등위접속사 but

- but은 '그러나', '~(이)지만'이라는 뜻으로 내용상 서로 반대되거나 대조되는 것을 연결한다.
  It was a cold **but** sunny morning.
  I grew up in a big city, **but** I like small towns.

A 다음 ( ) 안에서 의미상 가장 알맞은 말을 고르시오.

1 My bag is old (and / but) clean.
2 I didn't eat anything, (and / but) I feel full.
3 It is raining, (and / but) I forgot my umbrella.
4 She sent me an email (and / but) gave me a call.
5 We played on the slide (and / but) on the swing.

B 다음 두 문장을 접속사 but을 이용하여 한 문장으로 만들 때, 빈칸에 알맞은 말을 쓰시오.

1 He is strong. He is not fast.
   → He is strong, ＿＿＿＿＿ ＿＿＿＿＿ ＿＿＿＿＿ ＿＿＿＿＿ fast.
2 I came early. I didn't get a good seat.
   → I came early, ＿＿＿＿＿ ＿＿＿＿＿ ＿＿＿＿＿ ＿＿＿＿＿ a good
     seat.
3 They had a quiet weekend. They had a fun weekend.
   → They had ＿＿＿＿＿ ＿＿＿＿＿ ＿＿＿＿＿ ＿＿＿＿＿ weekend.
4 Jay loves hip-hop music. I don't like it.
   → Jay loves hip-hop music, ＿＿＿＿＿ ＿＿＿＿＿ ＿＿＿＿＿
     ＿＿＿＿＿ it.

C 다음 우리말과 같은 뜻이 되도록 ( ) 안의 말을 배열하여 문장을 완성하시오.

1 그녀는 슬펐지만 울지 않았다. (she, but, cry, didn't)
   She was sad, ＿＿＿＿＿＿＿＿＿＿＿＿＿＿＿.
2 이 문제는 단순하지만 어렵다. (difficult, but, is, simple)
   This question ＿＿＿＿＿＿＿＿＿＿＿＿＿＿＿.
3 나는 시험에 떨어졌지만, 다시 시도할 것이다. (again, I'll, but, try)
   I failed the test, ＿＿＿＿＿＿＿＿＿＿＿＿＿＿＿.
4 그는 짧지만 매우 감동적인 연설을 했다. (very touching, but, speech, a short)
   He gave ＿＿＿＿＿＿＿＿＿＿＿＿＿＿＿.

등위접속사 or

- or는 '또는', '~(이)거나'라는 뜻으로 선택을 나타낸다.
  Are you coming to Korea in July **or** August?
  They can take the bus **or** they can walk to school.

- 〈either A or B〉는 'A이거나 B'라는 뜻이다.
  Either my brother **or** I should do the dishes.

A 다음 [ ] 안에서 알맞은 말을 고르시오.

1 I want to be an artist (but / or) a teacher.

2 He is (both / either) Australian or British.

3 Natalie went on a picnic, (but / or) Ben didn't.

4 Which kind of coffee do you want, hot (and / or) iced?

B 다음 두 문장을 접속사 or를 이용하여 한 문장으로 만들 때, 빈칸에 알맞은 말을 쓰시오.

1 Do you want to come with William? Do you want to come with Jack?

→ Do you want to come with ______________ ______________ ______________?

2 He may be waiting at the bus stop. He may be waiting in the café.

→ He may be waiting ____________ at the bus stop ____________ in the café.

3 Did she call you? Did she forget again?

→ Did she call you, ____________ ____________ ____________ ____________ again?

4 You can pay by credit card. You can pay with cash.

→ You can pay ____________ ____________ ____________ ____________

____________ ____________.

C 다음 우리말과 같은 뜻이 되도록 [ ] 안의 말을 배열하여 문장을 완성하시오.

1 그들은 우산이나 비옷을 가져와야 한다. (or, umbrellas, bring, raincoats)

They should ____________________________.

2 저 여자아이의 이름은 Justine이거나 Julia이다. (either, Justine, Julia, or, is)

That girl's name ____________________________.

3 그는 캠핑을 가거나 집에 있을 것이다. (stay, or, camping, at, go, home)

He is going to ____________________________.

4 우리는 외식하거나 내가 집에서 뭔가 요리할 수 있다. (can, I, or, eat out, we, cook, can)

____________________________ something at home.

○ so는 '그래서'라는 뜻으로 절과 절을 연결하며, 이때 so 앞의 절은 원인을 나타내고 뒤의 절은 결과를 나타낸다.
　It rained all day long, **so** we couldn't go on a picnic.
　There was a lot of traffic, **so** I was twenty minutes late for work.

A　다음 ( ) 안에서 알맞은 말을 고르시오.

1　My final exams are over, (but / so) I can go out to play.

2　We'll either go paragliding (or / so) go skydiving on the trip.

3　The movie looked interesting, (but / so) it was boring.

4　Isabella was tired, so (very sleepy / she went to bed early).

B　자연스러운 문장이 되도록 알맞게 연결하시오.

1　The soup was salty,　　　　　・　　・ ⓐ so I wore my jacket.

2　It was cold outside,　　　　　・　　・ ⓑ so I used a flashlight.

3　The light was broken,　　　　・　　・ ⓒ so I added water to it.

4　I didn't listen carefully,　　 ・　　・ ⓓ so I can introduce them to you.

5　I have a lot of foreign friends, ・　・ ⓔ so I didn't understand the lesson.

C　다음 〈보기〉에서 알맞은 접속사를 골라 두 문장을 한 문장으로 만드시오. (단, 한 번씩만 사용할 것)

〈보기〉	and	but	or	so

1　He wasn't feeling well. He didn't go to school.

　→ ______________________________________

2　I called her name. She didn't look at me.

　→ ______________________________________

3　You can make an exchange. You can get a refund.

　→ ______________________________________

4　We went to the store. We bought some batteries.

　→ ______________________________________

시간을 나타내는 접속사 when / while

- 종속접속사는 주절(문장에서 중심이 되는 절)과 종속절(주절의 내용을 보충하는 절)을 연결하는 말이다. 종속절은 맨 앞에 쓰이는 접속사의 뜻에 따라 시간, 이유, 조건 등을 나타낸다.

- 접속사 when은 '~할 때', while은 '~하는 동안(에)'라는 뜻이다.
  You were with James **when** I saw you.
  While I'm out, please take care of my children.

> **+ Plus** 종속절이 주절의 앞에 올 때는 종속절 끝에 콤마를 쓴다.
> **When** he was young, he lived in Jeju. / He lived in Jeju **when** he was young.

- 시간을 나타내는 접속사가 이끄는 절에서는 미래의 일이더라도 현재시제를 쓴다.
  I'll reply **when** I **get** back to my office. (~~will get~~)

A 다음 〈보기〉와 같이 접속사 when을 이용하여 두 문장을 한 문장으로 만드시오.

> 〈보기〉 The balloon popped. It surprised me.
> → When the balloon popped, it surprised me.

1 You called me. I was sleeping.

→ ______________________________________

2 Alice heard a strange sound. She felt scared.

→ ______________________________________

3 David crossed the street. He saw the accident.

→ ______________________________________

B 다음 우리말과 같은 뜻이 되도록 접속사 when 또는 while과 [ ] 안의 말을 이용하여 문장을 완성하시오.

1 나는 프랑스에 있을 때 그림 한 점을 샀다. (be)
I bought a painting ____________ ____________ ____________ in France.

2 그는 길을 걷는 동안 자주 노래를 부른다. (walk)
____________ ____________ ____________ ____________ on the street, he often sings.

3 그들은 졸업할 때 사업을 시작할 것이다. (graduate)
____________ ____________ ____________, they will start a business.

4 그녀는 책을 읽을 때 안경을 쓴다. (read)
She wears glasses ____________ ____________ ____________ a book.

5 우리는 저녁을 먹고 있는 동안에 우리의 여행에 대해 이야기했다. (eat)
____________ ____________ ____________ ____________ dinner, we talked about our trip.

시간을 나타내는 접속사 before / after

- 접속사 before는 '~하기 전에', after는 '~한 후에'라는 뜻이다.
  I usually ask the price **before** I buy something.
  You can't exchange these shoes **after** you wear them.

> **+ Plus** before와 after가 접속사로 쓰일 때는 뒤에 절이 오지만, 전치사로 쓰일 때는 뒤에 (동)명사(구)가 온다.
> I do homework **after** *dinner*. (나는 저녁 식사 후에 숙제를 한다.)

A 다음 우리말과 같은 뜻이 되도록 〈보기〉에서 알맞은 접속사를 골라 문장을 완성하시오.

〈보기〉	before	after	when	while

1 이 차를 마시고 나면 당신은 기분이 좋을 거예요.

You'll feel good ______________ you drink this tea.

2 나는 장을 보러 갈 때 너무 많은 물건을 산다 .

I buy too many things ______________ I go shopping.

3 해가 지기 전에 우리는 공원에 도착했다.

______________ the sun set, we arrived at the park.

4 그녀는 잠을 자는 동안에 돼지꿈을 꿨다.

______________ she was sleeping, she dreamed of a pig.

B 다음 우리말과 같은 뜻이 되도록 접속사와 [ ] 안의 말을 이용하여 문장을 완성하시오.

1 네가 읽고 난 후에 그 책을 빌릴 수 있을까? (read)

Can I borrow the book ______________ ______________ ______________ it?

2 나는 그가 외국으로 가기 전에 그를 보고 싶다. (go, abroad)

I want to see him ______________ ______________ ______________ ______________.

3 우리가 이야기하는 동안에 Grace는 많이 웃었다. (talk)

Grace laughed a lot ______________ ______________ ______________ ______________.

4 그들은 점심을 먹은 후에 체육관에 갔다. (eat, lunch)

______________ ______________ ______________ ______________, they went to the gym.

5 너는 너무 늦기 전에 치과에 가야 해. (it, too late)

You should go to the dentist ______________ ______________ ______________

______________ ______________.

이유, 조건을 나타내는 접속사 because / if

- 접속사 because는 '~하기 때문에'라는 뜻으로 이유나 원인을 나타낸다.
  I didn't go out **because** it was raining.

- 접속사 if는 '~한다면'이라는 뜻으로 조건을 나타낸다. 조건을 나타내는 접속사가 이끄는 절에서는 미래의 일이더라도 현재시제를 쓴다.
  If it **rains**, I won't go out. (~~will rain~~)

>  **내신만점 Tip** 시간이나 조건을 나타내는 접속사가 이끄는 절에서는 미래의 일이더라도 현재시제를 쓴다는 것을 기억하자.

A 다음 [ ] 안에서 알맞은 말을 고르시오.

1 (If / Because) you listen to the song, you'll like it.

2 They are happy (if / because) they won the game.

3 Rachel will be upset if I (tell / will tell) her the truth.

B 다음 [ ] 안에서 알맞은 말을 고르시오.

1 If he accepts the job, •   • ⓐ he was late.

2 He couldn't see well •   • ⓑ if he fails the test.

3 He will be disappointed •   • ⓒ he'll start work tomorrow.

4 Because the traffic was bad, •   • ⓓ because he didn't have his glasses.

C 다음 우리말과 같은 뜻이 되도록 접속사 because 또는 if와 [ ] 안의 말을 이용하여 문장을 완성하시오.

1 내가 운전면허증을 딴다면 차를 살 것이다. (get)
   _____________ _____________ _____________ a driver's license, I will buy a car.

2 그녀는 몸이 좋지 않아서 결석했다. (feel)
   She was absent _____________ _____________ _____________ _____________ well.

3 네가 배가 고프다면, 뭘 좀 먹자. (hungry)
   _____________ _____________ _____________ _____________, let's eat something.

4 그 영화가 재미없어서 우리는 집에 가고 싶었다. (film, interesting)
   _____________ _____________ _____________ _____________ _____________, we wanted

   to go home.

5 그들은 충분한 돈을 모으면 하와이로 여행을 갈 것이다. (save, enough)
   They will travel to Hawaii _____________ _____________ _____________ _____________

   _____________.

명사절을 이끄는 접속사 that

- 접속사 that은 '~라는 것'이라는 뜻으로 문장에서 주어, 보어, 목적어 역할을 하는 명사절을 이끈다. 주어로 쓰인 that절은 3인칭 단수 취급한다.

  That we are friends is important.　　　　(주어)

  The issue is **that** there's not enough time.　　(보어)

  I think **(that)** his English is quite good.　　(목적어)

  > **+ Plus**　that절이 목적어 역할을 하는 경우, 접속사 that은 생략할 수 있다.

- that절이 주어 역할을 하는 경우, 보통 주어 자리에 가주어 it을 쓰고 that절을 뒤로 보낸다.

  That it snowed was surprising.

  　　　주어

  → **It** was surprising **that** it snowed.

  　가주어　　　　　　　　진주어

A 다음 밑줄 친 부분을 어법에 맞게 고쳐 쓰시오.

1　I believe <u>it</u> dreams can come true.

2　The fact <u>is he</u> lied to us again.

3　<u>That</u> was lucky that we found a solution.

B 다음 문장을 가주어 It을 이용한 문장으로 바꾸어 쓰시오.

1　That she became a comedian is amazing.

　→ ______________________________________

2　That I broke the window is a secret.

　→ ______________________________________

3　That I forgot my wallet was unlucky.

　→ ______________________________________

C 다음 우리말과 같은 뜻이 되도록 [ ] 안의 말을 알맞게 배열하여 문장을 완성하시오.

1　나는 그 노래가 좋다고 생각하지 않는다. (good, the song, is, that)

　I don't think ____________________________.

2　그를 초대하지 않은 것은 나의 실수였다. (invite, didn't, that, I, him)

　____________________________ was my mistake.

3　문제는 내가 전화기를 가져오지 않은 것이다. (didn't, that, I, my phone, bring)

　The problem is ____________________________.

4　당신은 그녀가 농구 선수라는 것을 알고 있었나요? (that, a basketball player, she, is)

　Did you know ____________________________?

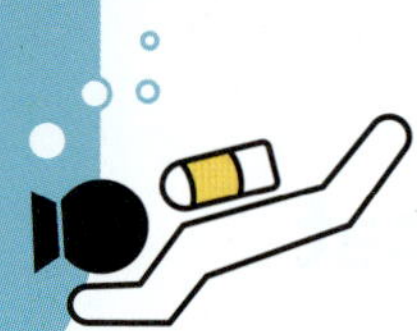

01-03 다음 빈칸에 알맞은 말을 고르시오.

01

> I like bananas __________ melons. They are sweet.

① and ② but ③ or
④ that ⑤ so

02

> __________ you don't have an umbrella, you can borrow mine.

① That ② Before ③ After
④ But ⑤ If

03

> I enjoyed the film, __________ I didn't like the main character.

① and ② but ③ or
④ because ⑤ so

04 내신기출

다음 빈칸에 공통으로 들어갈 말은?

> • It is important __________ you prepare for the class.
> • I thought __________ this umbrella was yours.

① before ② after ③ if
④ when ⑤ that

05

다음 빈칸에 because[Because]가 들어갈 수 없는 것은?

① I ate sandwiches __________ I was hungry.
② I was listening to music __________ she called me.
③ __________ it snowed a lot, we couldn't leave.
④ Be careful with the bottles __________ they break easily.
⑤ __________ there was nothing to eat, we ordered a pizza.

06-07 다음 우리말을 영어로 바르게 옮긴 것을 고르시오.

06

> 내가 일을 끝낸 후에 너에게 전화할게.

① I'll call you that I finish my work.
② I'll call you after I'll finish my work.
③ I'll call you before I finish my work.
④ I'll call you after I finish my work.
⑤ I finish my work before I'll call you.

07

> 나는 서점이나 미술관에 갈 것이다.

① I will go to both bookstore and art museum.
② I will go to either a bookstore and an art museum.
③ I will go to either a bookstore or an art museum.
④ I will go to a bookstore after I go to an art museum.
⑤ I will not go to a bookstore but to an art museum.

08-10 다음 빈칸에 알맞은 말이 바르게 짝지어진 것을 고르시오.

08

> • ___________ he was sick, he couldn't go on the field trip.
> • ___________ you are interested in art, let's take the drawing class.

① When – That
② After – That
③ Because – If
④ After – Before
⑤ Because – That

09

> • I heard ___________ you like rock music.
> • Is today Thursday ___________ Friday?

① when – but
② when – after
③ if – or
④ that – but
⑤ that – or

10

> A: What did you do ___________ you came back home?
> B: I ate dinner ___________ watched a movie.

① when – that
② before – that
③ after – and
④ when – but
⑤ after – but

11 내신기출

다음 중 빈칸에 들어갈 말이 나머지와 <u>다른</u> 것은?

① I thought ___________ you were busy.
② It is not true ___________ he failed the test.
③ It is my fault ___________ you missed the train.
④ Brush your teeth ___________ you eat those chocolates.
⑤ The problem is ___________ he plays computer games too much.

12

다음 중 대화가 자연스럽지 <u>않은</u> 것은?

① A: Which do you like better, milk or juice?
  B: I prefer juice.
② A: Do you like to dance?
  B: Yes, but I'm not good at it.
③ A: Why did you walk home?
  B: I couldn't take the bus because I lost my wallet.
④ A: What will you do on Sunday?
  B: I'll either meet Julie or stay home.
⑤ A: Are you going to invite both Jason and Ann?
  B: Yes. I'll invite only Jason.

13

다음 중 밑줄 친 부분이 어법상 옳은 것은?

① I like both skating <u>or</u> skiing.
② She sang a song, <u>but</u> nobody listened.
③ I took a shower <u>after</u> I went to bed.
④ He can buy either the shirt <u>and</u> the hat.
⑤ I will buy the book <u>and</u> borrow it from the library.

14-15 다음 두 문장을 한 문장으로 만들 때 빈칸에 알맞은 말을 고르시오.

14

> She studied hard. She passed the test.
> → She studied hard, __________ she passed the test.

① or ② so ③ but
④ if ⑤ that

15

> My parents and I set up the tent. Then we built a fire.
> → __________ my parents and I set up the tent, we built a fire.

① Before ② Because ③ If
④ After ⑤ While

16-17 다음 중 어법상 <u>틀린</u> 것을 고르시오.

16

① I know they will meet at the airport.
② He lost his phone while he was sleeping on the bus.
③ If it is not expensive, I'll get it.
④ I'll dance with either Brad and Andrew.
⑤ She didn't answer my calls because she was angry with me.

17

① Try on the shirt before you buy it.
② If the rumor is true, Brian will marry Helen.
③ She drinks hot milk when she wants to sleep well.
④ I don't like vegetables, but they are good for my health.
⑤ I went to a nice restaurant and having a great dinner.

18

(A), (B), (C)의 괄호 안에서 알맞은 것끼리 바르게 짝지어진 것은?

> (A) It is surprising [before / that] he took a taxi.
> (B) You should put on your coat [and / because] it is cold.
> (C) Did you go to a park or [watch / watched] a movie?

(A)	(B)	(C)
① before	and	watch
② before	because	watched
③ that	because	watch
④ that	because	watched
⑤ that	and	watch

19 고난도 내신기출

다음 중 어법상 <u>틀린</u> 문장의 개수는?

> (a) That Jake is a great cook is surprising.
> (b) I will be very sad if my puppy will die.
> (c) Turn off the lights when you will go out.
> (d) I didn't swim in the river if I was afraid of the deep water.

① 0개 ② 1개 ③ 2개 ④ 3개 ⑤ 4개

20 고난도 내신기출

다음 중 밑줄 친 부분을 생략할 수 <u>없는</u> 것은?

① I knew <u>that</u> he was lying.
② Tina said <u>that</u> she wanted to be an editor.
③ We hope <u>that</u> you will get better soon.
④ It is strange <u>that</u> Mike is absent from school.
⑤ Did you know <u>that</u> she is our teacher's daughter?

21

다음 우리말과 같은 뜻이 되도록 접속사와 주어진 말을 이용하여 문장을 완성하시오.

(1) 네가 아프면 이 약을 먹어. (feel sick)

→ Take this medicine ___________ ___________

___________ ___________.

(2) 나는 우리가 우승할 것이라고 믿는다. (win)

→ I believe ___________ ___________ ___________

___________.

22

주어진 말을 알맞게 배열하여 대화를 완성하시오.

(1) A: Why didn't you come yesterday?

B: I ___________________________ I had a cold.

(because, in, stayed, bed)

(2) A: Do you want something to eat?

B: No, thanks. I ___________________________.

(I, here, had, came, before, lunch)

23

각 상자에서 알맞은 말을 골라 문장을 완성하시오.
[단, 한 번씩만 사용할 것]

| and
but
or | I'll buy some at the bakery
I won the gold medal
you didn't reply |

(1) I sent a text message to you, ___________

___________.

(2) I'll bake some cookies, ___________

___________.

(3) I ran in the marathon, ___________

___________.

24

다음 일과표를 보고, 알맞은 접속사를 넣어 문장을 완성하시오.

Time	Things to do
10:00-11:30 a.m.	Go to my ballet lesson
2:00-3:00 p.m.	Walk my dog
3:00-6:00 p.m.	Practice violin on Mon. Read books on Tue. & Fri.
6:00-8:00 p.m.	Watch TV
8:00-9:00 p.m.	Write in my diary

(1) I go to my ballet lesson ___________ I walk my dog.

(2) I ___________ practice violin ___________ read books from three o'clock to six o'clock.

(3) I write in my diary ___________ I watch TV.

25 내신기출

다음 〈조건〉에 맞게 우리말을 영어로 옮겨 쓰시오.

> 〈조건〉 1. 적절한 접속사를 이용할 것
> 2. 어휘 be, late, angry, have, a book, a laptop을 이용할 것

(1) 그녀가 늦는다면, 나는 화가 날 것이다.

→ ___________________________

(2) 그는 책과 노트북 둘 다를 가지고 있다.

→ ___________________________

26 고난도 내신기출

다음 대화를 읽고, 어법상 <u>틀린</u> 부분을 <u>모두</u> 찾아 바르게 고쳐 쓰시오. [2군데]

> A: Did you stay at home?
> B: No. I went jogging or had a snack at a café.
> A: What are your plans for tonight?
> B: If my dad will come home early, I will eat out with him.

접속사

1 등위접속사

- 의미: 문법적으로 대등한 단어, 구, 절을 연결하는 말
- 종류
  - and: '그리고', '~와' (서로 비슷한 내용 연결)
  - ① ___________ : '그러나', '~(이)지만' (서로 반대·대조되는 내용 연결)
  - or: '또는', '~(이)거나' (선택)
  - so: '그래서' (원인과 결과 연결)

  〈② ___________ A and B〉: 'A와 B 둘 다'
  〈③ ___________ A or B〉: 'A이거나 B'

🛑 등위접속사로 연결되는 말은 문장에서의 역할과 형태가 대등해야 한다는 것 기억하기

2 종속접속사

- 의미: 주절(문장에서 중심이 되는 절)과 종속절(주절의 내용을 보충하는 절)을 연결하는 말
- 종류

④ ___________	'~할 때'
while	'~하는 동안(에)'
before	'⑤ ___________'
after	'~한 후에'
because	'~하기 때문에'
⑥ ___________	'~한다면'
that	'~라는 것' – 명사절을 이끄는 접속사(주어, 보어, 목적어 역할) – 주어 역할인 경우 보통 주어 자리에 가주어 ⑦ ___________을 쓰고 that절을 뒤로 보냄 – 목적어 역할인 경우 접속사 that 생략 가능

🛑 시간이나 조건을 나타내는 종속절에서는 미래의 일도 현재시제를 쓴다는 것 기억하기

접속사 that의 여러 가지 역할 구분하기

CHECK

밑줄 친 부분이 어법상 맞으면 O, 틀리면 X 표시하고 바르게 고치시오.

1 He stayed at home and <u>watching</u> TV last night.
2 You can have either French fries <u>and</u> onion rings.
3 Do you want to have a snack or <u>drinking</u> some coffee?
4 It is impossible <u>that</u> he got home so early.
5 <u>When</u> I got on the bus, I met Tim.
6 If it <u>will snow</u>, we will cancel the trip.
7 It is surprising <u>if</u> the main character dies in the movie.

CHAPTER 13

전치사

전치사는 명사[구]나 대명사 앞에 쓰여 시간, 장소 등을 나타내는 말입니다.

시간의 전치사 in / on / at

○ 전치사는 명사(구)나 대명사 앞에 쓰여 시간, 장소 등을 나타내는 말이다.
Summer vacation starts **in** July.
I'll be **at** home all day.

+ Plus 전치사 뒤에 대명사가 올 때는 반드시 목적격을 쓴다.
They left **before** *me*. / Nora sat **near** *him* in class.

○ 전치사 in, on, at은 '~에'라는 뜻으로 특정한 시간이나 때를 나타낸다.

in	연도, 월, 계절, 오전, 오후 등 비교적 긴 시간을 나타낼 때 **in** 2022, **in** June, **in** winter, **in** the morning
on	날짜, 요일, 특정한 날을 나타낼 때 **on** February 4, **on** Friday, **on** New Year's Day
at	구체적인 시각, 하루의 때, 특정한 시점을 나타낼 때 **at** 7:30, **at** midnight, **at** that time

---

A 다음 빈칸에 들어갈 수 <u>없는</u> 것에 ✔ 표시하시오.

1 I was born in ___________. ☐ 2015 ☐ August 7 ☐ spring
2 The parade starts at ___________. ☐ the morning ☐ noon ☐ nine o'clock
3 We have a math test on ___________. ☐ Monday ☐ April 15 ☐ November

B 다음 밑줄 친 부분을 어법에 맞게 고쳐 쓰시오.

1 They moved here <u>on</u> 2020.
2 My class ends <u>on</u> 3:40.
3 People eat turkey <u>in</u> Thanksgiving Day.
4 I will go to Europe <u>at</u> September.
5 Let's meet <u>in</u> noon and have lunch.
6 What are you going to do <u>at</u> Sunday?

C 다음 빈칸에 in, on, at 중 알맞은 전치사를 쓰시오.

1 It snowed a lot ___________ January.
2 I sometimes have a snack ___________ midnight.
3 My aunt got married ___________ May 5.
4 We didn't know each other ___________ that time.
5 He usually watches TV ___________ the evening.
6 How about playing soccer ___________ Saturday afternoon?

시간의 전치사
around / before / after / for / during / until / by

전치사 around, before, after, for, during, until, by는 시간의 전후 관계, 기간, 기한 등을 나타낸다.

around	~경에, ~ 무렵에	**around** noon, **around** lunchtime, **around** sunset
before	~ 전에	**before** breakfast, **before** 8:30, **before** dark
after	~ 후에	**after** the meeting, **after** nine o'clock, **after** dinner
for	~ 동안	**for** a week, **for** three hours, **for** two years
during	~ 동안	**during** winter vacation, **during** the weekend, **during** class
until	~까지 (지속)	**until** next Monday, **until** tomorrow, **until** 5:00 p.m.
by	~까지는 (완료)	**by** this weekend, **by** twelve o'clock, **by** tomorrow morning

내신만점 Tip 시간의 전치사 for 뒤에는 숫자를 포함하는 구체적인 기간, during 뒤에는 특정한 때를 나타내는 명사(구)가 온다는 것을 기억하자.

A 다음 우리말과 같은 뜻이 되도록 빈칸에 알맞은 전치사를 쓰시오.

1 나는 자정 무렵에 잠자리에 들었다.

I went to bed ____________ midnight.

2 그들은 영화를 보는 동안 큰 소리로 떠들었다.

They talked loudly ____________ the movie.

3 우리 방과 후에 도서관에 가도 될까?

Can we go to the library ____________ school?

4 그는 몇 주 동안 동남아시아를 여행했다.

He traveled in Southeast Asia ____________ a few weeks.

5 Stephan은 내일 아침까지 여기에 머물 것이다.

Stephan will stay here ____________ tomorrow morning.

B 다음 우리말과 같은 뜻이 되도록 전치사와 [ ] 안의 말을 이용하여 문장을 완성하시오.

1 너는 쇼핑 전에 목록을 작성해야 한다. (shopping)

You should make a list ____________ ____________.

2 Brian은 2시간 동안 하이킹을 갔다. (hour)

Brian went hiking ____________ ____________ ____________.

3 나는 보고서를 다음 수요일까지 끝내야 한다. (next)

I have to finish my report ____________ ____________ ____________.

4 여러분은 월요일에 3시경에 저를 만나러 와도 좋아요. (three)

You can come and see me ____________ ____________ ____________ ____________.

장소·위치의 전치사 in / on / at

○ 전치사 in, on, at은 '~에'라는 뜻으로 장소나 위치를 나타낸다.

in	~(안)에	도시, 국가 등 비교적 넓은 장소나 건물·사물의 내부를 나타낼 때 **in** Seoul, **in** Korea, **in** a building, **in** a box
on	~(위)에	접촉해 있는 상태를 나타낼 때 **on** the table, **on** the ground, **on** the skin
at	~에	비교적 좁은 장소나 하나의 지점을 나타낼 때 **at** home, **at** the airport, **at** my uncle's

---

A 다음 빈칸에 들어갈 수 **없는** 것에 ✔ 표시하시오.

1 We saw him at ____________. ☐ Canada ☐ school ☐ the station

2 There is a book on ____________. ☐ the floor ☐ the shelf ☐ my room

3 I found my phone in ____________. ☐ his car ☐ the door ☐ the backpack

B 다음 빈칸에 in, on, at 중 알맞은 전치사를 쓰시오.

1 Lucas is lying ____________ the carpet.

2 They played games ____________ home.

3 Look at those stars ____________ the sky.

4 Joan will stay ____________ her grandmother's.

5 One of my best friends studies ____________ London.

6 The German couple lives ____________ the 3rd floor.

C 다음 우리말과 같은 뜻이 되도록 전치사와 [ ] 안의 말을 이용하여 문장을 완성하시오.

1 네 주머니 안에 저것들을 넣어. (pocket)

Put those things ____________ ____________ ____________.

2 나는 이 벽에 시계를 걸 것이다. (wall)

I will hang a clock ____________ ____________ ____________.

3 그는 버스 정류장에서 딸을 기다렸다. (bus stop)

He waited for his daughter ____________ ____________ ____________.

4 그 아이들은 땅 위에 앉아 있었다. (ground)

The children were sitting ____________ ____________ ____________.

5 인터넷은 세계에서 가장 큰 도서관이다. (world)

The Internet is the biggest library ____________ ____________ ____________.

장소·위치의 전치사 near / over / under / behind / to

○ 전치사 near, over, under, behind, to는 장소나 위치 관계를 나타낸다.

near	~ 근처에	**near** the station, **near** here, **near** my house
over	~ 위에 (표면에 접촉해 있지 않은 상태)	**over** my head, **over** the roof, **over** the horizon
under	~ 아래에	**under** the desk, **under** the sea, **under** a bridge
behind	~ 뒤에	**behind** the car, **behind** the building, **behind** the tree
to	~로 (목적지)	**to** the department store, **to** the west, **to** the left

---

A 다음 우리말과 같은 뜻이 되도록 〈보기〉에서 알맞은 말을 골라 문장을 완성하시오.

> 〈보기〉   behind   near   over   to   under

1 Michael은 침대 밑에 숨었다.

Michael hid ____________ the bed.

2 나는 내 가방을 그 의자 뒤에 두었다.

I put my bag ____________ the chair.

3 그녀는 그의 머리 위로 공을 던졌다.

She threw the ball ____________ his head.

4 이 건물 근처에 제과점이 있나요?

Is there a bakery ____________ this building?

5 그는 우리에게 호수 공원으로 가는 길을 알려 주었다.

He showed us the way ____________ Lake Park.

B 다음 우리말과 같은 뜻이 되도록 전치사와 [ ] 안의 말을 이용하여 문장을 완성하시오.

1 나는 저 버스 뒤에 내 차를 주차했다. (bus)

I parked my car ____________ ____________ ____________.

2 우리 가게 근처에 놀이터가 있다. (store)

There is a playground ____________ ____________ ____________.

3 헬리콥터들이 그 도시 위를 날고 있었다. (city)

Helicopters were flying ____________ ____________.

4 그는 그 나무 아래 앉아 일기를 썼다. (tree)

He sat ____________ ____________ ____________ and wrote his journal.

장소·위치의 전치사
in front of / next to / across from / between A and B

○ 둘 이상의 단어가 모여 하나의 전치사 역할을 하기도 한다.

○ in front of, next to, across from, between A and B는 장소나 위치 관계를 나타낸다.

in front of	~ 앞에	We met **in front of** the theater.
next to	~ 옆에 (= beside)	I was standing **next to** my favorite singer.
across from	~ 맞은편에 (= opposite)	The bakery **across from** the Art Center opens at ten.
between A and B	A와 B 사이에	The supermarket is **between** the bank **and** my house.

A 다음 두 문장이 같은 뜻이 되도록 빈칸에 알맞은 말을 쓰시오.

1 I'm sitting behind the Sarah.

→ Sarah is sitting ___________ ___________ ___________ me.

2 Can you see the girl sitting beside George?

→ Can you see the girl sitting ___________ ___________ George?

3 The lamp is in the middle of the sofa and the bookshelf.

→ The lamp is ___________ the sofa ___________ the bookshelf.

4 I'm at the new Italian restaurant opposite my school.

→ I'm at the new Italian restaurant ___________ ___________ my school.

B 다음 우리말과 같은 뜻이 되도록 전치사와 [ ] 안의 말을 이용하여 문장을 완성하시오.

1 음악실은 그들의 교실 옆에 있다. (classroom)

The music room is ___________ ___________ ___________.

2 Ella는 그 쇼핑몰 앞에서 너를 기다리고 있어. (mall)

Ella is waiting for you ___________ ___________

___________.

3 그 바닷가 맞은편에 있는 호텔은 전망이 아름답다. (beach)

The hotel ___________ ___________ ___________ ___________ has a beautiful

view.

C 다음 우리말과 같은 뜻이 되도록 [ ] 안의 말을 알맞게 배열하여 문장을 완성하시오.

1 그는 내 문 앞에 상자 하나를 두고 갔다. (a box, my door, front, he, in, left, of)

____

2 박물관 맞은편에 도서관이 있다. (a library, the museum, is, across, there, from)

____

3 우리는 그네와 미끄럼틀 사이에 나무를 심을 것이다. (the slide, plant, between, we'll, the swings, and, a tree)

____

기타 전치사 for / with / by / about / from A to B

◉ 하나의 전치사가 여러 의미로 쓰일 수 있으며, 목적, 이유, 수단, 주제 등 다양한 의미를 나타낸다.

for	~을 위해 (목적) / ~ 때문에 (이유)	I'm packing **for** the trip.
with	~와 함께 (동반) / ~으로 (도구)	He hit the ball **with** a bat.
by	~으로 (방법 / 교통·통신 수단)	They talked **by** video call.
about	~에 대하여 (주제)	We are learning **about** different countries.
from A to B	A부터 B까지 (시간·위치·범위)	My father works **from** 10:00 a.m. **to** 7:00 p.m.

+ Plus 목적·이유를 나타내는 전치사 for와 방법·수단을 나타내는 전치사 by 뒤에는 (대)명사 외에도 동명사(v-ing)가 자주 쓰이며, '~해서', '~함으로써'라는 의미를 나타낸다.
I'm sorry **for** *being* late. / You can save money **by** *cooking* at home.

A 다음 우리말과 같은 뜻이 되도록 빈칸에 알맞은 전치사를 쓰시오.

1 나는 그 파일을 이메일로 보낼 것이다.

I'll send the file ______________ email.

2 그는 역사에 관한 책을 썼다.

He wrote a book ______________ history.

3 그녀는 가위로 종이를 잘랐다.

She cut the paper ______________ scissors.

4 그들은 학교 축구 시합을 위해 훈련하고 있다.

They are training ______________ the school soccer match.

5 여기서부터 서울 타워까지 운전해서 얼마나 걸리나요?

How long does it take to drive ______________ here ______________ Seoul Tower?

B 다음 우리말과 같은 뜻이 되도록 전치사와 [ ] 안의 말을 이용하여 문장을 완성하시오.

1 너의 하루에 대해 나에게 말해 줄래? (day)

Can you tell me ______________ ______________ ______________?

2 나는 내 실수 때문에 그들에게 사과했다. (mistake)

I apologized to them ______________ ______________ ______________.

3 봄은 3월부터 5월까지 계속된다. (March, May)

Spring lasts ______________ ______________ ______________ ______________.

4 우리는 우리 조부모님과 함께 저녁을 먹었다. (grandparents)

We had dinner ______________ ______________ ______________.

5 Olivia는 규칙적으로 운동함으로써 더 튼튼해졌다. (exercise regularly)

Olivia became stronger ______________ ______________ ______________.

01-03 다음 빈칸에 알맞은 말을 고르시오.

01

> She went for a walk __________ the morning.

① at　　　② until　　　③ in
④ to　　　⑤ behind

02

> Brian gave his little brother a gift __________ Christmas.

① in　　　② until　　　③ at
④ to　　　⑤ on

03

> I don't stay up late __________ night.

① at　　　② on　　　③ beside
④ to　　　⑤ under

04 　내신기출

다음 중 밑줄 친 부분의 쓰임이 나머지와 <u>다른</u> 것은?
① Turn <u>to</u> the left at that corner.
② My classmate gave a pencil <u>to</u> me.
③ We went <u>to</u> the ice cream shop after lunch.
④ He decided <u>to</u> change his travel plans.
⑤ Emily works from nine <u>to</u> six on weekdays.

05-06 다음 빈칸에 알맞은 말이 바르게 짝지어진 것을 고르시오.

05

> • Elizabeth contacted me __________ text message.
> • The store is open __________ Tuesday to Saturday.

① by – in　　　② by – for
③ by – from　　　④ with – on
⑤ with – from

06

> • You should come home __________ ten o'clock.
> • I can see the kite flying __________ the sky.

① at – on　　　② at – for
③ for – in　　　④ before – in
⑤ under – at

07-08 다음 중 빈칸에 들어갈 말이 나머지와 <u>다른</u> 것을 고르시오.

07

① The car key is __________ the table.
② Look at the picture __________ the wall.
③ I danced with Brian __________ the party.
④ She put her bag __________ the floor.
⑤ There are three buttons __________ my coat.

08

① Let's go __________ the park now.
② Will you come __________ my office?
③ We moved __________ a new apartment.
④ There's an art gallery __________ my house.
⑤ You can walk __________ the station in ten minutes.

09

> • I jogged __________ 45 minutes before breakfast.
> • She is working hard __________ her future.

① at   ② for   ③ in
④ to   ⑤ with

10

> • More and more people are coming __________ Korea.
> • Your cell phone is next __________ your wallet.

① to   ② on   ③ in
④ from   ⑤ with

11

다음 중 밑줄 친 부분과 의미가 같지 <u>않은</u> 것은?

① I sat <u>across from</u> Ian at the table.
    → opposite Ian

② The girl is sitting <u>next to the cute boy</u>.
    → beside the cute boy

③ Students will <u>have math class after lunch</u>.
    → have lunch before math class

④ <u>The parking lot is behind the building</u>.
    → The building is in front of the parking lot

⑤ We must finish the project <u>by Friday morning</u>.
    → after Friday morning

12

> 책상 옆에 있는 기타는 네 것이니?

① Is the guitar in the desk yours?
② Is the guitar on the desk yours?
③ Is the guitar under the desk yours?
④ Is the guitar next to the desk yours?
⑤ Is the guitar behind the desk yours?

13

> 당신은 자정까지 도서관에서 공부할 수 있다.

① You can study at the library until midnight.
② You can study at the library for midnight.
③ You can study at the library after midnight.
④ You can study at the library before midnight.
⑤ You can study at the library around midnight.

14

다음 중 어느 빈칸에도 들어갈 수 <u>없는</u> 것은?

> • The person __________ you is my mother.
> • We parked __________ the bank.
> • Mike was __________ her.
> • The snack shop was __________ my school.

① with   ② about
③ behind   ④ next to
⑤ across from

 다음 중 밑줄 친 부분이 어법상 **틀린** 것을 고르시오.

15

① It often rains <u>in</u> fall.
② I have no classes <u>at</u> Sunday.
③ My father came home <u>at</u> midnight.
④ We should get there <u>by</u> one o'clock.
⑤ It's <u>between</u> the bank <u>and</u> the laundry shop.

16

① The kids sat <u>under</u> the tree.
② Her office is <u>beside</u> to City Hall.
③ The artist painted <u>with</u> a brush.
④ He lived there <u>from</u> 2019 to 2024.
⑤ The boy is standing <u>in front of</u> his desk.

17

① Let's go shopping <u>on</u> Friday.
② There was a fire <u>in</u> the building.
③ They plan to meet <u>at</u> 7:30 p.m.
④ She worked out <u>during</u> lunchtime.
⑤ Maria only slept <u>in</u> an hour last night.

18

다음 중 우리말을 영어로 바르게 옮긴 것은?

① 테이블 앞에 상자가 있다.
　　There is a box behind the table.
② 우리는 정오 무렵에 점심을 먹는다.
　　We eat lunch after noon.
③ 그는 극장 맞은편에 서 있다.
　　He is standing next to the theater.
④ 그 나라는 태국과 베트남 사이에 있다.
　　The country is from Thailand to Vietnam.
⑤ 나는 다음 주까지 두바이에 머무를 예정이다.
　　I'm going to stay in Dubai until next week.

19 고난도

[A], [B], [C]의 괄호 안에서 알맞은 것끼리 바르게 짝 지어진 것은?

(A) I held an umbrella [over / with] her head.
(B) He traveled from Seattle [to / in] Boston.
(C) My friend was waiting for me [on / at] the bus stop.

	(A)	(B)	(C)
①	over	in	on
②	over	to	on
③	over	to	at
④	with	to	at
⑤	with	in	at

20 고난도 내신기출

다음 중 어법상 옳은 것을 <u>모두</u> 고르면? [3개]

① There is a boat under the bridge.
② She studied fashion on New York.
③ He arrived here on October 22.
④ We do the dishes after dinner.
⑤ I was at a summer camp during two weeks.

21

다음 우리말과 같은 뜻이 되도록 〈보기〉에서 알맞은 전치사를 골라 문장을 완성하시오.

〈보기〉	with	during	around

(1) 오후 3시 무렵 눈이 멈췄다.
It stopped snowing ___________ 3:00 p.m.

(2) 그녀는 반 친구들과 함께 영화를 보러 갔다.
She went to the movies ___________ her classmates.

(3) 공연 중에는 조용히 해 주십시오.
Please keep quiet ___________ the performance.

22

다음 우리말과 같은 뜻이 되도록 전치사와 주어진 말을 이용하여 문장을 완성하시오.

너는 다음 월요일까지 그 책을 다 읽을 수 있니? (next)

→ Can you finish reading the book ___________ ___________ ___________?

23

다음 우리말과 같은 뜻이 되도록 주어진 말을 알맞게 배열하여 문장을 완성하시오.

(1) 우리는 건강한 음식에 관한 다큐멘터리를 봤다.
(healthy food, watched, about, we, a documentary)
→ ___________

(2) 공원 맞은편에 장난감 가게가 있다.
(from, a toy shop, there, the park, across, is)
→ ___________

24 　내신기출

다음 그림을 보고, 전치사를 이용하여 위치를 나타내는 문장을 완성하시오.

(1) The bakery is ___________ the flower shop ___________ the bookstore.
(2) There is a bicycle ___________ ___________ ___________ the bakery.

25

다음 표를 보고, 질문에 답하시오.

Dan's Plan	
12:00 p.m.	go to the library
1:00 p.m. – 3:00 p.m.	play tennis
4:00 p.m. – 6:00 p.m.	meet some friends

(1) Q: When will Dan go to the library?
A: He'll go there ___________ noon.
(2) Q: How long will Dan play tennis?
A: He'll play tennis ___________ ___________ ___________.
(3) Q: When will Dan be with his friends?
A: He'll be with them ___________ four o'clock ___________ six o'clock.

26 　고난도

다음 현장 학습 안내문을 읽고, 틀린 부분을 모두 찾아 바르게 고쳐 쓰시오. (3군데)

School Field Trip! We will go to the National Museum at May 21. We will stay there during three hours. We will go there together with bus. So let's meet in front of the school at nine o'clock.

CHAPTER 13
전치사

1 시간의 전치사

in (비교적 긴 시간) '~에'	on (특정한 날) '~에'	① __________ (특정한 시점) '~에'
② __________ '~경에', '~ 무렵에'	before '~ 전에'	after '~ 후에'
for, during '~ 동안'	③ __________ (지속) '~까지'	④ __________ (완료) '~까지는'

❗ 시간을 나타내는 전치사 in, on, at의 쓰임을 구분하여 알아두기

    <for+숫자 포함 구체적인 기간>, <during+특정한 기간을 나타내는 명사>라는 것 잊지 말기

2 장소·위치의 전치사

in (비교적 넓은 곳) '~에'	⑤ __________ (접촉해 있는 상태) '~에'	at (비교적 좁은 곳) '~에'
near '~ 근처에'	⑥ __________ (표면에 접촉해 있지 않은 상태) '~ 위에'	under '~ 아래에'
behind '~ 뒤에'	to (목적지) '~로'	in front of '~ 앞에'
next to '~ 옆에'	⑦ __________ '~ 맞은편에'	⑧ __________ A and B 'A와 B 사이에'

❗ 장소·위치를 나타내는 전치사 in, on, at의 쓰임을 구분하여 알아두기

3 기타 전치사

⑨ __________ '~을 위해', '~ 때문에'	with '~와 함께', '~으로'	by '~으로'
about '~에 대하여'	⑩ __________ A to B 'A부터 B까지'	

CHECK

밑줄 친 부분이 어법상 맞으면 O, 틀리면 X 표시하고 바르게 고치시오.

1 You didn't answer my calls <u>during</u> two days. (너는 이틀 동안 내 전화를 받지 않았다.)

2 A new semester usually begins <u>on</u> March in Korea. (한국에서 새 학기는 보통 3월에 시작한다.)

3 I should hand in my essay <u>until</u> next week. (나는 다음 주까지 에세이를 제출해야 한다.)

4 He stayed <u>at</u> the hotel all day. (그는 온종일 그 호텔에 머물렀다.)

5 Birds flew <u>over</u> the roof. (새들이 지붕 위로 날아갔다.)

6 A cat was sitting <u>across from</u> my house. (고양이 한 마리가 우리 집 앞에 앉아 있었다.)

7 She received the information <u>with</u> email. (그녀는 이메일로 정보를 받았다.)

8 They thanked me <u>for</u> my support. (그들은 내 지원 때문에 나에게 감사했다.)

MEMO

MEMO

NE능률

문마중

LEVEL 1

정답 및 해설

문제로 **마**스터하는 중학 영문법

본책 정답 및 해설

CHAPTER 01 기초 문법

POINT 01 영어의 8품사　　p.9

A 1 ⓒ　2 ⓐ　3 ⓓ　4 ⓑ　5 ⓖ　6 ⓗ　7 ⓔ
　8 ⓕ
B 1 puppy　2 cold　3 carefully　4 at　5 but
　6 They　7 Oh　8 cleans

POINT 02 문장 성분　　p.10

A 1 ⓔ　2 ⓑ　3 ⓓ　4 ⓒ　5 ⓐ
B 1 Steve는 뜨거운 커피를 마신다.
　2 나는 콘서트에서 음악을 들었고 춤을 추었다.
　3 새들이 매우 아름답게 노래한다.
　4 그 시험은 어려워 보인다.

POINT 03 구와 절　　p.11

A 1 구　2 절　3 구　4 절　5 구
B 1 절　2 절　3 구　4 절　5 구　6 절　7 절
　8 구

문법 정리 노트　　p.12

① 대명사　　② 전치사　　③ 동사　　④ 주어
⑤ 주어+동사

CHECK

1 X, 명사는 사람, 동물, 사물 등의 이름을 나타내는 말이
다.　2 O　3 O
4 X, 문장은 〈주어+동사〉를 포함해야 한다.
5 X, 목적어는 동사의 대상을 나타낸다.
6 X, 보어이다.　7 O　8 O

CHAPTER 02 인칭대명사와 be동사

POINT 01 인칭대명사와 be동사의 현재형　　p.14

A 1 are　2 is　3 are　4 am　5 are
B 1 She's　2 It's　3 They're　4 I'm　5 You're
C 1 It's　2 You are　3 I am

POINT 02 be동사의 과거형　　p.15

A 1 was　2 was　3 were　4 were　5 was
B 1 are　2 were　3 was　4 is　5 were
C 1 was　2 is　3 were　4 We were
　5 He was

POINT 03 be동사의 부정문　　p.16

A 1 is not　2 aren't　3 wasn't　4 are not
B 1 I'm not　2 weren't　3 We're not[We aren't]
　4 She's not[She isn't]
C 1 I am not　2 Mark was not
　3 Some people aren't　4 My mother is not

POINT 04 be동사의 의문문　　p.17

A 1 Are we　2 Is it　3 Was she　4 Were you
　5 Are they
B 1 Are you　2 it is　3 Was he　4 we were

POINT 05 There is/are ~　　p.18

A 1 are　2 was　3 There were not
　4 Is, there is
B 1 There isn't　2 There was
　3 Are there hamburgers
C 1 There aren't any coins in her purse.
　2 Is there a restaurant near here?
　3 There were two birds on the roof.

POINT 06 인칭대명사의 격
　- 주격/소유격/목적격/소유대명사　　p.19

A 1 his　2 It　3 my　4 her　5 Our　6 him
　7 theirs
B 1 Their, us　2 My, hers　3 He, Laura's

4 mine, them **5** you, yours

01 ②	02 ④	03 ⑤	04 ③	05 ③	06 ④
07 ③	08 ①	09 ⑤	10 ④	11 ②	12 ④
13 ②	14 ②	15 ④	16 ②	17 ③	18 ②
19 ④	20 ②				

서술형 집중공략　　　　　　　　　　p.23

21 (1) are, them (2) hers, Teddy's

22 (1) He was not (2) It is, Its

23 (1) Were Julie and David in the same class?
(2) There is a jacket on the bench. It is mine.

24 yours, isn't, Mine

25 (1) is, His (2) are, They are (3) Are, I'm not, I'm

26 (1) The blanket is not[isn't] his.
(2) Was your son a soccer player?

01 주어가 3인칭 복수이고, now로 보아 현재의 일이므로 are를 써야 한다.

02 주어가 3인칭 단수이고, last year로 보아 과거의 일이므로 Was를 써야 한다.

03 ⑤의 are는 '(~에) 있다'의 의미이고, ①,②,③,④의 be동사는 모두 '~이다'의 의미이다.

04 대답하는 사람의 입장에서 you and your sister를 받는 주격 대명사는 we이며, A에 대한 대답으로 긍정의 경우 Yes, we are., 부정의 경우 No, we aren't.가 와야 한다.

05 〈There is/are+명사〉의 현재형 의문문이고 a bus stop은 단수명사이므로, A에 대한 대답으로 긍정의 경우 Yes, there is., 부정의 경우 No, there isn't.가 와야 한다.

06 첫 번째 빈칸에는 that boy를 받는 3인칭 단수 주격 대명사 he가 와야 하고, 두 번째 빈칸에는 명사 son을 수식하는 소유격 My가 와야 한다.

07 첫 번째 빈칸에는 주어 it에 대한 be동사의 부정형인 isn't가 와야 하고, 두 번째 빈칸에는 '그의 것'이라는 의미의 소유대명사 his가 와야 한다.

08 〈There is/are+명사〉에서 be동사 뒤의 명사가 cookies인 복수명사이므로 첫 번째 빈칸에는 are가 와야 하고, 두 번째 빈칸에는 '너/너희들'이라는 의미의 목적격 you가 와야 한다.

09 ⑤ 현재 Andrew 선생님이 교무실에 계시냐는 질문에 과거에 계셨다는 대답은 자연스럽지 않다.

10 The bags는 3인칭 복수이므로 be동사의 부정형으로 were not이 와야 하고, '우리의 것'이라는 의미를 나타내는 소유대명사 ours가 와야 한다.

11 '~가 있다'라는 의미를 나타내는 〈There is/are+명사〉에서 be동사 뒤의 명사가 a pine tree인 단수명사이므로 동사는 is가 와야 하고, garden 앞에는 '그녀의'라는 의미를 나타내는 소유격 her가 와야 한다.

12 ④ be동사 과거형의 부정문에서 주어 You 뒤에는 weren't가 와야 한다.

13 ② '그들의 것'이라는 의미의 소유대명사 theirs가 와야 한다.

14 ②의 her는 소유격이고, ①,③,④,⑤는 목적격이다.

15 ④의 his는 소유대명사이고, ①,②,③,⑤는 소유격이다.

16 B의 응답에서 주어가 각각 I와 we이므로 빈칸에는 Are you가 와야 한다.

17 ①,②,④에는 주어가 3인칭 단수이므로 Is(is)가 와야 하고, ⑤에는 뒤의 명사가 a dog인 단수명사이므로 is가 와야 한다. ③에는 주어가 복수명사이므로 Are가 와야 한다.

18 ② be동사의 부정문은 be동사 뒤에 not을 쓴다.

19 (A) 주어가 you이므로 Were가 알맞다.
(B) 동사 helps의 목적어로 목적격 them이 알맞다.
(C) 주어가 3인칭 복수인 Jason and his brother이므로 be동사는 are가 와야 한다.

20 (c) Dan and I는 1인칭 복수이므로 be동사는 are가 와야 한다.
(d) country를 수식하는 소유격 your가 와야 한다.

21 (1) '~가 있다'라는 의미를 나타내는 〈There is/are+명사〉에서 be동사 뒤의 명사가 many animals인 복수명사이므로 첫 번째 빈칸에는 are을 쓴다. 두 번째 빈칸에는 동사 like의 목적어로 앞 문장의 many animals를 받는 3인칭 복수 목적격인 them이 와야 한다.
(2) 문맥상 she와 Teddy는 각각 '그녀의 것', 'Teddy의 것'이라는 의미의 소유대명사 hers와 Teddy's가 되어야 한다.

22 (1) 주어는 3인칭 단수 He이고 과거의 일에 대해 말하고 있으므로 be동사의 과거형 was를 쓴다. be동사의 부정문은 동사 뒤에 not을 쓴다.
(2) 앞의 a cat을 대신하는 주격 대명사 It과 '(~에) 있다'라는 의미인 be동사의 3인칭 단수형 is를 쓴다. '그것의'라는 의미로 fur를 수식하는 소유격 Its를 쓴다.

23 (1) 주어가 3인칭 복수인 Julie and David이므로 be동사는 Were가 되어야 한다.
(2) 〈There is/are+명사〉에서 be동사 뒤의 명사가 a jacket인 단수명사이므로 동사는 is가 되어야 한다. '나의 것'이라는 의미의 소유대명사 mine이 되어야 한다.

24 Amy의 대답으로 보아, Sam의 질문에는 빨간색 모자가 '너의 것'인지 물어보는 말이 와야 알맞다. Amy가 부정하

는 대답에는 it 뒤에 isn't가 와야 하고, '나의 것'이라는 의미의 소유대명사 Mine이 와야 한다.

25 (1) 주어가 3인칭 단수이므로 첫 번째 빈칸에는 is를 쓴다. 두 번째 빈칸에는 nickname을 수식하는 소유격 His가 와야 한다.

(2) 주어가 3인칭 복수이므로 첫 번째 빈칸에는 are를 쓴다. Junho and Alice를 받는 주격 대명사는 They이고 이때 be동사는 are를 쓴다.

(3) 주어가 2인칭 단수이므로 첫 번째 빈칸에는 Are를 쓴다. Alice는 영국 출신이므로, 부정의 대답으로 No, I'm not.이 와야 한다. '나는 ~이다'라는 의미로는 I am의 줄임말 I'm을 쓴다.

26 (1) 주어인 The blanket은 3인칭 단수이므로 동사는 is를, '그의 것'이라는 의미의 소유대명사는 his를 쓴다. be동사의 부정문은 be동사 뒤에 not을 쓴다.

(2) 주어인 '당신의 아들'은 3인칭 단수이고, 과거의 일에 대해 물어보고 있으므로 동사는 Was를 쓴다. '당신의'는 소유격 your로 표현한다. be동사의 의문문은 〈be동사+주어 ~?〉의 어순이 되어야 알맞다.

문법 정리 노트   p.24

① mine   ② yours   ③ his   ④ her
⑤ us   ⑥ theirs   ⑦ was   ⑧ were
⑨ be동사, not   ⑩ Is/Are there

CHECK

1 O   2 X, Is
3 X, We are not[We're not/We aren't]
4 O   5 X, they are   6 O

1 앞 문장의 milk을 대신하는 주격 대명사 It과 be동사의 3인칭 단수형 is가 와야 하는데, 줄여서 It's로 쓸 수 있다.

2 주어가 he이고, B의 응답으로 보아 현재의 일이므로 Is를 써야 한다.

3 be동사의 부정문은 be동사 뒤에 not을 쓴다.

4 동사 like의 목적어로 앞 문장의 an old piano를 받는 3인칭 단수 목적격 it이 알맞다.

5 A의 질문에서 주어가 3인칭 복수인 Cindy and Ellie이므로 B의 응답에서는 주어로 they가 와야 하고 be동사 are를 쓴다.

6 〈There is/are+명사〉에서 be동사 뒤의 명사가 a tall building인 단수명사이므로 동사는 is가 알맞다.

POINT 01   일반동사의 현재형 - 1인칭/2인칭 주어   p.26

A   1 I have plans this evening.
2 You need my advice.
3 We feel happy on Christmas.
4 You and Julia get the prize.
5 My Family and I live in London.

B   1 make   2 speak   3 work   4 practice
5 watch

POINT 02   일반동사의 현재형 - 3인칭 주어   p.27

A   1 X, eats   2 O   3 X, call   4 X, knows   5 O
6 O   7 X, get

B   1 looks   2 begins   3 wants   4 closes
5 ride   6 sends   7 climb

POINT 03   일반동사의 3인칭 단수 현재형   p.28

A   1 flies   2 teaches   3 has   4 enjoys
5 cries   6 uses   7 plays   8 does
9 washes   10 reads

B   1 goes   2 brushes   3 fixes   4 envies
5 makes

POINT 04   일반동사의 과거형 - 규칙 변화   p.29

A   1 snowed   2 studied   3 opened
4 stopped   5 asked   6 moved   7 visited

B   1 dropped   2 trusted   3 arrived   4 stayed
5 planned   6 tried   7 showed

POINT 05   일반동사의 과거형 - 불규칙 변화 I   p.30

A   1 met   2 came   3 ate   4 went   5 said
6 found   7 gave   8 saw   9 felt

B   1 caught   2 heard   3 thought   4 left
5 built

POINT 06   일반동사의 과거형 - 불규칙 변화 II   p.31

A   1 O   2 X, read   3 X, hurt   4 O   5 X, shut

6 ○ **7** ○ **8** X, set

B 1 hit **2** cost **3** cut **4** put **5** read

POINT 07 일반동사의 현재형 부정문   p.32

A 1 don't eat **2** doesn't **3** don't **4** get
5 don't

B 1 doesn't like **2** don't practice
3 doesn't look **4** don't have

C 1 It doesn't work **2** We don't go
3 She doesn't spend

POINT 08 일반동사의 과거형 부정문   p.33

A 1 didn't pass **2** move **3** didn't
4 understand

B 1 didn't tell **2** didn't want **3** didn't finish

C 1 I didn't turn **2** Ross didn't write
3 They didn't have **4** She felt, she didn't cry

POINT 09 일반동사의 현재형 의문문   p.34

A 1 I look **2** eat **3** Do **4** doesn't

B 1 Do you need **2** Does Kate have
3 Do we take

C 1 Does he love **2** Do they know
3 she play, doesn't **4** Do you walk, I don't
5 Does, go, it does

POINT 10 일반동사의 과거형 의문문   p.35

A 1 Do **2** Did **3** Does **4** Did

B 1 Did he catch **2** Did they help
3 Did you lose

C 1 Did, leave, didn't **2** Did, like, they did
3 Did you have, did

내신 대비 실전 TEST   pp.36-38

01 ④ **02** ③ **03** ④ **04** ② **05** ① **06** ②
07 ④ **08** ④ **09** ⑤ **10** ③ **11** ④
12 ②, ⑤ **13** ④ **14** ③ **15** ⑤ **16** ③
17 ⑤ **18** ⑤ **19** ③ **20** ②

서술형 집중공략   p.39

21 (1) didn't[did not] watch the movie
(2) takes a walk

22 (1) Do Sharon and Brad eat meat? /
Sharon and Brad don't[do not] eat meat.
(2) Did Joe hit 20 home runs last season? /
Joe didn't[did not] hit 20 home runs last
season.

23 (1) studied at the library
(2) didn't[did not] study at the library

24 Does he cook

25 (1) didn't visit her grandmother
(2) ate pizza with her friends
(3) did her homework

26 bring → brought / don't → doesn't

01 3인칭 단수 현재형인 designs가 쓰였으므로, 주어는 3인칭 단수인 She가 적절하다.

02 주어가 1인칭, 2인칭이거나 3인칭 복수일 때 부정문에서 don't를 사용하므로 빈칸에는 They가 적절하다.

03 주어가 2인칭(you)일 때 일반동사의 현재형 의문문은 Do로 시작한다.

04 주어가 3인칭 단수(she)이므로 일반동사의 과거형 의문문에 대한 대답은 Yes, she did. 또는 No, she didn't. 이다.

05 주어가 3인칭 단수(Matt)이므로 일반동사의 현재형 의문문에 대한 대답은 Yes, he does. 또는 No, he doesn't.이다.

06 ② 일반동사의 현재형 의문문 Do they ~?에 대한 대답은 Yes, they do.나 No, they don't.가 자연스러운데, No, they didn't.라고 과거형으로 대답하는 것은 어색하다.

07 ④ 주어가 1인칭 복수(We)인 일반동사의 부정문은 〈주어+don't+동사원형〉의 형태이므로 sells를 sell로 써야 한다.

08 ④ 주어가 3인칭 단수(He)이고 these days는 현재를 나타내는 표현이므로 go를 goes로 써야 한다.

09 첫 번째 빈칸에는 3인칭 단수 주어(Frank)의 현재형 의문문에 사용되는 Does가, 두 번째 빈칸에는 3인칭 단수 주어(She)의 현재형 부정문에 사용되는 does가 와야 한다.

5

10 첫 번째 문장은 yesterday로 보아 과거의 일을 나타내므로 didn't가, 두 번째 문장은 일반동사의 과거형 의문문에 대한 부정의 대답이므로 didn't가 와야 한다.

11 주어가 3인칭 단수(He)이므로 현재형 부정문은 〈주어+doesn't+동사원형〉의 형태로 쓴다.

12 Yesterday는 과거를 나타내는 표현이므로 동사의 과거형을 써야 한다. ②와 ⑤가 각각 buy와 give의 올바른 과거형이다. ① look의 과거형은 looked, ③ cost의 과거형은 cost, ④ pay의 과거형은 paid이다.

13 3인칭 단수(Victoria)를 주어로 하는 일반동사의 현재형 의문문에 대한 긍정의 대답이므로 첫 번째 빈칸에는 does가, 두 번째 빈칸에는 study의 3인칭 단수 현재형인 studies가 와야 한다.

14 B의 대답으로 보아 A에는 일반동사의 과거형 의문문이 와야 하므로 첫 번째 빈칸에는 Did가, 두 번째 빈칸에는 open이 와야 한다.

15 ⑤는 주어가 3인칭 복수(your parents)인 의문문이므로 Does 대신 Do 또는 Did가 와야 한다.

16 ③ 일반동사 stop의 과거형은 stopped이다.

17 ⑤의 does는 '하다'라는 의미를 가진 일반동사 do의 3인칭 단수 현재형이고, 나머지는 일반동사의 부정문과 의문문을 만들 때 사용되는 does이다.

18 ①, ②, ③, ④에는 일반동사의 과거형 부정문과 의문문을 만들 때 사용되는 did가 와야 한다. ⑤에는 right now로 보아 현재의 일을 나타내므로 주어가 1인칭일 때 일반동사의 현재형 부정문을 만들 때 사용되는 do가 와야 한다.

19 (a)는 3인칭 단수(he)를 주어로 하는 일반동사의 현재형 의문문이므로 주어 앞에 Does를 써야 한다.
(b)는 주어가 1인칭 복수(We)인 일반동사의 현재형 부정문이므로 don't를 써야 한다.

20 ② 일반동사의 과거형 부정문은 〈주어+didn't+동사원형〉의 형태로 쓰므로 didn't finish가 되어야 한다.

21 (1) 일반동사의 과거형 부정문은 〈주어+didn't+동사원형〉의 형태로 쓴다.
(2) 주어(Julie)가 3인칭 단수이므로 take의 3인칭 단수 현재형인 takes를 쓴다.

22 (1) 주어가 3인칭 복수(Sharon and Brad)인 일반동사의 현재형 의문문은 Do로 시작한다. 부정문은 동사원형 앞에 don't를 쓴다.
(2) 일반동사의 과거형 의문문은 Did로 시작한다. 부정문은 동사원형 앞에 didn't를 쓴다.

23 (1) yesterday는 과거를 나타내는 표현이므로 study의 과거형 studied를 쓴다.
(2) last weekend는 과거를 나타내는 표현이고 하지 않은 일이므로 동사원형 앞에 didn't를 쓴다.

24 B의 대답으로 보아 주어가 3인칭 단수(he)인 현재형 의문문이므로 〈Does+주어+동사원형 ~?〉의 형태로 쓴다.

25 (1) Suji는 월요일에 할머니를 찾아뵙지 않았으므로 didn't를 이용하여 과거형 부정문을 쓴다
(2) Suji는 수요일에 친구들과 피자를 먹었으므로 eat의 과거형인 ate를 쓴다.
(3) Suji는 금요일에 숙제를 했으므로 do의 과거형인 did를 쓴다.

26 B의 첫 번째 말에서 a month ago는 과거를 나타내는 표현이므로 bring의 과거형인 brought를 써야 한다. B의 두 번째 말에서 주어가 3인칭 단수(he)이고 현재형 부정문이므로 동사원형 앞에 doesn't를 써야 한다.

1 주어가 3인칭 복수(Grace and Justin)인 일반동사의 현재형 부정문은 동사원형 앞에 don't를 쓴다.

2 일반동사 enjoy의 3인칭 단수 현재형은 enjoys이다.

3 last week는 과거를 나타내는 표현이므로 go의 과거형 went가 알맞다.

4 yesterday는 과거를 나타내는 표현이므로 일반동사의 과거형 의문문을 만들 때 사용되는 Did가 와야 한다.

5 주어(My brother)가 3인칭 단수이므로 play의 3인칭 단수 현재형인 plays가 알맞다.

6 일반동사 sit의 과거형은 sat이다.

7 주어가 3인칭 단수(The bus)인 일반동사의 현재형 부정문이므로 doesn't가 와야 한다.

8 주어가 3인칭 단수(Brenda)인 현재형 의문문은 〈Does+주어+동사원형 ~?〉의 형태로 써야 하므로 have가 알맞다.

CHAPTER 04 명사와 관사

POINT 01 셀 수 있는 명사 - 규칙 변화 I p.42

A 1 cats 2 tomatoes 3 foxes 4 flowers 5 stars 6 presents 7 pianos 8 watches 9 friends 10 cards 11 buses 12 brushes 13 photos 14 computers 15 ships 16 benches 17 addresses 18 heroes

B 1 arms 2 dishes 3 sandwiches 4 houses 5 classes 6 questions 7 beaches 8 bananas 9 boxes 10 egg, potatoes 11 shirts, sweaters

POINT 02 셀 수 있는 명사 - 규칙 변화 II p.43

A 1 countries 2 keys 3 factories 4 shelves 5 donkeys 6 bodies 7 armies 8 flies 9 hobbies 10 halves 11 ways 12 parties 13 roofs 14 puppies 15 diaries 16 lives 17 wolves 18 families

B 1 leaves 2 Monkeys 3 lives 4 babies 5 roofs 6 toys 7 knives 8 stories 9 ladies, wives 10 cities, buildings 11 holidays

POINT 03 셀 수 있는 명사 - 불규칙 변화 p.44

A 1 teeth 2 men 3 fish 4 deer 5 feet 6 oxen 7 Mice 8 sheep 9 women 10 children

B 1 mice 2 teeth 3 fish 4 women 5 Children 6 geese

POINT 04 셀 수 없는 명사 p.45

A 1 Sugar 2 is 3 ink 4 France 5 information

B 1 is 2 music 3 honey 4 luck 5 advice

C 1 news 2 water 3 money 4 health 5 America

POINT 05 셀 수 없는 명사의 수량 표현 p.46

A 1 piece 2 bottles 3 apple juice 4 bowls of rice 5 pair of pants

B 1 cups of tea 2 pair of sunglasses 3 bottles of cola 4 a piece of paper 5 two bowls of soup 6 two slices of bread

POINT 06 부정관사 a/an p.47

A 1 a 2 an 3 X 4 a 5 an 6 a 7 an 8 a 9 an 10 a

B 1 an answer 2 a magazine 3 an hour 4 a university student 5 once a day

POINT 07 정관사 the p.48

A 1 the 2 a 3 the 4 the 5 an 6 the 7 the 8 The, the 9 a, The

B 1 the Internet 2 a book 3 The bottles 4 The moon, the earth 5 a cat, The cat

POINT 08 관사의 생략 p.49

A 1 X 2 the 3 X 4 X 5 the 6 X 7 X 8 an, a 9 X 10 X

B 1 school, the school 2 bus, The bus 3 a guitar, the guitar 4 bed, the bed

내신 대비 실전 TEST pp.50-52

01 ② 02 ④ 03 ③ 04 ④ 05 ② 06 ④
07 ⑤ 08 ① 09 ③ 10 ④ 11 ③ 12 ③
13 ② 14 ⑤ 15 ⑤ 16 ③ 17 ④ 18 ③
19 ⑤ 20 ④

서술형 집중공략 p.53

21 mice

22 (1) play a violin → play the violin
(2) baby → babies / photoes → photos

23 geese, oxen, deer, donkey

24 ate two bowls of rice

25 (1) three slices of pizza, two glasses of milk
(2) two pieces of cake, a[one] bottle of juice

26 an, X, X

01 -ch로 끝나는 명사는 뒤에 -es를 붙여 복수형으로 쓴다.

02 부정관사 a는 셀 수 있는 명사의 단수형 앞에 사용한다.

03 ①, ②, ④, ⑤는 모두 셀 수 없는 명사로 관사 없이 쓸 수 있지만, ③의 book은 셀 수 있는 명사로 a book이나 books로 써야 한다.

04 scissors와 juice는 수량을 표현할 때 단위 명사로 각각 pair와 glass를 쓰며, 복수형은 단위 명사에 -(e)s를 붙여서 나타낸다.

05 Internet, radio 같은 일부 매체 앞에는 정관사 the를 쓴다. '~마다(= per)'의 의미를 나타낼 때는 명사 앞에 부정관사 a를 쓴다.

06 ④ child의 복수형은 children이다.

07 ⑤ butter는 셀 수 없는 명사이므로 항상 단수형으로 쓴다.

08 ① air는 셀 수 없는 명사이므로 부정관사와 함께 쓰지 않는다.

09 ③ coffee는 셀 수 없는 명사이므로 부정관사와 함께 쓰지 않는다.

10 cheese와 같이 셀 수 없는 명사의 수량은 〈수량+단위 명사+of+셀 수 없는 명사〉의 형태로 나타내며, 복수형은 단위 명사에 -(e)s를 붙인다. cheese는 '조각'의 수량을 표현할 때 단위 명사로 slice 또는 piece를 사용한다.

11 태양(sun)과 같이 세상에 하나뿐인 대상 앞에는 정관사 the를 쓴다. 수식어(on your left)의 꾸밈을 받는 명사 (woman) 앞에는 정관사 the를 쓴다.

12 paper와 cake는 수량을 표현할 때 단위 명사 piece를 사용한다.

13 ②의 feet는 셀 수 있는 명사 foot의 복수형이고, 나머지는 모두 셀 수 없는 명사이다.

14 셀 수 없는 명사 furniture는 수량을 표현할 때 단위 명사 piece를 사용하며 복수형은 piece에 -s를 붙인다. 주어진 단어를 배열하면 We bought two pieces of furniture.이므로 네 번째 오는 단어는 pieces이다.

15 ⑤ '안경'을 뜻하는 glasses는 항상 복수형으로 쓰며, 단위 명사 pair를 사용해서 수량을 표현하는데 안경은 일반적으로 한 번에 한 개만 착용하므로 a pair of가 되어야 한다.

16 ③ hour는 셀 수 있는 명사이며 앞에 수량을 나타내는 eight이 왔으므로 복수형 hours가 되어야 한다.

17 ④ 〈by+교통/통신수단〉의 형태로 쓸 때는 명사 앞에 관사를 쓰지 않는다.

18 〈보기〉와 ③의 a는 막연한 하나를 가리킨다. ①은 '~마다', ②, ④, ⑤는 '하나'라는 의미로 쓰였다.

19 ⑤ 일반적으로 식사(breakfast)를 나타내는 명사 앞에는 관사를 쓰지 않는다.

20 (a) of France가 capital을 뒤에서 수식하고 있으므로 capital 앞에는 정관사 the가 와야 한다.
(c) woman의 복수형은 women이다.

21 집에서 모두 네 마리의 쥐를 발견한 것이므로, mouse의 복수형인 mice를 쓴다.

22 (1) '악기를 연주하다'라는 의미를 나타낼 때는 악기의 이름 앞에 정관사 the를 쓴다.
(2) 첫 번째 문장에서 be동사 were 뒤에는 복수명사가 오므로 baby의 복수형 babies로 쓴다. 두 번째 문장에서 photo의 복수형은 photos이다.

23 goose의 복수형은 geese, ox의 복수형은 oxen이다. deer는 단수형과 복수형의 형태가 같으며, donkey는 한 마리가 있으며 앞에 관사 a가 왔으므로 단수형으로 쓴다.

24 rice와 같이 셀 수 없는 명사의 수량은 〈수량+단위 명사+of+셀 수 없는 명사〉의 형태로 나타내며, 복수형은 단위 명사에 -(e)s를 붙인다. rice는 단위 명사로 bowl을 사용한다.

25 (1) 셀 수 없는 명사의 수량은 〈수량+단위 명사+of+셀 수 없는 명사〉의 형태로 나타내며, pizza는 단위 명사로 slice를, milk는 glass를 사용한다. 이때 복수형은 단위 명사에 -(e)s를 붙인다.
(2) cake는 단위 명사로 piece를, juice는 bottle을 사용하여 수량을 표현한다. 이때 복수형은 단위 명사에 -(e)s를 붙여 나타낸다.

26 • hour는 셀 수 있는 명사이며 발음이 모음으로 시작하므로 앞에 부정관사 an을 쓴다.
• 침대가 잠을 자는 곳이라는 본래의 용도로 쓰였으므로 bed 앞에 관사를 쓰지 않는다.
• 학교가 공부하는 곳이라는 본래의 용도로 쓰였으므로 school 앞에 관사를 쓰지 않는다.

1 명사 sheep은 단수형과 복수형이 같다.

2 하늘(sky)과 같이 세상에 하나뿐인 대상을 나타내는 명사 앞에는 정관사 the를 쓴다.

3 셀 수 없는 명사의 수량은 〈수량+단위 명사+of+셀 수 없는 명사〉의 형태로 나타내며, 복수형은 단위 명사에 -(e)s를 붙인다.

4 '~마다(= per)'의 의미를 나타낼 때는 명사 앞에 부정관사 a를 쓴다.

5 태양(sun)과 같이 세상에 하나뿐인 대상을 나타내는 명사 앞에는 정관사 the를 쓴다.

6 hour는 셀 수 있는 명사이며 발음이 모음으로 시작하므로 앞에 부정관사 an을 쓴다.

CHAPTER 05 대명사

POINT 01 지시대명사   p.56

A 1 this   2 that   3 these   4 Those   5 That   6 this
B 1 These   2 that   3 this   4 those
C 1 these   2 That   3 this   4 those   5 This

POINT 02 부정대명사 one   p.57

A 1 one   2 it   3 ones   4 one   5 ones
B 1 One   2 ones   3 one
C 1 ones   2 One   3 them   4 one   5 It   6 one, ones

POINT 03 부정대명사 some/any   p.58

A 1 some   2 any   3 some   4 any   5 Some   6 any   7 some   8 some, any   9 any, some   10 some, any
B 1 any   2 ones   3 one   4 Some

POINT 04 비인칭 주어 it   p.59

A 1 It is spring now.
2 It is about five kilometers.
3 It was cloudy yesterday.
4 What day is it today?
5 It takes half an hour.
B 1 It is dark   2 It is my birthday
3 It takes three hours   4 It is ten to six
5 It is 500 meters   6 It was rainy, it is sunny

POINT 05 재귀대명사   p.60

A 1 herself   2 itself   3 themselves   4 himself   5 myself   6 yourselves   7 ourselves
B 1 myself   2 yourself   3 herself   4 themselves   5 itself   6 ourselves   7 himself

POINT 06 재귀대명사의 용법   p.61

A 1 X   2 O   3 X   4 X   5 O   6 X   7 O
B 1 herself baked   2 angry at myself
3 book itself   4 talks to himself
5 artists, themselves

내신 대비 실전 TEST   pp.62-64

01 ③   02 ③   03 ①   04 ④   05 ④   06 ③
07 ②   08 ③   09 ①   10 ②   11 ①   12 ④
13 ⑤   14 ④   15 ⑤   16 ③   17 ⑤   18 ③
19 ②   20 ④

서술형 집중공략   p.65

21 (1) Are those your pets
   (2) These are, tablet PCs, the old ones
22 (1) One (2) It
23 (1) It (2) it (3) one
24 (1) cares about himself (2) pants, loose ones
25 (1) Did Mike himself move the box?[Did Mike move the box himself?]
   (2) They looked at themselves in the mirror.
26 (1) any (2) some (3) That

01 앞에서 언급된 것과 같은 종류의 불특정한 사물을 가리킬 때 부정대명사 one을 쓴다.
02 긍정문에서 '조금', '약간'이라는 뜻의 부정대명사 some 이 적절하다.
03 앞에서 언급된 특정한 대상 the movie를 받는 대명사는 it이다.
04 ④의 this는 지시대명사이고 나머지는 모두 명사를 수식하는 지시형용사이다.
05 '조금(의)', '약간(의)'이라는 뜻으로 의문문에서는 any를, 긍정문에서는 some을 사용한다.
06 A의 빈칸에는 앞에 나온 purse와 같은 종류의 불특정한 것을 나타내는 one이, B의 빈칸에는 this purse라는 특정 대상을 받는 It이 적절하다.
07 A의 빈칸에는 '조금(의)', '약간(의)'이라는 뜻으로 긍정문에 쓰이는 some이, B의 빈칸에는 주어 I를 강조하는 재귀대명사 myself가 적절하다.

08 ③ 부정문에서는 some이 아닌 any를 사용한다.

09 〈보기〉와 ②,③,④,⑤의 It은 비인칭 주어인 반면, ①의 It은 특정한 대상을 가리키는 인칭대명사이다.

10 〈보기〉와 ①,③,④,⑤는 강조 용법의 재귀대명사인 반면, ②의 herself는 동사의 목적어로 쓰인 재귀 용법의 재귀대명사이다.

11 (c) 앞에 나온 단수명사인 tie와 같은 종류의 불특정한 것을 나타내는 one이 와야 한다.
(e) 문장의 주어가 3인칭 복수(They)이므로 take care of의 목적어로 재귀대명사 themselves가 와야 한다.

12 문장의 주어가 1인칭 복수(We)이므로 be proud of의 목적어로 재귀대명사 ourselves가 온다.

13 ⑤ 부정문에서는 some이 아닌 any를 쓴다.

14 날씨와 특정한 날을 나타내는 비인칭 주어 It이 들어가야 한다.

15 각각 동사 enjoyed와 know의 목적어 역할을 하는 재귀대명사가 필요한데, 문장의 주어가 3인칭 복수명사이므로 themselves가 와야 한다.

16 ‘조금(의)’, ‘약간(의)’이라는 뜻으로 부정문과 의문문에서는 any를 쓴다.

17 ①,②,③,④의 재귀대명사는 동사나 전치사의 목적어로 쓰인 반면, ⑤의 themselves는 주어를 강조하는 재귀대명사로 생략이 가능하다.

18 ③ ‘조금(의)’, ‘약간(의)’이라는 뜻으로 긍정문에서는 some을 쓴다.

19 ② over there로 보아 멀리 있는 대상을 가리키므로 지시대명사 That이 와야 한다.

20 (A) 시간을 나타내는 비인칭 주어 It이 알맞다.
(B) ‘조금’, ‘약간’이라는 뜻으로 긍정문에 쓰이는 Some이 알맞다.
(C) 재귀대명사 herself가 쓰였으므로 주어 자리에는 3인칭 단수명사인 child가 알맞다.

21 (1) 지시대명사 that의 복수형으로 those를 쓴다.
(2) 지시대명사 This의 복수형으로 These를 쓴다. 부정대명사 one의 복수형은 ones이다.

22 (1) 일반인을 가리킬 때 부정대명사 One을 쓴다.
(2) 특정한 사물 a nice bag을 받는 인칭대명사 It을 쓴다.

23 (1) 날씨를 나타내는 비인칭 주어 It을 써야 한다.
(2) 특정한 사물인 my black jacket을 받는 대명사 it을 써야 한다.
(3) 앞에 나온 jacket과 같은 종류의 불특정한 것을 나타내는 부정대명사 one을 써야 한다.

24 (1) 주어가 He이므로 전치사 about의 목적어로 재귀대명사 himself를 써야 한다.
(2) 항상 복수형으로 쓰는 명사 pants(바지)와 같은 종류의 불특정한 것을 나타내는 ones를 써야 한다.

25 (1) 주어인 Mike를 강조하는 재귀대명사 himself를 이용한다. 강조 용법의 재귀대명사는 강조하는 말 바로 뒤 또는 문장의 맨 끝에 쓴다.
(2) 문장의 주어가 3인칭 복수(They)이므로 looked at의 목적어로 재귀대명사 themselves를 쓴다.

26 (1) ‘조금(의)’, ‘약간(의)’이라는 뜻으로 의문문에서는 any를 쓴다.
(2) ‘조금(의)’, ‘약간(의)’이라는 뜻으로 긍정문에서는 some을 쓴다.
(3) pink one은 단수이므로 이를 수식하는 지시형용사로는 That을 써야 한다.

문법 정리 노트   p.66

① this   ② those   ③ ones   ④ some
⑤ any   ⑥ ourselves   ⑦ yourself
⑧ themselves

CHECK

1 X, that   **2** O   **3** X, themselves   **4** O
5 X, ones   **6** O

1 동사가 3인칭 단수형(looks)이므로 주어 자리의 지시대명사는 That이 되어야 한다.

2 날씨를 나타낼 때 문장의 주어로 비인칭 주어 It을 쓴다.

3 문장의 주어가 3인칭 복수(The children)이므로 enjoyed의 목적어로 재귀대명사 themselves를 쓴다.

4 주어인 Logan을 강조하는 재귀대명사 himself는 문장의 맨 끝이나 주어 바로 뒤에 쓴다.

5 앞에서 언급한 three skirts 중 불특정한 2개를 가리키므로 복수형 부정대명사 ones를 쓴다.

6 ‘조금’, ‘약간’이라는 뜻으로 부정문에서는 any를 쓴다.

CHAPTER 06 시제

POINT 01 현재시제   p.68

A 1 are   2 get   3 rises   4 is   5 has
B 1 is   2 are   3 goes   4 comes   5 opens
C 1 boils   2 studies   3 are   4 practice   5 eat

A 1 snowed　2 came　3 wrote　4 read
5 painted
B 1 sat　2 put　3 am, was　4 was, gave
5 drives, drove
C 1 had　2 sent　3 met　4 baked

A 1 sleeping　2 writing　3 tying　4 sitting
5 riding　6 meeting　7 running　8 dying
9 driving　10 swimming
B 1 I'm looking for my student ID.
2 He is sending a text message.
3 They are having lunch together.
C 1 raining　2 putting　3 drinking　4 smiling
5 lying　6 arriving

A 1 am learning　2 was flying　3 are making
4 were talking　5 is climbing
B 1 I'm writing　2 Cathy was crying
3 We were choosing　4 He is solving
5 My brothers are taking
6 The children were jumping

A 1 am　2 was not　3 visiting　4 is
5 weren't
B 1 not waiting　2 were lying　3 isn't playing
4 weren't wasting
C 1 I'm not thinking　2 He wasn't doing
3 Tina isn't packing
4 They weren't watching
5 I aren't hiding

A 1 exercising　2 I talking　3 Was　4 Are
5 sleeping
B 1 Are you　2 No, he wasn't
3 Yes, they are　4 Were, we weren't

C 1 Is Vicky washing
2 Were you looking for
3 Are they cutting
4 Was he lying

내신 대비 실전 TEST　pp.74-76

01 ③	02 ①	03 ④	04 ③	05 ②	06 ③
07 ③	08 ②	09 ⑤	10 ⑤	11 ③	12 ②
13 ④	14 ②, ⑤		15 ⑤	16 ④	17 ④
18 ③	19 ①	20 ③			

서술형 집중공략　p.77

21 (1) is (2) brought (3) cleans
22 My friends were not dancing on stage.
23 (1) He is staying at his cousin's house. /
Was he staying at his cousin's house?
(2) Are they eating strawberries for dessert? /
They weren't[were not] eating strawberries
for dessert.
24 (1) is sitting (2) is lying (3) are running
25 (1) No, she wasn't, was drawing a picture
(2) No, he isn't, is making some food
26 were, called, went out

01 yesterday로 보아 과거를 나타내는 시제를 써야 하므로
wore가 알맞다.
02 now가 있고 전화를 받으라는 말이 이어지므로 현재진행
형 〈be동사의 현재형+v-ing〉의 형태가 와야 한다. 주어
(Your phone)가 3인칭 단수이므로 be동사는 is가 알맞
다.
03 last night로 보아 과거를 나타내는 시제를 써야 하고, 주
어가 복수형이므로 were talking이 알맞다.
04 ③ -e로 끝나는 동사는 e를 빼고 -ing를 붙여 진행형을 만
들어야 하므로 moving으로 써야 한다.
05 ② know(알고 있다)는 상태를 나타내는 동사이므로 진행
형으로 쓰지 않는다.
06 ③ need(필요하다)는 상태를 나타내는 동사이므로 진행
형으로 쓰지 않는다.
07 이메일을 확인하고 있냐는 A의 질문에 B는 컴퓨터 게임
을 하는 중이라고 말하므로 ③이 알맞다.
08 어제 이 시간에 비가 많이 내리고 있었냐는 A의 질문에, B
는 비가 매우 많이 내리고 있었다고 말하므로 ②가 알맞다.
09 과거진행형을 만들기 위해 빈칸에 be동사의 과거형이 들어
가야 하는데, 주어가 you와 They이므로 were가 알맞다.
10 현재 진행 중인 일을 묻고 답하는 대화로 A의 빈칸에는

doing이, B의 빈칸에는 watching이 알맞다.

11 talking과 they aren't로 보아 A의 질문은 현재진행형이 되어야 하므로 빈칸에 Are가, B의 이어지는 말에서는 10 minutes ago가 있으므로 빈칸에 과거시제 talked가 알맞다.

12 주어진 말을 배열하면 'They / were / not / waving / at / us.'이므로 네 번째 단어는 waving이다.

13 ④ 현재 일요일마다 가게를 닫는지 묻는 말에 과거에 문을 열었던 일에 대해 답하는 것은 자연스럽지 않다.

14 ① 과거진행형의 의문문에서 주어가 2인칭(you)이므로 Was가 아닌 Were를 써야 한다.
③ last month로 보아 과거에 일어난 일을 이야기하고 있으므로 buy의 과거형인 bought를 써야 한다.
④ 과거진행형의 부정문은 〈be동사의 과거형＋not＋v-ing〉의 형태이므로, was not using으로 써야 한다.

15 ⑤ 역사적 사실은 과거시제로 써야 하므로 break의 과거형인 broke를 써야 한다.

16 ④ have(가지다)는 소유를 나타내는 동사이므로 진행형으로 쓰지 않는다.

17 ④ 과거의 특정 시점에 진행 중이던 일을 묻는 말이므로 과거진행형의 의문문 〈be동사의 과거형＋주어＋v-ing ~?〉의 형태가 되어야 하며 주어가 3인칭 복수(they)이므로 Were를 써야 한다.

18 과거진행형의 부정문으로 써야 하는데, 주어가 3인칭 복수(Ian and Sue)이므로 weren't chatting이 알맞다.

19 (c) every morning으로 보아 일상적인 습관을 나타내며, 주어가 3인칭 단수이므로 현재시제 takes가 되어야 한다.
(d) right now로 보아 현재 진행 중인 일을 나타내므로 am recording이 되어야 한다.

20 (A) 불변의 사실이므로 현재시제 is가 알맞다.
(B) 과거의 동작을 나타내므로 과거시제 found가 알맞다.
(C) 소유를 나타내는 동사는 진행형으로 쓰지 않으므로 had가 알맞다.

21 (1) tonight이 있으므로 현재시제로 쓴다.
(2) yesterday가 있으므로 과거시제로 쓴다.
(3) every day와 these days로 보아 현재의 일상적인 습관을 나타내고 있으므로 현재시제로 쓴다.

22 과거진행형의 부정문은 〈be동사의 과거형＋not＋v-ing〉의 형태로 쓴다.

23 (1) 현재진행형의 평서문은 〈be동사의 현재형＋v-ing〉, 과거진행형의 의문문은 〈be동사의 과거형＋주어＋v-ing ~?〉의 형태로 쓴다.
(2) 현재진행형의 의문문은 〈be동사의 현재형＋주어＋v-ing ~?〉, 과거진행형의 부정문은 〈be동사의 과거형＋not＋v-ing〉의 형태로 쓴다.

24 (1) 여자는 벤치에 앉아 있으므로 is sitting을 쓴다.

(2) 남자는 풀밭 위에 누워 있으므로 is lying을 쓴다.
(3) 아이들이 강을 따라 달리고 있으므로 are running을 쓴다.

25 (1) 한 시간 전에 Amy는 그림을 그리고 있었으므로 No, she wasn't.로 답하고, 과거진행형 was drawing을 써서 표현한다.
(2) Fred는 지금 음식을 만들고 있으므로 No, he isn't. 로 답하고, 현재진행형 is making을 써서 표현한다.

26 yesterday가 있으므로 과거시제로 쓴다. 과거에 이미 끝난 일(전화한 것, 쇼핑하러 간 것)에 대해 이야기하는 것이므로 과거시제로 쓴다.

문법 정리 노트 p.78

① be동사 ② v-ing ③ be동사의 과거형
④ be동사, not, v-ing ⑤ be동사, v-ing
⑥ not

CHECK

1 goes **2** lost **3** invented **4** is **5** wants
6 were not **7** Were

---

1 usually와 these days로 보아 현재의 일상적인 습관을 나타내고 있으므로 현재시제가 알맞다.

2 last night이 있으므로 과거시제가 알맞다.

3 역사적 사실은 과거시제로 쓴다.

4 right now로 보아 현재 진행 중인 일을 나타내므로 is가 알맞다.

5 want(원하다, 필요하다)는 상태를 나타내는 동사이므로 진행형으로 쓰지 않는다.

6 과거진행형의 부정문은 〈be동사의 과거형＋not＋v-ing〉의 형태로 쓴다.

7 watching과 this morning으로 보아 과거진행형의 의문문이므로 주어 앞에 be동사를 쓴다.

CHAPTER 07 조동사

POINT 01 **will** p.80

A 1 will join 2 open 3 will not 4 won't
B 1 will be 2 give 3 come 4 not ask

C 1 will begin   2 Will, call   3 won't sing
4 Will, be, I'll be

POINT 02   **be going to**   p.81

A 1 are   2 Is   3 not going   4 going
B 1 am going to wash
2 Are you going to learn
3 is going to be nice
4 aren't[are not] going to watch
C 1 Are you going to help me?
2 He isn't going to change his hairstyle.
3 I'm going to meet my friend in Japan.

POINT 03   **can**   p.82

A 1 play   2 you turn   3 cannot find   4 see
B 1 Can I   2 Can you   3 he can't
C 1 Can I open   2 Dorothy can use
3 You can't[cannot] use   4 Can you send

POINT 04   **can과 be able to**   p.83

A 1 is   2 Are   3 weren't   4 I was
B 1 am able to make   2 Are you able to do
3 were able to hear
4 wasn't[was not] able to use
5 are able to deliver
C 1 I'm able to tell   2 Is Joe able to run
3 We weren't able to lift
4 Peter isn't able to play
5 Was she able to catch

POINT 05   **may**   p.84

A 1 may I have   2 may I use
3 may not be true   4 may be sick
B 1 may not sit   2 May I try   3 may be bad
4 May I take   5 He may not know

POINT 06   **must**   p.85

A 1 come   2 not waste   3 must not   4 must
B 1 ⓒ   2 ⓐ   3 ⓑ   4 ⓓ
C 1 must be   2 She must not enter
3 We must follow   4 You must not talk

POINT 07   **have to**   p.86

A 1 have   2 has   3 doesn't   4 had
5 must not
B 1 has to work   2 Does, have to go
3 You have to meet   4 didn't have to wear
5 Do, have to finish   6 I had to walk

POINT 08   **should**   p.87

A 1 should, take   2 should apologize
3 shouldn't believe   4 should wear
5 shouldn't use
B 1 We shouldn't skip   2 You should listen
3 he can't be tired
4 They don't have to answer

내신 대비 실전 TEST   pp.88-90

01 ④   02 ①   03 ②   04 ③   05 ①   06 ④
07 ②   08 ②   09 ⑤   10 ⑤   11 ①   12 ⑤
13 ③   14 ③   15 ①   16 ④   17 ④   18 ③
19 ④   20 ④

서술형 집중공략 —————— p.91

21 (1) must be hungry (2) can't[cannot] be
22 (1) He isn't[He's not] going to say hello to
her.
Is he going to say hello to her?
(2) She didn't have to come back home by
ten.
Did she have to come back home by ten?
23 Were you able to get a good seat?
24 (1) must stay silent during the show
(2) must not take pictures during the show
25 (1) can drive (2) is not able to play
26 (1) must be kind (2) doesn't have to go to
school

01 안전하지 않기에 불을 갖고 놀면 안 된다는 내용이 되어야
하므로 금지를 나타내는 must not이 알맞다.
02 우산을 가져가라는 것으로 보아 오늘 오후에 비가 올 것이
라는 내용이 되어야 하므로 미래의 일을 나타내는 will이
알맞다.
03 어제 온종일 운동을 한 것으로 보아 Eric이 분명 피곤할
것이라고 추측하는 내용이 되어야 하므로 강한 추측을 나

타내는 must가 알맞다.

04 허가의 의미를 지니는 can은 may로 바꾸어 쓸 수 있다.

05 be going to는 미래의 일을 나타내는 will로 바꾸어 쓸 수 있다.

06 '~해야 한다'의 의미를 나타내는 should를 쓴다.

07 '~임이 틀림없다'라는 의미의 강한 추측을 나타내는 must를 쓴다.

08 〈Will you ~?〉에 대한 부정의 대답으로 No, I won't.가 알맞다.

09 빈칸 뒤에서 '다음 주 토요일이 어때?'라고 묻는 것으로 보아 빈칸에는 부정의 대답이 알맞다. 〈May/Can I ~?〉에 대한 부정의 대답은 'I'm afraid ~' 또는 'I'm sorry ~' 등을 주로 쓴다.

10 ⑤ should는 '~해야 한다'라는 의미를 나타내므로 B에서 과거세제인 had to를 이용해 답하는 것은 어색하다.

11 ②,③,④,⑤의 must는 '~해야 한다'라는 의무의 의미인 반면, ①의 must는 '~임이 틀림없다'라는 강한 추측의 의미이다.

12 ⑤ '~임이 틀림없다'라는 의미의 강한 추측을 나타낼 때는 must를 쓴다.

13 주어가 3인칭 단수이고 have to의 의문문은 〈Do/Does/Did+주어+have to ~?〉로 쓰므로, A의 빈칸에는 have가 알맞고 이에 대한 부정의 대답으로 B의 빈칸에는 doesn't가 알맞다.

14 늦게 일어나서 제시간에 도착할 수 없었다는 내용이 되어야 하므로 첫 번째 빈칸에는 wasn't가 알맞다. 그래서 모든 사람들에게 사과를 해야 했다는 내용이 되어야 하므로 두 번째 빈칸에는 had to가 알맞다.

15 문맥상 '~할 수 없다'라는 의미의 can't가 들어가야 한다.

16 ④ must not은 '~하면 안 된다'라는 의미이고, have to의 부정형인 don't have to는 '~할 필요가 없다'라는 의미이다.

17 ④ 조동사는 주어의 인칭이나 수에 관계없이 형태가 변하지 않으므로 mays는 may가 되어야 한다.

18 ③ '~할 수 있다'는 의미의 can 또는 are able to를 써야 한다.

19 (c) can을 이용해 카메라를 수리할 수 있는지 묻는 질문에, (b) be able to의 부정형을 이용한 대답이 이어지고, (d) should를 이용해 그렇다면 무엇을 해야 하는지 묻자, (a) have to로 답하는 말이 이어지는 것이 자연스럽다.

20 (a) 조동사 뒤에는 항상 동사원형을 쓰므로 won은 win이 되어야 한다.
(c) '~해야 했다'라는 과거의 의무를 나타내려면 had to를 써서 had to clean이 되어야 한다.

21 (1) 문맥상 '~임이 틀림없다'라는 의미의 강한 추측을 나타내는 must를 이용해서 써야 한다.
(2) 문맥상 '~일 리가 없다'라는 의미의 강한 부정적 추측

22 (1) be going to의 부정문은 〈주어+be동사+not+going to+동사원형〉, 의문문은 〈be동사+주어+going to+동사원형 ~?〉으로 쓴다.
(2) have to의 과거시제 부정형은 didn't have to를 쓰며, 과거시제 의문문은 〈Did+주어+have to ~?〉로 쓴다.

23 가능을 나타내는 be able to의 의문문은 〈be동사+주어+able to+동사원형 ~?〉으로 쓴다.

24 해야 하는 일은 must, 해서는 안 되는 일은 must not을 이용해서 쓴다.

25 할 수 있는 일은 can 또는 be able to, 할 수 없는 일은 can't[cannot] 또는 〈be동사+not+able to+동사원형〉을 이용해서 쓴다.

26 (1) 항상 반 친구들을 돕는다고 했으므로, '친절한 게 틀림없다'라는 의미의 강한 추측을 나타내는 must be kind를 써야 한다.
(2) 오늘이 일요일이라고 했으므로, '학교에 갈 필요가 없다'라는 의미의 doesn't have to go to school을 써야 한다.

문법 정리 노트   p.92

① 동사원형   ② ~할 것이다   ③ be able to
④ may   ⑤ must not   ⑥ have to
⑦ ~할 필요가 없다

CHECK

1 (1) must (2) don't have to (3) able to
2 (1) X, I introduce (2) O (3) X, be
(4) X, Do I have (5) X, won't[will not]

1 (1) '~임이 틀림없다'라는 의미의 강한 추측을 나타낼 때는 must를 쓴다.
(2) '~할 필요가 없다'라는 의미를 나타낼 때는 don't have to를 쓴다. must not은 '~하면 안 된다'라는 의미이다.
(3) '~할 수 없다'라는 의미를 나타낼 때는 〈be동사+not+able to+동사원형〉을 쓴다.

2 (1) 조동사 뒤에는 항상 동사원형을 쓴다.
(2) 허락을 구하는 의문문은 〈May/Can I+동사원형 ~?〉으로 쓴다.
(3) 조동사 뒤에는 항상 동사원형을 써야 한다.
(4) have to의 의문문은 〈Do/Does/Did+주어+have to ~?〉로 쓴다.
(5) will의 부정형은 won't[will not]로 쓴다.

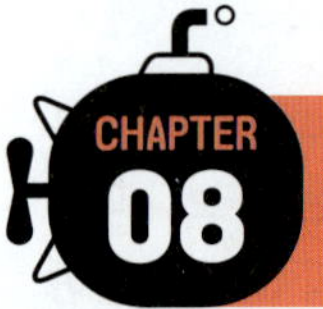

CHAPTER 08 형용사, 부사, 비교

POINT 01 형용사의 역할　　p.94

A 1 hair　2 the window　3 questions
4 Her dress　5 nothing
B 1 dangerous　2 nice
3 famous photographer　4 delicious
5 someone important
C 1 simple game　2 me angry
3 clothes, wet　4 everything necessary

POINT 02 수량 형용사　　p.95

A 1 many　2 a little　3 Few　4 A lot of
B 1 carrot　2 much　3 information　4 a little
C 1 much juice　2 a few keys
3 little energy　4 a lot of cookies

POINT 03 부사의 역할과 형태　　p.96

A 1 easily　2 simple　3 happily　4 late
5 Luckily　6 great　7 hardly　8 quietly
9 well　10 high
B 1 kind, kindly　2 heavily, heavy
3 terrible, terribly　4 fast, fast　5 well, good

POINT 04 빈도부사　　p.97

A 1 ①　2 ②　3 ②
B 1 always　2 often　3 sometimes
4 never　5 usually
C 1 seldom goes to school
2 should always be careful
3 often calls his grandmother

POINT 05 원급 비교　　p.98

A 1 as light as　2 not as[so] expensive as
3 as slowly as　4 as comfortable as
5 not as[so] interesting as　6 as well as
B 1 as wide as　2 not as[so] thick as
3 as fast as

POINT 06 비교급과 최상급 만드는 방법　　p.99

A 1 louder, loudest
2 cuter, cutest
3 thinner, thinnest
4 prettier, prettiest
5 more famous, most famous
6 worse, worst
7 smaller, smallest
8 more careful, most careful
9 heavier, heaviest
10 nicer, nicest
11 less, least
12 more interesting, most interesting
B 1 better　2 biggest　3 worse　4 easier
5 most expensive　6 highest

POINT 07 비교급 비교　　p.100

A 1 healthier than　2 less than
3 harder than　4 more important than
5 higher than　6 cheaper than
7 better than　8 more difficult than
9 faster than　10 more exciting than
B 1 more slowly　2 earlier than
3 more active than　4 much heavier than
5 more serious than
6 a lot more expensive than

POINT 08 최상급 비교　　p.101

A 1 smallest　2 the youngest　3 fastest
4 the most　5 games
B 1 the hottest　2 the best　3 the happiest
4 the richest　5 the most dangerous
C 1 the hardest　2 the worst mistake
3 the most popular　4 the most impressive
5 one of the oldest houses

내신 대비 실전 TEST pp.102-104

01 ③　02 ①　03 ②　04 ④　05 ④　06 ③
07 ②　08 ②　09 ⑤　10 ③　11 ④　12 ⑤
13 ④　14 ③　15 ②　16 ①　17 ③　18 ④
19 ③　20 ①

서술형 집중공략 p.105

21 (1) shorter than (2) the tallest
22 (1) usually plays the guitar
　　(2) sometimes takes pictures
　　(3) often reads books
23 (1) bigger than (2) the most diligent
24 (1) I will never forget you.
　　(2) She is one of the smartest students
25 (1) older than (2) as fast as (3) the lightest
26 hardly, thinner, the worst

01 동사 looked 뒤에 주격 보어로 형용사가 와서 주어의 상태나 성질을 보충 설명해 준다. ③ lovely는 '사랑스러운'을 뜻하는 형용사이고, 나머지는 모두 부사이다.

02 '…만큼 ~한/하게'라는 뜻을 나타내는 비교 표현은 〈as+형용사/부사의 원급+as〉의 형태로 쓴다.

03 '…보다 더 ~한'이라는 뜻을 나타내는 〈비교급+than〉이 되어야 하므로 형용사 cold의 비교급 colder가 알맞다.

04 ④는 명사와 형용사의 관계이고, 나머지는 모두 형용사와 부사의 관계이다.

05 ④ 비교급을 강조할 때 much, even, still, a lot, far 등을 쓸 수 있으며, very는 쓸 수 없다.

06 ③ 수량 형용사 a little은 셀 수 없는 명사 앞에 쓴다.

07 ② 앞에 more가 있으므로 비교급 wiser는 빈칸에 쓸 수 없다.

08 ② 〈자음+-y〉로 끝나는 단어의 비교급/최상급은 y를 i로 바꾸고 -er/-est를 붙인다. 따라서 ugly의 비교급은 uglier, 최상급은 ugliest로 쓴다.

09 첫 번째 빈칸 앞에 the가 쓰인 것으로 보아 최상급 largest가 알맞고, 두 번째 빈칸 뒤에 than이 쓰인 것으로 보아 비교급 higher가 알맞다.

10 첫 번째 빈칸에는 -thing으로 끝나는 대명사의 경우 형용사가 뒤에서 수식하므로 something hot이 알맞고, 두 번째 빈칸에는 found의 목적격 보어로 형용사를 써야 하므로 impressive가 알맞다.

11 water는 셀 수 없는 명사이므로 '약간의'라는 뜻을 나타내는 수량 형용사는 a little을 앞에 쓴다. 셀 수 없는 명사는 항상 단수형으로 쓴다.

12 '가장 ~한 … 중의 하나'라는 의미는 〈one of the+최상급+복수명사〉의 형태로 나타낸다.

13 ④ '…만큼 ~한/하게'라는 뜻을 나타내는 〈as+형용사/부사의 원급+as〉의 as가 와야 한다. 나머지는 '…보다 더 ~한'이라는 뜻을 나타내는 〈비교급+than〉의 than이 와야 한다.

14 주어진 문장이 '나는 Joe만큼 독일어를 잘 말하지 못한다.'라는 의미이므로, 'Joe가 나보다 독일어를 더 잘 말한다.'라는 ③이 같은 의미의 문장이다.

15 ② made의 목적격 보어 자리에 형용사 happy가 와야 한다.

16 ① 〈as+형용사/부사의 원급+as〉 비교 표현이므로 less가 아닌 little이 와야 한다.

17 ③ 셀 수 있는 명사의 복수형 앞에서 '거의 없는'이라는 뜻을 나타내는 수량 형용사는 few이다.

18 ④ '늦게'라는 의미를 나타내는 부사는 late이며, lately는 '최근에'라는 뜻이다.

19 (A) made의 목적격 보어 자리에 형용사 horrible이 와야 한다.
　　(B) juice는 셀 수 없는 명사이므로 '많은'이라는 뜻을 나타내는 수량 형용사는 much를 앞에 쓴다.
　　(C) '잘'이라는 의미의 부사 well이 알맞다.

20 (c) 셀 수 있는 명사 sandwich의 복수형 앞에서 '약간의'라는 뜻을 나타내는 수량 형용사는 a few이다.
　　(e) 〈as+형용사/부사의 원급+as〉 또는 〈not+as[so]+형용사/부사의 원급+as〉의 형태가 되어야 하므로, is as near as 또는 is not as[so] near as로 쓴다.

21 (1) Jenny가 Phillip보다 키가 작으므로 〈비교급+than〉의 형태로 쓴다.
　　(2) Jack이 세 학생 중에서 가장 키가 크므로 〈the+최상급〉의 형태로 쓴다.

22 (1) 일주일 중 6일 기타를 연주하므로 plays the guitar를 usually와 함께 쓴다. 빈도부사는 일반동사 앞에 쓴다.
　　(2) 일주일 중 하루 사진을 찍으므로 takes pictures를 sometimes와 함께 쓴다.
　　(3) 일주일 중 4일 책을 읽으므로 reads books를 often과 함께 쓴다.

23 (1) '서울은 뉴욕만큼 크지 않다.'라는 것은 '뉴욕이 서울보다 더 크다.'라는 의미이므로 bigger than을 쓴다.
　　(2) 'Tony가 반의 다른 모든 소년들보다 더 부지런하다.'라는 것은 'Tony가 반에서 가장 부지런한 소년이다.'라는 의미이므로 the most diligent를 쓴다.

24 (1) 빈도부사 never는 조동사 뒤, 일반동사 앞에 쓴다.
　　(2) '가장 ~한 … 중의 하나'라는 의미는 〈one of the+최상급+복수명사〉의 형태로 나타낸다.

25 (1) Luis가 Becky보다 나이가 더 많으므로 older than을 쓴다.
　　(2) Cooper와 Max는 속도에서 같은 점수를 받았으므로 as fast as를 쓴다.

16

(3) Becky는 네 마리의 개들 중에서 무게가 가장 적게 나가므로 the lightest를 쓴다.

26 첫 번째 빈칸에는 문맥상 '거의 ~않다'라는 의미의 부사 hardly가 적절하다. 두 번째 빈칸에는 뒤의 than으로 보아 전보다 '더 마른'이라는 의미의 비교급 thinner를 쓴다. 세 번째 빈칸에는 내내 아팠던 이번 여름 방학이 인생에서 '가장 나쁜' 방학들 중 하나였다는 의미가 되는 것이 자연스러우므로 the worst를 쓴다.

문법 정리 노트 p.106

① a few　② much　③ 형용사+ly ④ 뒤
⑤ 앞　⑥ sometimes　⑦ often
⑧ as　⑨ than　⑩ 복수명사

CHECK

1 ○　**2** X, fast　**3** ○　**4** X, bigger
5 X, is always　**6** X, members
7 X, the cutest　**8** ○

1 형용사는 보통 수식하는 명사 앞에 쓴다.
2 '빠르게'라는 뜻의 부사는 형용사와 형태가 같은 fast이다.
3 빈도부사는 일반동사의 앞에 쓴다.
4 than 앞에는 비교급을 쓰며 the를 붙이지 않는다.
5 빈도부사는 be동사의 뒤에 쓴다.
6 '가장 ~한 … 중의 하나'라는 의미는 〈one of the+최상급 +복수명사〉의 형태로 나타낸다.
7 형용사 cute의 최상급은 cutest로 최상급 비교 표현에서는 앞에 the를 붙여 the cutest로 쓴다.
8 '…만큼 ~한/하게'라는 뜻을 나타내는 비교 표현은 〈as+형용사/부사의 원급+as〉의 형태로 쓴다.

CHAPTER 09 의문문, 명령문, 감탄문

POINT 01 who, what, which p.108

A **1** What　**2** Who　**3** Which　**4** What
B **1** Who is coming　**2** What did you make
3 Who drew this picture
4 Which seat do you want
C **1** Who is　**2** What do, eat

POINT 02 when, where p.109

A **1** Where　**2** When　**3** Where　**4** When
B **1** Where are they　**2** When did you buy
3 Where did he see
4 When[What time] does the movie
C **1** Where was she　**2** When did Mark call
3 Where do they live
4 What time will you meet
5 Where does he download

POINT 03 why p.110

A **1** Why　**2** Where　**3** do
4 What time　**5** Why don't
B **1** ©　**2** ⓓ　**3** ⓑ　**4** ⓐ　**5** ⓔ
C **1** Why did they　**2** Why is he studying
3 When was her sister
4 Why did you come to work
5 Where will you travel
6 Why does Luna read

POINT 04 how p.111

A **1** How　**2** How long　**3** How　**4** How often
B **1** How old　**2** How much　**3** How
4 How tall　**5** How many
C **1** How did you talk　**2** How far is
3 How was your first day
4 How often do they go

POINT 05 부가 의문문 p.112

A **1** do　**2** doesn't　**3** can't they
4 did she　**5** weren't you
B **1** does he　**2** can't she　**3** didn't you
4 did she　**5** won't they
C **1** is it, it isn't　**2** can't she, she can
3 did you, I didn't　**4** doesn't he, he does

POINT 06 부정 의문문 p.113

A **1** Isn't this yours?
2 Wasn't it expensive?

3 Don't you feel thirsty?
4 Can't they deliver it?
5 Didn't he take notes?
6 Aren't they designers?
7 Doesn't he play tennis well?
8 Won't she move to New York?
9 Weren't you interested in animals?
B 1 Isn't, she is   2 Won't you, No, I
3 Doesn't he, he does
4 Can't they, they can't
5 Didn't she, she did

POINT 07   명령문   p.114

A 1 Be   2 Do not   3 have   4 Let's not
5 Don't   6 or   7 and
B 1 Let's take   2 Don't go out   3 Study, or
4 turn on   5 Visit, and   6 Don't listen to
7 Get up   8 Let's not go

POINT 08   감탄문   p.115

A 1 What a huge   2 the story is
3 How peaceful   4 small these shoes
5 a lovely dress
B 1 How friendly the dog is!
2 What a nice car he has!
3 How exciting the game was!
4 What a long message she sent!
C 1 What a clever dog it is!
2 How difficult this problem was!
3 How fast he ran in the race!
4 What great films the director makes!

01 ④	02 ④	03 ③	04 ⑤	05 ⑤	06 ④
07 ③	08 ①	09 ④	10 ①	11 ②	12 ①
13 ②	14 ③	15 ④	16 ③	17 ③	18 ②
19 ④	20 ②				

서술형 집중공략   p.119

21 (1) Who is (2) Why did she
22 (1) How fresh (2) Let's go
23 (1) Where is David (2) Don't throw trash
24 (1) When did you send him
(2) doesn't play computer games, does he
25 What → How / Let → Let's
26 (A) won't (B) Did[Didn't] (C) How (D) What

01 B에서 전화기가 있는 장소를 답하고 있으므로 질문에 Where가 와야 한다.
02 빈칸 뒤에 〈a+형용사+명사+주어+동사!〉가 이어지므로 감탄문을 만드는 What이 와야 한다.
03 시제가 과거이고 일반동사가 쓰인 긍정문이 앞에 나오므로 부정의 부가 의문문 didn't you가 와야 한다.
04 ⑤의 빈칸에는 '어느 것'이라는 뜻으로 정해진 범위 안의 대상에 대해 물을 때 쓰는 Which가 와야 한다. 나머지는 모두 Why를 쓴다.
05 ⑤의 빈칸 뒤에는 〈형용사+명사+주어+동사!〉가 이어지므로 What이, 나머지는 모두 뒤에 〈형용사+주어+동사!〉가 이어지므로 How가 와야 한다.
06 언제 런던을 방문했는지 묻고 있으므로 ④가 알맞다.
07 빈칸 뒤에 도움이 필요하냐는 말이 이어지고 있는 것으로 보아, 중국어를 할 수 있다는 긍정의 답변이 오는 것이 알맞다. A에서 조동사 can을 이용해 질문을 했으므로 Yes, I can.이 와야 한다.
08 빈칸 뒤에 그녀의 영화를 좋아한다는 말이 이어지는 것으로 보아, 그녀가 훌륭한 배우라는 긍정의 답변이 오는 것이 알맞다. be동사를 이용한 부정 의문문에 대한 긍정의 대답으로 Yes, she is.가 와야 한다.
09 ④ '~하지 마라'라는 뜻의 부정 명령문은 〈Don't[Do not]+동사원형〉의 형태로 쓴다.
10 의문문에서 '무엇', '무슨'이라는 뜻을 나타내고, 감탄문에도 쓰이는 What이 와야 한다.
11 의문문에서 '어떤', '얼마나 ~한'이라는 뜻을 나타내고, 감탄문에도 쓰이는 How가 와야 한다.
12 ①의 의문사 What은 '무엇'이라는 뜻으로 쓰인 반면, ②, ③,④,⑤의 What은 명사 앞에 쓰여 '무슨'이라는 뜻을 나타낸다.
13 ② 누가 초콜릿을 주었냐고 묻는 질문에 그것을 좋아한다

고 답하는 것은 자연스럽지 않다.

14 ③ 번지 점프를 하러 가자고 권유하는 표현에 긍정의 대답인 Yes라고 말한 뒤에 '~하지 말자'라는 뜻의 let's not이 이어지는 것은 자연스럽지 않다.

15 첫 번째 B에서 빈도를 나타내는 대답이 나오므로 첫 번째 빈칸에는 How often, 두 번째 B에서 이유를 나타내는 대답이 나오므로 두 번째 빈칸에는 Why가 와야 한다.

16 ③ 시계(it=this watch)가 멋지지 않냐고 묻는 시점이 현재이고 뒤에 형용사가 오므로 Isn't it으로 써야 한다.

17 ③ (a)에는 빈도를 묻는 (How) often, (b)에는 셀 수 없는 명사 앞에 쓰여 양을 묻는 (How) much, (c)와 (e)에는 셀 수 있는 명사 앞에 쓰여 수를 묻는 (How) many, (d)에는 길이나 기간을 묻는 (How) long이 올 수 있다. (How) tall은 키나 높이를 물을 때 쓴다.

18 ② 의문사가 문장에서 주어 역할을 하는 경우 3인칭 단수 취급하므로 wants가 되어야 한다.

19 (A) 뒤에 〈부사+주어+동사!〉가 이어지므로 감탄문을 만드는 How가 와야 한다.
(B) '~하지 마라'라는 뜻의 부정 명령문은 〈Don't[Do not]+동사원형〉의 형태로 쓴다.
(C) 명사 앞에서 '어느'라는 뜻으로 정해진 범위 안의 대상에 대해 물을 때 쓰는 Which가 와야 한다.

20 (c) 의문사가 있는 일반동사의 의문문은 〈의문사+do동사+주어+동사원형 ~?〉의 형태로 쓴다.
(d) 권유의 부정 명령문은 〈Let's not+동사원형〉의 형태로 쓴다.

21 (1) '누구'라는 뜻으로 사람에 대해 물을 때 쓰는 의문사 who를 이용한다. 의문사가 주어일 때는 〈의문사+동사 ~?〉의 형태로 쓴다.
(2) '왜'라는 뜻으로 원인이나 이유를 물을 때 쓰는 의문사 why를 이용한다. 의문사가 있는 일반동사의 과거시제 의문문은 〈의문사+did+주어+동사원형 ~?〉의 형태로 쓴다.

22 (1) how로 시작하는 감탄문은 〈How+형용사/부사+주어+동사!〉의 형태로 쓴다.
(2) 〈Why don't we ~?〉는 '우리 ~하지 않을래?'라는 뜻으로 제안할 때 쓰는 표현이며, 〈Let's+동사원형〉로 바꿔 쓸 수 있다.

23 (1) 의문사가 있는 be동사의 의문문은 〈의문사+be동사+주어 ~?〉의 형태로 쓴다.
(2) 부정 명령문은 〈Don't[Do not]+동사원형〉의 형태로 쓴다.

24 (1) 의문사가 있는 일반동사의 과거시제 의문문은 〈의문사+did+주어+동사원형 ~?〉의 형태로 쓴다.
(2) 부가 의문문은 평서문 뒤에 〈동사+주어?〉의 형태로 쓴다.

25 '얼마나 먼/멀리'라는 뜻으로 거리를 물을 때는 How far

를 쓴다. 권유의 명령문은 동사원형 앞에 Let's를 쓴다.

26 (A) 부가 의문문이므로 조동사 will의 부정형인 won't가 와야 한다.
(B) 의문문에 대한 대답으로 Yes, they did.가 이어지므로 Did 또는 Didn't가 와야 한다.
(C) 아주 좋았다고 답하는 것으로 보아 어땠는지를 물을 때 사용하는 의문사 How가 와야 한다.
(D) 빈칸 뒤에 〈형용사+명사+주어+동사!〉가 이어지므로 감탄문을 만드는 What이 와야 한다.

문법 정리 노트　　　p.120

① 의문사　　② 부정　　③ 긍정　　④ not
⑤ 동사원형　⑥ Don't[Do not]　　⑦ Let's
⑧ Let's not　⑨ What　　⑩ How

CHECK

1 O　**2** X, Be　**3** X, not go　**4** O　**5** X, isn't
6 X, What　**7** X, How much　**8** X, Why　**9** O

1 what으로 시작하는 감탄문은 〈What+a/an+형용사+명사(+주어+동사)!〉의 형태로 쓴다.

2 명령문은 동사원형으로 시작한다.

3 권유의 부정 명령문은 〈Let's not+동사원형〉의 형태로 쓴다.

4 B의 대답이 Yes, he did.이므로 A의 질문은 Did 또는 Didn't로 시작한다.

5 앞 문장이 긍정문일 때는 부정의 부가 의문문을 쓴다.

6 B에서 무엇을 하고 있는지 답하고 있으므로 질문에 What이 와야 한다.

7 셀 수 없는 명사(money) 앞에는 How much를 쓴다.

8 B에서 이유를 답하고 있으므로 질문에 Why가 와야 한다.

9 의문사가 주어일 때는 3인칭 단수 취급하며, 〈의문사+동사 ~?〉의 형태로 쓴다.

CHAPTER 10 문장의 형식

A **1** <u>He</u> <u>sings</u> well. X
　　주어　동사

2 Marie became a scientist.
　주어　　동사　　보어

3 The phone on the table rang. X
　주어　　　　　　　　동사

4 The dress in the shop is pretty.
　주어　　　　　　　동사 보어

5 We were playing in the backyard. X
　주어　　동사

6 This city is famous for its film festival.
　주어　동사　　　　보어

B **1** She will arrive, 1
2 is a high school student, 2
3 They are walking, 1
4 The leaves turn yellow, 2
5 I am usually nervous, 2
6 my parents moved to Boston, 1

POINT 02　2형식 - 감각동사+형용사　　p.123

A **1** soft　**2** good　**3** look like　**4** wonderful
B **1** sweet　**2** like a good　**3** terrible　**4** sick
C **1** taste sour　**2** felt hungry
3 sounds British　**4** smelled like medicine

POINT 03　3형식 / 4형식　　p.124

A **1** gave　**2** watch　**3** the book
B **1** I want a cheeseburger
2 teaches children math
3 He lent me $10
4 We saw Kevin
5 will show us her new car
C **1** made him a pie
2 He fixed my computer
3 tell me the way
4 She knows, famous people
5 gave us Christmas gifts

POINT 04　4형식 → 3형식
- 전치사 to를 쓰는 경우　　p.125

A **1** her a package
2 the story to you
3 gave me his bicycle
4 an umbrella to David
5 two glasses of water to us
6 will teach them Japanese

B **1** showed my picture to
2 wrote an email to
3 me the comic book
4 gave these tickets to us
5 send a report to our teacher

POINT 05　4형식 → 3형식
- 다른 전치사를 쓰는 경우　　p.126

A **1** for　**2** to　**3** for them　**4** got
B **1** fresh salad for him
2 a favor of you
3 buys flowers for his wife
C **1** made a doghouse for
2 cooks dinner for us
3 get some orange juice for you
4 bought, doughnuts for the kids

POINT 06　5형식
- 목적격 보어가 명사/형용사인 경우　　p.127

A **1** sad　**2** Diane an angel　**3** healthy
B **1** She found the book interesting.
2 The news made us angry.
3 He calls his daughter "sweetie."
C **1** found, easy　**2** left the door open
3 keep your uniform clean
4 made him a good player

POINT 07　5형식
- 목적격 보어가 to부정사인 경우　　p.128

A **1** to read　**2** to be　**3** to close
4 to stop　**5** to take care of
B **1** tell him to leave
2 want me to be confident
3 Luke allowed her to use
C **1** want me to call
2 expected them to come
3 ask Helen to lend
4 allowed us to stay

POINT 08　5형식 - 지각동사/사역동사　　p.129

A **1** shake[shaking]　**2** eat　**3** to be
4 stay　**5** knock[knocking]

B 1 made us clean 2 see the stars shine
　　3 She had them paint
　　4 help Mia write her report
　　5 I heard the students shout

C 1 felt, touch[touching] 2 let me wear
　　3 We watched, float[floating]
　　4 helped Maggie to become

내신 대비 **실전 TEST**　　pp.130-132

01 ③　02 ①　03 ②　04 ⑤　05 ②　06 ⑤
07 ④　08 ①　09 ②　10 ①　11 ④　12 ①
13 ③　14 ③　15 ⑤　16 ⑤　17 ③
18 ③, ④　　19 ①　20 ②

서술형 집중공략　　p.133

21 (1) Sam the ball (2) some bread for them
22 (1) felt the rain fall[falling] on his head
　(2) helped me (to) wash the dishes
23 (1) ordered Ned to stay silent
　(2) heard her shout[shouting] at people
24 (1) smells delicious (2) told us the big news
　(3) made her happy
25 (1) some cookies for Jeremy
　(2) a book to Sophia
26 (1) to read an English book
　(2) clean the bathroom
　(3) take care of her sister

01 동사 buy는 4형식 문장에서 3형식 문장으로 바꿀 때 간접목적어 앞에 전치사 for를 쓴다.

02 5형식 문장에서 지각동사 watch는 목적격 보어로 동사원형이나 현재분사를 쓴다.

03 5형식 문장에서 동사 expect는 목적격 보어로 to부정사를 쓴다.

04 ⑤ 동사 make는 4형식 문장에서 3형식 문장으로 바꿀 때 간접목적어 앞에 전치사 for를 쓴다. ①, ②, ③, ④는 모두 간접목적어 앞에 전치사 to를 쓴다.

05 ② 2형식 문장에서 감각동사 look 뒤에는 주격 보어로 형용사가 온다.

06 ⑤ 빈칸에는 감각동사와 같이 주격 보어로 형용사를 쓰는 동사가 와야 한다.

07 ④ 5형식 문장에서 동사 make 뒤에는 목적격 보어로 명사(구)나 형용사(구)가 올 수 있으며, '~하게 하다'라는 의미의 사역동사로 쓰일 경우에는 동사원형이 온다.

08 '~하게 하다', '~하도록 시키다'라는 의미를 지닌 사역동사 have, let은 목적격 보어로 동사원형을 쓴다.

09 5형식 문장에서 동사 keep은 목적격 보어로 형용사를 쓰며, want는 목적격 보어로 to부정사를 쓴다.

10 2형식 문장의 보어 자리에는 형용사가 와야 하며, 사역동사 let은 목적격 보어로 동사원형을 쓴다.

11 지각동사 see는 목적격 보어로 동사원형이나 현재분사를 쓴다. 동사 send는 4형식 문장에서 3형식 문장으로 바꿀 때 간접목적어 앞에 전치사 to를 쓴다.

12 동사 lend는 4형식 문장에서 3형식 문장으로 바꿀 때 간접목적어 앞에 전치사 to를 쓰며, 5형식 문장에서 동사 ask는 목적격 보어로 to부정사를 쓴다.

13 5형식 문장에서 목적격 보어 자리에 형용사와 동사원형을 쓸 수 있는 동사는 make이다.

14 ③ 동사 buy는 4형식 문장에서 3형식 문장으로 바꿀 때 간접목적어 앞에 전치사 for를 쓴다.

15 ⑤ 〈I can teach+간접목적어(you)+직접목적어(Spanish)〉 또는 〈I can teach+직접목적어(Spanish)+to+간접목적어(you)〉의 형태로 써야 한다.

16 ⑤ 지각동사 hear는 목적격 보어로 동사원형이나 현재분사를 쓴다.

17 ③은 〈주어+동사+간접목적어+직접목적어〉 형태의 4형식 문장인 반면, 나머지는 모두 〈주어+동사+목적어+목적격 보어〉 형태의 5형식 문장이다.

18 ③ 사역동사 have는 목적격 보어로 동사원형을 쓴다.
　④ 5형식 문장에서 동사 find는 목적격 보어로 형용사를 쓴다.

19 (A) 감각동사 taste는 주격 보어로 형용사를 쓴다.
　(B) 동사 ask는 4형식 문장에서 3형식 문장으로 바꿀 때 간접목적어 앞에 전치사 of를 쓴다.
　(C) 지각동사 see는 목적격 보어로 동사원형이나 현재분사를 쓴다.

20 (a) 2형식 문장에서 감각동사 look 뒤에 명사가 올 때는 전치사 like를 함께 쓴다.
　(c) 동사 make는 4형식 문장에서 3형식 문장으로 바꿀 때 간접목적어(my brothers) 앞에 전치사 for를 써야 한다.
　(d) 동사 give는 4형식 문장에서 3형식 문장으로 바꿀 때 간접목적어(me) 앞에 전치사 to를 써야 한다.

21 (1) 〈주어+동사+직접목적어+전치사+간접목적어〉 형태의 3형식 문장은 〈주어+동사+간접목적어+직접목적어〉 형태의 4형식 문장으로 바꿀 수 있다.
　(2) 동사 get은 4형식 문장에서 3형식 문장으로 바꿀 때 간접목적어 앞에 전치사 for를 쓴다.

22 (1) 주어진 두 문장은 〈주어+지각동사(feel)+목적어+목적격 보어(동사원형/현재분사)〉의 형태로 쓸 수 있다.
　(2) 주어진 두 문장은 〈주어+준사역동사(help)+목적어+목적격 보어(동사원형/to부정사)〉의 형태로 쓸 수 있다.

23 (1) 동사 order는 목적격 보어로 to부정사를 쓴다.

(2) 지각동사 hear는 목적격 보어로 동사원형이나 현재분사를 쓴다.

24 (1) 감각동사 smell은 주격 보어로 형용사를 쓴다.
(2) 4형식 문장에서 동사 tell은 〈주어+동사+간접목적어(us)+직접목적어(the big news)〉의 형태로 쓴다.
(3) 5형식 문장에서 동사 make는 〈주어+동사+목적어+목적격 보어(형용사)〉의 형태로 쓴다.

25 (1) 동사 buy는 4형식 문장에서 3형식 문장으로 바꿀 때 간접목적어 앞에 전치사 for를 쓴다.
(2) 동사 lend는 4형식 문장에서 3형식 문장으로 바꿀 때 간접목적어 앞에 전치사 to를 쓴다.

26 (1) 동사 want는 목적격 보어로 to부정사를 쓴다.
(2) 사역동사 have는 목적격 보어로 동사원형을 쓴다.
(3) 사역동사 make는 목적격 보어로 동사원형을 쓴다.

문법 정리 노트   p.134

① 형용사   ② 목적어   ③ 목적격 보어
④ 전치사   ⑤ to   ⑥ for   ⑦ of
⑧ to부정사   ⑨ 동사원형

CHECK

1 X, great   2 O   3 X, to   4 X, warm   5 O
6 O   7 X, carry

1 감각동사 sound는 주격 보어로 형용사를 쓴다.
2 동사 expect는 목적격 보어로 to부정사를 쓴다.
3 동사 give는 간접목적어 앞에 전치사 to를 쓴다.
4 동사 keep은 목적격 보어로 형용사를 쓴다.
5 동사 buy는 4형식 문장일 때 〈주어+동사+간접목적어+직접목적어〉의 형태로 쓴다.
6 지각동사 see는 목적격 보어로 동사원형이나 현재분사를 쓴다.
7 사역동사 let은 목적격 보어로 동사원형을 쓴다.

CHAPTER 11   to부정사와 동명사

POINT 01   to부정사의 명사적 용법 - 주어 역할   p.136

A 1 to travel   2 It, to go   3 To start, is

---

4 To jog along the river
5 It is not easy to learn

B 1 To become   2 It, to keep
3 To watch, is   4 It is, to open
5 It was difficult to understand

POINT 02   to부정사의 명사적 용법 - 보어/목적어 역할   p.137

A 1 to come   2 to become   3 to bake
4 to write

B 1 is to repair cars
2 don't want to be late
3 She needed to buy
4 promised not to tell

C 1 expect to win   2 is to play
3 decided not to join   4 plan is to read

POINT 03   to부정사의 명사적 용법 - 의문사+to부정사   p.138

A 1 what to do   2 when to go   3 how to drive
B 1 who to sit with
2 how to play the guitar
3 where to stay in London
4 when to wake up tomorrow
5 what to wear to the party
C 1 when to come   2 who(m) to invite
3 where to go   4 what to buy
5 how to use

POINT 04   to부정사의 형용사적 용법 - (대)명사 수식   p.139

A 1 to leave   2 money to spend   3 to help
4 important to say   5 to do
B 1 to talk   2 to use   3 to eat   4 to wear
C 1 a good way to stay healthy
2 anything interesting to do
3 has some homework to finish
4 many places to visit

POINT 05   to부정사의 부사적 용법 - 목적   p.140

A 1 to buy   2 to buy   3 in order to join

B 1 came early to help
2 drinks coffee to stay
3 ran in order to catch
4 do to be successful

C 1 to tell you
2 to swim with them
3 to pack her things
4 to share his ideas

POINT 06 to부정사의 부사적 용법
- 감정의 원인 / 결과 p.141

A 1 to read 2 too hot to drink
3 too tired to study

B 1 too hot to eat
2 lived to be
3 strong enough to lift
4 happy to get a message

C 1 sad to hear
2 too busy to have
3 grew up to become
4 old enough to watch

POINT 07 동명사 - 주어/보어 역할 p.142

A 1 Meeting 2 getting 3 Driving 4 listening
5 Reading 6 taking 7 Playing

B 1 Making a film takes
2 was helping others
3 Riding roller coasters scares
4 Drinking soda is not good
5 is getting up late in the morning

POINT 08 동명사 - 목적어 역할 p.143

A 1 walking 2 driving 3 to make
4 helping 5 visiting

B 1 playing soccer professionally
2 missing the train
3 trying to fix the computer

C 1 finished washing
2 Don't stop challenging
3 I'm good at drawing
4 We should avoid using

내신 대비 실전 TEST pp.144-146

01 ② 02 ④ 03 ① 04 ② 05 ② 06 ④
07 ③ 08 ⑤ 09 ④ 10 ④ 11 ② 12 ①
13 ③ 14 ① 15 ③ 16 ③ 17 ② 18 ⑤
19 ⑤ 20 ②

서술형 집중공략 p.147

21 (1) too expensive to buy
(2) It is, to climb high mountains
22 (1) playing the violin
(2) Riding a bike
23 anything to eat, to buy
24 (1) He was surprised to hear the noise.
(2) Do you mind opening the window?
25 (1) old enough to go hiking
(2) too young to take a diving class
26 (1) what to do
(2) someone helpful to guide

01 to부정사가 주어 역할을 하는 경우, 보통 주어 자리에 가주어 It을 쓰고 to부정사를 문장 뒤로 보낸다.
02 동사 avoid는 동명사를 목적어로 쓴다.
03 '어떻게 ~할지', '~하는 방법'의 뜻을 나타내기 위해 to부정사 앞에 how가 와야 한다.
04 〈보기〉와 ②의 동명사는 동사의 목적어로 쓰였다. ①은 주어, ③, ④는 보어, ⑤는 전치사의 목적어로 쓰였다.
05 동사 plan은 to부정사를 목적어로 쓴다. to부정사가 주어 역할을 하는 경우, 보통 주어 자리에 가주어 It을 쓰고 to부정사를 문장 뒤로 보낸다.
06 〈too+형용사/부사+to부정사〉는 '너무 ~해서 …할 수 없다'라는 뜻을 나타낸다.
07 동사 want는 to부정사를 목적어로, give up은 동명사를 목적어로 쓴다.
08 B가 길을 알려 주고 있으므로 '어떻게 ~할지', '~하는 방법'의 뜻을 나타내기 위해 to부정사 앞에 how가 와야 한다.
09 〈-thing / -one / -body+형용사+to부정사〉의 순서로 쓴다.
10 '…할 만큼 충분히 ~하다'는 〈형용사 / 부사+enough+to부정사〉로 쓸 수 있다.
11 ② 동사 enjoy는 동명사를 목적어로 쓴다.
12 ① 동사 plan은 to부정사를 목적어로 쓴다.
13 ③은 결과를 나타내는 부사적 용법의 to부정사이고, 나머지는 모두 (대)명사를 수식하는 형용사적 용법의 to부정사이다.
14 ①은 동사의 목적어로 쓰인 명사적 용법의 to부정사이고, 나머지는 모두 부사적 용법의 to부정사이다.

15 ③ 동사 quit은 동명사를 목적어로 쓴다.

16 ③ '(…해서) ~하다'라는 뜻으로 결과를 나타내는 부사적 용법의 to부정사가 되어야 한다.

17 ② 지각동사는 목적격 보어로 동사원형 또는 현재분사를 쓴다.

18 주어진 말을 배열하면 'I can't decide what to cook for dinner.'이므로 네 번째에 오는 단어는 what이다.

19 (A) 동사 mind는 동명사를 목적어로 쓴다.
(B) 문장의 주어 자리이므로 '~하는 것'이라는 뜻의 동명사를 쓴다.
(C) to부정사가 주어 역할을 하는 경우, 보통 주어 자리에 가주어 It을 쓰고 to부정사를 문장 뒤로 보낸다.

20 (b) 진주어 to lose weight를 대신하여 주어 자리에 가주어 It이 와야 한다.
(d) 전치사 in의 목적어로 동명사가 와야 한다.

21 (1) '…하기에는 너무 ~하다'라는 뜻의 〈too+형용사/부사+to부정사〉를 쓴다.
(2) to부정사가 주어 역할을 하는 경우 보통 주어 자리에 가주어 It을 쓰고 to부정사를 문장 뒤로 보낸다.

22 (1) 전치사 at의 뒤에 목적어 역할을 하는 동명사가 와야 한다.
(2) 주어 역할을 하는 동명사구를 쓴다.

23 A에서 anything을 수식하는 형용사적 용법의 to부정사를 쓴다. 이때 to부정사는 수식하는 (대)명사 뒤에 온다. B에서 '~하러'라는 뜻으로 목적을 나타내는 부사적 용법의 to부정사를 쓴다.

24 (1) 형용사(surprised) 뒤에 감정의 원인을 나타내는 부사적 용법의 to부정사를 쓴다.
(2) 동사 mind 뒤에 목적어 역할을 하는 동명사 opening을 쓴다.

25 (1) Emma는 산을 등반하기에 충분히 나이가 들었음을 〈형용사/부사+enough+to부정사〉를 이용해 나타낸다.
(2) Andy는 너무 어려서 다이빙 수업을 들을 수 없음을 〈too+형용사/부사+to부정사〉를 이용해 나타낸다.

26 (1) '무엇을 ~할지'의 뜻을 나타내기 위해 to부정사 앞에 what을 쓴다.
(2) 〈-thing/-one/-body+형용사+to부정사〉의 순서로 쓴다.

① to, 동사원형   ② 목적어   ③ 형용사
④ 목적   ⑤ too   ⑥ enough
⑦ 동사원형, -ing   ⑧ to부정사   ⑨ 동명사

CHECK

1 X, to introduce   **2** O   **3** X, asking   **4** O
5 X, deep enough to swim   **6** X, seeing
7 X, to dance

1 someone을 뒤에서 수식하여 '~하는', '~할'이라는 뜻을 나타내는 to부정사가 와야 한다.

2 형용사(lucky) 뒤에 to부정사를 써서 '~해서', '~하니'라는 뜻으로 감정의 원인을 나타낼 수 있다.

3 동사 keep은 동명사를 목적어로 쓴다.

4 〈too+형용사/부사+to부정사〉는 '너무 ~해서 …할 수 없다'라는 뜻을 나타낸다.

5 '…할 만큼 충분히 ~하다'라는 뜻을 나타낼 때는 〈형용사/부사+enough+to부정사〉 어순으로 쓴다.

6 전치사 of의 목적어 역할을 하는 동명사가 와야 한다.

7 동사 want는 to부정사를 목적어로 쓴다.

CHAPTER 12 접속사

POINT 01   등위접속사 and   p.150

A **1** beautiful   **2** ate   **3** sing a song   **4** take
B **1** gentle and smart
   2 Frank and Sarah
   3 and long, blond hair
C **1** and talked about them
   2 both Chinese and Japanese
   3 to buy a laptop and to travel to Australia

POINT 02   등위접속사 but   p.151

A **1** but   **2** but   **3** but   **4** and   **5** and
B **1** but he is not   **2** but I didn't get
   3 a quiet but fun   **4** but I don't like
C **1** but she didn't cry
   2 is simple but difficult

3 but I'll try again

4 a short but very touching speech

POINT 03 등위접속사 or p.152

A **1** or **2** either **3** but **4** or

B **1** William or Jack **2** either, or

3 or did she forget

4 by credit card or with cash

C **1** bring umbrellas or raincoats

2 is either Justine or Julia

3 go camping or stay at home

4 We can eat out or I can cook

POINT 04 등위접속사 so p.153

A **1** so **2** or **3** but

4 she went to bed early

B **1** ⓒ **2** ⓐ **3** ⓑ **4** ⓔ **5** ⓓ

C **1** He wasn't feeling well, so he didn't go to school.

2 I called her name, but she didn't look at me.

3 You can make an exchange or get a refund.

4 We went to the store, and we bought some batteries.

POINT 05 시간을 나타내는 접속사 when / while p.154

A **1** When you called me, I was sleeping.[I was sleeping when you called me.]

2 When Alice heard a strange sound, she felt scared.[Alice felt scared when she heard a strange sound.]

3 When David crossed the street, he saw the accident.[David saw the accident when he crossed the street.]

B **1** when I was **2** While he is walking

3 When they graduate **4** when she reads

5 While we were eating

POINT 06 시간을 나타내는 접속사 before / after p.155

A **1** after **2** when **3** Before **4** While

B **1** after you read

2 before he goes abroad

3 while we were talking

4 After they ate lunch

5 before it is too late

POINT 07 이유, 조건을 나타내는 접속사 because / if p.156

A **1** If **2** because **3** tell

B **1** ⓒ **2** ⓓ **3** ⓑ **4** ⓐ

C **1** If I get **2** because she didn't feel

3 If you are hungry

4 Because the film wasn't interesting

5 if they save enough money

POINT 08 명사절을 이끄는 접속사 that p.157

A **1** that **2** is that he **3** it

B **1** It is amazing that she became a comedian.

2 It is a secret that I broke the window.

3 It was unlucky that I forgot my wallet.

C **1** that the song is good

2 That I didn't invite him

3 that I didn't bring my phone

4 that she is a basketball player

내신 대비 실전 TEST pp.158-160

01 ①	02 ⑤	03 ②	04 ⑤	05 ②	06 ④
07 ③	08 ③	09 ⑤	10 ③	11 ④	12 ⑤
13 ②	14 ②	15 ④	16 ④	17 ⑤	18 ③
19 ④	20 ④				

서술형 집중공략 p.161

21 (1) if you feel sick (2) that we will win

22 (1) stayed in bed because

(2) had lunch before I came here

23 (1) but you didn't reply

(2) or I'll buy some at the bakery

(3) and I won the gold medal

24 (1) before (2) either, or (3) after

25 (1) If she is late, I'll be angry. [I'll be angry if she is late.]

(2) He has both a book and a laptop.

26 or → and / will come → comes

01 '~와'라는 뜻의 등위접속사 and가 와야 한다.

02 '~한다면'이라는 뜻으로 조건을 나타내는 종속접속사 If가 와야 한다.

03 앞의 내용과 반대되는 내용을 이어주는 등위접속사 but이 와야 한다.

04 첫 번째 빈칸에는 가주어 It에 대한 진주어인 명사절을 이끄는 접속사 that이, 두 번째 빈칸에는 목적어 역할을 하는 명사절을 이끄는 접속사 that이 와야 한다.

05 ②의 빈칸에는 '~할 때'라는 뜻의 when과 같이 시간을 나타내는 종속접속사가 들어가야 한다.

06 '~한 후에'라는 뜻의 종속접속사 after를 이용한다. 시간을 나타내는 접속사가 이끄는 절에서는 미래의 일이더라도 현재시제를 쓴다.

07 'A이거나 B'라는 뜻의 〈either A or B〉를 쓴다.

08 첫 번째 빈칸에는 '~하기 때문에'라는 뜻으로 이유를 나타내는 종속접속사 Because가, 두 번째 빈칸에는 '~한다면'이라는 뜻으로 조건을 나타내는 종속접속사 If가 와야 한다.

09 첫 번째 빈칸에는 목적어 역할을 하는 명사절을 이끄는 접속사 that이, 두 번째 빈칸에는 '또는'이라는 뜻의 등위접속사 or가 와야 한다.

10 첫 번째 빈칸에는 '~한 후에'라는 뜻의 종속접속사 after가, 두 번째 빈칸에는 '그리고'라는 뜻의 등위접속사 and가 와야 한다.

11 ④의 빈칸에는 앞뒤 내용의 시간적 순서상 '~한 후에'라는 뜻의 종속접속사 after가 오고, 나머지는 모두 명사절을 이끄는 접속사 that이 와야 한다.

12 ⑤ Jason과 Ann 둘 다를 초대하겠냐는 질문에, Yes라고 답한 후에 Jason만 초대하겠다고 말하는 것은 어색하다.

13 ① 'A와 B 둘 다'라는 뜻의 〈both A and B〉가 되어야 하므로 and로 써야 한다.
③ 접속사 앞뒤 내용의 시간적 순서상 '~하기 전에'라는 뜻의 종속접속사 before가 와야 한다.
④ 'A이거나 B'라는 뜻의 〈either A or B〉가 되어야 하므로 or로 써야 한다.
⑤ 문맥상 '또는'이라는 뜻의 등위접속사 or가 와야 한다.

14 빈칸 앞의 절은 원인을 나타내고 뒤의 절은 결과를 나타내므로 '그래서'라는 뜻의 등위접속사 so가 와야 한다.

15 내용의 시간적 순서상 불을 지핀 것이 텐트를 친 후의 일이므로 '~한 후에'라는 뜻의 종속접속사 After가 와야 한다.

16 ④ 'A이거나 B'라는 뜻의 〈either A or B〉를 쓰거나, 'A와 B 둘 다'라는 뜻의 〈both A and B〉를 쓴다.

17 ⑤ and는 문법적으로 대등한 단어, 구, 절을 연결하는 등위접속사이므로 went와 대등한 형태가 되도록 having을 have의 과거형 had로 고쳐야 한다.

18 (A) 가주어 It에 대한 진주어인 명사절을 이끄는 접속사 that이 와야 한다.
(B) 괄호 뒤에서 앞 내용에 대한 이유가 이어지고 있으므로 종속접속사 because가 와야 한다.
(C) or는 문법적으로 대등한 단어, 구, 절을 연결하는 등위접속사이므로 go와 대등한 형태가 되도록 watch가 와야 한다.

19 (b), (c) 조건이나 시간을 나타내는 접속사가 이끄는 절에서는 미래의 일이더라도 현재시제를 쓴다.
(d) 종속절에서 주절에 대한 이유가 나오므로 이유를 나타내는 종속접속사 because를 써야 한다.

20 ④의 that은 가주어 It에 대한 진주어인 명사절을 이끄는 접속사로 생략할 수 없는 반면, ①, ②, ③, ⑤의 that은 목적어 역할을 하는 명사절을 이끄는 접속사로 생략이 가능하다.

21 (1) '~한다면'이라는 뜻으로 조건을 나타내는 종속접속사 if를 이용한다.
(2) 목적어 역할을 하는 명사절을 이끄는 접속사 that을 이용한다.

22 (1) 이유를 나타내는 종속접속사 because가 I had a cold 앞에 와서 '감기에 걸렸기 때문에 침대에 누워 있었다.'라는 의미가 되도록 배열한다.
(2) '나는 여기에 오기 전에 점심을 먹었다.'라는 의미가 되어야 하므로 종속접속사 before가 I came here 앞에 오도록 배열한다.

23 (1) 문자 메시지를 보냈다는 내용은 상대가 답변을 하지 않았다는 내용과 어울리며, 두 문장은 서로 반대되는 내용이므로 등위접속사 but으로 연결한다.
(2) 쿠키를 구울 것이라는 내용은 빵집에서 살 것이라는 내용과 어울리며, 둘 중 하나를 선택하는 경우이므로 등위접속사 or로 연결한다.
(3) 마라톤을 뛰었다는 내용은 금메달을 땄다는 내용과 어울리며, 시간의 순서를 나타내는 '그리고'라는 뜻의 등위접속사 and로 연결한다.

24 (1) 개를 산책시키기 전에 발레 수업을 받으므로 종속접속사 before를 쓴다.
(2) 3시부터는 요일에 따라 바이올린을 연습하거나 책을 읽으므로 〈either A or B〉를 쓴다.
(3) TV 시청 후에 일기를 쓰므로 종속접속사 after를 쓴다.

25 (1) 조건을 나타내는 종속접속사 if를 이용한다. 조건을 나타내는 접속사가 이끄는 절에서는 미래의 일이더라도 현재시제를 쓴다.
(2) 'A와B 둘 다'라는 뜻의 〈both A and B〉를 쓴다.

26 조깅을 하러 갔다는 내용과 카페에서 간식을 먹었다는 내용을 '그리고'라는 뜻의 등위접속사 and로 연결해야 한다. 조건을 나타내는 접속사가 이끄는 절에서는 미래의 일이

더라도 현재시제를 써야 하므로 will come을 comes로 고친다.

문법 정리 노트 p.162

① but ② both ③ either ④ when
⑤ ~하기 전에 ⑥ if ⑦ it

CHECK

1 X, watched 2 X, or 2 X, (to) drink 4 O
5 O 6 X, snows 7 X, that

1 and는 문법적으로 대등한 단어, 구, 절을 연결하는 등위접속사이므로 과거형 watched를 써야 한다.
2 'A이거나 B'라는 뜻의 〈either A or B〉를 쓴다.
3 or는 문법적으로 대등한 단어, 구, 절을 연결하는 등위접속사이므로 (to) drink를 써야 한다.
4 that절이 주어 역할을 하는 경우, 보통 주어 자리에 가주어 it을 쓰고 that절을 뒤로 보낸다.
5 접속사 when은 '~할 때'라는 뜻이다.
6 조건을 나타내는 접속사가 이끄는 절에서는 미래의 일이더라도 현재시제를 쓴다.
7 가주어 It에 대한 진주어인 명사절을 이끄는 접속사 that을 써야 한다.

CHAPTER 13 전치사

POINT 01 시간의 전치사 in / on / at p.164

A 1 August 7 2 the morning 3 November
B 1 in 2 at 3 on 4 in 5 at 6 on
C 1 in 2 at 3 on 4 at 5 in 6 on

POINT 02 시간의 전치사 around / before / after / for / during / until / by p.165

A 1 around 2 during 3 after 4 for 5 until
B 1 before shopping
2 for two hours
3 by next Wednesday
4 around three on Monday

POINT 03 장소·위치의 전치사 in / on / at p.166

A 1 Canada 2 my room 3 the door
B 1 on 2 at 3 in 4 at 5 in 6 on
C 1 in your pocket
2 on this wall
3 at the bus stop
4 on the ground
5 in the world

POINT 04 장소·위치의 전치사 near / over / under / behind / to p.167

A 1 under 2 behind 3 over 4 near 5 to
B 1 behind that bus
2 near our store
3 over the city
4 under the tree

POINT 05 장소·위치의 전치사 in front of / next to / across from / between A and B p.168

A 1 in front of 2 next to
3 between, and 4 across from
B 1 next to their classroom
2 in front of the mall
3 across from the beach
C 1 He left a box in front of my door.
2 There is a library across from the museum.
3 We'll plant a tree between the swings and the slide.

POINT 06 기타 전치사 for / with / by / about / from A to B p.169

A 1 by 2 about 3 with 4 for 5 from, to
B 1 about your day
2 for my mistake
3 from March to May
4 with our grandparents
5 by exercising regularly

01 오전(morning)을 나타낼 때는 in이 와야 한다.

02 특정한 날(Christmas)을 나타낼 때는 on이 와야 한다.

03 하루의 때(night)를 나타낼 때는 전치사 at이 와야 한다.

04 ④의 to는 동사 decided의 목적어로 쓰인 to부정사인 반면, 나머지는 모두 전치사 to로 쓰였다.

05 첫 번째 빈칸에는 교통·통신 수단 앞에서 '~으로'라는 뜻을 나타내는 전치사 by가, 두 번째 빈칸에는 'A부터 B까지'를 뜻하는 전치사 from A to B의 from이 와야 한다.

06 첫 번째 빈칸에는 '~ 전에'를 뜻하는 전치사 before가, 두 번째 빈칸에는 비교적 넓은 장소를 나타낼 때 쓰는 전치사 in이 와야 한다.

07 ③의 빈칸에는 비교적 좁은 장소나 하나의 지점을 나타내는 전치사 at이, 나머지는 모두 접촉한 상태를 나타내는 전치사 on이 와야 한다.

08 ④의 빈칸에는 near(~ 근처에), in front of(~ 앞에), behind(~ 뒤에) 등 위치 관계를 나타내는 전치사를 쓸 수 있는 반면, 나머지는 모두 '~로'라는 뜻으로 목적지를 나타내는 전치사 to가 와야 한다.

09 첫 번째 빈칸에는 '~ 동안'이라는 뜻으로 구체적인 기간을 나타내는 전치사 for가, 두 번째 빈칸에는 '~을 위해'라는 뜻으로 목적을 나타내는 전치사 for가 와야 한다.

10 첫 번째 빈칸에는 '~로'라는 뜻으로 목적지를 나타내는 전치사 to가, 두 번째 빈칸에는 '~ 옆에'라는 뜻을 나타내는 전치사 next to의 to가 와야 한다.

11 ⑤ 전치사 by는 '~까지는'이라는 뜻으로 동작이 완료되는 기한을 나타내고, after는 '~ 후에'라는 뜻이다.

12 '~ 옆에'라는 뜻으로 전치사 next to가 와야 한다.

13 '~까지'라는 뜻으로 동작이 지속되는 기간을 나타내는 전치사 until이 와야 한다.

14 ② '~에 대하여'라는 뜻의 전치사 about은 주제를 나타내는 명사(구) 앞에 쓴다.

15 ② 요일 앞에는 전치사 on을 써야 한다.

16 ② beside는 그 자체로 '~ 옆에'라는 뜻을 나타내는 전치사이므로 to와 함께 쓸 수 없다. 따라서 beside를 next로 고쳐야 한다.

17 ⑤ '~ 동안'이라는 뜻으로 숫자를 포함하는 구체적인 기간 앞에는 전치사 for를 써야 한다.

18 ① '~ 앞에'라는 뜻으로 전치사 in front of를 써야 한다.
　 ② '~ 무렵에'라는 뜻으로 전치사 around를 써야 한다.
　 ③ '~ 맞은편에'라는 뜻으로 전치사 across from을 써야 한다.
　 ④ 'A와 B 사이에'라는 뜻으로 전치사 between A and B를 써야 한다.

19 (A) '~ 위에'라는 뜻으로 표면에 접촉해 있지 않은 상태를 나타내는 전치사 over를 쓴다.
　 (B) 'A부터 B까지'라는 뜻으로 전치사 from A to B를 쓴다.
　 (C) '~에서'라는 뜻으로 한 지점을 나타내는 전치사 at을 쓴다.

20 ② New York과 같은 도시명 앞에는 전치사 in을 써야 한다.
　 ⑤ '~ 동안'이라는 뜻으로 숫자를 포함하는 구체적인 기간 앞에는 전치사 for를 써야 한다.

21 (1) '~ 무렵에'라는 뜻으로 전치사 around를 쓴다.
　 (2) '~와 함께'라는 뜻으로 동반을 나타내는 전치사 with를 쓴다.
　 (3) '~ 동안'이라는 뜻으로 특정한 기간을 나타내는 명사(구) 앞에는 전치사 during을 쓴다.

22 '~까지는'이라는 뜻으로 동작이 완료되는 기한을 나타내는 전치사 by를 쓴다.

23 (1) '~에 대하여'라는 뜻의 전치사 about을 주제를 나타내는 명사 a documentary 앞에 쓴다.
　 (2) 장난감 가게가 공원 맞은편에 있다고 했으므로 '~ 맞은편에'라는 뜻의 전치사 across from을 the park 앞에 쓴다.

24 (1) 'A와 B 사이에'라는 뜻으로 전치사 between A and B를 쓴다.
　 (2) '~ 앞에'라는 뜻으로 전치사 in front of를 쓴다.

25 (1) Dan은 정오에 도서관에 갈 예정이므로 구체적인 시각이나 하루의 때를 나타내는 전치사 at을 쓴다.
　 (2) Dan은 1시부터 3시까지 두 시간 동안 테니스를 칠 예정이므로 숫자를 포함하는 구체적인 기간을 나타내는 전치사 for를 쓴다.
　 (3) Dan은 4시부터 6시까지 친구들과 있을 예정이므로 'A부터 B까지'라는 뜻의 전치사 from A to B를 쓴다.

26 날짜 앞에는 전치사 on을, '~ 동안'이라는 뜻으로 숫자를 포함하는 구체적인 기간을 나타낼 때는 전치사 for를 써야 한다. 교통·통신 수단 앞에는 전치사 by를 써야 한다.

1 '~ 동안'이라는 뜻으로 숫자를 포함하는 구체적인 기간 앞에는 전치사 for를 쓴다.

2 월 앞에는 전치사 in을 쓴다.

3 '~까지는'이라는 뜻으로 동작이 완료되는 기한을 나타내는 전치사 by를 쓴다.

4 '~에서'라는 뜻으로 한 지점을 나타내는 전치사 at을 쓴다.

5 '~ 위에'라는 뜻으로 표면에 접촉해 있지 않은 상태를 나타내는 전치사 over를 쓴다.

6 '~ 앞에'라는 뜻으로 전치사 in front of를 쓴다.

7 교통·통신 수단 앞에는 전치사 by를 쓴다.

8 '~ 때문에'라는 뜻으로 이유를 나타내는 전치사 for를 쓴다.

01 last weekend로 보아 과거의 일을 나타내므로 catch의 과거형 caught가 와야 한다.

02 '…만큼 ~하지 않은/않게'라는 뜻을 나타내는 비교 표현 〈not+as[so]+형용사/부사의 원급+as〉로 as가 와야 한다.

03 첫 번째 빈칸에는 'A와 B 둘 다'라는 뜻을 나타내는 〈both A and B〉의 and가, 두 번째 빈칸에는 '…해라, 그러면 ~할 것이다'라는 뜻을 나타내는 〈명령문+and ~〉의 and가 와야 한다.

04 내가 Stephen의 뒤에 서 있다는 것은 Stephen이 내 앞에 서 있다는 것이므로 '~ 앞에'라는 뜻의 전치사 in front of를 쓴다.

05 주어가 3인칭 단수(he)이고 과거의 일이므로, A에 대한 대답으로 부정의 경우 No, he wasn't.가 와야 한다.

06 B의 대답에서 회사에 가는 방법을 말하고 있으므로 '어떻게'라는 뜻으로 수단, 방법 등을 물을 때 쓰는 의문사 How가 와야 한다.

07 능력·가능(~할 수 있다)을 나타내는 can은 be able to로 바꾸어 쓸 수 있다. be able to의 의문문은 〈be동사+주어+able to+동사원형 ~?〉으로 쓴다.

08 '~임이 틀림없다'라는 의미의 강한 추측을 나타낼 때는 must를 쓴다.

09 시제가 과거이고 일반동사가 쓰인 긍정문이 앞에 나오므로 부정의 부가 의문문 didn't you가 와야 한다.

10 〈보기〉와 ④는 (대)명사를 수식하는 형용사적 용법의 to부정사이다. ①은 목적을 나타내는 부사적 용법, ②는 진주어로 쓰인 명사적 용법, ③은 목적어로 쓰인 명사적 용법, ⑤는 감정의 원인을 나타내는 부사적 용법의 to부정사이다.

11 셀 수 없는 명사의 수량은 〈수량+단위 명사+of+셀 수 없는 명사〉의 형태로 나타내며, 복수형은 단위 명사에 -(e)s를 붙인다.

12 ⑤ foot의 복수형은 feet이다.

13 주어가 3인칭 단수(She)이므로 현재형 부정문은 〈주어+doesn't[does not]+동사원형〉의 형태로 쓴다.

14 과거진행형의 의문문은 〈be동사의 과거형+주어+v-ing ~?〉의 형태로 쓴다.

15 일반동사의 과거형 의문문은 〈Did+주어+동사원형 ~?〉의 형태로 쓴다.

16 감탄문은 〈What+a/an+형용사+명사(+주어+동사)!〉 또는 〈How+형용사/부사+주어+동사!〉의 형태로 쓴다.

17 ② 사역동사 make는 목적격 보어로 동사원형을 쓰므로 to cry는 cry가 되어야 한다.

18 빈도부사 never는 조동사 뒤, 일반동사 앞에 쓴다.

19 be going to의 부정문은 〈주어+be동사+not+going to+동사원형〉으로 쓴다.

20 ③ 동사 finish는 동명사를 목적어로 쓴다.

21 첫 번째 빈칸에는 뒤에 복수명사가 있으므로 지시형용사 These 또는 Those가, 두 번째 빈칸에는 앞에 나온 apples와 같은 종류의 불특정한 것을 나타내는 부정대명사 ones가 와야 한다.

22 첫 번째 빈칸에는 뒤에 than이 쓰인 것으로 보아 비교급 easier가, 두 번째 빈칸에는 '가장 ~한'이라는 뜻을 나타내

는 최상급 the easiest가 와야 한다.

23 전치사 about 뒤에 목적어 역할을 하는 동명사를 쓴다.

24 '얼마나 큰'이라는 뜻으로 키를 물을 때는 how tall을 쓴다. 의문사가 있는 be동사의 의문문은 〈의문사＋be동사＋주어 ~?〉의 형태로 쓴다. where는 '어디서', '어디에'라는 뜻으로 장소, 위치 등을 물을 때 쓴다. 의문사가 있는 일반동사의 의문문은 〈의문사＋do동사＋주어＋동사원형 ~?〉의 형태로 쓴다.

25 ④ 'A부터 B까지'를 뜻하는 전치사 from A to B를 써야 한다.
⑤ '가장 ~한 … 중의 하나'라는 의미는 〈one of the ＋최상급＋복수명사〉의 형태로 나타내므로 countries가 되어야 한다.

26 동사 enjoy와 consider는 동명사를 목적어로 쓰고, decide와 plan은 to부정사를 목적어로 쓴다.

01 가주어 It에 대한 진주어인 명사절을 이끄는 접속사 that이 와야 한다.

02 3형식 문장에서 간접목적어(me) 앞에 전치사 to를 쓰는 동사는 give이다. 나머지 동사는 모두 간접목적어 앞에 전치사 for를 쓴다.

03 조건을 나타내는 접속사가 이끄는 절에서는 미래의 일이더라도 현재시제를 쓰며 주어가 3인칭 단수이므로 comes가 와야 한다.

04 '악기를 연주하다'라는 의미를 나타낼 때는 악기의 이름 앞에 정관사 the를 쓴다.

05 〈by＋교통/통신수단〉을 나타낼 때는 명사 앞에 관사를 쓰지 않는다.

06 '~마다(= per)'의 의미를 나타낼 때는 명사 앞에 부정관사 a를 쓴다.

07 ③ 동사 plan은 to부정사를 목적어로 쓴다.

08 '누구'라는 뜻으로 사람에 대해 물을 때 쓰는 의문사 who를 이용한다. 의문사가 주어일 때는 〈의문사＋동사 ~?〉의 형태로 쓴다.

09 last month로 보아 과거시제를 써야 하므로 첫 번째 빈칸에는 didn't walk가, 두 번째 빈칸에는 뒤에 현재의 일상적인 습관을 나타내는 these days가 있고 주어가 3인칭 단수(he)이므로 walks가 와야 한다.

10 첫 번째 빈칸에는 뒤에 복수명사가 있으므로 지시형용사 these가, 두 번째 빈칸에는 앞에 나온 sneakers와 같은 종류의 불특정한 것을 나타내는 부정대명사 ones가 와야 한다.

11 첫 번째 빈칸에는 '너의 것'이라는 의미의 소유대명사 yours가, 두 번째 빈칸에는 뒤에 있는 명사 new bike를 수식하는 소유격 my가 와야 한다.

12 현재의 일상적인 행동을 나타내며, 주어가 3인칭 단수(my mother, my father)이므로 동사는 3인칭 단수 현재형을 쓴다.

13 권유의 명령문 〈Let's＋동사원형 ~〉은 '우리 ~하지 않을래?'라는 뜻으로 제안할 때 쓰는 표현 〈Why don't we ~?〉로 바꾸어 쓸 수 있다.

14 money는 셀 수 없는 명사이므로 앞에서 '거의 없는'이라는 뜻을 나타내는 수량 형용사 little을 쓴다. 셀 수 있는 명사 coin의 복수형 앞에서 '약간의'라는 뜻을 나타내는 수량 형용사 a few를 쓴다.

15 주어가 3인칭 단수(She)이므로 〈is going to＋동사원형〉으로 쓴다.

16 주어가 3인칭 단수(Paul)이므로 〈has to＋동사원형〉으로 쓴다.

17 〈보기〉와 ④의 must는 '~임이 틀림없다'라는 강한 추측의 의미인 반면, 나머지는 모두 '~해야 한다'라는 의무의 의미이다.

18 이어지는 대답에서 시각을 말하고 있으므로 첫 번째 빈칸에는 What time을 쓴다. 이어지는 대답에서 빈도를 말하고 있으므로 두 번째 빈칸에는 How often을 쓴다.

19 첫 번째 빈칸에는 'A이거나 B'라는 뜻을 나타내는 〈either A or B〉의 or가, 두 번째 빈칸에는 '…해라, 그러지 않으면 ~할 것이다'라는 뜻을 나타내는 〈명령문＋or ~〉의 or가 와야 한다.

20 첫 번째 빈칸에는 진주어 to eat 이하를 대신하는 가주어 It이, 두 번째 빈칸에는 시간을 나타내는 비인칭 주어 It이 와야 한다.

21 동사 looks 뒤에 주어의 상태나 성질을 보충 설명해 주는 주격 보어로 형용사를 써야 하므로 happily를 happy로 고쳐야 한다.

22 감탄문은 〈What＋a/an＋형용사＋명사(＋주어＋동사)!〉 또는 〈How＋형용사/부사＋주어＋동사!〉의 형태로 쓴다. 복수명사 dolls가 있으므로 빈칸에는 What beautiful dolls가 알맞다.

23 ②의 cutting은 현재진행형 〈be동사+v-ing〉의 현재분사이고 나머지는 모두 동명사이다.

24 이유를 나타내는 종속절 앞에 접속사 because를 쓴다. 종속절이 주절의 앞에 올 때는 종속절 끝에 콤마를 쓴다.

25 ① 지각동사 hear는 목적격 보어로 동사원형이나 현재분사를 쓰므로 knocks는 knock 또는 knocking이 되어야 한다.

26 (c) '어떻게 ~할지', '~하는 방법'의 뜻을 나타내려면 how 뒤에 to부정사가 와야 한다.

(d) -thing, -one, -body로 끝나는 대명사를 형용사와 to부정사가 함께 수식하는 경우에는 〈-thing / -one / -body+형용사+to부정사〉의 순서로 쓴다.

27 (1) Jake가 Tom보다 체중이 많이 나가므로 형용사 heavy의 비교급을 써서 heavier than으로 나타낸다.

(2) Tom은 Steve보다 체중이 적게 나가므로 형용사 light의 비교급을 써서 lighter than으로 나타낸다.

(3) Steve가 셋 중에서 가장 체중이 많이 나가므로 형용사 heavy의 최상급을 써서 the heaviest로 나타낸다.

문제로 **마**스터하는 **중**학 영문법

문마중

LEVEL
1

Workbook
정답 및 해설

CHAPTER 01 기초 문법

POINT 01 영어의 8품사 p.2

A 1 ⓒ 2 ⓔ 3 ⓑ 4 ⓕ 5 ⓐ 6 ⓖ 7 ⓗ 8 ⓓ

B 1 phone 2 hard 3 takes 4 under 5 and

POINT 02 문장 성분 p.2

A 1 ⓓ 2 ⓐ 3 ⓔ 4 ⓑ 5 ⓒ

B 1 거북이는 느리게 걷는다.
2 그 소년은 축구를 한다.
3 그 식당은 아주 유명해졌다.
4 저기 있는 건물은 박물관이다.

POINT 03 구와 절 p.3

A 1 구 2 절 3 구 4 구 5 절
B 1 절 2 구 3 절 4 구 5 절

CHAPTER 02 인칭대명사와 be동사

POINT 01 인칭대명사와 be동사의 현재형 p.4

A 1 are 2 is 3 am 4 are 5 is
B 1 He's 2 We're 3 It's 4 You're 5 I'm
C 1 They're 2 I am 3 She is

POINT 02 be동사의 과거형 p.5

A 1 was 2 were 3 was 4 were
B 1 am 2 were 3 was 4 are
C 1 was 2 They were 3 He was 4 I were

POINT 03 be동사의 부정문 p.6

A 1 are not 2 isn't 3 weren't 4 are not
B 1 wasn't 2 I'm not 3 He's not[He isn't]
4 They're not[They aren't]
C 1 We are not 2 I am not
3 The restaurant is not
4 My parents were not

POINT 04 be동사의 의문문 p.7

A 1 Are you 2 Was it 3 Am I 4 Is he
5 Were they
B 1 Is she 2 they are 3 Was he 4 I'm not
5 we were

POINT 05 There is/are ~ p.8

A 1 is 2 were 3 There was not
4 Are, aren't
B 1 There isn't 2 There were
3 Is there a bank
C 1 Are there people at the beach?
2 There was a special gift for everyone.
3 There is not a window in this room.

POINT 06 인칭대명사의 격 - 주격/소유격/목적격/소유대명사 p.9

A 1 Her 2 theirs 3 You 4 us 5 His
6 yours 7 me 8 its
B 1 We, their 2 Our, Its 3 His, hers
4 mine, my 5 Anne's, them

REVIEW TEST pp.10-11

01 ② 02 ④ 03 ④ 04 were 05 wasn't
06 Are 07 ② 08 ① 09 It, Its, it 10 ①
11 Are you interested in sports?
12 He was not a famous actor.
13 ③ 14 ⑤ 15 ② 16 is, is 17 is, He
18 Are, I'm not

01 주어가 2인칭 단수이고 현재의 일이므로 Are를 써야 한다.

02 대답하는 사람의 입장에서 you를 받는 주격 대명사는 수에 따라 I 또는 we이며, 부정의 대답이므로 I wasn't 또는 we weren't를 써야 한다.

03 첫 번째 빈칸에는 주어 My uncle에 대한 be동사 is가 와야 하고, 두 번째 빈칸에는 명사 books를 수식하는

My uncle의 소유격 his가 와야 한다.

04 〈There is/are+명사〉에서 be동사 뒤의 명사가 rabbits 인 복수명사이고 과거의 일이므로 동사는 were를 써야 한다.

05 주어가 3인칭 단수이고 과거의 일이므로 be동사의 부정 형으로 wasn't를 써야 한다.

06 주어가 3인칭 복수이고 현재의 일이므로 Are를 써야 한다.

07 〈보기〉와 ①,③,④,⑤의 her는 소유격이고, ②의 her는 목 적격이다.

08 〈보기〉와 ②,③,④,⑤의 his는 소유대명사이고, ①의 His 는 소유격이다.

09 첫 번째 빈칸에는 앞의 a bag을 대신하는 주격 대명사 It 을 쓴다. 두 번째 빈칸에는 '그것의'라는 의미로 pockets 를 수식하는 소유격 Its를 쓴다. 세 번째 빈칸에는 동사 use의 목적어로 앞의 a bag을 받는 3인칭 단수 목적격 인 it을 쓴다.

10 ①의 is는 '~이다'의 의미이고, ②,③,④,⑤의 be동사는 모 두 '(~에) 있다'의 의미이다.

11 be동사의 의문문은 〈be동사+주어 ~?〉의 어순이 되어야 알맞다.

12 be동사의 부정문은 be동사 뒤에 not을 쓴다.

13 주어는 '그'를 의미하는 3인칭 단수 주격 대명사 He가 와 야 한다. 고유명사의 소유격은 명사에 's를 붙여서 쓰므로 brother 앞에 Sam's가 와야 한다.

14 ⑤ 주어가 3인칭 복수인 they이므로 be동사는 Are가 와 야 한다.

15 ② '너의 것'이라는 의미의 소유대명사 yours가 와야 한 다.

16 주어가 3인칭 단수이므로 두 빈칸에 모두 is를 쓴다.

17 주어가 3인칭 단수이므로 첫 번째 빈칸에는 is를 쓴다. 두 번째 빈칸에는 앞의 Mr. Brown을 받는 주격 대명사 He 를 쓴다.

18 주어가 2인칭 단수이므로 첫 번째 빈칸에는 Are를 쓴다. Ping은 중국 출신이므로, 부정의 대답으로 No, I'm not. 이 와야 한다.

CHAPTER 03 일반동사

A 1 I love the new movie.
 2 You speak French fluently.
 3 We play basketball on weekends.
 4 You and your sister walk to school.
 5 Daniel and I work at a restaurant.
B 1 read　2 cook　3 exercise　4 meet
 5 listen

A 1 X, speaks　2 O　3 O　4 X, want　5 O
 6 X, visits　7 X, go
B 1 shines　2 study　3 cleans　4 live
 5 opens　6 meet

A 1 worries　2 has　3 dresses　4 sells
 5 washes　6 does　7 fixes　8 teaches
B 1 studies　2 has　3 watches　4 goes
 5 finishes

A 1 lived　2 cleaned　3 tried　4 baked
 5 dropped　6 carried　7 enjoyed
B 1 closed　2 planned　3 cried　4 helped
 5 studied　6 received

A 1 lost　2 had　3 bought　4 found　5 built
 6 paid　7 met　8 sent
B 1 got　2 left　3 ate　4 came　5 made

A 1 O　2 X, cut　3 O　4 X, put　5 X, hit　6 O
 7 X, read　8 O
B 1 shut　2 put　3 set　4 cut　5 hit

A 1 don't work　2 doesn't　3 don't　4 look
B 1 doesn't know　2 don't agree
 3 doesn't drink　4 don't play
C 1 She doesn't enjoy　2 They don't live

3 He doesn't wear

POINT 08   일반동사의 과거형 부정문   p.19

A 1 didn't believe   2 like   3 didn't   4 sleep
B 1 didn't text   2 didn't join   3 didn't buy
C 1 I didn't feel   2 He didn't return
   3 We didn't take   4 They didn't eat

POINT 09   일반동사의 현재형 의문문   p.20

A 1 you have   2 run   3 Do   4 does
B 1 Do you know   2 Does Taylor work
   3 Do they play
C 1 Does she speak   2 Do they need, don't
   3 Does, start, it doesn't   4 Do you eat, I do

POINT 10   일반동사의 과거형 의문문   p.21

A 1 Does   2 Did   3 Do   4 Did
B 1 Did Roy paint   2 Did he finish
   3 Did they open
C 1 Did you hear, I did
   2 Did she check, she didn't
   3 Did they solve, they did

REVIEW TEST   pp.22-23

01 ③   02 ②   03 ④   04 doesn't watch
05 Did you buy   06 ③   07 ①   08 ③   09 ②
10 She doesn't eat onions.   11 Does Jack keep a diary?   12 ④   13 ③   14 ⑤
15 Jessie didn't[did not] see her aunt this morning.   16 Did Robert send an email?

01 B의 대답으로 보아 A에는 일반동사의 현재형 의문문이 와야 하고 주어가 3인칭 단수(Nick)이므로 주어 앞에 Does를 쓴다.

02 주어가 2인칭(you)이므로 일반동사의 과거형 의문문에 대한 대답은 Yes, I/we did. 또는 No, I/we didn't.이다.

03 work와 drive의 3인칭 단수 현재형은 각각 works, drives이다.

04 주어가 3인칭 단수(Andy)이므로 현재형 부정문은 〈주어+doesn't+동사원형〉의 형태로 쓴다.

05 일반동사의 과거형 의문문은 〈Did+주어+동사원형 ~?〉

06 ③에서 last year는 과거를 나타내는 표현이므로 move의 과거형 moved를 써야 한다.

07 ①은 3인칭 단수(your sister)를 주어로 하는 일반동사의 현재형 의문문이므로 주어 앞에 Does를 써야 한다.

08 일반동사의 현재형 의문문 Does he ~?에 대한 대답은 Yes, he does.나 No, he doesn't.가 자연스러운데, No, he didn't.라고 과거형으로 대답하는 것은 어색하다.

09 대답의 주어가 he이고 과거형 did가 왔으므로 질문은 일반동사의 과거형 의문문 〈Did+he+동사원형 ~?〉이 알맞다.

10 주어가 3인칭 단수(She)인 현재형 부정문은 〈주어+doesn't+동사원형〉의 형태로 쓴다.

11 주어가 3인칭 단수(Jack)인 일반동사의 현재형 의문문은 〈Does+주어+동사원형 ~?〉의 형태로 쓴다.

12 ① 주어가 3인칭 단수(Ann)인 일반동사의 현재형 부정문이므로 동사원형 앞에 doesn't를 써야 한다. ② leave의 과거형은 left이다. ③, ⑤ 일반동사의 의문문이므로 주어 뒤에 각각 동사원형 read, open을 써야 한다.

13 ① 3인칭 단수(she)를 주어로 하는 일반동사의 현재형 의문문이므로 주어 앞에 Does를 써야 한다. ② last night는 과거를 나타내는 표현이므로 go의 과거형 went를 써야 한다. ④ cut의 과거형은 cut이다. ⑤ 주어가 1인칭이므로 동사원형 carry를 써야 한다.

14 주어가 3인칭 단수(your brother)인 일반동사의 현재형 의문문은 〈Does+주어+동사원형 ~?〉의 형태로 쓴다.

15 일반동사의 과거형 부정문은 〈주어+didn't+동사원형〉의 형태로 쓴다.

16 일반동사의 과거형 의문문은 〈Did+주어+동사원형 ~?〉의 형태로 쓴다.

CHAPTER 04 명사와 관사

POINT 01   셀 수 있는 명사 - 규칙 변화 I   p.24

A 1 balls   2 potatoes   3 boxes   4 dishes
   5 beaches   6 houses   7 photos   8 classes
   9 roses   10 chairs   11 windows
   12 churches   13 wishes   14 buildings
   15 foxes   16 pianos   17 dresses

18 sandwiches

B 1 maps 2 Tomatoes 3 cookies 4 buses
5 trees 6 boxes 7 clubs 8 peaches
9 brushes 10 glasses 11 flowers

POINT 02 셀 수 있는 명사 - 규칙 변화 II p.25

A 1 stories 2 wolves 3 holidays 4 guys
5 elves 6 berries 7 ladies 8 lives
9 knives 10 cities 11 enemies
12 donkeys 13 leaves 14 roofs
15 bodies 16 journeys 17 wives
18 companies

B 1 boys 2 thieves 3 families 4 days
5 activities 6 cities 7 keys 8 chefs
9 shelves, toys 10 leaves 11 countries

POINT 03 셀 수 있는 명사 - 불규칙 변화 p.26

A 1 Oxen 2 women 3 fish 4 Mice 5 feet
6 men 7 children 8 teeth 9 Sheep

B 1 Geese 2 Children 3 men 4 feet
5 deer

POINT 04 셀 수 없는 명사 p.27

A 1 Paris 2 is 3 friendship 4 butter
5 advice

B 1 Monday 2 was 3 Water 4 kindness
5 milk

C 1 hope 2 gold 3 smoke 4 time
5 furniture

POINT 05 셀 수 없는 명사의 수량 표현 p.28

A 1 bowl 2 pieces 3 cheese 4 cups of tea
5 pair of shoes

B 1 glasses of milk 2 piece of pizza
3 bottles of soda 4 a pair of gloves
5 two bowls of rice 6 three loaves of bread

POINT 06 부정관사 a/an p.29

A 1 a 2 an 3 X 4 a 5 an 6 a 7 X
8 an 9 a

B 1 an hour 2 a volunteer 3 a garden
4 an umbrella 5 once a month

POINT 07 정관사 the p.30

A 1 the 2 the 3 an 4 the 5 the 6 a
7 the 8 the 9 the

B 1 The bag 2 the radio 3 the cello
4 The sky 5 a tree, The tree

POINT 08 관사의 생략 p.31

A 1 X 2 X 3 the 4 X 5 X 6 the 7 X
8 an 9 X 10 X, a

B 1 train, The train 2 bed, The bed
3 TV, the TV 4 a piano, the piano

REVIEW TEST pp.32-33

01 ③ 02 ④ 03 ③ 04 ② 05 ④ 06 ②
07 ④ 08 by the subway → by subway
09 A novel → The novel
10 plays the baseball → plays baseball
11 ④ 12 ② 13 made a bowl of soup
14 two cups of tea a day 15 ④ 16 ④
17 ⑤

01 〈모음+y〉끝나는 명사는 뒤에 -s를 붙여 복수형으로 쓴다.
02 부정관사 a는 셀 수 있는 명사의 단수형 앞에 사용한다.
03 셀 수 있는 명사 lemon의 복수형인 lemons는 be동사 is의 주어 자리에 들어갈 수 없다.
04 coffee와 bread는 수량을 표현할 때 사용하는 단위 명사로 각각 cup과 slice/piece가 알맞고, 복수형은 단위 명사에 -(e)s를 붙여서 나타낸다.
05 Internet, radio 같은 일부 매체 앞이나, 앞에 언급된 명사를 가리킬 때는 정관사 the를 쓴다. paper는 단위 명사 piece를 사용해서 수량을 표현하며, 하나일 때는 앞에 부정관사 a를 쓴다.
06 침대가 잠을 자는 곳이라는 본래의 용도로 쓰였으므로 bed 앞에 관사를 쓰지 않는다.
07 '안경'을 뜻하는 glasses는 항상 복수형으로 쓰며, 단위 명사 pair를 사용해서 수량을 표현한다. 하나일 때는 앞에 부정관사 a를 써서 a pair of가 온다.
08 〈by+교통/통신수단〉의 형태로 쓸 때는 명사 앞에 관사를 쓰지 않는다.
09 앞에 언급된 명사를 가리킬 때는 정관사 the를 쓴다.
10 운동 경기의 이름을 나타내는 명사 앞에는 관사를 쓰지 않는다.
11 〈보기〉와 ④의 a는 '~마다(= per)'라는 의미로 쓰였다. ①

과 ③은 '하나'라는 의미로 쓰였고, ②와 ⑤는 막연한 하나를 가리킨다.

12 '~마다(= per)'라는 의미와 막연한 하나를 나타낼 때 명사 앞에 부정관사 a나 an을 쓰는데, hour와 actress는 발음이 모음으로 시작하므로 an을 쓴다.

13 셀 수 없는 명사의 수량은 〈수량+단위 명사+of+셀 수 없는 명사〉의 형태로 나타내며, 하나일 때는 앞에 부정관사 a/an을 쓴다.

14 셀 수 없는 명사의 수량은 〈수량+단위 명사+of+셀 수 없는 명사〉의 형태로 나타내며, 복수형은 단위 명사에 -(e)s를 붙인다. '~마다(= per)'의 의미를 나타낼 때는 명사 앞에 부정관사 a를 쓴다.

15 '악기를 연주하다'라는 의미를 나타낼 때는 악기의 이름 앞에 정관사 the를 쓴다.

16 ④ star는 셀 수 있는 명사이고 앞에 millions of가 있으므로 복수형 stars가 되어야 한다.

17 ⑤ time은 셀 수 없는 명사이므로 항상 단수형으로 쓴다.

CHAPTER 05 대명사

POINT 01 지시대명사 p.34

A 1 this 2 These 3 those 4 That 5 these
B 1 Those 2 this 3 These 4 that
C 1 That 2 these 3 This 4 those 5 that

POINT 02 부정대명사 one p.35

A 1 one 2 ones 3 It 4 one 5 ones
B 1 One 2 ones 3 one
C 1 One 2 it 3 ones 4 them 5 one
6 them, ones

POINT 03 부정대명사 some/any p.36

A 1 any 2 some 3 any 4 some 5 any
6 some 7 any 8 Some 9 any, some
10 some, any
B 1 Some 2 any 3 ones 4 one

POINT 04 비인칭 주어 it p.37

A 1 It rained for a week.
2 It is not far from here.
3 It is bright in here.
4 It is Monday again.
5 What day of the week is It?
B 1 What time is it
2 It took five months
3 It is cold and dry
4 It is their wedding day
5 It is about eight kilometers

POINT 05 재귀대명사 p.38

A 1 myself 2 itself 3 ourselves 4 herself
5 themselves 6 yourself 7 himself
B 1 herself 2 myself 3 themselves
4 himself 5 yourselves 6 ourselves

POINT 06 재귀대명사의 용법 p.39

A 1 ○ 2 ○ 3 X 4 X 5 ○ 6 X 7 ○
B 1 idea itself 2 protect themselves
3 himself washed 4 take care of yourself
5 We fixed, ourselves 6 talk about herself

REVIEW TEST pp.40-41

01 ③ 02 ③ 03 ④ 04 This 05 those
06 ④ 07 ① 08 ④ 09 ②
10 These are my notebooks
11 It was warm
12 He introduced himself
13 ⑤ 14 ③ 15 ② 16 ③

01 시간을 나타내는 비인칭 주어 It이 알맞다.

02 주어 I를 강조하는 재귀대명사 myself가 알맞다.

03 one은 '한 개/사람(의)'이라는 뜻을 나타내는 수사로 쓰일 수 있다. 또한 앞에서 언급된 명사와 같은 종류의 불특정한 대상을 가리키거나 일반적인 '사람'을 가리키는 부정대명사로도 쓰인다.

04 동사가 3인칭 단수형(causes)이므로 주어 자리의 지시대명사는 This가 되어야 한다.

05 '저 사람들'이라는 복수의 대상을 가리키므로 지시대명사 that의 복수형 those가 되어야 한다.

06 〈보기〉와 ①,②,③,⑤의 재귀대명사는 동사나 전치사의 목적어로 쓰인 반면, ④의 themselves는 주어를 강조하는

재귀대명사로 생략이 가능하다.

07 〈보기〉와 ②,③,④,⑤의 It[it]은 시간, 날씨, 요일, 거리 등을 나타낼 때 쓰는 비인칭 주어인 반면, ①의 It은 특정 대상을 가리키는 인칭대명사이다.

08 '조금(의)', '약간(의)'이라는 뜻으로 의문문에서는 any를, 긍정문에서는 some을 사용한다.

09 ② 긍정문에서는 any가 아닌 some을 사용한다.

10 주어가 '이것들'이라는 복수의 대상을 가리키므로 지시대명사 These를 쓴다.

11 날씨를 나타낼 때는 비인칭 주어 It을 쓴다.

12 주어가 He이므로 introduced의 목적어로 재귀대명사 himself를 쓴다.

13 A에서 언급한 cups와 같은 종류의 불특정한 것을 나타내는 복수형 부정대명사 ones 앞에 '조금(의)', '약간(의)'이라는 뜻의 some이 와야 한다.

14 ③ 조금(의)', '약간(의)'이라는 뜻으로 부정문에서는 any를 쓴다.

15 ② 3인칭 복수형 재귀대명사는 themselves이다.

16 ③의 빈칸에는 일반적인 '사람'을 가리키는 부정대명사 One이 들어가야 한다. ①과 ②에는 날씨와 시간을 나타내는 비인칭 주어 It이, ④와 ⑤에는 특정 대상을 가리키는 인칭대명사 It[it]이 들어갈 수 있다.

CHAPTER 06 시제

POINT 01 현재시제 p.42

A 1 are 2 has 3 reads 4 goes
B 1 has 2 study 3 is 4 owns
C 1 make 2 walks 3 gives 4 is

POINT 02 과거시제 p.43

A 1 lied 2 bought 3 lived 4 took 5 wrote
B 1 was 2 didn't 3 finished
4 were, worked 5 is, made
C 1 ate 2 got 3 graduated 4 spent

POINT 03 진행형 만드는 방법 p.44

A 1 reading 2 saying 3 living 4 winning
5 opening 6 taking 7 getting 8 lying
9 moving 10 watching 11 beginning
12 bringing 13 tying 14 dancing
B 1 I'm writing his address.
2 He is playing with his toy car.
3 She is having breakfast right now.
C 1 tying 2 waiting 3 cutting
4 entering 5 riding 6 coming

POINT 04 현재진행형과 과거진행형 p.45

A 1 am cleaning 2 was drawing
3 are cooking 4 were watching
5 is studying
B 1 He was looking 2 I'm washing
3 She is practicing 4 Gary was singing
5 The players are training
6 My friends were standing

POINT 05 진행형의 부정문 p.46

A 1 is not 2 wearing 3 were 4 wasn't
5 aren't
B 1 not using 2 are playing 3 isn't driving
4 weren't fighting
C 1 She wasn't cleaning 2 I'm not enjoying
3 They weren't looking
4 Joe aren't studying

POINT 06 진행형의 의문문 p.47

A 1 doing 2 he painting 3 Were 4 brushing
5 Are
B 1 Is he 2 Are you 3 Was it, it wasn't
4 Were, No, they weren't
C 1 Is Carter calling 2 Was she holding
3 Are they shopping 4 Were you playing

REVIEW TEST pp.48-49

01 ② 02 ① 03 ④ 04 ① 05 ⑤ 06 ①
07 works out 08 had fun 09 ⑤
10 Jane was not reading the newspaper.
11 He is cooking for his wife. 12 ⑤ 13 ④
14 ② 15 was doing yoga 16 had
17 was eating lunch with Ben

01 A가 〈be동사의 현재형＋주어＋v-ing ~?〉로 현재 진행 중인 일을 묻고 있으므로, 긍정의 대답으로 〈Yes, 주어＋be동사의 현재형〉이 알맞다.

02 과거의 동작을 나타내므로 과거시제 ate가 알맞다.

03 과거의 특정 시점에 진행 중이던 일을 묻는 말이므로 과거진행형의 의문문 〈be동사의 과거형＋주어＋v-ing ~?〉의 형태가 되어야 한다.

04 ① -e로 끝나는 동사는 e를 빼고 -ing를 붙여 진행형을 만들어야 하므로 smiling으로 써야 한다.

05 A의 질문에 yesterday가 있으므로 두 빈칸에 들어가는 동사 모두 과거시제가 알맞다.

06 첫 번째 문장은 now가 있고 현재의 상태를 나타내므로 현재시제가 알맞다. 두 번째 문장의 want(원하다, 필요하다)는 상태를 나타내는 동사이므로 진행형으로 쓰지 않는다.

07 every day가 있고 현재의 일상적인 습관을 나타내고 있으므로 현재시제로 쓴다.

08 last summer가 있으므로 과거시제로 쓴다.

09 대답이 과거진행형이므로 질문도 과거진행형의 의문문 형태가 알맞다.

10 과거진행형의 부정문은 〈be동사의 과거형＋not＋v-ing〉의 형태로 쓴다.

11 현재진행형은 〈be동사의 현재형＋v-ing〉의 형태로 쓴다.

12 과거진행형의 의문문은 〈be동사의 과거형＋주어＋v-ing ~?〉의 형태로 쓴다.

13 ④ 과거시제 didn't do 또는 과거진행형 wasn't doing이 되어야 한다.

14 ② yesterday가 있으므로 과거시제 met이 되어야 한다.

15 Laura는 어제 아침에 요가를 하고 있었으므로 과거진행형 〈be동사의 과거형＋v-ing〉의 형태로 쓴다.

16 11시부터 12시까지는 한 일이 없었다는 것을 표현해야 하므로 과거시제 had를 쓴다.

17 12시 30분에는 Ben과 점심을 먹고 있었으므로 과거진행형 〈be동사의 과거형＋v-ing〉의 형태로 쓴다.

CHAPTER 07 조동사

POINT 01 will p.50

A 1 will meet 2 will not 3 leave 4 won't
B 1 won't[will not] 2 visit 3 not help

4 your brother cook
C 1 She will start 2 Will you send
3 We won't watch 4 Will he arrive, he'll be

POINT 02 be going to p.51

A 1 I'm 2 drive 3 Are 4 not going
B 1 is going to show
2 isn't[is not] going to stop
3 Are you going to have
4 aren't[are not] going to play
C 1 Are you going to fix your bike?
2 I'm not going to read that book.
3 The students are going to clean the classroom.

POINT 03 can p.52

A 1 can 2 can't 3 you open 4 could
B 1 Can you 2 they can 3 you can't
C 1 Steve can't[cannot] eat 2 We can solve
3 You can't[cannot] touch 4 Can I bring

POINT 04 can과 be able to p.53

A 1 to hear 2 is 3 Were 4 not able
B 1 aren't[are not] able to stay
2 is able to speak 3 were able to find
4 Are you able to pay
5 wasn't[was not] able to finish
C 1 We are able to grow
2 Were you able to save
3 Mia isn't able to go 4 I was able to wake

POINT 05 may p.54

A 1 may I borrow 2 may not come
3 may be driving 4 may not use
B 1 may arrive 2 may enter 3 May I see
4 She may not like 5 You may not take

POINT 06 must p.55

A 1 tell 2 must not 3 be 4 must
B 1 ⓑ 2 ⓒ 3 ⓓ 4 ⓐ
C 1 He must be 2 You must not write
3 We must show 4 They must not park

POINT 07 　have to　　　　p.56

A 1 have to　2 to stop　3 has　4 had to
5 doesn't　6 must not　7 don't have to
B 1 have to drive　2 Do, have to wait
3 don't have to bring　4 They had to find
5 Did she have to work
6 Adam doesn't have to worry

POINT 08 　should　　　　p.57

A 1 should see　2 shouldn't make
3 You should study　4 should I bring
5 You shouldn't eat
B 1 She shouldn't spend
2 You should take off
3 He can't be serious
4 We don't have to go

REVIEW TEST　　　　pp.58-59

01 ⑤　**02** ③　**03** ①　**04** Are, going to
05 wasn't able to　**06** may　**07** ⑤　**08** ③
09 ①　**10** You should not eat so much sugar.
11 Do we have to stay here?
12 ⑤　**13** ⑤　**14** ④　**15** 모두가 Tim을 좋아한다.
그는 매우 친절한 게 틀림없다.
16 너는 미안해할 필요 없어. 그것은 내 잘못이었어.

01 그가 거짓말을 하고 있을지도 모르니 그를 믿으면 안 된다
는 내용이 되어야 하므로 shouldn't가 알맞다.
02 옷이 자신에게 어울리지 않았다는 것으로 보아 그것을 사
지 않겠다는 내용이 되어야 하므로 will not이 알맞다.
03 '~일지도 모른다'라는 추측의 의미를 나타내는 may가 알
맞다.
04 '~할 것이다'라는 의미를 나타내는 be going to의 의문문
은 〈be동사+주어+going to+동사원형 ~?〉으로 쓴다.
05 '~할 수 없었다'라는 의미를 나타내려면 can't의 과거형
couldn't 또는 be able to의 과거형 wasn't able to
를 써야 한다.
06 '~일지도 모른다'라는 추측의 의미를 나타내는 may를 써
야 한다.
07 〈보기〉와 ①,②,③,④의 must는 '~해야 한다'라는 의무의
의미인 반면, ⑤의 must는 '~임이 틀림없다'라는 강한 추
측의 의미이다.
08 〈보기〉와 ①,②,④,⑤의 can은 '~할 수 있다'라는 능력이
나 가능의 의미인 반면, ③의 can은 '~해도 좋다'라는 허
가의 의미이다.
09 '~해도 좋다'라는 의미로 허가를 나타내는 may가 들어가
야 한다.
10 '~하지 않아야 한다'라는 의미를 나타내려면 〈주어
+shouldn't[should not]+동사원형〉으로 쓴다.
11 have to의 의문문은 〈Do/Does/Did+주어+have to
~?〉로 쓴다.
12 ⑤ 〈May I ~?〉라고 묻는 말에 답할 때는 주어 you를 써
야 자연스럽다.
13 '~하지 않을 것이다'라는 의미를 나타내려면 be going to
의 부정문 〈주어+be동사+not+going to+동사원형〉
으로 쓴다.
14 ④ 허가를 나타내는 may의 부정형은 may not을 써서
may not leave가 되어야 한다.
15 앞 문장에서 모두가 Tim을 좋아한다고 했으므로 must는
'~임이 틀림없다'라는 추측의 의미로 해석하는 것이 적절
하다.
16 have to의 부정형 don't have to는 '~할 필요가 없다'
라는 의미를 나타낸다.

CHAPTER 08　형용사, 부사, 비교

POINT 01 　형용사의 역할　　　　p.60

A 1 roses　2 us　3 His shoes　4 someone
B 1 happy　2 talented musician　3 difficult
4 clean　5 anything hot
C 1 sky, clear　2 strange animal
3 something different　4 this puzzle easy

POINT 02 　수량 형용사　　　　p.61

A 1 a little　2 little　3 much　4 A lot of
B 1 many　2 people　3 little　4 sandwiches
C 1 many toys　2 little information
3 a few vegetables　4 a lot of advice

POINT 03 　부사의 역할과 형태　　　　p.62

A 1 carefully　2 quick　3 lately　4 Sadly
5 high　6 gently　7 early　8 well　9 hard

10 safe

B **1** quiet, quietly   **2** good, well
3 angrily, angry   **4** simple, simply
5 late, late

POINT 04 빈도부사   p.63

A **1** ①   **2** ②   **3** ②

B **1** usually   **2** seldom   **3** sometimes
4 never   **5** often

C **1** are always kind
2 usually takes a shower
3 will never say bad things

POINT 05 원급 비교   p.64

A **1** as heavy as   **2** as carefully as
3 not as[so] shy as   **4** as difficult as
5 as loudly as   **6** not as[so] clean as

B **1** as tall as   **2** not as[so] hot as
3 as quickly as

POINT 06 비교급과 최상급 만드는 방법   p.65

A **1** smarter, smartest
2 larger, largest
3 funnier, funniest
4 more expensive, most expensive
5 bigger, biggest
6 better, best
7 longer, longest
8 more useful, most useful
9 lazier, laziest
10 more difficult, most difficult
11 wiser, wisest
12 more dangerous, most dangerous

B **1** hottest   **2** more   **3** fastest   **4** earlier
5 harder   **6** most popular

POINT 07 비교급 비교   p.66

A **1** bigger than   **2** more than
3 faster than   **4** easier than
5 better than   **6** more useful than
7 earlier than   **8** cheaper than
9 more interesting than

10 more quickly than

B **1** healthier than   **2** later than
3 much more difficult than
4 more clearly than
5 a lot more important than

POINT 08 최상급 비교   p.67

A **1** largest   **2** the most   **3** buildings
4 most   **5** the highest

B **1** the fastest   **2** the longest   **3** the worst
4 the most difficult   **5** the most popular

C **1** the lightest laptop   **2** the best movie
3 the most important chapter
4 one of the most famous artists

REVIEW TEST   pp.68-69

01 ④   **02** ⑤   **03** ③   **04** ②   **05** ②
06 not as[so] fun as   **07** more important than
08 the largest   **09** ①
10 You should always be honest.
11 He is one of the richest people in the world.
12 ④   **13** ⑤   **14** ②   **15** as long as
16 longer than   **17** the most expensive

01 early는 형용사와 부사의 형태가 같다.

02 -ful/-ous/-less/-ing/-ive로 끝나거나 3음절 이상의 단어는 앞에 more, most를 붙여 비교급, 최상급을 만든다.

03 ③ 동사 look 뒤에 주격 보어로 형용사가 와서 주어의 상태나 성질을 보충 설명해 준다. ③ easily는 '쉽게'를 뜻하는 부사이고, 나머지는 모두 형용사이다.

04 ② water는 셀 수 없는 명사이므로, 셀 수 있는 명사 앞에 쓰는 수량 형용사 a few는 쓸 수 없다.

05 첫 번째 빈칸 뒤에 than이 쓰인 것으로 보아 비교급 taller가 알맞고, 두 번째 빈칸 앞에 the가 쓰인 것으로 보아 최상급 tallest가 알맞다.

06 '…만큼 ~하지 않은'이라는 뜻을 나타내는 비교 표현은 〈not+as[so]+형용사의 원급+as〉의 형태로 쓴다.

07 '…보다 더 ~한'이라는 뜻을 나타내는 비교 표현은 〈비교급+than〉의 형태로 쓴다.

08 '가장 ~한'이라는 뜻을 나타내는 비교 표현은 〈the+최상급〉의 형태로 쓴다.

09 ①의 hard는 동사를 수식하는 부사이고, 나머지는 모두 명사·대명사를 수식하거나 주격·목적격 보어로 쓰인 형용

사이다.

10 빈도부사는 조동사의 뒤에 쓴다.

11 '가장 ~한 … 중의 하나'라는 의미는 〈one of the+최상급+복수명사〉의 형태로 나타낸다.

12 '대개'라는 뜻의 빈도부사는 usually이며 일반동사 앞에 쓴다.

13 ⑤ 셀 수 있는 명사의 복수형 앞에서 '약간의'라는 뜻을 나타내는 수량 형용사는 a few를 쓴다.

14 ② 뒤에 than이 있고 앞에는 비교급을 강조하는 much가 있으므로 shorter가 되어야 한다.

15 하이킹과 스쿠버 다이빙은 활동 시간이 같으므로 〈as+형용사/부사의 원급+as〉의 형태로 쓴다.

16 스쿠버 다이빙은 자전거 타기보다 오래 걸리므로 〈비교급+than〉의 형태로 쓴다.

17 스쿠버 다이빙은 세 활동 중에서 비용이 가장 비싸므로 〈the+최상급〉의 형태로 쓴다.

CHAPTER 09 의문문, 명령문, 감탄문

POINT 01 who, what, which — p.70

A 1 Who 2 What 3 Which 4 What
B 1 Who is the man 2 What are they cooking
3 Who can help me 4 Which do you prefer
C 1 Who won 2 What does, do
3 Which, did you choose
4 What, are they listening

POINT 02 when, where — p.71

A 1 When 2 Where 3 What 4 Where
B 1 Where is Helen 2 When did he finish
3 Where will you wait
4 When[What time] does the train
C 1 When is 2 Where did she buy
3 What time will you have
4 Where are they staying

POINT 03 why — p.72

A 1 Why 2 Where 3 Why don't
4 When 5 Why
B 1 ⓔ 2 ⓓ 3 ⓑ 4 ⓒ 5 ⓐ
C 1 Why is she 2 Why did they save
3 Where are your friends
4 Why did you see 5 When does he go
6 Why are you wearing

POINT 04 how — p.73

A 1 How old 2 How 3 How many 4 How
B 1 How long 2 How 3 How much
4 How far 5 How often
C 1 How does the cake 2 How tall is
3 How did she fix 4 How often do they go
5 How many people are there

POINT 05 부가 의문문 — p.74

A 1 didn't they 2 can't you 3 does she
4 aren't they 5 was it
B 1 is it 2 won't you 3 do we 4 didn't he
5 weren't they
C 1 isn't it, it is 2 does he, he doesn't
3 can't we, we can 4 did you, I didn't

POINT 06 부정 의문문 — p.75

A 1 Doesn't it look great?
2 Weren't they late?
3 Can't she speak French?
4 Won't you walk the dog?
5 Didn't we watch this movie?
6 Aren't they home now?
7 Don't you know the answer?
8 Wasn't he ready for the meeting?
9 Isn't it going to snow tomorrow?
B 1 Aren't, I'm not 2 Won't he, Yes, he
3 Didn't she, she didn't 4 Isn't, Yes, it is
5 Doesn't he, No, he doesn't

POINT 07 명령문 — p.76

A 1 Wash 2 Do not 3 take 4 Don't
5 Let's not 6 or 7 Let's 8 and
B 1 hurry 2 Be 3 Don't open 4 Exercise
5 Let's find 6 turn off 7 Don't lie

8 Let's not spend

A 1 How fast   2 her hair is   3 What nice
    4 What fun   5 a pretty T-shirt
B 1 How cute their baby is!
    2 What delicious cookies these are!
    3 How sleepy I felt during class!
    4 What a charming voice Jude has!
C 1 How comfortable this sofa is!
    2 What a shy boy you are!
    3 How hard they worked yesterday!
    4 What great food the restaurant serves!

REVIEW TEST   pp.78-79

01 ②   02 ④   03 ③   04 ④   05 ②
06 Andrew has, doesn't he
07 When did you go   08 ④   09 ②   10 ②
11 ①   12 Which do you like, dogs or cats?
13 What a warm coat this is!   14 ③   15 ①
16 Where will you meet your friends?
17 Let's go to Jeju next month.
18 How beautiful the picture is!

01 B에서 누가 수학 문제를 풀었는지를 답하고 있으므로 질문에 Who가 와야 한다.

02 before로 보아 시제가 과거이고 B의 대답이 No, I didn't.이므로 질문에 Didn't가 와야 한다.

03 첫 번째 빈칸에는 부가 의문문이므로 조동사 can의 부정형인 can't가, 두 번째 빈칸에는 앞에 긍정의 대답 Yes가 있으므로 can이 와야 한다.

04 첫 번째 빈칸에는 구체적인 시각을 물을 때 쓰는 What time의 What이 와야 한다. 두 번째 B에서 이유를 나타내는 대답이 나오므로 두 번째 빈칸에는 Why가 와야 한다.

05 ② Won't you로 시작하는 부정 의문문에 대한 대답으로 Yes, I will. 또는 No, I won't.가 오는 것이 자연스럽다.

06 부가 의문문은 평서문 뒤에 〈동사+주어?〉의 형태로 쓴다.

07 '언제'라는 뜻으로 시간, 날짜 등을 물을 때 쓰는 의문사 when을 이용한다. 의문사가 있는 일반동사의 과거시제 의문문은 〈의문사+did+주어+동사원형 ~?〉의 형태로 쓴다.

08 대답의 twice a week로 보아 How often을 사용해서 빈도를 묻는 의문문이 알맞다.

09 대답의 I don't로 보아 do you 또는 don't you로 묻는

의문문이 알맞다.

10 의문문에서 '어떤', '얼마나 ~한'이라는 뜻을 나타내고, 감탄문에도 쓰이는 How가 와야 한다.

11 의문문에서 '무엇', '무슨'이라는 뜻을 나타내고, 감탄문에도 쓰이는 What이 와야 한다.

12 의문사가 있는 일반동사의 의문문은 〈의문사+do동사+주어+동사원형 ~?〉의 형태로 쓴다.

13 what으로 시작하는 감탄문은 〈What+a/an+형용사+명사(+주어+동사)!〉의 형태로 쓴다.

14 '~해라, 그러면 …할 것이다'라는 뜻이므로 〈긍정 명령문+and ~〉로 쓴다.

15 ① '~하지 마라'라는 뜻의 부정 명령문은 〈Don't[Do not]+동사원형〉의 형태로 쓰므로, Don't[Do not] be upset about it.이 되어야 한다.

16 '어디서', '어디에'라는 뜻으로 장소, 위치 등을 물을 때 쓰는 의문사 where를 이용한다. 의문사가 있는 조동사의 의문문은 〈의문사+조동사+주어+동사원형 ~?〉의 형태로 쓴다.

17 〈Why don't we ~?〉는 '우리 ~하지 않을래?'라는 뜻으로 제안할 때 쓰는 표현이며, 〈Let's+동사원형〉으로 바꿔 쓸 수 있다.

18 how로 시작하는 감탄문은 〈How+형용사/부사+주어+동사!〉의 형태로 쓴다.

CHAPTER 10 문장의 형식

A 1 They work hard. X
       주어   동사

   2 Max is a web designer.
     주어 동사   보어

   3 The sun sets in the west. X
     주어   동사

   4 These chairs are comfortable.
     주어   동사   보어

   5 He slept for 13 hours yesterday. X
     주어 동사

   6 Kelly and I became best friends.
     주어   동사   보어

B 1 The trees are growing, 1
    2 My brother was angry, 2

44

3 They studied hard, 1
4 It is getting dark, 2
5 is our neighbor's daughter, 2
6 We will travel to Japan, 1

POINT 02 2형식 - 감각동사 + 형용사 p.81

A 1 salty **2** sounds **3** cold **4** looks like
B 1 delicious **2** feels like **3** great **4** sour
C 1 looks kind **2** smells sweet
3 sounds like thunder
4 the milk taste strange

POINT 03 3형식 / 4형식 p.82

A 1 lent **2** open **3** the lesson
B 1 made us smoothies
2 I found my keys
3 bought me this T-shirt
4 Alice is reading a magazine
5 should send them some flowers
C 1 give him a chance
2 They want two tickets
3 lent me his notebook
4 met her old friend
5 show you the answer

POINT 04 4형식 → 3형식
- 전치사 to를 쓰는 경우 p.83

A 1 her room to them
2 us some snacks
3 some roses to Linda
4 pass me the pencil
5 tell the truth to him
6 a text message to me
B 1 teaches history to
2 writing a letter to
3 lend me your running shoes
4 showed her new phone to us
5 give a gift to him

POINT 05 4형식 → 3형식
- 다른 전치사를 쓰는 경우 p.84

A 1 for **2** to **3** bought **4** for the child

B 1 a book for his friend
2 buy a present for her
3 made a pair of mittens for me
C 1 cook spaghetti for
2 asked a favor of
3 buy some eggs for me
4 made a photo album for him

POINT 06 5형식
- 목적격 보어가 명사/형용사인 경우 p.85

A 1 delicious **2** her a liar **3** angry
B 1 I kept the window open.
2 This movie made her a star.
3 His friends call him Superman.
C 1 leave me alone
2 named the cat Oreo
3 found the show boring
4 keep you warm

POINT 07 5형식
- 목적격 보어가 to부정사인 경우 p.86

A 1 to fix **2** to help **3** to eat
4 to win **5** to come
B 1 want me to go to sleep early
2 told us to be quiet
3 He expected them to exercise
C 1 allowed us to sing
2 tell Nancy to do
3 ordered him to get
4 expect her to study

POINT 08 5형식 - 지각동사/사역동사 p.87

A 1 sing[singing] **2** to clean **3** wait
4 run[running] **5** know
B 1 hear the baby cry
2 have him carry
3 felt his heart beating
4 help you find your seat
5 She saw her sister washing
C 1 let us use **2** I watched, play[playing]
3 helped him to understand
4 made us turn off

01 2형식 문장에서 감각동사 look 뒤에는 주격 보어로 형용사가 온다. look 뒤에 명사가 올 때는 전치사 like를 함께 쓴다.

02 빈칸에는 tell, order, ask, want 등과 같이 목적격 보어로 to부정사를 쓰는 동사가 와야 한다. 사역동사 make는 목적격 보어로 동사원형을 쓴다.

03 빈칸에는 give, send, lend, show 등과 같이 4형식 문장에서 3형식 문장으로 바꿀 때 간접목적어 앞에 전치사 to를 쓰는 동사가 와야 한다. 동사 buy는 전치사 for를 쓴다.

04 첫 번째 빈칸에는 2형식 문장에서 3인칭 단수 주어와 주격 보어인 명사 사이에 be동사 is가 들어가야 한다. 두 번째 빈칸에는 준사역동사 help의 목적격 보어로 동사원형 또는 to부정사가 들어가야 한다.

05 동사 show는 4형식 문장에서 3형식 문장으로 바꿀 때 간접목적어 앞에 전치사 to를 쓴다.

06 ①은 〈주어+동사〉 형태의 1형식 문장인 반면, 나머지는 모두 〈주어+동사+목적어〉 형태의 3형식 문장이다.

07 ⑤는 〈주어+동사+목적어〉 형태의 3형식 문장인 반면, 나머지는 모두 〈주어+동사+주격 보어〉 형태의 2형식 문장이다.

08 3형식과 4형식 문장에서 '만들다'라는 뜻을 나타내면서, 5형식 문장에서는 '~하게 하다'라는 뜻을 나타내며 목적격 보어로 동사원형을 쓰는 동사 make가 알맞다.

09 ②에서 a desk는 4형식 문장의 직접목적어로 쓰인 반면, 나머지는 모두 5형식 문장의 목적격 보어로 쓰였다.

10 〈주어+지각동사(see)+목적어+목적격 보어(동사원형/현재분사)〉의 형태로 쓴다.

11 〈주어+동사(expect)+목적어+목적격 보어(to부정사)〉의 형태로 쓴다.

12 '~하도록 허락하다'라는 의미를 지닌 사역동사 let은 목적격 보어로 동사원형을 쓰고, 동사 allow는 목적격 보어로 to부정사를 쓴다.

13 ⑤ 5형식 문장에서 동사 want는 목적격 보어로 to부정사를 쓴다.

14 ② 〈Tim told+간접목적어(me)+직접목적어(his secret)〉 또는 〈Tim told+직접목적어(his secret)+to+간접목적어(me)〉의 형태로 써야 한다.

15 〈주어+동사+직접목적어+전치사+간접목적어〉 형태의 3형식 문장은 〈주어+동사+간접목적어+직접목적어〉 형태의 4형식 문장으로 바꿀 수 있다.

16 동사 give는 4형식 문장에서 3형식 문장으로 바꿀 때 간접목적어 앞에 전치사 to를 쓴다.

17 동사 buy는 4형식 문장에서 3형식 문장으로 바꿀 때 간접목적어 앞에 전치사 for를 쓴다.

CHAPTER 11 to부정사와 동명사

POINT 01　**to부정사의 명사적 용법 - 주어 역할**　p.90

A **1** to bake　**2** It, to follow　**3** To touch, is
4 To write a good essay is
5 It is interesting to watch

B **1** To be　**2** It, to see　**3** It was, to get up
4 To talk, makes　**5** It is helpful to memorize

POINT 02　**to부정사의 명사적 용법 - 보어/목적어 역할**　p.91

A **1** to get　**2** to deliver　**3** to travel　**4** to start
B **1** refused to say　**2** is to teach children
3 decided not to sell
4 Her dream is to sing
C **1** is to protect　**2** want to visit
3 My goal is to walk
4 promised not to be late

POINT 03　**to부정사의 명사적 용법 - 의문사+to부정사**　p.92

A **1** when to start　**2** where to sit
3 what to buy

B **1** how to swim last year
2 when to leave my house
3 what to bring to the picnic
4 who to invite to the party

5 where to go for dinner
C **1** what to say　**2** how to turn
3 where to park　**4** when to meet
5 who(m) to choose

POINT 04　**to부정사의 형용사적 용법**
- (대)명사 수식　　　　p.93

A **1** to learn　**2** time to waste
3 to wear　**4** nothing to eat
5 something interesting to show
B **1** to watch　**2** to share　**3** to join　**4** to write
C **1** time to say goodbye
2 anything good to read
3 looking for a place to stay
4 needs someone to talk to

POINT 05　**to부정사의 부사적 용법**
- 목적　　　　p.94

A **1** to win　**2** to buy　**3** in order to save
B **1** work hard to earn
2 wrote an email to thank
3 got up early to cook
4 moved to the city to find
C **1** to remember that day
2 to ask for advice
3 to help the children
4 order to build muscle

POINT 06　**to부정사의 부사적 용법**
- 감정의 원인 / 결과　　　　p.95

A **1** to get　**2** too shocked to speak
3 too late to join
B **1** grew up to become
2 too sick to go
3 brave enough to try
4 were disappointed to lose
C **1** too full to finish
2 glad to see
3 high enough to touch
4 came home to find

POINT 07　**동명사 - 주어/보어 역할**　　　　p.96

A **1** winning　**2** Swimming　**3** Eating
4 planting　**5** Climbing　**6** watching
7 Reading
B **1** Living without water is
2 was solving the problem
3 Writing the essay gave me
4 is speaking in front of people
5 Traveling to other countries is

POINT 08　**동명사 - 목적어 역할**　　　　p.97

A **1** reading　**2** riding　**3** to work　**4** staying
5 getting
B **1** talking during class　**2** singing well
3 helping my little brother
C **1** stopped playing
2 enjoy going skiing
3 am good at making
4 give up looking for

REVIEW TEST　　　　pp.98-99

01 ③　**02** ②　**03** ④　**04** a book to read
05 Learning a new language　**06** ④　**07** ③
08 ④　**09** ⑤　**10** I'm sorry for making you cry.
11 He was excited to run in the race.
12 He didn't know when to tell her the truth.
13 ⑤　**14** ②　**15** too lazy to keep a job
16 too full to eat

01 '~하기 위해', '~하러'라는 뜻으로 목적을 나타내는 부사적 용법의 to부정사가 와야 한다.
02 '(…해서) ~하다'라는 뜻으로 결과를 나타내는 부사적 용법의 to부정사가 와야 한다.
03 첫 번째 빈칸에는 '어떻게 ~할지', '~하는 방법'의 뜻을 나타내는 〈how+to부정사〉가 와야 한다. 두 번째 빈칸에는 동사 need의 목적어로 to부정사를 쓴다.
04 형용사적 용법의 to부정사는 수식하는 (대)명사 뒤에 온다.
05 동명사는 '~하는 것'이라는 뜻으로 문장에서 주어로 쓰일 수 있다.
06 〈보기〉와 ①, ②, ③, ⑤의 밑줄 친 부분은 '~하기 위해', '~하러'라는 뜻으로 목적을 나타내는 부사적 용법의 to부정사이다. ④는 동사의 목적어로 쓰인 명사적 용법의 to부정사이다.
07 〈보기〉와 ①, ②, ④, ⑤의 밑줄 친 부분은 문장에서 주어, 보어, 목적어로 쓰인 명사적 용법의 to부정사이다. ③은

(대)명사를 수식하는 형용사적 용법의 to부정사이다.

08 첫 번째 빈칸에는 문장에서 주어 역할을 하는 동명사가 들어가야 하고, 두 번째 빈칸에는 동사 avoid의 목적어 역할을 하는 동명사가 들어가야 한다.

09 '너무 ~해서 …할 수 없다'라는 뜻을 나타내려면 〈too+형용사/부사+to부정사〉의 형태로 써야 한다.

10 전치사 for의 목적어 역할을 하는 동명사가 와야 한다.

11 형용사(excited) 뒤에 감정의 원인을 나타내는 부사적 용법의 to부정사가 와야 한다.

12 동사(didn't know) 뒤에 목적어 역할을 하는 〈의문사+to부정사〉가 와야 한다.

13 '…할 만큼 충분히 ~하다'라는 뜻을 나타내는 〈형용사/부사+enough+to부정사〉를 쓴다.

14 ② give up은 동명사를 목적어로 쓴다.

15 '너무 ~해서 …할 수 없다'라는 뜻의 〈too+형용사/부사+to부정사〉로 쓸 수 있다.

16 '너무 ~해서 …할 수 없다'라는 뜻의 〈too+형용사/부사+to부정사〉로 쓸 수 있다.

CHAPTER 12 접속사

POINT 01 등위접속사 and   p.100

A 1 carefully   2 fixed   3 we made breakfast
4 read
B 1 a writer and a professor
2 swimming and watching movies
3 the museum and Namdaemun Market
C 1 and made a phone call
2 both the piano and the violin
3 and we decided to take a walk

POINT 02 등위접속사 but   p.101

A 1 and   2 but   3 but   4 and
B 1 old but very useful
2 but I'm not hungry
3 but it started to rain
C 1 small but cozy room
2 but she sat far away from him
3 are expensive but very comfortable

4 but we didn't understand it

POINT 03 등위접속사 or   p.102

A 1 and   2 Either   3 but   4 or
B 1 or in the evening   2 either, or
3 or he will send
C 1 today June 25 or June 26
2 your red shirt or your blue one
3 come with us or you can wait
4 either study abroad or get a job

POINT 04 등위접속사 so   p.103

A 1 so   2 but   3 or   4 I was tired
B 1 ©   2 ⓓ   3 ⓐ   4 ⓔ   5 ⓑ
C 1 We didn't have enough money, so we couldn't buy it.
2 She opened the book, and she started to read.
3 I knocked on the door, but no one answered.
4 You can go to the park, or you can visit the zoo.

POINT 05 시간을 나타내는 접속사 when / while   p.104

A 1 When she is cold, she drinks tea.[She drinks tea when she is cold.]
2 When he saw the dog, he ran away.[He ran away when he saw the dog.]
3 When Dad comes back, we will have the dinner.[We will have the dinner when Dad comes back.]
B 1 When we arrived   2 While he was cooking
3 when she sees   4 while he is taking
5 When I went to
6 while I was waiting for them

POINT 06 시간을 나타내는 접속사 before / after   p.105

A 1 When   2 before   3 while   4 after
B 1 Before we start   2 After the rain stops
3 when we met yesterday

4 before it gets dark
5 after the party ended

POINT 07 이유, 조건을 나타내는 접속사 because / if p.106

A 1 if 2 because 3 gets
B 1 ⓓ 2 ⓐ 3 ⓑ 4 ⓒ
C 1 if you work 2 because we heard
  3 Because she forgot
  4 If you like action films
  5 because he hurt his leg

POINT 08 명사절을 이끄는 접속사 that p.107

A 1 that 2 It 3 a fact that the Earth
B 1 It is amazing that she speaks three languages.
  2 It is a problem that he often loses things.
  3 It surprised everyone that they missed the meeting.
C 1 that we should try again
  2 That they stole something
  3 It was good that
  4 that he is planning a party

REVIEW TEST pp.108-109

01 ③ 02 ② 03 ② 04 while you were out
05 before his mom came home
06 if I have time 07 ② 08 ③ 09 ⑤ 10 ③
11 Because it was raining, we stayed home.
   [We stayed home because it was raining.]
12 When you come in, take off your shoes.
   [Take off your shoes when you come in.]
13 ④ 14 ③
15 아무도 다치지 않은 것은 다행이었다.
16 그는 운전하는 동안에 음악을 듣는다.

01 빈칸 앞의 절은 원인을 나타내고 뒤의 절은 결과를 나타내므로 '그래서'라는 뜻의 등위접속사 so가 와야 한다.
02 앞의 내용과 반대되는 내용을 이어주는 등위접속사 but이 와야 한다.
03 첫 번째 빈칸에는 '또는', '~(이)거나'라는 뜻으로 선택을 나타내는 등위접속사 or가, 두 번째 빈칸에는 '~하기 때문에'

라는 뜻으로 이유를 나타내는 종속접속사 because가 와야 한다.
04 '~하는 동안(에)'이라는 뜻의 종속접속사 while을 이용한다.
05 '~하기 전에'라는 뜻의 종속접속사 before를 이용한다.
06 '~한다면'이라는 뜻으로 조건을 나타내는 종속접속사 if를 이용한다.
07 ②의 when은 '언제'라는 뜻으로 쓰인 의문사인 반면, 나머지는 모두 '~할 때'라는 뜻의 종속접속사 when이다.
08 ③의 after는 명사 앞에 쓰인 전치사인 반면, 나머지는 모두 '~한 후에'라는 뜻의 종속접속사 after이다.
09 첫 번째 빈칸에는 가주어 It에 대한 진주어인 명사절을 이끄는 접속사 that이, 두 번째 빈칸에는 목적어 역할을 하는 명사절을 이끄는 접속사 that이 와야 한다.
10 ③의 That은 주어 역할을 하는 명사절을 이끄는 접속사로 생략할 수 없는 반면, ①, ②, ④, ⑤의 that은 목적어 역할을 하는 명사절을 이끄는 접속사로 생략이 가능하다.
11 종속접속사 because를 이유를 나타내는 절 앞에 오도록 배열한다.
12 종속접속사 when을 시간을 나타내는 절 앞에 오도록 배열한다.
13 'A이거나 B'라는 뜻의 〈either A or B〉가 되어야 한다.
14 조건을 나타내는 접속사가 이끄는 절에서는 미래의 일이더라도 현재시제를 쓰므로 will ask를 ask로 써야 한다.
15 It은 가주어, that이 이끄는 절이 진주어이다.
16 접속사 while은 '~하는 동안(에)'이라는 뜻이다.

CHAPTER 13 전치사

POINT 01 시간의 전치사 in / on / at p.110

A 1 the afternoon 2 May 23 3 July
B 1 at 2 in 3 on 4 at 5 in 6 on
C 1 at 2 on 3 in 4 at 5 in 6 On

POINT 02 시간의 전치사 around / before / after / for / during / until / by p.111

A 1 around 2 for 3 by 4 during 5 before
B 1 after lunch
  2 during the meeting

3 until next weekend
4 for 45 minutes
5 around noon

POINT 03 장소·위치의 전치사 in / on / at p.112

A 1 the table 2 the air 3 the ground
B 1 in 2 on 3 at 4 in 5 on 6 at
C 1 at home
2 on that bookshelf
3 In our country
4 on the fifth floor

POINT 04 장소·위치의 전치사 near / over / under / behind / to p.113

A 1 under 2 behind 3 near 4 over 5 to
B 1 under the bridge
2 near your house
3 behind this curtain
4 over the stream

POINT 05 장소·위치의 전치사 in front of / next to / across from / between A and B p.114

A 1 across from 2 next to
3 in front of 4 between, and
B 1 across from him
2 in front of this building
3 next to the door
C 1 My house is across from the radio station.
2 She threw the ball between Charlie and me.
3 Some teenagers are standing in front of the concert hall.

POINT 06 기타 전치사 for / with / by / about / from A to B p.115

A 1 with 2 by 3 about 4 for 5 from, to
B 1 about the news
2 with my friends
3 for breaking
4 by video call
5 from the airport to the city

REVIEW TEST p.116
01 ④ 02 ③ 03 ⑤ 04 under her desk
05 around noon 06 went to, with
07 ③ 08 ② 09 ② 10 ①
11 The sun rose over the mountain.
12 Korea is between China and Japan.
13 Is there a gym near your school?
14 ④ 15 ② 16 next to 17 across from

01 전치사 between은 '~ 사이에'라는 뜻으로 둘 이상의 대상 간의 위치 관계를 나타낸다.

02 첫 번째 빈칸에는 'A부터 B까지'라는 뜻을 나타내는 전치사 from A to B의 from이, 두 번째 빈칸에는 교통·통신 수단 앞에서 '~으로'라는 뜻을 나타내는 전치사 by가 와야 한다.

03 첫 번째 빈칸에는 '~ 후에'를 뜻하는 전치사 after가, 두 번째 빈칸에는 '~ 앞에'라는 뜻을 나타내는 in front of의 in이 와야 한다.

04 '~ 아래에'라는 뜻으로 전치사 under를 쓴다.

05 '~ 무렵에'라는 뜻으로 전치사 around를 쓴다.

06 went 뒤에는 '~로'라는 뜻으로 목적지를 나타내는 전치사 to를, his brother 앞에는 '~와 함께'라는 뜻으로 동반을 나타내는 전치사 with를 쓴다.

07 ③의 빈칸에는 오전(morning)과 함께 쓰는 전치사 in이 와야 한다. ①, ④에는 접촉한 상태의 위치를 나타내는 전치사 on이, ②, ⑤에는 요일, 특정한 날 앞에 쓰는 전치사 on이 와야 한다.

08 ②의 빈칸에는 비교적 넓은 장소를 나타낼 때 쓰는 전치사 in이 와야 한다. ①, ④, ⑤에는 비교적 좁은 장소나 하나의 지점을 나타내는 전치사 at이, ③에는 하루의 때를 나타내는 전치사 at이 와야 한다.

09 첫 번째 빈칸에는 '~을 위해'라는 뜻으로 목적을 나타내는 전치사 for가, 두 번째 빈칸에는 '~ 동안'이라는 뜻으로 구체적인 기간을 나타내는 전치사 for가 와야 한다.

10 첫 번째 빈칸에는 Boston과 같은 도시명 앞에 쓰는 전치사 in이, 두 번째 빈칸에는 '~(안)에'라는 뜻으로 사물의 내부를 나타내는 전치사 in이 와야 한다.

11 '~ 위에'라는 뜻으로 표면에 접촉해 있지 않은 상태를 나타내는 전치사 over를 the mountain 앞에 쓴다.

12 'A와 B 사이에'라는 뜻을 나타내는 전치사 between A and B의 어순으로 쓴다.

13 학교 근처에 체육관이 있는지 묻고 있으므로 '~ 근처에'라는 뜻의 전치사 near를 your school 앞에 쓴다.

14 '~까지는'이라는 뜻으로 동작이 완료되는 기한을 나타내는 전치사 by를 쓴다.

15 ② '~ 동안'이라는 뜻으로 숫자를 포함하는 구체적인 기간

앞에는 전치사 for를 써야 한다.

16 beside는 '~ 옆에'라는 뜻의 전치사로 next to로 바꾸어 쓸 수 있다.

17 opposite은 '~ 맞은편에'라는 뜻의 전치사로 across from으로 바꾸어 쓸 수 있다.

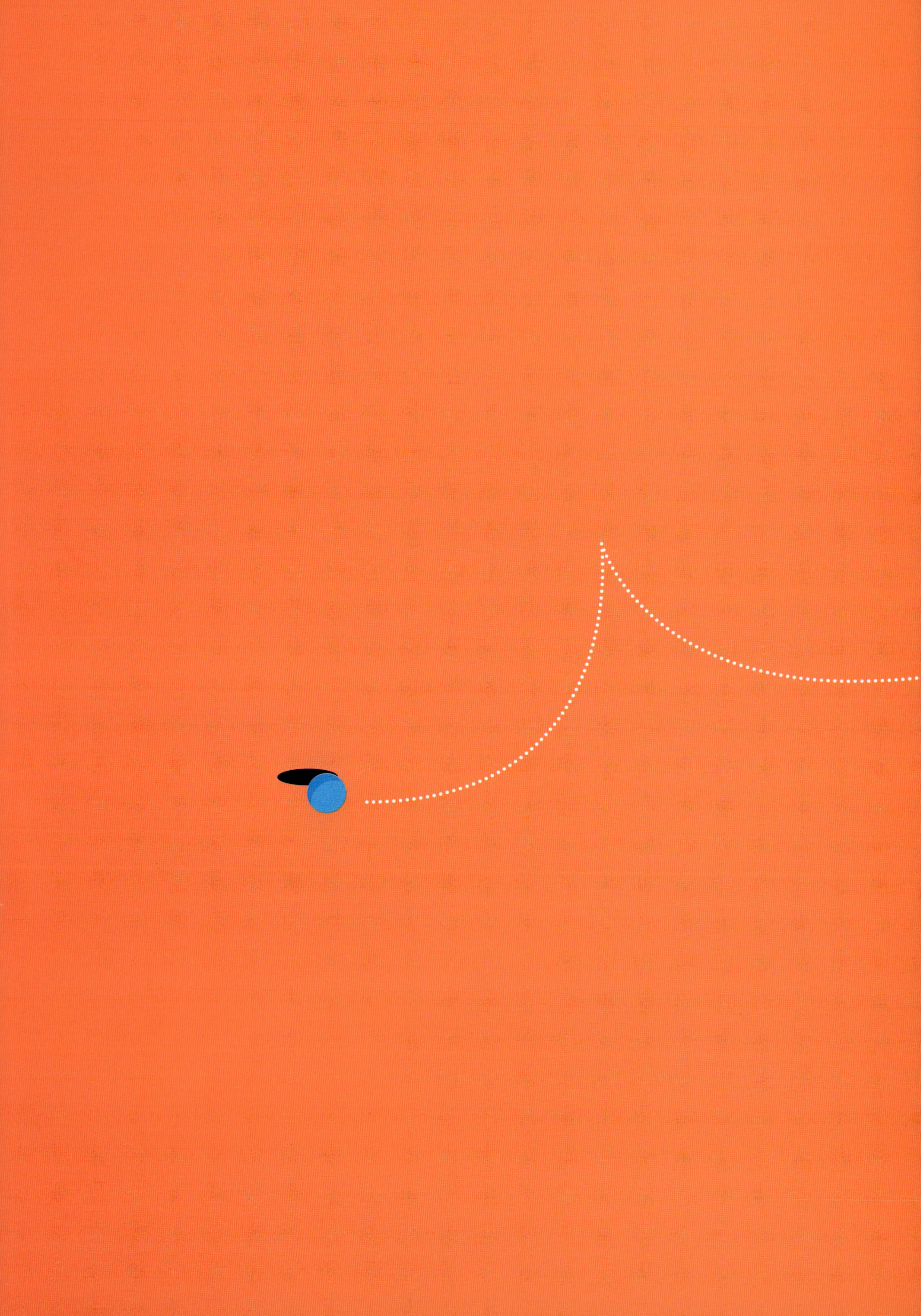

반 __________ 이름 __________ 맞은 개수 __________ 개

[01-02] 다음 빈칸에 알맞은 말을 고르시오.

01

I was sick last weekend. I ____________ a bad cold.

① catch ② catches ③ catched
④ caught ⑤ catching

02

These lamps are not so bright ____________ those ones.

① and ② than ③ to
④ that ⑤ as

03 다음 빈칸에 공통으로 들어갈 말은?

• I want both cookies ____________ ice cream for dessert.
• Add some salt, ____________ the soup will taste better.

① and ② so ③ or
④ but ⑤ that

서술형
04 다음 두 문장이 같은 뜻이 되도록 빈칸에 알맞은 말을 쓰시오.

I was standing behind Stephen in the line.

→ Stephen was standing ____________ ____________ ____________ me in the line.

[05-06] 다음 대화의 빈칸에 알맞은 말을 고르시오.

05

A: Was he at the beach with you yesterday?
B: No, he ____________. He stayed at home.

① is ② isn't ③ was
④ wasn't ⑤ weren't

06

A: ____________ does your father get to work?
B: He takes the subway to work.

① Why ② Where ③ How
④ What time ⑤ How long

07 다음 밑줄 친 부분과 바꾸어 쓸 수 있는 말은?

A: Can you speak Chinese?
B: Yes, I can speak it very well.

① Able you to ② Do you able
③ Are able you ④ Able you are to
⑤ Are you able to

[08-09] 다음 우리말과 같은 뜻이 되도록 빈칸에 알맞은 말을 고르시오.

08

그는 천재임이 틀림없다.
→ He ____________ be a genius.

① cannot ② may ③ must
④ may not ⑤ doesn't have to

09

너는 어젯밤에 문을 잠갔지, 그렇지 않니?
→ You locked the door last night, ____________?

① are you ② aren't you ③ don't you
④ did you ⑤ didn't you

10 다음 중 〈보기〉의 밑줄 친 부분과 쓰임이 같은 것은?

〈보기〉 I don't have anything to do tonight.

① He went to the gym to exercise.
② It is wonderful to help others.
③ He refused to answer my questions.
④ Please give me a pen to write with.
⑤ We were glad to see you again.

서술형
11 다음 우리말과 같은 뜻이 되도록 주어진 말을 이용하여 문장을 완성하시오.

나는 프린터에 종이 다섯 장을 넣었다. (piece, paper)

→ I put ____________ ____________ ____________ ____________ in the printer.

12 다음 중 밑줄 친 부분이 어법상 틀린 것은?

① Water and oil don't mix.
② I don't have much time now.
③ There is an egg in the basket.
④ We have four classes on Monday.
⑤ She is wearing cute socks on her foots.

13 - 15 다음 문장을 지시대로 바꾸어 쓰시오.

13 She knows Henry's parents. (부정문으로)

→ _______________________________________

14 They were watching the fireworks in the park. (의문문으로)

→ _______________________________________

15 He had a good time at the concert. (의문문으로)

→ _______________________________________

16 다음 우리말을 영어로 바르게 옮긴 것은?

> 그것은 정말 흥미진진한 경기였어!

① How exciting game it was!
② What exciting a game was it!
③ What an exciting game it was!
④ How exciting it was a game!
⑤ What was it an exciting game!

17 다음 중 어법상 틀린 것은?

① The sun rises in the east.
② This song makes me to cry.
③ The children looked very happy.
④ I told an interesting story to Paul.
⑤ He showed me the way to the station.

18 - 19 주어진 말을 알맞게 배열하여 대화를 완성하시오.

18 A: The food at this restaurant is terrible.
B: I agree. _______________________ this place again. (never, visit, will, I)

19 A: Will you and your sister go to the amusement park tomorrow?
B: No, _______________________ there. (to, going, we, not, are, go) We have other plans.

20 다음 빈칸에 들어갈 수 없는 말은?

> She _____________ to open her own bakery.

① decided　② hoped　③ finished
④ wanted　⑤ planned

21 - 22 다음 빈칸에 알맞은 말이 바르게 짝지어진 것을 고르시오.

21

> _____________ red apples don't look very fresh. Let's buy the green _____________.

① This – it
② These – ones
③ That – ones
④ Those – it
⑤ These – it

22

> History is _____________ than science to me. Actually, I think history is _____________ subject of all.

① easy – easier
② the easier – most easy
③ more easy – easiest
④ easier – the easiest
⑤ the easiest – easier

23 다음 두 문장을 한 문장으로 만들 때, 빈칸에 알맞은 말을 쓰시오.

I will be late for the meeting. I'm worried about it.

→ I'm worried about _____________ _____________ for the meeting.

24 의문사와 주어진 말을 이용하여 대화를 완성하시오.

Sally: _____________ _____________ _____________ he? (tall)

Brian: He is 170 cm tall.

Sally: _____________ _____________ he _________? (live)

Brian: He lives in Daegu.

25 다음 중 어법상 틀린 것을 모두 고르면? (2개)

① You don't have to call me back.
② It is not easy to take care of babies.
③ Roy ate five slices of pizza for dinner.
④ I have a class from 9:00 a.m. and 1:00 p.m. today.
⑤ Canada is one of the largest country in the world.

26 다음 Jinsu가 작성한 표를 보고, 빈칸에 알맞은 말을 쓰시오.

좋아하는 것	I love eating fast food.
새해 결심	I will become healthier in the new year.
결심을 이루기 위한 계획	I will eat more vegetables. I will drink more water.

Jinsu enjoys _____________ fast food. But he decided _____________ _____________ healthier in the new year. In order to become healthier, he is considering _____________ more vegetables. He is also planning _____________ _____________ more water for his health.

반 _________ 이름 ___________ 맞은 개수 _________ 개

01-03 다음 빈칸에 알맞은 말을 고르시오.

01

It is not true ___________ he always tells the truth.

① it ② to ③ that
④ this ⑤ near

02

Maggie ___________ some chicken soup to me.

① made ② got ③ bought
④ gave ⑤ cooked

03

If Andrew ___________ to school tomorrow, I will talk to him about the project.

① come ② comes ③ came
④ coming ⑤ will come

서술형

04-06 다음 빈칸에 a, an, the 중 알맞은 말을 쓰시오. (불필요하면 X 표시할 것)

04 He practiced playing ___________ violin all morning.

05 It takes about an hour to get to Jeju by ___________ plane.

06 I go to see a musical with my parents once ___________ month.

07 다음 빈칸에 들어갈 수 <u>없는</u> 말은?

I ___________ working out at the gym.

① enjoyed ② finished ③ planned
④ gave up ⑤ considered

서술형

08 다음 우리말과 같은 뜻이 되도록 주어진 말을 이용하여 문장을 완성하시오.

누가 너에게 이 카드를 보냈니? (send)

→ ___________ this card to you?

09-11 다음 빈칸에 알맞은 말이 바르게 짝지어진 것을 고르시오.

09

Jason ___________ to school last month, but he ___________ to school these days.

① not walk – walk ② didn't walk – walked
③ doesn't walk – walks ④ doesn't walk – walked
⑤ didn't walk – walks

10

A: I like ___________ black sneakers. They are on sale.
B: How about those white ___________? They are cheap, too.

① one – it ② this – them ③ that – one
④ it – others ⑤ these – ones

11

A: Is that blue bike over there ___________?
B: Yes, it's ___________ new bike. I got it for my birthday gift.

① you – mine ② your – my ③ yours – my
④ your – me ⑤ yours – mine

서술형

12 다음 두 문장이 같은 뜻이 되도록 빈칸에 알맞은 말을 쓰시오.

It is my mother's job to cook dinner every day, and it is my father's job to wash the dishes every day.

→ Every day, my mother ___________ dinner and my father ___________ the dishes.

13 다음 두 문장이 같은 뜻이 되도록 빈칸에 들어갈 알맞은 말은?

Let's go out for a walk for a while.
→ ___________ go out for a walk for a while?

① When do we ② Why do you ③ Which do we
④ Why don't we ⑤ How do we

14 다음 우리말과 같은 뜻이 되도록 빈칸에 들어갈 말이 바르게 짝지어진 것은?

나는 돈이 거의 없어. 동전 몇 개만 있을 뿐이야.
→ I have ___________ money. I only have ___________ coins.

① little – a few ② a few – little ③ a little – few
④ little – few ⑤ few – a little

15 – 16 다음 문장을 지시대로 바꾸어 쓰시오.

15 She will pick me up at the airport. (be going to를 사용하여)

→ ____

16 Paul must finish his homework by 6:00. (have to를 사용하여)

→ ____

17 다음 중 〈보기〉의 밑줄 친 부분과 의미가 같은 것은?

> 〈보기〉 You didn't have lunch. You <u>must</u> be very hungry.

① <u>Must</u> I take the test again?
② You <u>must</u> pay $5 for the ticket.
③ We <u>must</u> not cross the road here.
④ He <u>must</u> be a kind person to say so.
⑤ You <u>must</u> write the answers in pencil.

18 다음 대화의 빈칸에 알맞은 말을 쓰시오.

Tiffany: ____________ ____________ did you come to the library?

Julie: I came here at 10:30.

Tiffany: ____________ ____________ do you study here?

Julie: I study here once or twice a week.

19 – 20 다음 빈칸에 공통으로 들어갈 말을 고르시오.

19
> • Either you ____________ your sister must clean the table.
> • Go to bed now, ____________ you'll feel tired tomorrow.

① and ② so ③ or
④ but ⑤ that

20
> • ____________ is important to eat healthy food.
> • ____________ takes thirty minutes from here to your house.

① That ② If ③ It
④ This ⑤ One

21 다음 문장에서 어법상 틀린 부분을 찾아 바르게 고쳐 쓰시오.

> Jake looks happily today, doesn't he?

22 다음 문장을 감탄문으로 바꿀 때, 빈칸에 알맞은 말은?

> These are very beautiful dolls.
> → ____________________ these are!

① How beautiful dolls ② What beautiful dolls
③ What dolls beautiful ④ How a beautiful doll
⑤ What a beautiful doll

23 다음 중 밑줄 친 부분의 쓰임이 나머지와 <u>다른</u> 것은?

① Do you mind <u>sitting</u> on the floor?
② The cook is <u>cutting</u> the onions.
③ <u>Driving</u> on a snowy day is dangerous.
④ His job is <u>taking</u> pictures of models.
⑤ I will keep <u>calling</u> him until he answers.

24 [ ] 안에 주어진 말을 이용하여 두 문장을 한 문장으로 바꾸어 쓰시오.

She is rude. People don't like her. (because)

→ ____

25 다음 중 어법상 틀린 것은?

① I didn't hear him knocks on the door.
② The man asked me to tell him the time.
③ She found her reading club interesting.
④ Will you write me letters from Rome?
⑤ This building looks like a spaceship.

26 다음 중 어법상 옳은 것끼리 짝지어진 것은?

> (a) Did you have lunch at noon?
> (b) Are you able to ride a motorcycle?
> (c) I don't know how does play the drums.
> (d) I have important something to tell you.
> (e) He is fast enough to win the 100-meter race.

① (a), (b), (e) ② (a), (c), (d) ③ (b), (c), (d)
④ (b), (c), (e) ⑤ (c), (d), (e)

27 다음 표를 보고, 주어진 말을 이용하여 비교하는 문장을 완성하시오.

Jake	Steve	Tom
55 kg	60 kg	52 kg

(1) Jake is ____________ ____________ Tom. (heavy)

(2) Tom is ____________ ____________ Steve. (light)

(3) Steve is ____________ ____________ boy of the three. (heavy)

NE능률

문마중

LEVEL 1

Workbook

01 기초 문법

POINT 01 영어의 8품사

A 다음 단어의 품사가 무엇인지 〈보기〉에서 골라 알맞은 기호를 쓰시오.

> 〈보기〉 ⓐ 명사 ⓑ 대명사 ⓒ 동사 ⓓ 형용사 ⓔ 부사 ⓕ 전치사 ⓖ 접속사 ⓗ 감탄사

1	have	→ (　　)	2	usually	→ (　　)
3	we	→ (　　)	4	with	→ (　　)
5	student	→ (　　)	6	although	→ (　　)
7	aha	→ (　　)	8	happy	→ (　　)

B 다음 문장에서 [ ] 안의 품사에 해당하는 단어를 찾아 쓰시오.

1 I want a new phone. (명사)　　　　　　　　　→ ___________

2 They study hard. (부사)　　　　　　　　　　→ ___________

3 He takes the subway every day. (동사)　　　→ ___________

4 A cat is sleeping under the chair. (전치사)　→ ___________

5 Zoe sang a song, and her sister danced. (접속사)　→ ___________

POINT 02 문장 성분

A 다음 밑줄 친 부분의 문장 성분으로 알맞은 것을 〈보기〉에서 골라 기호를 쓰시오.

> 〈보기〉 ⓐ 주어　　ⓑ 동사　　ⓒ 목적어　　ⓓ 보어　　ⓔ 수식어

1 The small bird is <u>cute</u>.　　　　　　　　　　(　　)

2 Did <u>you</u> eat pizza yesterday?　　　　　　　(　　)

3 She washes her hair <u>in the morning</u>.　　　(　　)

4 We <u>talked</u> about many things.　　　　　　(　　)

5 My dad teaches <u>math</u> at a middle school.　(　　)

B 다음 문장을 밑줄 친 부분에 유의하여 우리말로 해석하시오.

1 The turtle walks <u>slowly</u>.

→ _______________________________________

2 The boy plays <u>soccer</u>.

→ _______________________________________

3 The restaurant became <u>very popular</u>.

→ _______________________________________

4 That building <u>over there</u> is a museum.

→ _______________________________________

POINT 03 구와 절

A 다음 단어 덩어리가 구인지 절인지 고르시오.

1 by email ☐ 구 ☐ 절

2 when you leave ☐ 구 ☐ 절

3 listening to music ☐ 구 ☐ 절

4 because of bad weather ☐ 구 ☐ 절

5 that they are from England ☐ 구 ☐ 절

B 다음 문장의 밑줄 친 부분이 구인지 절인지 쓰시오.

1 We took a walk <u>after we had dinner</u>. → _____________

2 The flower shop is <u>next to the bakery</u>. → _____________

3 I think <u>that they need some rest</u>. → _____________

4 <u>Reading books</u> is important for learning. → _____________

5 Noah failed the test, <u>but Olivia passed it</u>. → _____________

CHAPTER 02 인칭대명사와 be동사

POINT 01 인칭대명사와 be동사의 현재형

A 다음 빈칸에 알맞은 be동사의 현재형을 쓰시오.

1 You ______________ a great dancer.

2 It ______________ under the bridge.

3 I ______________ 160 cm tall.

4 They ______________ at the airport.

5 She ______________ late for the concert.

B 다음 밑줄 친 부분을 줄임말로 바꿔 쓰시오.

1 <u>He is</u> from Japan.

2 <u>We are</u> in the bookstore.

3 <u>It is</u> a popular restaurant.

4 <u>You are</u> always full of energy.

5 <u>I am</u> at a cafe with my family.

C 다음 우리말과 같은 뜻이 되도록 문장을 완성하시오.

1 그들은 학교 도서관에 있다.

______________ in the school library.

2 나는 그 밴드의 열혈팬이다.

______________ ______________ a big fan of the band.

3 그녀는 모두에게 매우 친절하다.

______________ ______________ very friendly to everyone.

be동사의 과거형

A 다음 빈칸에 알맞은 be동사의 과거형을 쓰시오.

1 I ___________ proud of my team.

2 They ___________ brave soldiers.

3 It ___________ near the supermarket.

4 You ___________ right about the weather.

B 다음 [ ] 안에서 알맞은 말을 고르시오.

1 I (am / was) in a meeting right now.

2 We (are / were) at the beach yesterday.

3 She (is / was) a great leader last year.

4 My friends (are / were) busy with their homework now.

C 다음 우리말과 같은 뜻이 되도록 문장을 완성하시오.

1 어제 그 공연은 꽤 지루했다.

The show yesterday ___________ quite boring.

2 그들은 작년에 그 대학교 학생들이었다.

___________ ___________ students at the university last year.

3 그는 하루 종일 사무실에 있었다.

___________ ___________ in the office all day.

4 Sarah와 나는 오늘 아침 공원에 있었다.

Sarah and ___________ ___________ at the park this morning.

be동사의 부정문

A 다음 ( ) 안에서 알맞은 말을 고르시오.

1 You (not are / are not) late.

2 She (isn't / aren't) a morning person.

3 We (wasn't / weren't) in the same room.

4 Rick and Jerry (is not / are not) brothers.

B 다음 밑줄 친 부분을 줄임말로 바꿔 쓰시오.

1 It <u>was not</u> in the car.

2 <u>I am not</u> good at sports.

3 <u>He is not</u> my homeroom teacher.

4 <u>They are not</u> happy with the decision.

C 다음 문장을 부정문으로 바꿀 때, 빈칸에 알맞은 말을 쓰시오.

1 We are ready for the presentation.

→ ______________ ______________ ______________ ready for the presentation.

2 I'm a member of the art club.

→ ______________ ______________ ______________ a member of the art club.

3 The restaurant is open today.

→ ______________ ______________ ______________ ______________ open today.

4 My parents were at home last night.

→ ______________ ______________ ______________ ______________ at home last night.

POINT 04 be동사의 의문문

A 다음 우리말과 같은 뜻이 되도록 문장을 완성하시오.

1 너는 그 팀의 선수니?

______________ ______________ a player on the team?

2 그것이 어젯밤 냉장고 안에 있었니?

______________ ______________ in the refrigerator last night?

3 제가 그 일을 하기에는 너무 어린가요?

______________ ______________ too young for the job?

4 그는 그 결과에 자랑스러워하나요?

______________ ______________ proud of the results?

5 그들은 어제 서울에 있었나요?

______________ ______________ in Seoul yesterday?

B 다음 빈칸에 알맞은 말을 넣어 대화를 완성하시오.

1 A: ______________ ______________ a worker at this company?

B: No, she isn't.

2 A: Are they still at the gym?

B: Yes, ______________ ______________.

3 A: ______________ ______________ on vacation last week?

B: No, he wasn't.

4 A: Are you a good cook?

B: No, ______________ ______________.

5 A: Were you and your friends excited about the news?

B: Yes, ______________ ______________.

POINT 05 There is/are ~

A 다음 [ ] 안에서 알맞은 말을 고르시오.

1 There (is / are) a problem with my phone.

2 There (was / were) chairs around the table.

3 (There was not / There not was) a cloud in the sky.

4 A: (Is / Are) there two bathrooms in the house?

   B: No, there (isn't / aren't).

B 다음 문장을 지시대로 바꿀 때, 빈칸에 알맞은 말을 쓰시오.

1 There is a notebook on the desk. (부정문)

→ ________________ ______________ a notebook on the desk.

2 There are three cars in the parking lot. (과거형)

→ ________________ ______________ three cars in the parking lot.

3 There is a bank near the station. (의문문)

→ ____________ ____________ ____________ ____________ near the station?

C 다음 우리말과 같은 뜻이 되도록 [ ] 안의 말을 알맞게 배열하여 문장을 완성하시오.

1 해변에 사람들이 있나요? (people, are, at the beach, there)

____

2 모두를 위한 특별한 선물이 있었다. (there, for everyone, was, a special gift)

____

3 이 방에는 창문이 없다. (not, in this room, is, a window, there)

____

인칭대명사의 격 - 주격/소유격/목적격/소유대명사

A 다음 밑줄 친 부분을 어법에 맞게 고쳐 쓰시오.

1 <u>She</u> voice is beautiful.

2 The small house is <u>their</u>.

3 <u>Your</u> are a smart student.

4 Please join <u>our</u> for dinner.

5 <u>He</u> ideas are very creative.

6 Is the umbrella <u>your</u> or mine?

7 They help <u>my</u> with the housework.

8 The hotel is famous for <u>it</u> location.

B 다음 우리말과 같은 뜻이 되도록 문장을 완성하시오.

1 우리는 그들의 독특한 옷을 좋아한다.

___________ like ___________ unique clothes.

2 우리의 고양이는 회색이다. 그것의 털은 부드럽다.

___________ cat is gray. ___________ fur is soft.

3 그의 구두는 새것이고 그녀의 것은 낡았다.

___________ shoes are new, and ___________ are old.

4 그 반지는 나의 것이다. 그것은 나의 제일 친한 친구가 준 선물이다.

The ring is ___________. It was a gift from ___________ best friend.

5 Anne의 이야기들은 모험으로 가득하다. 나는 그것들을 정말 좋아한다.

___________ stories are full of adventure. I love ___________.

CHAPTER 02 REVIEW TEST

 다음 빈칸에 알맞은 말을 고르시오.

01

A: ___________ you Brian?
B: Yes, I am.

① Am　　② Are　　③ Is
④ Was　　⑤ Were

02

A: Were you at school yesterday?
B: No, ___________.

① I am　　② we are　　③ I'm not
④ I wasn't　　⑤ we were

03

다음 빈칸에 알맞은 말이 바르게 짝지어진 것은?

A: My uncle ___________ a writer.
B: Oh, really? Are ___________ books fiction?

① am – his　　② are – his
③ is – them　　④ is – his
⑤ are – their

서술형

04-06 다음 우리말과 같은 뜻이 되도록 빈칸에 알맞은 be동사를 쓰시오.

04

그 공원에는 토끼들이 있었다.

→ There ___________ rabbits in the park.

05

Emily는 어제 바쁘지 않았다.

→ Emily ___________ busy yesterday.

06

너희 부모님은 괜찮으시니?

→ ___________ your parents okay?

07-08 다음 중 〈보기〉의 밑줄 친 부분과 쓰임이 다른 것을 고르시오.

07

〈보기〉 Ms. Smith likes her dog.

① This is her scarf.
② We see her every day.
③ Her sister is Chloe.
④ Is her new shirt blue?
⑤ Today is her birthday.

08

〈보기〉 That book is his.

① His hobby is skiing.
② Those children are his.
③ The socks on the sofa are his.
④ Her name is Kate and his is Toby.
⑤ My favorite color is blue and his is red.

09　서술형

다음 빈칸에 알맞은 인칭대명사를 쓰시오.

I have a bag. ___________ is light. ___________ pockets are big. I use ___________ every day.

10

다음 중 밑줄 친 부분의 의미가 나머지와 <u>다른</u> 것은?

① Mary <u>is</u> my friend.
② I <u>am</u> in the living room.
③ She <u>isn't</u> home today.
④ <u>Are</u> you with Peter now?
⑤ Your cap <u>is</u> on the table.

11 - 12 다음 우리말과 같은 뜻이 되도록 주어진 말을 알맞게 배열하여 문장을 완성하시오.

11

> 너는 스포츠에 관심 있니?
> (you, interested, are, sports, in)

→ ______________________________

12

> 그는 유명한 배우가 아니었다.
> (not, a famous actor, was, he)

→ ______________________________

13

다음 밑줄 친 우리말을 영어로 바르게 옮긴 것은?

> A: Is he your brother?
> B: No, he isn't. <u>그는 Sam의 형이야.</u>

① Sam is his brother.
② He is Sams brother.
③ He is Sam's brother.
④ Sam's brother is his.
⑤ He is a brother Sam.

14 - 15 다음 중 밑줄 친 부분이 어법상 <u>틀린</u> 것을 고르시오.

14

① I'm <u>not</u> a good singer.
② Mr. Kim <u>wasn't</u> there.
③ There <u>is</u> a bird in the cage.
④ <u>Were</u> you free yesterday?
⑤ <u>Is</u> they her friends?

15

① Tell <u>me</u> your secret.
② Are those pencils <u>your</u>?
③ <u>I</u> am good at English.
④ She is <u>Dan's</u> daughter.
⑤ We visit <u>him</u> every weekend.

16 - 18 다음 표를 보고, 빈칸에 알맞은 말을 쓰시오.

Name	Age	Nationality	Job
Mira	13	Korea	Student
Mr. Brown	31	Canada	Teacher
Ping	25	China	Cook

16

Mira __________ 13 years old. She __________ a student.

17

Mr. Brown __________ 31 years old. __________ is a teacher.

18

Mira: __________ you from Korea?
Ping: No, __________ __________ . I am from China.

03 일반동사

일반동사의 현재형 - 1인칭/2인칭 주어

A 다음 두 문장 중에서 어법상 옳은 것에 ✔ 표시하시오.

1 ☐ I loves the new movie.

☐ I love the new movie.

2 ☐ You speaks French fluently.

☐ You speak French fluently.

3 ☐ We play basketball on weekends.

☐ We plays basketball on weekends.

4 ☐ You and your sister walks to school.

☐ You and your sister walk to school.

5 ☐ Daniel and I work at a restaurant.

☐ Daniel and I works at a restaurant.

B 다음 우리말과 같은 뜻이 되도록 〈보기〉에서 알맞은 말을 골라 빈칸에 적절한 형태로 써넣으시오.

〈보기〉 cook	exercise	listen	meet	read

1 너는 여가 시간에 책을 읽는다.

You ____________ books in your free time.

2 우리는 매일 저녁 요리를 한다.

We ____________ dinner every evening.

3 나는 일주일에 세 번 운동을 한다.

I ____________ three times a week.

4 그들은 토요일마다 친구들을 만난다.

They ____________ their friends every Saturday.

5 Bob과 나는 아침에 음악을 듣는다.

Bob and I ____________ to music in the morning.

일반동사의 현재형 - 3인칭 주어

A 다음 밑줄 친 부분이 어법상 맞으면 ○, 틀리면 X 표시하고 바르게 고치시오. (단, 현재형으로 쓸 것)

1 He <u>speak</u> three languages.

2 They always <u>help</u> each other.

3 It <u>grows</u> slowly in the winter.

4 The kids <u>wants</u> some ice cream.

5 My brother <u>reads</u> comics every evening.

6 Carrie <u>visit</u> the museum once a month.

7 Her friends <u>goes</u> to the park after school.

B 다음 우리말과 같은 뜻이 되도록 [ ] 안의 말을 이용하여 문장을 완성하시오.

1 그것은 하늘에서 밝게 빛난다. (shine)

It _____________ brightly in the sky.

2 그 학생들은 시험을 위해 열심히 공부한다. (study)

The students _____________ hard for their exams.

3 그녀는 일요일마다 자신의 방을 청소한다. (clean)

She _____________ her room on Sundays.

4 그들은 바닷가 작은 도시에 산다. (live)

They _____________ in a small town near the beach.

5 그 빵집은 평일 오전 10시에 문을 연다. (open)

The bakery _____________ at 10:00 a.m. on weekdays.

6 Ryan과 Tina는 매일 아침 버스 정류장에서 만난다. (meet)

Ryan and Tina _____________ at the bus stop every morning.

POINT 03

일반동사의 3인칭 단수 현재형

A 다음 밑줄 친 부분을 어법에 맞게 고쳐 쓰시오. (단, 현재형으로 쓸 것)

1 He <u>worry</u> about his health.

2 It <u>have</u> a unique design.

3 She <u>dress</u> quickly for work.

4 The store <u>sell</u> a winter jacket.

5 My father <u>wash</u> our clothes by hand.

6 The student <u>do</u> her best at all times.

7 Anthony <u>fix</u> the machine every weekend.

8 Mr. Green <u>teach</u> history at the school.

B 다음 우리말과 같은 뜻이 되도록 〈보기〉에서 알맞은 말을 골라 빈칸에 적절한 형태로 써넣으시오.

| 〈보기〉 go finish have study watch |

1 Jenny는 대학에서 미술을 공부한다.

Jenny ______________ art at university.

2 그 의사는 경험이 많다.

The doctor ______________ a lot of experience.

3 내 여동생은 금요일 밤마다 영화를 본다.

My sister ______________ movies on Friday nights.

4 그는 아침 식사 전에 체육관에 간다.

He ______________ to the gym before breakfast.

5 Ellis 씨는 보통 5시에 일을 마친다.

Ms. Ellis usually ______________ her work at five.

POINT 04 일반동사의 과거형 - 규칙 변화

A 다음 밑줄 친 부분을 어법에 맞게 고쳐 쓰시오.

1 I <u>live</u> in that house five years ago.

2 They <u>clean</u> the windows yesterday.

3 We <u>try</u> a new restaurant last Saturday.

4 He <u>bake</u> a cake for my birthday yesterday.

5 Alice <u>drop</u> her phone on the floor this morning.

6 My brother and I <u>carry</u> many books yesterday.

7 The show was great. We <u>enjoy</u> it very much.

B 다음 우리말과 같은 뜻이 되도록 [ ] 안의 말을 이용하여 문장을 완성하시오.

1 그녀는 회의 후에 문을 닫았다. (close)

She ______________ the door after the meeting.

2 그들은 함께 휴가를 계획했다. (plan)

They ______________ their vacation together.

3 그 아이는 몇 시간 동안 큰 소리로 울었다. (cry)

The child ______________ loudly for hours.

4 Jason은 나의 숙제를 도와주었다. (help)

Jason ______________ me with my homework.

5 우리는 어젯밤 새로운 어휘를 공부했다. (study)

We ______________ the new vocabulary last night.

6 나는 어제 내 친구에게서 소포 하나를 받았다. (receive)

I ______________ a package from my friend yesterday.

일반동사의 과거형 - 불규칙 변화 Ⅰ

A 다음 [ ] 안의 말을 빈칸에 적절한 형태로 써넣으시오.

1 Ken ______________ his job last year. (lose)

2 I ______________ a headache last night. (have)

3 She ______________ a new dress last Friday. (buy)

4 He ______________ a wallet on the street yesterday. (find)

5 They ______________ the treehouse ten years ago. (build)

6 We ______________ $80 for dinner last night. (pay)

7 I ______________ some friends at the cafe this morning. (meet)

8 Erica ______________ a present to him last month. (send)

B 다음 우리말과 같은 뜻이 되도록 〈보기〉에서 알맞은 말을 골라 빈칸에 적절한 형태로 써넣으시오.

〈보기〉	come	eat	get	make	leave

1 나는 어젯밤 늦게 Lily에게서 전화를 받았다.

   I ______________ a call from Lily late last night.

2 그녀는 동료들과 함께 사무실을 나갔다.

   She ______________ the office with her coworkers.

2 Max는 어제 점심에 샌드위치를 먹었다.

   Max ______________ a sandwich for lunch yesterday.

4 오늘 아침에 그 기차는 제시간에 왔다.

   The train ______________ on time this morning.

5 우리는 모든 사람들 앞에서 실수를 했다.

   We ______________ a mistake in front of everyone.

일반동사의 과거형 - 불규칙 변화 Ⅱ

A 밑줄 친 부분이 어법상 맞으면 O, 틀리면 X 표시하고 바르게 고치시오.

1 The shirt <u>cost</u> $50 last week.

2 Liz <u>cuts</u> the rope two days ago.

3 They <u>set</u> their goals last month.

4 I <u>puted</u> the keys on the desk yesterday.

5 The bird <u>hitted</u> the wall this morning.

6 Kevin <u>hurt</u> his leg during the game yesterday.

7 She <u>reads</u> the story to her children last night.

8 We <u>shut</u> the window an hour ago because of the rain.

B 다음 우리말과 같은 뜻이 되도록 〈보기〉에서 알맞은 말을 골라 빈칸에 적절한 형태로 써넣으시오.

〈보기〉	cut	hit	put	set	shut

1 Jamie는 조용히 문을 닫았다.

Jamie _____________ the door quietly.

2 우리는 침대 밑에 신발을 두었다.

We _____________ our shoes under the bed.

3 나는 오전 7시에 알람을 맞춰 놓았다.

I _____________ the alarm clock for 7:00 a.m.

4 그들은 그 종이를 작은 조각들로 잘랐다.

They _____________ the paper into small pieces.

5 그 트럭은 빠른 속도로 나무를 박았다.

The truck _____________ the tree at high speed.

일반동사의 현재형 부정문

A 다음 ( ) 안에서 알맞은 말을 고르시오.

1 We (not work / don't work) on Sundays.

2 My sister (don't / doesn't) watch the news.

3 You (don't / doesn't) understand the situation.

4 The hat doesn't (look / looks) good on me.

B 다음 문장을 부정문으로 바꿀 때, 빈칸에 알맞은 말을 쓰시오.

1 He knows the truth.

→ He ________________ ________________ the truth.

2 I agree with her opinion.

→ I ________________ ________________ with her opinion.

3 Ella drinks coffee in the afternoon.

→ Ella ________________ ________________ coffee in the afternoon.

4 My friends play video games often.

→ My friends ________________ ________________ video games often.

C 다음 우리말과 같은 뜻이 되도록 ( ) 안의 말을 이용하여 문장을 완성하시오.

1 그녀는 매운 음식을 즐기지 않는다. (enjoy)

________________ ________________ ________________ spicy food.

2 그들은 같은 나라에 살지 않는다. (live)

________________ ________________ ________________ in the same country.

3 그는 학교에서 교복을 입지 않는다. (wear)

________________ ________________ ________________ a uniform at school.

일반동사의 과거형 부정문

A 다음 [ ] 안에서 알맞은 말을 고르시오.

1 I (believed not / didn't believe) his story.

2 My parents didn't (like / liked) the movie.

3 She (doesn't / didn't) go there yesterday.

4 Carl didn't (sleep / sleeps) well last night.

B 다음 문장을 부정문으로 바꿀 때, 빈칸에 알맞은 말을 쓰시오.

1 You texted me back.

→ You ________________ ________________ me back.

2 Daisy joined us for lunch.

→ Daisy ________________ ________________ us for lunch.

3 We bought a birthday cake for Adam.

→ We ________________ ________________ a birthday cake for Adam.

C 다음 우리말과 같은 뜻이 되도록 [ ] 안의 말을 이용하여 문장을 완성하시오.

1 나는 오늘 아침에 몸이 좋지 않았다. (feel)

________________ ________________ ________________ well this morning.

2 그는 내 책을 제때 돌려주지 않았다. (return)

________________ ________________ ________________ my book on time.

3 우리는 작년에 같은 수업을 듣지 않았다. (take)

________________ ________________ ________________ the same class last year.

4 그들은 그 식당에서 야채를 먹지 않았다. (eat)

________________ ________________ ________________ their vegetables at the restaurant.

일반동사의 현재형 의문문

A 다음 밑줄 친 부분을 어법에 맞게 고쳐 쓰시오.

1 Do <u>have you</u> a pet?

2 Does Matt <u>runs</u> fast?

3 <u>Does</u> they need help with it now?

4 A: Does the store open early? – B: Yes, it <u>doesn't</u>.

B 다음 문장을 의문문으로 바꿀 때, 빈칸에 알맞은 말을 쓰시오.

1 You know the answer.

→ ＿＿＿＿＿＿ ＿＿＿＿＿＿ ＿＿＿＿＿ the answer?

2 Taylor works in this office.

→ ＿＿＿＿＿＿ ＿＿＿＿＿＿ ＿＿＿＿＿ in this office?

3 They play baseball after school.

→ ＿＿＿＿＿＿ ＿＿＿＿＿＿ ＿＿＿＿＿ baseball after school?

C 다음 [ ] 안의 말을 이용하여 대화를 완성하시오.

1 A: ＿＿＿＿＿＿ ＿＿＿＿＿＿ ＿＿＿＿＿ Chinese? (speak)

B: Yes, she does.

2 A: ＿＿＿＿＿＿ ＿＿＿＿＿＿ ＿＿＿＿＿ tickets for the concert? (need)

B: No, they ＿＿＿＿＿＿. It is a free event.

3 A: ＿＿＿＿＿ the movie ＿＿＿＿＿ at 9:00 p.m.? (start)

B: No, ＿＿＿＿＿＿ ＿＿＿＿＿. It starts at 8:00 p.m.

4 A: ＿＿＿＿＿＿ ＿＿＿＿＿＿ ＿＿＿＿＿ breakfast every day? (eat)

B: Yes, ＿＿＿＿＿＿ ＿＿＿＿＿. I usually have pancakes.

POINT 10 일반동사의 과거형 의문문

A 다음 [ ] 안에서 알맞은 말을 고르시오.

1 (Does / Did) he live in Seoul now?

2 (Do / Did) you visit her yesterday?

3 (Do / Did) they exercise regularly these days?

4 (Does / Did) Chloe travel abroad last summer?

B 다음 문장을 의문문으로 바꿀 때, 빈칸에 알맞은 말을 쓰시오.

1 Roy painted the picture.

→ ______________ ______________ ______________ the picture?

2 He finished the project last week.

→ ______________ ______________ ______________ the project last week?

3 They opened a restaurant five years ago.

→ ______________ ______________ ______________ a restaurant five years ago?

C 다음 우리말과 같은 뜻이 되도록 [ ] 안의 말을 이용하여 대화를 완성하시오.

1 A: 너는 그 소식을 들었어? (hear)

______________ ______________ ______________ the news?

B: Yes, ______________ ______________. I heard it this morning.

2 A: 그녀가 이메일을 확인했나요? (check)

______________ ______________ ______________ her email?

B: No, ______________ ______________. She was too busy.

3 A: 그들은 그 문제를 해결했나요? (solve)

______________ ______________ ______________ the problem?

B: Yes, ______________ ______________.

[01-02] 다음 빈칸에 알맞은 말을 고르시오.

01

A: ___________ Nick go to the gym?
B: No, he doesn't.

① Do　　　　　② Is
③ Does　　　　④ Did
⑤ Has

02

A: Did you invite him to the event?
B: Yes, ___________.

① I do　　　　② I did
③ you do　　　④ you did
⑤ I was

03

다음 빈칸에 알맞은 말이 바르게 짝지어진 것은?

My father ___________ for a bus company.
He ___________ a bus.

① is – drive　　　② do – drives
③ work – drive　　④ works – drives
⑤ workes – drives

[서술형]

[04-05] 다음 우리말과 같은 뜻이 되도록 주어진 말을 이용하여 문장을 완성하시오.

04

Andy는 공포 영화를 보지 않는다. (watch)

→ Andy ___________ ___________ horror movies.

05

너는 선물을 샀니? (buy)

→ ___________ ___________ ___________ a present?

[06-07] 다음 중 밑줄 친 부분이 어법상 틀린 것을 고르시오.

06

① Do you <u>listen</u> to pop music?
② He <u>speaks</u> English very well.
③ They <u>move</u> to Busan last year.
④ My brother <u>likes</u> mystery stories.
⑤ Sarah <u>enjoys</u> shopping with her friends.

07

① <u>Do</u> your sister wear glasses?
② He <u>looked</u> at me and smiled.
③ <u>Do</u> you talk to your parents a lot?
④ My mother <u>bought</u> a backpack for me.
⑤ <u>Did</u> you <u>have breakfast this morning</u>?

08

다음 중 대화가 자연스럽지 <u>않은</u> 것은?

① A: Do you know Tom?
　 B: Yes, I do.
② A: Do they take a bus to school?
　 B: No, they don't. They walk to school.
③ A: Does he play the piano?
　 B: No, he didn't.
④ A: Does she like math?
　 B: Yes, she does. It's her favorite subject.
⑤ A: Did you see Erica yesterday?
　 B: No, I didn't.

09

다음 대답이 나올 수 있는 질문으로 알맞은 것은?

> Yes, he did.

① Does he have a car?

② Did he pass the exam?

③ Was he with you yesterday?

④ Is he a high school student?

⑤ Did you go swimming with him?

10-11 다음 우리말과 같은 뜻이 되도록 주어진 말을 알맞게 배열하여 문장을 완성하시오.

10

> 그녀는 양파를 먹지 않는다.
> (doesn't, she, onions, eat)

→ ___________________________________

11

> Jack은 일기를 쓰나요?
> (keep, Jack, a diary, does)

→ ___________________________________

12-13 다음 중 어법상 옳은 것을 고르시오.

12

① Ann don't study at night.

② I leaved my phone in a taxi.

③ Does he reads books every day?

④ We traveled to Paris last summer.

⑤ Did the store opened at nine o'clock?

13

① Do she live with her friend?

② I go to bed early last night.

③ They didn't see the stop sign.

④ She cutted the picture yesterday.

⑤ I always carries my earphones with me.

14

다음 밑줄 친 우리말을 영어로 바르게 옮긴 것은?

> A: 너희 오빠는 일찍 일어나니?
> B: No, he doesn't.

① Your brother got up early?

② Your brother get up early?

③ Do your brother get up early?

④ Does your brother gets up early?

⑤ Does your brother get up early?

15-16 다음 문장을 지시대로 바꾸어 쓰시오.

15

> Jessie saw her aunt this morning.

→ _________________________________ (부정문)

16

> Robert sent an email.

→ _________________________________ (의문문)

POINT 01 셀 수 있는 명사 - 규칙 변화 I

A 다음 명사의 복수형을 쓰시오.

1 ball ___________ 2 potato ___________

3 box ___________ 4 dish ___________

5 beach ___________ 6 house ___________

7 photo ___________ 8 class ___________

9 rose ___________ 10 chair ___________

11 window ___________ 12 church ___________

13 wish ___________ 14 building ___________

15 fox ___________ 16 piano ___________

17 dress ___________ 18 sandwich ___________

B 다음 밑줄 친 부분을 어법에 맞게 고쳐 쓰시오.

1 I have two <u>map</u> of Seoul.

2 <u>Tomato</u> are good for your health.

3 She ate five chocolate <u>cookie</u>.

4 Lots of <u>bus</u> go to the stadium.

5 The <u>tree</u> in the woods were very tall.

6 Please move these <u>box</u> for me.

7 Jennie joined three <u>club</u> last year.

8 There are fresh <u>peach</u> in the fridge.

9 I cleaned the shoes with two <u>brush</u>.

10 We need more <u>glass</u> for the party.

11 There are many <u>flower</u> in his garden.

셀 수 있는 명사 - 규칙 변화 II

A 다음 명사의 복수형을 쓰시오.

1 story __________ **2** wolf __________

3 holiday __________ **4** guy __________

5 elf __________ **6** berry __________

7 lady __________ **8** life __________

9 knife __________ **10** city __________

11 enemy __________ **12** donkey __________

13 leaf __________ **14** roof __________

15 body __________ **16** journey __________

17 wife __________ **18** company __________

B 다음 밑줄 친 부분을 어법에 맞게 고쳐 쓰시오.

1 The <u>boy</u> are best friends.

2 Two <u>thief</u> ran away quickly.

3 Many <u>family</u> live in this town.

4 Brian works four <u>day</u> a week.

5 The children enjoyed various <u>activity</u>.

6 Seoul, Beijing, and Tokyo are big <u>city</u>.

7 The <u>key</u> on the table are mine.

8 All the <u>chef</u> wear white uniforms.

9 The <u>shelf</u> are full of <u>toy</u>.

10 There were fallen <u>leafs</u> on the ground.

11 Different <u>country</u> have different cultures.

셀 수 있는 명사 - 불규칙 변화

A 다음 밑줄 친 부분을 어법에 맞게 고쳐 쓰시오.

1 <u>Ox</u> are strong animals.

2 Many <u>woman</u> enjoy yoga.

3 Patrick caught three <u>fishes</u>.

4 <u>Mouse</u> are afraid of cats.

5 My brother has very big <u>foot</u>.

6 There are five <u>man</u> in the store.

7 All the <u>child</u> in the class were quiet.

8 Brush your <u>tooths</u> three times a day.

9 <u>Sheeps</u> have thick wool on their bodies.

B 다음 우리말과 같은 뜻이 되도록 [ ] 안의 말을 이용하여 문장을 완성하시오.

1 거위들은 시끄러운 소리를 낸다. (goose)

 _______________ make loud noises.

2 아이들은 많은 잠이 필요하다. (child)

 _______________ need a lot of sleep.

3 그 남자들은 같은 회사에서 일한다. (man)

 The _______________ work at the same company.

4 그녀의 발은 진흙으로 덮여 있었다. (foot)

 Her _______________ were covered in mud.

5 우리는 호수 근처에서 사슴 두 마리를 보았다. (deer)

 We saw two _______________ near the lake.

셀 수 없는 명사

A 다음 [ ] 안에서 알맞은 말을 고르시오.

1 Emily lives in (a Paris / Paris).

2 Love (is / are) a powerful feeling.

3 Their (friendship / friendships) was strong.

4 There is (a butter / butter) on the table.

5 The teacher gives helpful (advice / advices).

B 다음 밑줄 친 부분을 어법에 맞게 고쳐 쓰시오.

1 A Monday is my favorite day.

2 The news were very interesting.

3 Waters is important to all living things.

4 Mr. Ross showed kindnesses to everyone.

5 I have milks and doughnuts every morning.

C 다음 〈보기〉에서 알맞은 말을 골라 빈칸에 적절한 형태로 써넣으시오. [단, 한 번씩만 사용할 것]

〈보기〉	furniture	gold	hope	smoke	time

1 Her words give us ____________.

2 We found some shiny ____________.

3 They saw ____________ in the air.

4 I don't have enough ____________ for a hobby.

5 My family bought new ____________ yesterday.

셀 수 없는 명사의 수량 표현

A 다음 밑줄 친 부분을 어법에 맞게 고쳐 쓰시오.

1 He ate a <u>bowls</u> of salad for lunch.

2 We need ten <u>piece</u> of paper for the test.

3 I added a slice of <u>cheeses</u> to my sandwich.

4 She drank three <u>cup of teas</u> during breakfast.

5 Robin tried on a <u>pairs of shoe</u> at the store.

B 다음 우리말과 같은 뜻이 되도록 〈보기〉와 [ ] 안의 말을 이용하여 문장을 완성하시오. [단, 한 번씩만 사용할 것]

〈보기〉	bottle	bowl	glass	loaf	pair	piece

1 나는 자기 전에 우유 두 잔을 마셨다. (milk)

   I had two ________________ before bed.

2 그녀는 피자 한 조각을 나와 나눠 먹었다. (pizza)

   She shared a ________________ with me.

3 Jane은 탄산음료 다섯 병을 가져왔다. (soda)

   Jane brought five ________________.

4 그는 서랍에서 장갑 한 켤레를 찾았다. (glove)

   He found ________________ in his drawer.

5 Steve는 회의 후에 밥 두 그릇을 먹었다. (rice)

   Steve ate ________________ after the meeting.

6 우리는 제과점에서 빵 세 덩이를 샀다. (bread)

   We bought ________________ from the bakery.

부정관사 a/an

A 다음 빈칸에 a와 an 중 알맞은 말을 쓰시오. (불필요하면 X 표시할 것)

1 The price is $10 ______________ day.

2 I called you ______________ hour ago.

3 There is ______________ sugar in the jar.

4 We found ______________ wallet on the ground.

5 Ben is ______________ engineer at the company.

6 I want ______________ cup of hot cocoa, please.

7 She gave me ______________ advice on my project.

8 He read ______________ article about history.

9 The city holds a festival twice ______________ year.

B 다음 우리말과 같은 뜻이 되도록 부정관사와 ( ) 안의 말을 이용하여 문장을 완성하시오.

1 그 차는 한 시간에 50킬로미터를 간다. (hour)

   The car is going 50 km ______________ ______________.

2 Linda는 병원에서 자원봉사자로 일한다. (volunteer)

   Linda works as ______________ ______________ at a hospital.

3 그들은 정원이 있는 집에 산다. (garden)

   They live in a house with ______________ ______________.

4 저에게 우산 하나를 빌려줄 수 있나요? (umbrella)

   Can you lend me ______________ ______________?

5 우리는 한 달에 한 번 가족 여행을 간다. (once, month)

   We go on a family trip ______________ ______________ ______________.

정관사 the

A 다음 ( ) 안에서 알맞은 말을 고르시오.

1 Rome is (a / the) capital of Italy.

2 What time does (a / the) sun rise?

3 They arrived (an / the) hour later.

4 He practices (a / the) trumpet every day.

5 I found some information on (a / the) Internet.

6 We clean the house twice (a / the) week.

7 Pass me (a / the) red pepper on the table, please.

8 Larry bought a new car. He washed (a / the) car yesterday.

9 This is her most famous novel. A lot of people read (a / the) novel.

B 다음 우리말과 같은 뜻이 되도록 관사와 ( ) 안의 말을 이용하여 문장을 완성하시오.

1 의자 옆에 있는 그 가방은 내 것이다. (bag)

_______________ _______________ next to the chair is mine.

2 그는 어젯밤에 라디오를 들었다. (radio)

He listened to _______________ _______________ last night.

3 Emily는 밴드에서 첼로를 연주한다. (cello)

Emily plays _______________ _______________ in a band.

4 오늘 아침에 하늘이 잔뜩 흐렸다. (sky)

_______________ _______________ was very cloudy this morning.

5 우리는 나무 한 그루를 심었다. 그 나무는 크게 자랐다. (tree)

We planted _______________ _______________. _______________ _______________ grew tall.

관사의 생략

A 다음 빈칸에 알맞은 관사를 쓰시오. (불필요하면 X 표시할 것)

1 We have ____________ lunch at home every day.

2 Do you go to ____________ work by bus?

3 She put the pillow on ____________ bed.

4 He plays ____________ golf with Alexa after work.

5 Paul contacted me by ____________ phone.

6 Diana plays ____________ flute in the school orchestra.

7 Students don't go to ____________ school on weekends.

8 I had ____________ early dinner with my family.

9 My brother went to ____________ bed two hours ago.

10 They go to Busan by ____________ plane once ____________ week.

B 다음 우리말과 같은 뜻이 되도록 관사와 [ ] 안의 말을 이용하여 문장을 완성하시오. (관사가 불필요하면 생략할 것)

1 (train) 너는 기차를 타고 여기 왔니?   Did you come here by ____________?

그 기차는 오전 9시에 도착한다.   ____________ arrives at 9:00 a.m.

2 (bed) 나는 어젯밤에 일찍 잤다.   I went to ____________ early last night.

그 침대는 아주 편했다.   ____________ was very comfortable.

3 (TV) 나는 저녁 식사 후 TV를 본다.   I watch ____________ after dinner.

그녀는 TV를 껐다.   She turned off ____________.

4 (piano) 방에 피아노 한 대가 있다.   There is ____________ in the room.

Noah는 피아노를 잘 친다.   Noah plays ____________ well.

01

다음 중 명사의 단수형과 복수형이 잘못 연결된 것은?

① cat – cats
② watch – watches
③ toy – toies
④ mouse – mice
⑤ man – men

02 - 03 다음 빈칸에 들어갈 수 없는 말을 고르시오.

02

I bought a ___________ at the market.

① book
② shirt
③ pan
④ sugar
⑤ gift

03

There is ___________ in the fridge.

① milk
② ice
③ lemons
④ honey
⑤ butter

04 - 05 다음 빈칸에 알맞은 말이 바르게 짝지어진 것을 고르시오.

04

Jane had a ___________ of coffee and two ___________ of cake.

① cup – piece
② cup – pieces
③ glass – slice
④ glasses – slices
⑤ bottle – bowl

05

Jack downloaded an image from ___________ Internet and printed ___________ image on ___________ piece of paper.

① a – an – a
② an – the – an
③ a – an – the
④ the – the – a
⑤ the – a – a

06 - 07 다음 빈칸에 알맞은 말을 고르시오.

06

Dave is a night owl. He usually ___________ ___________ around midnight.

① go to bed
② goes to bed
③ goes to a bed
④ goes to an bed
⑤ goes to the bed

07

A: Look! I have ___________.
B: Wow, they look great on you.

① a new glass
② a new glasses
③ new pair of glasses
④ a new pair of glasses
⑤ the new pairs of glass

서술형

08 - 10 어법상 틀린 부분을 찾아 바르게 고쳐 쓰시오.

08

Emily goes to school by the subway.
(Emily는 지하철을 타고 학교에 간다.)

09

Tim gave me a novel. A novel was interesting.
(Tim이 나에게 소설을 한 권 주었다. 그 소설은 흥미로웠다.)

10

Dan plays the baseball every Sunday.
(Dan은 일요일마다 야구를 한다.)

11

다음 중 〈보기〉의 밑줄 친 부분과 쓰임이 같은 것은?

〈보기〉 Leo goes to the gym twice a week.

① Jessica has a dog and two cats.
② I wrote a story about aliens.
③ The pen cost a dollar and ten cents.
④ I see him about three times a year.
⑤ Her mother is a doctor at the hospital.

12

다음 빈칸에 공통으로 들어갈 말은?

• He earns $10 ___________ hour.
• Charlotte became ___________ actress.

① a　　　　　② an
③ the　　　　④ this
⑤ per

13-14　다음 우리말과 같은 뜻이 되도록 주어진 말을 알맞게 배열하여 문장을 완성하시오.

13

나는 할머니께 수프 한 그릇을 만들어 드렸다.
I ___________________ for my grandmother.
(soup, a, made, of, bowl)

14

Harper는 하루에 차 두 잔을 마신다.
Harper drinks ___________________.
(day, two, of, a, tea, cups)

15

다음 밑줄 친 우리말을 영어로 바르게 옮긴 것은?

Josh likes music. 그는 기타를 친다.

① He plays an guitar.
② He plays guitars.
③ He plays a guitars.
④ He plays the guitar.
⑤ He plays the guitars.

16-17　다음 중 어법상 틀린 것을 고르시오.

16

① I need some advice.
② Jay went to Spain last year.
③ There are two files on the desk.
④ There are millions of star in the sky.
⑤ Sheep produce meat, milk, and wool.

17

① They have three children.
② I didn't bring an umbrella today.
③ Tom wrote a note on a piece of paper.
④ She bought a bottle of orange juice.
⑤ Do you have enough times for the meeting?

POINT 01 지시대명사

A 다음 [ ] 안에서 알맞은 말을 고르시오.

1 Is (this / these) fast or slow?

2 (These / Those) snacks in my hand are for you.

3 I'll take (that / those). They look perfect.

4 (This / That) store across the street sells fresh fruit.

5 She painted (this / these) walls last weekend.

B 다음 우리말과 같은 뜻이 되도록 빈칸에 알맞은 지시대명사를 쓰시오.

1 저분들은 Luna의 조부모님이다.

_______________ are Luna's grandparents.

2 그는 이것을 부엌으로 옮길 것이다.

He will move _______________ into the kitchen.

3 이것들은 나에게 너무 작다.

_______________ are too small for me.

4 문 근처에 있는 저거 네 우산이니?

Is _______________ your umbrella near the door?

C 다음 밑줄 친 부분을 어법에 맞게 고쳐 쓰시오.

1 <u>Those</u> boat under the bridge is his.

2 Are <u>this</u> your books on this shelf?

3 <u>That</u> part right here seems broken.

4 Don't touch <u>that</u> wires on the ceiling.

5 Can you see <u>this</u> woman over there?

부정대명사 one

A 다음 [ ] 안에서 알맞은 말을 고르시오.

1 I made two sandwiches. Do you want (it / one)?

2 Those socks are dirty. Put on clean (one / ones).

3 This bag feels heavy. (It / One) hurts my shoulder.

4 He lost his pencil, so he borrowed (it / one) from his friend.

5 A: Do you sell large notebooks? – B: No, just small (one/ ones).

B 다음 우리말과 같은 뜻이 되도록 빈칸에 알맞은 부정대명사를 쓰시오.

1 사람은 거짓말을 해선 안 된다.

____________ should not lie.

2 사각 테이블을 원하세요 아니면 원형 테이블을 원하세요?

Do you want square tables or round ____________?

3 나는 이 영화를 좋아하지 않아. 다른 것을 보자.

I don't like this movie. Let's watch a different ____________.

C 다음 빈칸에 one, ones, it, them 중 알맞은 말을 쓰시오.

1 ____________ should make decisions carefully.

2 He got a bike for his birthday. He rides ____________ every day.

3 These spoons are plastic. We need metal ____________ for the soup.

4 I took some pictures there and posted ____________ on my blog.

5 She didn't like the blue jacket, so she bought the red ____________.

6 Those curtains are too dark. I'll replace ____________ with brighter ____________.

A 다음 빈칸에 some과 any 중 알맞은 말을 쓰시오.

1 I need to get some tools. I don't have ______________.

2 We baked cookies. Would you like ______________?

3 Is there ______________ paper in the printer?

4 Try ______________ of this soup. It's delicious.

5 Don't send ______________ messages tonight.

6 We have extra pens. Why don't you take ______________?

7 I checked the drawer, but I didn't find ______________ candles.

8 Grace made many dresses. ______________ were colorful.

9 I didn't read ______________ books, but she read ______________.

10 I wanted to buy ______________ roses for my mom, but the store didn't have

______________.

B 다음 우리말과 같은 뜻이 되도록 〈보기〉에서 알맞은 말을 골라 문장을 완성하시오.

〈보기〉 any	one	ones	some

1 몇 명의 친구들이 저녁을 먹으러 왔다. 몇몇이 선물을 가져왔다.

Several of my friends came to dinner. ______________ brought gifts.

2 Mason이 담요를 다 가져갔다. 우리는 어떤 것도 받지 못했다.

Mason took all the blankets. He didn't leave ______________ for us.

3 의자 몇 개는 부서졌어. 멀쩡한 것들을 몇 개 가져오자.

Some of these chairs are broken. Let's get some good ______________.

4 너 충전기 필요하니? Amelia가 가방에 하나 갖고 있어.

Do you need a charger? Amelia has ______________ in her backpack.

비인칭 주어 it

A 다음 두 문장 중에서 밑줄 친 It[it]이 비인칭 주어인 것에 ✔ 표시하시오.

1 ☐ It is a raincoat.

☐ It rained for a week.

2 ☐ It is not interesting.

☐ It is not far from here.

3 ☐ It is bright in here.

☐ It was in my pocket.

4 ☐ It is Monday again.

☐ He didn't do it again.

5 ☐ Did it arrive on time?

☐ What day of the week is it?

B 다음 우리말과 같은 뜻이 되도록 [ ] 안의 말을 이용하여 문장을 완성하시오.

1 지금 몇 시야? (what time)

_______________ _______________ _______________ _______________ now?

2 총 5개월이 걸렸다. (take, month)

_______________ _______________ _______________ _______________ in total.

3 겨울에는 춥고 건조하다. (cold, dry)

_______________ _______________ _______________ _______________ in winter.

4 오늘은 그들의 결혼식 날이다. (wedding day)

_______________ _______________ _______________ today.

5 공항까지 약 8킬로미터이다. (about, kilometer)

_______________ _______________ _______________ _______________ to the

airport.

재귀대명사

A 다음 빈칸에 알맞은 재귀대명사를 쓰시오.

1 I hurt ______________ at the gym.

2 The cat cleaned ______________.

3 We wrote letters to them ______________.

4 My mom ______________ called the doctor.

5 Some people don't love ______________.

6 Claire, you should believe in ______________.

7 Mr. Johnson ______________ answered the questions.

B 다음 우리말과 같은 뜻이 되도록 문장을 완성하시오.

1 여왕이 직접 그 마을을 방문했다.

The queen ______________ visited the town.

2 나는 나 자신을 위해 선물을 샀다.

I bought a gift for ______________.

3 그 아이들은 자기들끼리 놀고 있다.

The kids are playing by ______________.

4 Andrew는 직접 식사를 준비했다.

Andrew ______________ prepared the meal.

5 너희들은 콘서트에서 즐거운 시간을 보냈어?

Did you enjoy ______________ at the concert?

6 내 친구와 나는 반 학생들에게 우리 자신을 소개했다.

My friend and I introduced ______________ to the class.

A 다음 밑줄 친 재귀대명사를 생략할 수 있으면 ○, 없으면 X 표시하시오.

1 We cooked dinner <u>ourselves</u>.

2 He carried the box <u>himself</u>.

3 This plant grows by <u>itself</u>.

4 I found <u>myself</u> in a strange place.

5 The actress <u>herself</u> sang the song.

6 Please be honest with <u>yourselves</u>, guys.

7 The children <u>themselves</u> built the treehouse.

B 다음 우리말과 같은 뜻이 되도록 재귀대명사와 [ ] 안의 말을 이용하여 문장을 완성하시오.

1 나는 그 생각 자체가 마음에 들지 않았다. (idea)

I didn't like the ________________ ________________.

2 그것들은 뱀으로부터 자신들을 보호한다. (protect)

They ________________ ________________ from snakes.

3 그의 할아버지는 직접 설거지를 하셨다. (wash)

His grandfather ________________ ________________ the dishes.

4 너는 네 자신을 돌봐야 한다. (take care of)

You need to ________________ ________________ ________________ ________________.

5 우리는 직접 그 컴퓨터를 고쳤다. (fix)

________________ ________________ the computer ________________.

6 Lucy는 다른 사람들과 그녀 자신에 대해 이야기하지 않는다. (talk about)

Lucy doesn't ________________ ________________ ________________ with others.

01-02 다음 빈칸에 알맞은 말을 고르시오.

01

A: ____________ is already eleven o'clock.
B: Really? We're late!

① This   ② That
③ It   ④ One
⑤ Some

02

A: Look! I drew this picture ____________!
B: Good job!

① me   ② it
③ myself   ④ mine
⑤ yourself

03

다음 빈칸에 공통으로 들어갈 말은?

• I stayed at the hotel for ____________ night.
• ____________ should not speak ill of others.
• My brother broke my tablet PC. I need a
  new ____________.

① this[This]   ② that[That]
③ it[It]   ④ one[One]
⑤ you[You]

서술형

04-05 다음 밑줄 친 부분을 어법에 맞게 고쳐 쓰시오.

04

These causes some problems.
(이것은 몇몇 문제를 일으킨다.)

05

Are that your children?
(저 사람들이 당신의 아이들입니까?)

06-07 다음 중 〈보기〉의 밑줄 친 부분과 쓰임이 다른 것을 고르시오.

06

〈보기〉 We enjoyed ourselves at the beach.

① Lynn often talks to herself.
② My mom hit herself with the door by
   accident.
③ He was angry at himself for the mistake.
④ The kids cleaned their rooms themselves.
⑤ You should forgive yourself first.

07

〈보기〉 What day is it today?

① It wasn't his fault.
② It is already Friday.
③ It was cold last night.
④ It's my friend's birthday today.
⑤ It takes twenty minutes to get to school.

08

다음 빈칸에 알맞은 말이 바르게 짝지어진 것은?

A: Do you have ____________ information
   about the job?
B: Yes, I have ____________.

① an – it   ② some – it
③ some – any   ④ any – some
⑤ any – any

09

다음 중 대화가 자연스럽지 <u>않은</u> 것은?

① A: Would you like some tea?

　B: Yes, please.

② A: Do you have any brothers or sisters?

　B: Yes, I have any.

③ A: Those cookies taste good.

　B: Yes, but these ones taste better.

④ A: What is the weather like?

　B: It's rainy and windy.

⑤ A: This machine doesn't work.

　B: I'm sorry. I'll exchange it for a new one.

10-12 다음 우리말과 같은 뜻이 되도록 대명사와 주어진 말을 이용하여 문장을 완성하시오.

10

이것들은 수업을 위한 내 공책들이다. (notebook)

→ ___________ ___________ ___________ ___________

for class.

11

그날은 따뜻했다. (warm)

→ ___________ ___________ ___________ that day.

12

그는 다른 사람들에게 자신을 소개했다. (introduce)

→ ___________ ___________ ___________ to the

others.

13

다음 밑줄 친 우리말을 영어로 바르게 옮긴 것은?

A: Are there any clean cups?

B: No, but <u>더러운 것들 몇 개가 있어</u>.

① there is a dirty one

② there is this dirty one

③ there are any dirty ones

④ there are some dirty one

⑤ there are some dirty ones

14-15 다음 중 밑줄 친 부분이 어법상 <u>틀린</u> 것을 고르시오.

14

① <u>This</u> is my brother's laptop.

② All of <u>those</u> cakes look delicious.

③ They didn't ask <u>some</u> questions.

④ <u>These</u> towns are famous for their grapes.

⑤ <u>Some</u> of the students were late.

15

① Please tell me about <u>yourself</u>.

② They built the house <u>theirselves</u>.

③ She looked at <u>herself</u> in the mirror.

④ Fred hurt <u>himself</u> in an accident.

⑤ I posted a photo of <u>myself</u> on my blog.

16

다음 중 빈칸에 It[it]이 들어갈 수 <u>없는</u> 것은?

① ___________ is still cold.

② ___________ is late. Let's go to bed.

③ ___________ should believe in oneself.

④ ___________ is a good movie about love.

⑤ Did you see my email? I sent ___________

　ten minutes ago.

06 시제

POINT 01 현재시제

A 다음 [ ] 안의 말을 빈칸에 적절한 형태로 써넣으시오.

1 We ______________ ready to go now. (be)

2 Japan ______________ four seasons. (have)

3 Bob ______________ a lot these days. (read)

4 The Moon ______________ around the Earth. (go)

B 다음 밑줄 친 부분을 어법에 맞게 고쳐 쓰시오.

1 A day <u>had</u> 24 hours.

2 I <u>studied</u> math every day now.

3 Seoul <u>was</u> the capital of Korea.

4 Emily <u>owned</u> a bakery, and she bakes all the bread herself.

C 다음 우리말과 같은 뜻이 되도록 〈보기〉에서 알맞은 말을 골라 빈칸에 적절한 형태로 써넣으시오.

〈보기〉 be	give	make	walk

1 벌은 꿀을 만든다.

Bees ______________ honey.

2 그는 매일 저녁 개를 산책시킨다.

He ______________ his dog every evening.

3 태양은 우리에게 빛과 열을 준다.

The Sun ______________ us light and heat.

4 우리 집에서 학교까지는 2km이다.

It ______________ two kilometers from my house to school.

A 다음 [ ] 안의 말을 빈칸에 적절한 형태로 써넣으시오.

1 Sue _______________ to her mother yesterday. (lie)

2 My brother _______________ a bike last week. (buy)

3 They _______________ in Los Angeles ten years ago. (live)

4 Korea _______________ fourth place in the 2002 World Cup. (take)

5 Charles Dickens _______________ *A Christmas Carol* in 1843. (write)

B 다음 [ ] 안에서 알맞은 말을 고르시오.

1 It (is / was) chilly yesterday, so I turned on the heater.

2 He (doesn't / didn't) like kimchi at first, but now he does.

3 The book was really interesting. I (finish / finished) it in one day.

4 We (are / were) very tired last night because we (work / worked) all day.

5 Angela (is / was) usually very careful, but she (make / made) a mistake yesterday.

C 다음 우리말과 같은 뜻이 되도록 [ ] 안의 말을 이용하여 문장을 완성하시오.

1 그들은 한 시간 전에 점심을 먹었다. (eat)

   They _______________ lunch an hour ago.

2 Nathan은 지난달에 새 일자리를 얻었다. (get)

   Nathan _______________ a new job last month.

3 그녀는 2020년에 대학을 졸업했다. (graduate)

   She _______________ from college in 2020.

4 지난 여름에 우리는 바닷가에서 많은 시간을 보냈다. (spend)

   We _______________ a lot of time at the beach last summer.

진행형 만드는 방법

A 다음 동사를 <v-ing>의 형태로 바꾸어 쓰시오.

1	read	___________	**2**	say	___________
3	live	___________	**4**	win	___________
5	open	___________	**6**	take	___________
7	get	___________	**8**	lie	___________
9	move	___________	**10**	watch	___________
11	begin	___________	**12**	bring	___________
13	tie	___________	**14**	dance	___________

B 다음 두 문장 중에서 어법상 옳은 것에 ✔ 표시하시오.

1 ☐ I'm knowing Brandon's last name. ☐ I'm writing his address.

2 ☐ He is playing with his toy car. ☐ He is wanting a new sports car.

3 ☐ She is having two brothers. ☐ She is having breakfast right now.

C 다음 〈보기〉에서 알맞은 말을 골라 빈칸에 적절한 형태로 써넣으시오.

〈보기〉	come	cut	enter	ride	tie	wait

1 I am ___________ my shoes.

2 We are ___________ for the bus.

3 They are ___________ the grass in the park.

4 The teacher is ___________ the classroom.

5 My sister is ___________ a bike around the lake.

6 The children are ___________ home from school.

현재진행형과 과거진행형

A 다음 문장을 진행형으로 바꿀 때, 빈칸에 알맞은 말을 쓰시오.

1 I clean my room.

I ＿＿＿＿＿＿＿＿ ＿＿＿＿＿＿＿＿ my room.

2 Lisa drew a picture.

Lisa ＿＿＿＿＿＿＿＿ ＿＿＿＿＿＿＿＿ a picture.

3 They cook dinner together.

They ＿＿＿＿＿＿＿＿ ＿＿＿＿＿＿＿＿ dinner together.

4 We watched a movie last night.

We ＿＿＿＿＿＿＿＿ ＿＿＿＿＿＿＿＿ a movie last night.

5 My brother studies at the library.

My brother ＿＿＿＿＿＿＿＿ ＿＿＿＿＿＿＿＿ at the library.

B 다음 우리말과 같은 뜻이 되도록 [ ] 안의 말을 이용하여 문장을 완성하시오.

1 그는 나를 바라보고 있었다. (look)

＿＿＿＿＿＿＿＿ ＿＿＿＿＿＿＿＿ ＿＿＿＿＿＿＿＿ at me.

2 나는 설거지를 하는 중이다. (wash)

＿＿＿＿＿＿＿＿ ＿＿＿＿＿＿＿＿ the dishes.

3 그녀는 방에서 바이올린을 연습하는 중이다. (practice)

＿＿＿＿＿＿＿＿ ＿＿＿＿＿＿＿＿ ＿＿＿＿＿＿＿＿ the violin in her room.

4 Gary는 그들을 위해 노래를 부르고 있었다. (sing)

＿＿＿＿＿＿＿＿ ＿＿＿＿＿＿＿＿ ＿＿＿＿＿＿＿＿ a song for them.

5 그 선수들은 다음 시즌을 대비해 훈련하는 중이다. (player, train)

＿＿＿＿＿＿＿＿ ＿＿＿＿＿＿＿＿ ＿＿＿＿＿＿＿＿ ＿＿＿＿＿＿＿＿ for next season.

6 내 친구들은 우리 학교 앞에 서 있었다. (friend, stand)

＿＿＿＿＿＿＿＿ ＿＿＿＿＿＿＿＿ ＿＿＿＿＿＿＿＿ ＿＿＿＿＿＿＿＿ in front of our school.

진행형의 부정문

A 다음 [ ] 안에서 알맞은 말을 고르시오.

1 Eve (is not / not is) talking to Mark.

2 I am not (wear / wearing) a sweater.

3 We (did / were) not watching the game on TV.

4 He (wasn't / weren't) paying attention in class.

5 Lucas and Olivia (isn't / aren't) doing their homework.

B 다음 문장을 지시대로 바꿀 때, 빈칸에 알맞은 말을 쓰시오.

1 I'm using the program now. (현재진행형 부정문)

→ I'm _______________ _______________ the program now.

2 The children aren't playing in the yard. (현재진행형 긍정문)

→ The children _______________ _______________ in the yard.

3 Ted wasn't driving to the gas station. (현재진행형 부정문)

→ Ted _______________ _______________ to the gas station.

4 We aren't fighting with each other. (과거진행형 부정문)

→ We _______________ _______________ with each other.

C 다음 우리말과 같은 뜻이 되도록 [ ] 안의 말을 이용하여 문장을 완성하시오.

1 그녀는 주방을 청소하고 있지 않았다. (clean)

_______________ _______________ _______________ the kitchen.

2 나는 지금 그 영화를 즐기고 있지 않다. (enjoy)

_______________ _______________ _______________ the movie now.

3 그들은 나를 찾고 있지 않았다. (look)

_______________ _______________ _______________ for me.

4 Daniel과 Joe는 시험공부를 하고 있지 않다. (study)

Daniel and _______________ _______________ _______________ for the test.

진행형의 의문문

A 다음 [ ] 안에서 알맞은 말을 고르시오.

1 Am I (do / doing) this right?

2 Is (he painting / painting he) the wall?

3 (Was / Were) they waiting for you?

4 Was Chloe (brushed / brushing) her teeth?

5 (Is / Are) you writing on your blog now?

B 다음 빈칸에 알맞은 말을 넣어 대화를 완성하시오.

1 A: _______________ _______________ looking for a job?

  B: Yes, he is. He's checking job sites every day.

2 A: _______________ _______________ listening to music?

  B: Yes, I am. This is my favorite song.

3 A: _______________ _______________ raining this morning?

  B: No, _______________ _______________. It was sunny all morning.

4 A: _______________ the kids jumping on the bed?

  B: _______________, _______________ _______________. They were sitting quietly.

C 다음 우리말과 같은 뜻이 되도록 [ ] 안의 말을 이용하여 문장을 완성하시오.

1 Carter는 친구에게 전화하는 중이니? (call)

  _______________ _______________ _______________ his friend?

2 그녀가 큰 상자를 들고 있었나요? (hold)

  _______________ _______________ _______________ a large box?

3 그들은 옷을 사는 중이야? (shop)

  _______________ _______________ _______________ for clothes?

4 너희들은 보드게임을 하고 있었어? (play)

  _______________ _______________ _______________ board games?

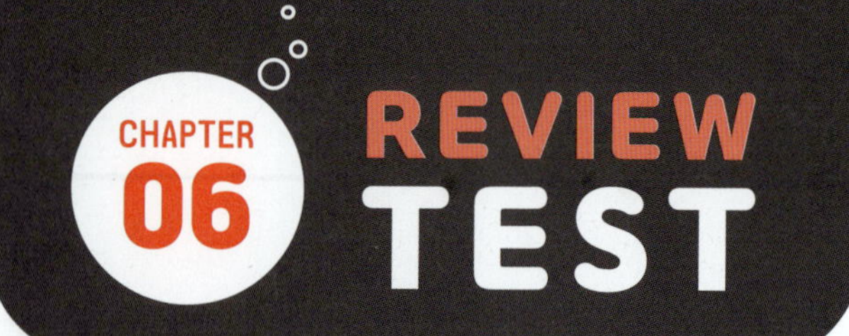

01 - 03 다음 빈칸에 알맞은 말을 고르시오.

01

A: Are you listening to me?
B: Yes, ___________.

① I do
② I am
③ I was
④ I don't
⑤ I'm not

02

A: Did she eat dessert?
B: Yes, she did. She ___________ some apple pie.

① ate
② eats
③ eating
④ is eating
⑤ was ate

03

Was Terry ___________ at that time?

① drive
② drives
③ drove
④ driving
⑤ driven

04

다음 중 밑줄 친 동사의 형태가 잘못된 것은?

① You were smileing at me.
② I'm not drinking milk right now.
③ Was she putting the toys away?
④ William is tying the rope.
⑤ Are they flying over the lake?

05 - 06 다음 빈칸에 알맞은 말이 바르게 짝지어진 것을 고르시오.

05

A: What ___________ you do yesterday?
B: I ___________ care of my sister all day.

① do – take
② do – took
③ did – take
④ did – takes
⑤ did – took

06

• He ___________ in the hospital now.
• I ___________ a slice of pizza.

① is – want
② was – want
③ is – am wanting
④ was – was wanting
⑤ did – am wanting

서술형

07 - 08 다음 우리말과 같은 뜻이 되도록 주어진 말을 이용하여 문장을 완성하시오.

07

Steve는 매일 운동을 한다. (work out)

→ Steve ___________ ___________ every day.

08

Jenny는 지난여름 하와이에서 즐거운 시간을 보냈다. (have fun)

→ Jenny ___________ ___________ in Hawaii last summer.

09

다음 대답이 나올 수 있는 질문으로 알맞은 것은?

> I was watching TV.

① What do you do?
② What are you doing now?
③ Do you watch TV at night?
④ Did you have a good time?
⑤ What were you doing at that time?

10-11 다음 우리말과 같은 뜻이 되도록 주어진 말을 알맞게 배열하여 문장을 완성하시오.

10

> Jane은 신문을 읽고 있지 않았다.
> (was, Jane, the newspaper, reading, not)

→ _______________________________

11

> 그는 그의 부인을 위해 요리를 하고 있다.
> (cooking, he, wife, for, is, his)

→ _______________________________

12

다음 밑줄 친 우리말을 영어로 바르게 옮긴 것은?

> I sent you a text message last night, but you didn't reply. <u>너는 자고 있었니?</u>

① Do you sleep?
② Does you sleep?
③ Are you sleeping?
④ Was you sleeping?
⑤ Were you sleeping?

13-14 다음 중 밑줄 친 부분이 어법상 틀린 것을 고르시오.

13

① <u>Is he staying</u> at a hotel now?
② The birds <u>are singing</u> happily.
③ They <u>were walking</u> together.
④ Tom <u>didn't doing</u> his homework.
⑤ Amy <u>agreed</u> with me at the last meeting.

14

① You <u>look</u> tired today.
② I <u>meet</u> my friend yesterday.
③ I usually <u>sleep</u> six hours a day.
④ Arthur <u>is studying</u> in his room.
⑤ How old <u>were</u> you at the time of the accident?

15-17 Laura의 어제 일정표를 보고, 주어진 말을 이용하여 문장을 완성하시오.

10:00-11:00	Yoga
11:00-12:00	-
12:00-13:00	Lunch with Ben

15

Laura __________ __________ __________
yesterday morning. (do)

16

Laura __________ nothing to do between 11:00 and 12:00 yesterday. (have)

17

Laura __________ __________ __________
__________ __________ at 12:30 yesterday.
(eat)

POINT 01 will

A 다음 ( ) 안에서 알맞은 말을 고르시오.

1 We (met / will meet) Emma next weekend.

2 She (will not / not will) forget your birthday.

3 Will the train (leave / leaves) at 10:00 a.m.?

4 Tom (will / won't) be in Korea next year. He'll go back to the US.

B 다음 밑줄 친 부분을 어법에 맞게 고쳐 쓰시오.

1 I <u>willn't</u> say anything tomorrow.

2 Linda will <u>visits</u> her grandparents soon.

3 They will <u>help not</u> us with the project.

4 Will <u>cook your brother</u> dinner tonight?

C 다음 우리말과 같은 뜻이 되도록 ( ) 안의 말을 이용하여 문장을 완성하시오.

1 그녀는 새로운 일을 시작할 것이다. (start)

______________ ______________ ______________ a new job.

2 이번 주 금요일에 메일을 보내 주시겠어요? (send)

______________ ______________ ______________ the email this Friday?

3 우리는 저 영화를 다시 보지 않을 것이다. (watch)

______________ ______________ ______________ that movie again.

4 A: 그가 시간 맞춰 집에 도착할까요? (arrive)

______________ ______________ ______________ home on time?

B: 아니요, 그는 조금 늦을 거예요. (be)

No, ______________ ______________ a bit late.

be going to

A 다음 [ ] 안에서 알맞은 말을 고르시오.

1 (I'm / I'll) going to buy a new laptop soon.

2 Is Ted going to (drive / drives) to Busan on Sunday?

3 (Do / Are) you going to study English after dinner?

4 She's (going not / not going) to take the test tomorrow.

B 다음 우리말과 같은 뜻이 되도록 be going to와 [ ] 안의 말을 이용하여 문장을 완성하시오.

1 Betty는 나에게 그녀의 사진들을 보여 줄 것이다. (show)

Betty _______________________ me her photos.

2 오늘 아침에 비가 그치지 않을 것이다. (stop)

The rain _______________________ this morning.

3 너는 집에서 저녁을 먹을 거니? (have)

_______________________ dinner at home?

4 Harry와 나는 방과 후에 배드민턴을 치지 않을 것이다. (play)

Harry and I _______________________ badminton after school.

C 다음 우리말과 같은 뜻이 되도록 [ ] 안의 말을 알맞게 배열하여 문장을 완성하시오.

1 너는 네 자전거를 고칠 거니? (going, your, are, bike, to, you, fix)

____

2 나는 그 책을 읽지 않을 것이다. (read, not, to, I'm, that book, going)

____

3 학생들은 교실을 청소할 것이다. (to, are, the classroom, going, the students, clean)

____

can

A 다음 ( ) 안에서 알맞은 말을 고르시오.

1 Amber (can / cans) ride a skateboard.

2 You (can't / not can) eat in the library.

3 Can (open you / you open) this bottle?

4 We (can / could) not go on a picnic yesterday because of the rain.

B 다음 빈칸에 알맞은 말을 넣어 대화를 완성하시오.

1 A: ______________ ______________ join us at the party later?

B: No, I can't. I have to study.

2 A: Can the children swim?

B: Yes, ______________ ______________. They enjoy playing in the pool.

3 A: Can I leave early today?

B: No, ______________ ______________. You still have work to do.

C 다음 우리말과 같은 뜻이 되도록 can과 ( ) 안의 말을 이용하여 문장을 완성하시오.

1 Steve는 매운 음식을 먹지 못한다. (eat)

______________ ______________ ______________ spicy food.

2 우리는 도움 없이 그 문제를 해결할 수 있다. (solve)

______________ ______________ ______________ the problem without help.

3 너는 그 그림을 만질 수 없다. (touch)

______________ ______________ ______________ that painting.

4 제가 모임에 친구를 데려가도 되나요? (bring)

______________ ______________ ______________ my friend to the meeting?

can과 be able to

A 다음 밑줄 친 부분을 어법에 맞게 고쳐 쓰시오.

1 I'm not able <u>hear</u> you clearly.

2 Dan <u>are</u> able to use this program now.

3 <u>Are</u> you able to get some rest last night?

4 Jackie was <u>able not</u> to hide her emotions.

B 다음 〈보기〉와 같이 be able to를 이용한 문장으로 바꾸어 쓰시오.

> 〈보기〉　Ryan can make kimchi. → Ryan is able to make kimchi.

1 We can't stay here forever.　　→ We ＿＿＿＿＿＿＿＿＿ here forever.

2 He can speak three languages. → He ＿＿＿＿＿＿＿＿＿ three languages.

3 They could find the station.　　→ They ＿＿＿＿＿＿＿＿＿ the station.

4 Can you pay the bill online?　　→ ＿＿＿＿＿＿＿＿＿ the bill online?

5 Eva couldn't finish her homework.

　　→ Eva ＿＿＿＿＿＿＿＿＿ her homework.

C 다음 우리말과 같은 뜻이 되도록 [ ] 안의 말을 이용하여 문장을 완성하시오.

1 우리는 여기에서 채소를 재배할 수 있다. (grow)

＿＿＿＿＿ ＿＿＿＿＿ ＿＿＿＿＿ ＿＿＿＿＿ ＿＿＿＿＿ vegetables here.

2 당신은 어제 그 파일을 저장할 수 있었어요? (save)

＿＿＿＿＿ ＿＿＿＿＿ ＿＿＿＿＿ ＿＿＿＿＿ the file yesterday?

3 Mia는 오늘 밤에 영화를 보러 갈 수 없다. (go)

＿＿＿＿＿ ＿＿＿＿＿ ＿＿＿＿＿ ＿＿＿＿＿ to the movies tonight.

4 나는 오늘 아침에 일찍 일어날 수 있었다. (wake)

＿＿＿＿＿ ＿＿＿＿＿ ＿＿＿＿＿ ＿＿＿＿＿ up early this morning.

may

A 다음 〈보기〉에서 알맞은 말을 골라 대화를 완성하시오.

> 〈보기〉   may be driving   may not come   may not use   may I borrow

1 A: Grace, ___________________ your umbrella?

B: Of course. Just bring it back tomorrow.

2 A: Lisa ___________________ to the concert tonight.

B: Really? She was so excited about it!

3 A: Why isn't Dad answering his phone?

B: He ___________________ right now.

4 A: We ___________________ our phones during the test.

B: Yeah, the teacher said we aren't allowed.

B 다음 우리말과 같은 뜻이 되도록 may와 [ ] 안의 말을 이용하여 문장을 완성하시오.

1 그 소포는 내일 도착할지도 모른다. (arrive)

The package _____________ _____________ tomorrow.

2 방문객들은 오전 10시 이후에 정원에 들어갈 수 있다. (enter)

Visitors _____________ _____________ the garden after 10:00 a.m.

3 제가 당신의 운전면허증을 봐도 될까요? (see)

_____________ _____________ _____________ your driver's license, please?

4 그녀는 나의 여행 계획을 좋아하지 않을지도 모른다. (like)

_____________ _____________ _____________ _____________ my plans for the trip.

5 여러분은 박물관 안에서 사진을 찍으면 안 됩니다. (take)

_____________ _____________ _____________ _____________ photos in the museum.

A   다음 [ ] 안에서 알맞은 말을 고르시오.

1   She must (tell / to tell) the truth.

2   We (must / must not) break the law. It's wrong.

3   You must (are / be) honest with your friends.

4   His jacket is wet. It (must / can't) be raining outside.

B   다음 밑줄 친 부분의 의미를 〈보기〉에서 골라 그 기호를 쓰시오.

> 〈보기〉   ⓐ ~해야 한다   ⓑ ~하면 안 된다   ⓒ ~임이 틀림없다   ⓓ ~일 리가 없다

1   Kids <u>must not</u> play on the road.   (   )

2   The alarm is ringing. It <u>must</u> be seven o'clock.   (   )

3   They <u>can't</u> be home already. The bus just left.   (   )

4   All students <u>must</u> bring gym clothes tomorrow.   (   )

C   다음 우리말과 같은 뜻이 되도록 must와 〈보기〉의 말을 이용하여 문장을 완성하시오.

> 〈보기〉   be   park   show   write

1   그는 Emily의 오빠임이 틀림없다.

  ____________ ____________ ____________ Emily's brother.

2   너는 연필로 답을 적으면 안 된다.

  ____________ ____________ ____________ ____________ your answer with a

pencil.

3   우리는 도서관에서 신분증을 보여 줘야 한다.

  ____________ ____________ ____________ our ID at the library.

4   그들은 문 앞에 주차하면 안 된다.

  ____________ ____________ ____________ in front of the gate.

have to

A 다음 ( ) 안에서 알맞은 말을 고르시오.

1 Do I (must / have to) take the class?

2 They have (stop / to stop) fighting.

3 Sue (has / have) to meet her teacher.

4 We (musted / had to) cancel the trip last month.

5 He (don't / doesn't) have to wear a suit to the event.

6 You (must not / don't have to) enter this room. It's for staff only.

7 We have a dishwasher. You (must not / don't have to) wash the dishes.

B 다음 우리말과 같은 뜻이 되도록 ( ) 안의 말을 이용하여 문장을 완성하시오.

1 너는 학교 근처에서 천천히 운전해야 한다. (drive)

You ________________ ________________ ________________ slowly near the school.

2 제가 줄을 서야 하나요? (wait)

________________ I ________________ ________________ ________________ in line?

3 우리는 점심을 가져갈 필요가 없다. (bring)

We ________________ ________________ ________________ ________________ our own lunch.

4 그들은 빨리 안전한 장소를 찾아야 했다. (find)

________________ ________________ ________________ ________________ a safe place quickly.

5 그녀는 어젯밤에 늦게까지 일해야 했나요? (work)

________________ ________________ ________________ ________________ ________________ late last

night?

6 Adam은 어떤 것에 대해서도 걱정할 필요가 없다. (worry)

________________ ________________ ________________ ________________ ________________ about

anything.

should

A 다음 〈보기〉에서 알맞은 말을 골라 should나 shouldn't를 이용하여 대화를 완성하시오.

> 〈보기〉　bring　　eat　　see　　make　　study

1 A: I'm feeling sick.

B: You ______________ ______________ a doctor.

2 A: You ______________ ______________ noise here.

B: Sorry, I'll be quiet.

3 A: I have a test tomorrow.

B: ______________ ______________ ______________ for it now.

4 A: Mom, ______________ ______________ ______________ a jacket?

B: Yes, you should. It's cold outside.

5 A: Can I have some chocolate?

B: No. ______________ ______________ ______________ too much before dinner.

B 다음 우리말과 같은 뜻이 되도록 〈보기〉와 [ ] 안의 말을 이용하여 문장을 완성하시오.

> 〈보기〉　should　　shouldn't　　don't have to　　can't

1 그녀는 자신의 돈을 다 쓰지 말아야 한다. (spend)

______________ ______________ ______________ all her money.

2 너는 신발을 벗어야 한다. (take off)

______________ ______________ ______________ ______________ your shoes.

3 그는 이 생각에 대해 진지할 리가 없다. (be serious)

______________ ______________ ______________ about this idea.

4 우리는 휴일에 학교에 갈 필요가 없다. (go)

______________ ______________ ______________ ______________ ______________ to

school on holidays.

CHAPTER 07 REVIEW TEST

01-02 다음 빈칸에 알맞은 말을 고르시오.

01

> He may be lying. You __________ trust him.

① have to   ② may   ③ will
④ can   ⑤ shouldn't

02

> A: Did you try on the red dress?
> B: Yes, but it didn't look good on me. So I
> __________ buy it.

① may   ② can   ③ will not
④ should   ⑤ am able to

03

다음 우리말과 같은 뜻이 되도록 빈칸에 들어갈 말로 알맞은 것은?

> 나는 네 전화에 바로 답신을 하지 않을지도 모른다.
> I __________ not return your calls right away.

① may   ② can   ③ must
④ will   ⑤ should

서술형

04-06 다음 우리말과 같은 뜻이 되도록 빈칸에 알맞은 말을 쓰시오.

04

> 너는 오늘 밤에 시험공부를 할 거니?

→ __________ you __________ __________ study
   for the test tonight?

05

> 그의 사촌은 기차를 탈 수 없었다.

→ His cousin __________ __________ __________
   catch the train.

06

> 그 기계는 고장 났을지도 모른다.

→ The machine __________ be broken.

07-08 다음 중 〈보기〉의 밑줄 친 부분과 쓰임이 <u>다른</u> 것을 고르시오.

07

> 〈보기〉 We <u>must</u> follow the traffic rules.

① We <u>must</u> help poor people.
② Students <u>must</u> wear school uniforms.
③ You <u>must</u> be careful with knives.
④ You <u>must</u> finish your report by 10:00 a.m.
⑤ He's so good. He <u>must</u> be a professional
   player.

08

> 〈보기〉 Josh <u>can</u> speak five languages.

① <u>Can</u> your sister drive?
② I <u>can</u> skate very well.
③ You <u>can</u> enter the building now.
④ <u>Can</u> you play this song on the guitar?
⑤ Music <u>can</u> express people's feelings.

09

다음 빈칸에 공통으로 들어갈 말은?

> • You ___________ go out and play now.
> • Sir, ___________ I ask a question?

① may
② cannot
③ will
④ must
⑤ have to

10-11 다음 우리말과 같은 뜻이 되도록 주어진 말을 알맞게 배열하여 문장을 완성하시오.

10

> 너는 설탕을 너무 많이 먹지 않아야 한다.
> (eat, not, so much sugar, should, you)

→ _______________________________________

11

> 우리는 여기 머물러야 하나요?
> (have, stay, do, here, we, to)

→ _______________________________________

12

다음 중 대화가 자연스럽지 <u>않은</u> 것은?

① A: Can you answer the phone?
   B: Sure.
② A: Should I bring an umbrella today?
   B: Yes, you should. It's going to rain.
③ A: Must I fill out this form?
   B: No, you don't have to.
④ A: Can you visit me tomorrow?
   B: I'm afraid I can't.
⑤ A: May I have your attention, please?
   B: No, I can't.

13

다음 밑줄 친 우리말을 영어로 바르게 옮긴 것은?

> A: Lucy is very angry at you.
> B: I know. <u>그녀는 나를 용서하지 않을 거야.</u>

① She can't forgive me.
② She must not forgive me.
③ She should not forgive me.
④ She is able to forgive me.
⑤ She isn't going to forgive me.

14

다음 중 밑줄 친 부분이 어법상 <u>틀린</u> 것은?

① <u>Can you read</u> the sign?
② She <u>will call</u> you in ten minutes.
③ I <u>can't understand</u> this book.
④ You <u>don't may leave</u> the classroom.
⑤ They <u>had to say</u> goodbye to their children.

15-16 다음 문장을 우리말로 해석하시오.

15

> Everybody likes Tim. He must be very kind.

→ _______________________________________

16

> You don't have to be sorry. It was my fault.

→ _______________________________________

08 형용사, 부사, 비교

형용사의 역할

A 다음 문장에서 형용사가 수식하는 말을 찾아 밑줄로 표시하시오.

1   She plants red roses.

2   The news made us angry.

3   His shoes were muddy.

4   I met someone friendly at the event.

B 다음 밑줄 친 부분을 어법에 맞게 고쳐 쓰시오.

1 The child looks <u>happily</u>.

2 He is a <u>musician talented</u>.

3 The test was <u>difficulty</u> for me.

4 They kept the room <u>cleanly</u>.

5 Do you have <u>hot anything</u> to drink?

C 다음 우리말과 같은 뜻이 되도록 〈보기〉와 [ ] 안의 말을 이용하여 문장을 완성하시오.

〈보기〉 easy	clear	different	strange

1   오늘 하늘이 맑다. (sky)

The ______________ is ______________ today.

2   우리는 숲에서 이상한 동물을 보았다. (animal)

We saw a ______________ ______________ in the woods.

3   나는 저녁 식사로 색다른 것을 원한다. (something)

I want ______________ ______________ for dinner.

4   Sarah는 이 퍼즐이 쉽다는 것을 알았다. (this puzzle)

Sarah found ______________ ______________ ______________.

수량 형용사

A 다음 [ ] 안에서 알맞은 말을 고르시오.

1 He poured (a few / a little) milk into his glass.

2 Lisa did (few / little) work today.

3 We don't have (many / much) time. Please hurry up.

4 (A little / A lot of) children are playing in the park.

B 다음 빈칸에 들어갈 수 <u>없는</u> 것에 ✔ 표시하시오.

1 She didn't have ____________ chocolate.　　☐ many　☐ much　☐ lots of

2 There isn't much ____________ on the road.　☐ snow　☐ traffic　☐ people

3 There were ____________ games at the event.　☐ few　☐ little　☐ a lot of

4 I brought a little ____________ for the hike.　☐ water　☐ food　☐ sandwiches

C 다음 우리말과 같은 뜻이 되도록 [ ] 안의 말을 이용하여 문장을 완성하시오.

1 그 상자 안에 장난감이 많이 있다. (toy)

   There are ____________ ____________ in the box.

2 그들은 그 프로젝트에 대한 정보가 거의 없다. (information)

   They have ____________ ____________ about the project.

3 그는 수프에 채소를 약간 넣었다. (vegetable)

   He added ____________ ____________ ____________ to the soup.

4 내 친구는 나에게 많은 조언을 해 주었다. (advice)

   My friend gave me ____________ ____________ ____________ ____________ .

부사의 역할과 형태

A 다음 [ ] 안에서 알맞은 말을 고르시오.

1 She carried the baby (careful / carefully).

2 Jeff gave a (quick / quickly) answer.

3 I'm not feeling very well (late / lately).

4 (Sad / Sadly), our team lost the game.

5 The bird flew (high / highly) in the sky.

6 We (gentle / gently) touched the flowers.

7 He finished his homework (early / earlily).

8 Ally performed (good / well) in the school play.

9 They are training (hard / hardly) for the Olympics.

10 This program keeps your computer (safe / safely).

B 다음 [ ] 안의 말을 빈칸에 적절한 형태로 써넣으시오.

1 (quiet) The library is very ______________.

She closed the door ______________.

2 (good) That was a ______________ choice.

They danced ______________ at the show.

3 (angry) Ted shouted ______________ at his friend.

Don't make her ______________ again.

4 (simple) This is a ______________ design.

He explained it ______________ to the class.

5 (late) We arrived ______________ to the meeting.

The bus was ______________ this morning.

빈도부사

A 다음 ( ) 안의 빈도부사가 들어갈 알맞은 위치를 고르시오.

1 (never)   It ① rains ② in this desert ③.

2 (often)   Jim ① is ② tired ③ after school.

3 (always)   Players ① must ② follow ③ the rules.

B 다음 우리말과 같은 뜻이 되도록 빈칸에 알맞은 빈도부사를 쓰시오.

1 나는 보통 자전거를 타고 학교에 간다.

I ______________ ride a bike to school.

2 그들은 패스트푸드를 거의 먹지 않는다.

They ______________ eat fast food.

3 너는 가끔 휴식을 취해야 한다.

You should ______________ take a break.

4 Jessica는 일에 절대 늦지 않는다.

Jessica is ______________ late for work.

5 우리는 토요일에 자주 축구를 한다.

We ______________ play soccer on Saturday.

C 다음 우리말과 같은 뜻이 되도록 ( ) 안의 말을 알맞게 배열하여 문장을 완성하시오.

1 그들은 항상 모두에게 친절하다. (kind, are, always)

They ______________________________ to everyone.

2 그는 보통 자기 전에 샤워를 한다. (a shower, takes, usually)

He ______________________________ before bed.

3 나는 절대 다른 사람들에 대해 나쁜 말을 하지 않을 것이다. (never, bad things, say, will)

I ______________________________ about others.

원급 비교

A 다음 우리말과 같은 뜻이 되도록 〈보기〉에서 알맞은 말을 골라 빈칸에 적절한 형태로 써넣으시오.

> 〈보기〉 carefully   clean   difficult   heavy   loudly   shy

1 저 상자는 바위만큼 무겁다.

That box is ________________________ a rock.

2 그는 엄마만큼 조심스럽게 케이크를 먹었다.

He ate the cake ________________________ his mom.

3 Jenny는 보이는 것만큼 부끄럼을 타지 않는다.

Jenny is ________________________ she looks.

4 이 퍼즐은 수학 시험만큼 어렵다.

This puzzle is ________________________ a math test.

5 나는 내 친구만큼 크게 웃지 않았다.

I didn't laugh ________________________ my friend.

6 그 방은 우리가 기대한 것만큼 깨끗하지 않았다.

The room was ________________________ we expected.

B 다음 〈보기〉와 같이 'as ~ as'를 이용하여 두 문장을 한 문장으로 만드시오.

> 〈보기〉 My bag is 30 cm wide. Your bag is 30 cm wide, too.
> → My bag is as wide as your bag.

1 Elizabeth is 150 cm tall. Her sister is 150 cm tall, too.

→ Elizabeth is ________________________ her sister.

2 It's very hot today. It is 24℃ in Seoul. It is 30℃ in Daegu.

→ Seoul is ________________________ Daegu.

3 Eric solved the problem in one minute. Eve solved it in one minute, too. They both solved it quickly.

→ Eve solved the problem ________________________ Eric did.

비교급과 최상급 만드는 방법

A 다음 단어의 비교급과 최상급을 쓰시오.

		비교급	최상급
1	smart		
2	large		
3	funny		
4	expensive		
5	big		
6	good		
7	long		
8	useful		
9	lazy		
10	difficult		
11	wise		
12	dangerous		

B 다음 [ ] 안에서 알맞은 말을 고르시오.

1 It was the (hotest / hottest) summer in ten years.

2 I have (more / much) money than you.

3 He is the (fastest / most fast) student in the class.

4 They woke up (early / earlier) than usual.

5 Sophia works (harder / more hard) than her friends.

6 This was the (popularest / most popular) film of the year.

비교급 비교

A 다음 [ ] 안의 말을 이용하여 비교급 문장을 완성하시오.

1 Your room is ___________________________ mine. (big)

2 She eats ___________________________ he does. (much)

3 Light travels much ___________________________ sound. (fast)

4 Making yogurt is ___________________________ you think. (easy)

5 Jackson sings ___________________________ before. (well)

6 The tablet is ___________________________ the laptop. (useful)

7 Chloe arrived ___________________________ the others. (early)

8 In some countries, wine is ___________________________ water. (cheap)

9 This book is even ___________________________ the movie. (interesting)

10 My sister learned Chinese ___________________________ I did. (quickly)

B 다음 우리말과 같은 뜻이 되도록 [ ] 안의 말을 이용하여 문장을 완성하시오.

1 현미가 백미보다 더 몸에 좋다. (healthy)

Brown rice is ___________ ___________ white rice.

2 버스는 우리가 예상한 것보다 더 늦게 왔다. (late)

The bus came ___________ ___________ we expected.

3 이번 시험은 지난번 것보다 훨씬 더 어려웠다. (much, difficult)

This exam was ___________ ___________ ___________ ___________ the

last one.

4 그는 반 친구들보다 더 분명하게 대답했다. (clearly)

He answered ___________ ___________ ___________ his classmates.

5 시간을 아끼는 것이 돈을 아끼는 것보다 훨씬 더 중요하다. (a lot, important)

Saving time is ___________ ___________ ___________

___________ saving money.

최상급 비교

A   다음 [ ] 안에서 알맞은 말을 고르시오.

1   Shanghai is the (larger / largest) city in China.

2   It was (much / the most) exciting trip of my life.

3   That is one of the tallest (building / buildings) in Asia.

4   Vincent is the (most / more) diligent of all the workers.

5   Mt. Everest is (highest / the highest) mountain in the world.

B   다음 [ ] 안의 말을 이용하여 최상급 문장을 완성하시오.

1   He always runs ___________________________ of all. (fast)

2   What is ___________________________ word in English? (long)

3   Zoe got ___________________________ grade in the class. (bad)

4   This is ___________________________ question on the test. (difficult)

5   Coffee is one of ___________________________ drinks in the world. (popular)

C   다음 우리말과 같은 뜻이 되도록 [ ] 안의 말을 이용하여 문장을 완성하시오.

1   이것은 시중에서 가장 가벼운 노트북이다. (light, laptop)

     This is ___________ ___________ ___________ on the market.

2   그것은 올해 최고의 영화였다. (good, movie)

     It was ___________ ___________ ___________ of the year.

3   나는 이 책에서 가장 중요한 장을 읽고 있다. (important, chapter)

     I'm reading ___________ ___________ ___________ ___________ in this book.

4   Dali는 스페인 출신의 가장 유명한 화가들 중 한 명이다. (famous, artist)

     Dali is ___________ ___________ ___________ ___________

     ___________ from Spain.

01

다음 중 형용사와 부사가 <u>잘못</u> 연결된 것은?

① wise – wisely　　② sudden – suddenly

③ simple – simply　　④ early – earlily

⑤ angry – angrily

02

다음 중 원급, 비교급, 최상급이 <u>잘못</u> 연결된 것은?

① much – more – most

② nice – nicer – nicest

③ big – bigger – biggest

④ busy – busier – busiest

⑤ beautiful – beautifuler – beautifulest

03 - 04 다음 빈칸에 들어갈 수 <u>없는</u> 말을 고르시오.

03

> Those books look ___________.

① boring　　② difficult

③ easily　　④ heavy

⑤ interesting

04

> Sean drank ___________ water.

① little　　② a few

③ a little　　④ lots of

⑤ a lot of

05

다음 빈칸에 알맞은 말이 바르게 짝지어진 것은?

> A: Is your brother ___________ than you?
> B: No, I'm the ___________ in my family.

① tall – tallest　　② taller – tallest

③ tall – taller　　④ taller – tall

⑤ tallest – tallest

서술형

06 - 08 다음 우리말과 같은 뜻이 되도록 주어진 말을 이용하여 문장을 완성하시오.

06

> 이 게임은 저것만큼 재미있지 않다. (fun)

→ This game is ___________ ___________ ___________ ___________ that one.

07

> 미래가 과거보다 더 중요하다. (important)

→ The future is ___________ ___________ ___________ the past.

08

> 대왕고래는 지구상에서 가장 큰 동물이다. (large)

→ The blue whale is ___________ ___________ animal on earth.

09

다음 중 밑줄 친 부분의 쓰임이 나머지와 <u>다른</u> 것은?

① She works very <u>hard</u>.
② We need a <u>new</u> computer.
③ I found the movie <u>interesting</u>.
④ I'd like to meet someone <u>nice</u>.
⑤ His face turned <u>red</u> at her comment.

10-11 다음 우리말과 같은 뜻이 되도록 주어진 말을 알맞게 배열하여 문장을 완성하시오.

10

> 너는 항상 솔직해야 한다.
> (always, honest, you, be, should)

→ ______________________________

11

> 그는 세계에서 가장 부유한 사람들 중 한 명이다. (the, one, he, people, of, richest, in the world, is)

→ ______________________________

12

다음 밑줄 친 우리말을 영어로 바르게 옮긴 것은?

> A: What do you do on weekends?
> B: <u>나는 대개 친구들과 축구를 해.</u>

① I play always soccer with my friends.
② I always play soccer with my friends.
③ I never play soccer with my friends.
④ I usually play soccer with my friends.
⑤ I play usually soccer with my friends.

13-14 다음 중 밑줄 친 부분이 어법상 <u>틀린</u> 것을 고르시오.

13

① We need <u>a little</u> sugar.
② I don't have <u>much</u> money.
③ <u>Many</u> children play outside.
④ It gave us <u>a lot of</u> information.
⑤ There are <u>a little</u> apples in the basket.

14

① I'm <u>as tired as</u> you are.
② This skirt is <u>much short than</u> that one.
③ I don't study <u>as hard as</u> I should.
④ There were <u>more</u> girls than boys in the class.
⑤ He is one of the <u>strongest</u> players on his team.

15-17 다음 표를 보고, 주어진 말을 이용하여 비교하는 문장을 완성하시오.

Activity	Time	Price
Hiking	2 hours	$20
Scuba Diving	2 hours	$100
Bike Riding	1 hour	$50

15

Hiking lasts __________ __________ __________ scuba diving. (long)

16

Scuba diving lasts __________ __________ bike riding. (long)

17

Scuba diving is __________ __________ __________ of the activities. (expensive)

09 의문문, 명령문, 감탄문

POINT 01

who, what, which

A 다음 [ ] 안에서 알맞은 말을 고르시오.

1 A: (Who / What) opened the window this morning? – B: Mr. Kim did.

2 A: (Who / What) subject do you like most? – B: My favorite subject is history.

3 A: (What / Which) of these bags is yours? – B: The blue one is mine.

4 A: (What / Which) did she buy at the market? – B: She bought some apples.

B 다음 [ ] 안의 말을 알맞게 배열하여 의문문을 완성하시오.

1 ______________________ in front of the store? (the man, is, who)

2 ______________________ for dinner? (cooking, they, are, what)

3 ______________________ with this project? (me, help, who, can)

4 ______________________, Italian or Chinese food? (you, which, prefer, do)

C 다음 우리말과 같은 뜻이 되도록 [ ] 안의 말을 이용하여 문장을 완성하시오.

1 누가 여우 주연상을 탔어요? (win)

______________ ______________ the Best Actress award?

2 그는 여가 시간에 무엇을 하나요? (do)

______________ ______________ he ______________ in his free time?

3 너는 이 중에서 어떤 사진을 골랐니? (choose)

______________ of the pictures ______________ ______________ ______________?

4 그들은 차 안에서 무슨 노래를 듣고 있어? (listen)

______________ song ______________ ______________ ______________ to in the car?

when, where

A 다음 대화의 빈칸에 알맞은 의문사를 쓰시오.

1 A: _______________ did they arrive? – B: They arrived an hour ago.

2 A: _______________ is the nearest bank? – B: It's just around the corner.

3 A: _______________ time does the class start? – B: It starts at 9:00 a.m.

4 A: _______________ are you going next summer? – B: I'm going to Italy.

B 다음 〈보기〉와 같이 밑줄 친 부분을 묻는 의문문을 완성하시오.

> 〈보기〉　My birthday is <u>November 18</u>. → When is your birthday?

1 Helen is sitting <u>on the bench</u>.　→ _______________________ sitting?

2 He finished the book <u>last night</u>. → _______________________ the book?

3 I will wait for you <u>in the lobby</u>. → _______________________ for me?

4 The train leaves <u>at 3:30 p.m.</u>　→ _______________________ leave?

C 다음 우리말과 같은 뜻이 되도록 [ ] 안의 말을 이용하여 문장을 완성하시오.

1 너희 기말고사가 언제니? (be)

_______________ _______________ your final exam?

2 그녀는 저 꽃병들을 어디에서 샀니? (buy)

_______________ _______________ _______________ _______________ those vases?

3 너는 내일 몇 시에 아침을 먹을 거니? (have)

_______________ _______________ _______________ _______________ _______________ breakfast

tomorrow?

4 그들은 시카고에서 어디에 묵고 있나요? (stay)

_______________ _______________ _______________ _______________ in Chicago?

why

A 다음 [ ] 안에서 알맞은 말을 고르시오.

1 A: (When / Why) are you so tired? – B: Because we stayed up late.

2 A: (Where / Why) is he hiding? – B: He's hiding behind the tree.

3 A: (Why / Why don't) we watch a movie tonight? – B: That sounds fun!

4 A: (When / Why) will she write her report?

B: She'll write it tomorrow afternoon.

5 A: (What / Why) are you looking at your phone?

B: Because I'm waiting for a message.

B 다음 질문에 대한 알맞은 대답을 찾아 연결하시오.

1 Why did he miss the bus? • • ⓐ Sure, let's do it!

2 Who called you last night? • • ⓑ I'd love to, thanks.

3 Why don't you join us for dinner? • • ⓒ Because it's full of books.

4 Why is her backpack so heavy? • • ⓓ Someone from the library.

5 Why don't we go to the mountains? • • ⓔ Because he forgot to set his alarm.

C 다음 〈보기〉와 같이 밑줄 친 부분을 묻는 의문문을 완성하시오.

> 〈보기〉 I skipped lunch <u>because I wasn't hungry</u>. → Why did you skip lunch?

1 She is upset <u>because she failed the test</u>. → ___________________ upset?

2 They saved money <u>for a trip</u>. → ___________________ money?

3 My friends are <u>from Japan</u>. → ___________________ from?

4 I saw a doctor <u>because of my headache</u>. → ___________________ a doctor?

5 He goes to the gym <u>in the morning</u>. → ___________________ to the gym?

6 I'm wearing my jacket <u>because it's cold</u>. → ___________________ your jacket?

A   다음 대화의 빈칸에 알맞은 말을 쓰시오.

1   A: _______________ are you? – B: I'm 12 years old.

2   A: _______________ is the weather in Seoul? – B: It's cloudy and cool.

3   A: _______________ oranges did he buy? – B: He bought five.

4   A: _______________ do you study English? – B: I read books and watch videos.

B   다음 〈보기〉에서 알맞은 말을 골라 대화를 완성하시오.

〈보기〉	How	How far	How long	How often	How much

1   A: _______________ is the movie? – B: It's about two hours long.

2   A: _______________ does he get to school? – B: He rides his bike.

3   A: _______________ is that sandwich? – B: It's eight dollars.

4   A: _______________ do we have to walk? – B: Just a few blocks.

5   A: _______________ do you visit your grandparents?

    B: I visit them every weekend.

C   다음 〈보기〉와 같이 밑줄 친 부분을 묻는 의문문을 완성하시오.

〈보기〉   Our science teacher is <u>really nice</u>. → How is your science teacher?

1   The cake smells <u>sweet and fruity</u>.   → _______________ smell?

2   That tower is <u>about 330 meters tall</u>. → _______________ that tower?

3   She fixed the toy <u>with glue</u>.   → _______________ the toy?

4   They go camping <u>twice a month</u>.   → _______________ camping?

5   There are <u>four people</u> in my family.   → _______________ in your family?

부가 의문문

A 다음 밑줄 친 부분을 어법에 맞게 고쳐 쓰시오.

1 They ordered a pizza, <u>did they</u>?

2 You can swim well, <u>don't you</u>?

3 She doesn't eat breakfast, <u>did she</u>?

4 The kids are in the garden, <u>are they</u>?

5 The homework wasn't too hard, <u>were you</u>?

B 다음 빈칸에 알맞은 부가 의문문을 쓰시오.

1 This bag isn't yours, _______________?

2 You will see a doctor, _______________?

3 We don't have art class today, _______________?

4 He got a high score on the test, _______________?

5 Emma and her friends were at the concert, _______________?

C 다음 빈칸에 알맞은 말을 넣어 대화를 완성하시오.

1 A: This book is really interesting, _______________ _______________?

   B: Yes, _______________ _______________. I like the main character.

2 A: Eric doesn't like seafood, _______________ _______________?

   B: No, _______________ _______________. He hates the smell.

3 A: We can take a break now, _______________ _______________?

   B: Yes, _______________ _______________. Let's rest for ten minutes.

4 A: You didn't bring an umbrella, _______________ _______________?

   B: No, _______________ _______________. I didn't know it was going to rain.

부정 의문문

A 다음 문장을 〈보기〉와 같이 부정 의문문으로 바꾸어 쓰시오.

> 〈보기〉 She is a nurse. → Isn't she a nurse?

1 It looks great. → ______________________

2 They were late. → ______________________

3 She can speak French. → ______________________

4 You will walk the dog. → ______________________

5 We watched this movie. → ______________________

6 They are home now. → ______________________

7 You know the answer. → ______________________

8 He was ready for the meeting. → ______________________

9 It is going to snow tomorrow. → ______________________

B [ ] 안의 우리말과 같은 뜻이 되도록 대화를 완성하시오.

1 A: ______________ you hungry now? (너는 지금 배고프지 않니?)

  B: No, ______________ ______________. I just had lunch.

2 A: ______________ ______________ join the music club? (그가 음악 동아리에 가입하지 않을까?)

  B: ______________, ______________ will. He's really into music.

3 A: ______________ ______________ call you yesterday? (그녀가 어제 너에게 전화하지 않았니?)

  B: No, ______________ ______________. I waited all day.

4 A: ______________ it too crowded here? (여기 너무 복잡하지 않아?)

  B: ______________, ______________ ______________. It's full of people.

5 A: ______________ ______________ go to the gym regularly? (그는 규칙적으로 체육관에 가지
  않아?)

  B: ______________, ______________ ______________. He runs outside instead.

A　다음 [ ] 안에서 알맞은 말을 고르시오.

1　(Wash / Washes) your hands before dinner.

2　(Not / Do not) eat too much candy.

3　Let's (took / take) a walk in the park.

4　(Don't / Let's) worry about me. I'm fine.

5　(Let's not / Not let's) watch a scary movie.

6　Wear your coat, (and / or) you'll catch a cold.

7　We are lost! (Don't / Let's) ask for directions.

8　Read this book, (and / or) you'll learn many things.

B　다음 〈보기〉에서 알맞은 말을 골라 명령문을 완성하시오.

〈보기〉	be	exercise	find	hurry
	lie	open	spend	turn off

1　The bus is coming! Let's ______________.

2　______________ quiet, please. The baby is sleeping.

3　______________ ______________ the window. It's cold outside.

4　______________ every day, and you will be healthy.

5　______________ ______________ the subway station together.

6　Please ______________ ______________ the lights when you leave.

7　______________ ______________ to your friends, or you will lose them.

8　______________ ______________ ______________ all our money. We need some for lunch.

감탄문

A 다음 밑줄 친 부분을 어법에 맞게 고쳐 쓰시오.

1 <u>What fast</u> the train is!

2 How short <u>is her hair</u>!

3 <u>What a nice</u> people they are!

4 <u>How fun</u> we had at the beach!

5 What <u>pretty a T-shirt</u> it is!

B 다음 문장을 〈보기〉와 같이 감탄문으로 바꾸어 쓰시오.

〈보기〉	They are very lovely flowers. I was very foolish.	→ What lovely flowers they are! → How foolish I was!

1 Their baby is very cute. → _________________________________

2 These are very delicious cookies. → _________________________________

3 I felt very sleepy during class. → _________________________________

4 Jude has a very charming voice. → _________________________________

C 다음 우리말과 같은 뜻이 되도록 [ ] 안의 말을 알맞게 배열하여 문장을 완성하시오.

1 이 소파는 정말 편하구나! (is, comfortable, sofa, how, this)

____

2 너는 정말 수줍음이 많은 소년이구나! (what, boy, are, you, a, shy)

____

3 그들은 어제 정말 열심히 일했구나! (worked, how, yesterday, they, hard)

____

4 그 식당은 정말 맛있는 음식을 제공하는구나! (restaurant, the, great, serves, what, food)

____

 다음 빈칸에 알맞은 말을 고르시오.

01

A: ___________ solved the math problem?
B: Lisa solved it.

① What ② Who ③ When
④ Where ⑤ How

02

A: ___________ you live in Busan before?
B: No, I didn't.

① Do ② Does ③ Don't
④ Didn't ⑤ Doesn't

03-04 빈칸에 알맞은 말이 바르게 짝지어진 것을 고르시오.

03

A: He can play the guitar, ___________ he?
B: Yes, he ___________.

① doesn't – does ② does – doesn't
③ can't – can ④ can – can't
⑤ can't – can't

04

A: ___________ time did you go to bed last night?
B: At three o'clock.
A: Really? ___________?
B: Because I had to finish my homework.

① When – How ② What – When
③ When – Why ④ What – Why
⑤ Which – What

05

다음 중 대화가 자연스럽지 <u>않은</u> 것은?

① A: What does he do?
　B: He is a pilot.
② A: Won't you come with us?
　B: Yes, I won't.
③ A: Where are the keys?
　B: They're on the kitchen table.
④ A: My grandmother made me this sweater.
　B: What a lovely sweater!
⑤ A: Which of these shirts do you prefer?
　B: I prefer the red one.

서술형

06-07 다음 우리말과 같은 뜻이 되도록 주어진 말을 이용하여 문장을 완성하시오.

06

Andrew는 여동생이 있어요, 그렇지 않나요? (have)

→ ___________ ___________ a sister, ___________
___________?

07

너는 언제 치과에 갔니? (go)

→ ___________ ___________ ___________
___________ to the dentist?

08-09 다음 대답이 나올 수 있는 질문으로 알맞은 것을 고르시오.

08

I visit them twice a week.

① Who did you visit yesterday?
② How did you visit your cousins?
③ When did you visit your cousins?
④ How often do you visit your cousins?
⑤ Why do you visit your cousins so often?

09

> No, I don't.

① When are you going to leave?
② You don't like baseball, do you?
③ How can you be so good at English?
④ Didn't you go to school yesterday?
⑤ Does your brother play computer games?

10 - 11 다음 빈칸에 공통으로 들어갈 말을 고르시오.

10

> • _________ useful the tool was!
> • _________ much time do you need?

① What　　② How　　③ When
④ Where　　⑤ Why

11

> • _________ an interesting book this is!
> • _________ is that black thing on the table?

① What　　② How　　③ Which
④ Who　　⑤ Why

서술형

12 - 13 다음 우리말과 같은 뜻이 되도록 주어진 말을 알맞게 배열하여 문장을 완성하시오.

12

> 너는 개와 고양이 중에 무엇을 좋아하니?
> (like, dogs or cats, do, which, you)

→ _________________________________

13

> 이 코트는 정말 따뜻하구나!
> (warm, this, a, what, coat, is)

→ _________________________________

14

다음 우리말을 영어로 바르게 옮긴 것은?

> 일찍 오세요, 그러면 좋은 자리를 잡을 거예요.

① Come early, or you'll get a good seat.
② Come early, but you'll get a good seat.
③ Come early, and you'll get a good seat.
④ Don't come early, or you'll get a good seat.
⑤ Don't come early, and you'll get a good seat.

15

다음 중 어법상 틀린 것은?

① Not be upset about it.
② Hand me the salt, please.
③ Let's visit him in the hospital.
④ Finish the work by 8 o'clock today.
⑤ Be honest and tell me what happened.

서술형

16 - 18 다음 문장을 지시대로 바꾸어 쓰시오.

16

> I will meet my friends <u>in front of the station</u>.
> (밑줄 친 부분을 묻는 의문문)

→ _________________________________

17

> Why don't we go to Jeju next month?
> (권유의 명령문)

→ _________________________________

18

> The picture is very beautiful.
> (감탄문)

→ _________________________________

10 문장의 형식

POINT 01 1형식 / 2형식

A 다음 문장에서 주어, 동사, 보어를 찾아 밑줄로 표시하고 성분을 쓰시오. (보어가 없으면 X 표시할 것)

1 They work hard.

2 Max is a web designer.

3 The sun sets in the west.

4 These chairs are comfortable.

5 He slept for 13 hours yesterday.

6 Kelly and I became best friends.

B 다음 우리말과 같은 뜻이 되도록 [ ] 안의 말을 알맞게 배열하여 문장을 완성하고, 몇 형식인지 쓰시오.

1 그 나무들은 빠르게 자라고 있다. (growing, are, the trees)

　　_______________________ fast.　　　　　　　〈　　　〉형식

2 내 남동생은 나에게 화가 났다. (was, brother, angry, my)

　　_______________________ at me.　　　　　　〈　　　〉형식

3 그들은 시험을 위해 열심히 공부했다. (hard, studied, they)

　　_______________________ for the exam.　　　〈　　　〉형식

4 밖이 어두워지고 있다. (is, dark, it, getting)

　　_______________________ outside.　　　　　　〈　　　〉형식

5 저 여자아이는 우리 이웃의 딸이다. (daughter, our, is, neighbor's)

　　That girl _______________________.　　　　〈　　　〉형식

6 우리는 내년에 일본으로 여행 갈 것이다. (Japan, we, travel, to, will)

　　_______________________ next year.　　　　　〈　　　〉형식

POINT 02

2형식 – 감각동사+형용사

A 다음 [ ] 안에서 알맞은 말을 고르시오.

1 This pizza tastes (salt / salty).

2 The music (smells / sounds) good.

3 I felt (cold / coldly) because of the wind.

4 Their dog (looks / looks like) a wolf.

B 다음 밑줄 친 부분을 어법에 맞게 고쳐 쓰시오.

1 The curry smells <u>deliciously</u>.

2 This pillow <u>feels</u> a rock.

3 You look <u>greatly</u> in your new suit.

4 That fruit tasted <u>like sour</u>.

C 다음 우리말과 같은 뜻이 되도록 〈보기〉와 [ ] 안의 말을 이용하여 문장을 완성하시오.

〈보기〉 smell   look   taste   sound

1 그 경찰은 친절해 보인다. (kind)

   The police officer ________________ ________________.

2 이 초콜릿 케이크는 달콤한 냄새가 난다. (sweet)

   This chocolate cake ________________ ________________.

3 저 소리는 천둥처럼 들린다. (thunder)

   That noise ________________ ________________ ________________.

4 그 우유는 맛이 이상한가요? (milk, strange)

   Does ________________ ________________ ________________ ________________?

3형식 / 4형식

A 다음 빈칸에 들어갈 수 <u>없는</u> 것에 ✔ 표시하시오.

1 He ___________ his homework.　　☐ started　☐ lent　☐ forgot

2 I'll ___________ you a story.　　☐ open　☐ tell　☐ show

3 She teaches ___________ science.　　☐ us　☐ children　☐ the lesson

B 다음 [ ] 안의 말을 알맞게 배열하여 문장을 완성하시오.

1 Toby ______________________. (us, smoothies, made)

2 ______________________ in the drawer. (keys, my, found, I)

3 My friend ______________________. (me, T-shirt, bought, this)

4 ______________________ now. (a magazine, is, Alice, reading)

5 You ______________________. (send, some, them, flowers, should)

C 다음 우리말과 같은 뜻이 되도록 [ ] 안의 말을 이용하여 문장을 완성하시오.

1 우리는 나중에 그에게 기회를 줄 것이다. (give, a chance)

We'll __________ __________ __________ __________ later.

2 그들은 그 콘서트의 표 두 장을 원한다. (want, ticket)

__________ __________ __________ __________ for the concert.

3 그는 어제 나에게 그의 공책을 빌려주었다. (lend, notebook)

He __________ __________ __________ __________ yesterday.

4 Nicole은 길에서 그녀의 옛 친구를 만났다. (meet, old friend)

Nicole __________ __________ __________ __________ on the street.

5 나는 수업 끝나고 그 답을 너에게 보여 줄 수 있다. (show, answer)

I can __________ __________ __________ __________ after class.

4형식 → 3형식 - 전치사 to를 쓰는 경우

A 다음 3형식 문장은 4형식 문장으로, 4형식 문장은 3형식 문장으로 바꾸어 쓰시오.

1 She showed them her room.

→ She showed ___________________________.

2 They'll bring some snacks to us.

→ They'll bring ___________________________.

3 Jake gave Linda some roses.

→ Jake gave ___________________________.

4 Can you pass the pencil to me?

→ Can you ___________________________?

5 Angela didn't tell him the truth.

→ Angela didn't ___________________________.

6 Send me a text message about our field trip.

→ Send ___________________________ about our field trip.

B 다음 우리말과 같은 뜻이 되도록 [ ] 안의 말을 이용하여 문장을 완성하시오.

1 그는 고등학생들에게 역사를 가르친다. (teach, history)

He ______________ ______________ ____________ high school students.

2 나는 부모님께 편지를 쓰고 있다. (write, a letter)

I'm ______________ ______________ ______________ ____________ my parents.

3 나에게 네 운동화를 좀 빌려줘. (lend, running shoes)

Please ______________ ______________ ______________ ______________.

4 Beth는 그녀의 새 전화기를 우리에게 보여 주었다. (show, new phone)

Beth ______________ ______________ ______________ ______________

______________.

5 그들은 그의 생일에 그에게 선물을 줄 것이다. (give, a gift)

They'll ______________ ______________ ______________ ______________

on his birthday.

4형식 → 3형식 - 다른 전치사를 쓰는 경우

A 다음 [ ] 안에서 알맞은 말을 고르시오.

1 He cooked dinner (to / for) us last night.

2 I won't tell your secret (to / of) anybody.

3 We (gave / bought) cookies for our guests.

4 She made a toy car (the child / for the child).

B 다음 문장을 3형식 문장으로 바꾸어 쓰시오.

1 Peter got his friend a book.

→ Peter got _______________________.

2 You should buy her a present.

→ You should _______________________.

3 My grandmother made me a pair of mittens.

→ My grandmother _______________________.

C 다음 우리말과 같은 뜻이 되도록 [ ] 안의 말을 이용하여 문장을 완성하시오.

1 나는 너에게 스파게티를 요리해 줄 수 있다. (cook, spaghetti)

I can ___________ ___________ ___________ you.

2 그들은 사서에게 도움을 청했다. (ask, a favor)

They ___________ ___________ ___________ ___________ the librarian.

3 나에게 달걀을 좀 사다 줄래? (buy, some eggs)

Will you ___________ ___________ ___________ ___________ ___________?

4 Grace는 그에게 사진첩을 만들어 주었다. (make, a photo album)

Grace ___________ ___________ ___________ ___________

___________.

5형식 - 목적격 보어가 명사/형용사인 경우

A 다음 우리말과 같은 뜻이 되도록 ( ) 안에서 알맞은 말을 고르시오.

1 우리는 그 음식이 맛있다고 생각했다.

We found the food (delicious / deliciously).

2 사람들은 그녀를 거짓말쟁이라고 불렀다.

People called (a liar her / her a liar).

3 내 남동생은 때때로 나를 화나게 한다.

My brother sometimes makes me (anger / angry).

B 다음 우리말과 같은 뜻이 되도록 ( ) 안의 말을 알맞게 배열하여 문장을 완성하시오.

1 나는 창문을 열어 두었다. (the window, I, kept, open)

____

2 이 영화는 그녀를 스타로 만들었다. (a star, made, this movie, her)

____

3 그의 친구들은 그를 '슈퍼맨'이라고 부른다. (him, Superman, call, his friends)

____

C 다음 우리말과 같은 뜻이 되도록 〈보기〉와 ( ) 안의 말을 이용하여 문장을 완성하시오.

〈보기〉	find	keep	leave	name

1 제발 저를 혼자 있게 내버려두세요. (alone)

Please _____________ _____________ _____________.

2 그들은 그 고양이를 Oreo라고 이름 지었다. (cat)

They _____________ _____________ _____________ _____________.

3 우리는 그 쇼가 지루하다는 것을 알게 되었다. (show, boring)

We _____________ _____________ _____________ _____________.

4 그 담요는 밤 동안에 너를 따뜻하게 유지해 줄 것이다. (will, warm)

The blanket will _____________ _____________ _____________ during the night.

5형식 – 목적격 보어가 to부정사인 경우

A 다음 〈보기〉에서 알맞은 말을 골라 빈칸에 적절한 형태로 써넣으시오.

> 〈보기〉 come   eat   fix   help   win

1 I want him ___________________ my bike.

2 Ella asked me ___________________ her.

3 They allowed us ___________________ snacks.

4 We expect Brian ___________________ the race.

5 Mr. Johnson told you ___________________ to his office.

B 다음 우리말과 같은 뜻이 되도록 [ ] 안의 말을 알맞게 배열하여 문장을 완성하시오.

1 부모님은 내가 일찍 자기를 원하신다. (go to sleep, me, to, want, early)

My parents ___________________________________.

2 선생님은 우리에게 조용히 하라고 말씀하셨다. (to, quiet, told, be, us)

The teacher ___________________________________.

3 그는 그들이 규칙적으로 운동하기를 기대했다. (them, exercise, he, to, expected)

___________________________________ regularly.

C 다음 우리말과 같은 뜻이 되도록 [ ] 안의 말을 이용하여 문장을 완성하시오.

1 그들은 우리가 축제에서 노래 부르는 것을 허락했다. (allow, sing)

They __________ __________ __________ __________ at the festival.

2 너는 Nancy에게 숙제를 하라고 말했니? (tell, do)

Did you __________ __________ __________ __________ her homework?

3 그녀는 그에게 자신의 차에서 나오라고 지시했다. (order, get)

She __________ __________ __________ __________ out of her car.

4 우리는 그녀가 외국에서 공부할 것이라고 예상하지 못했다. (expect, study)

We didn't __________ __________ __________ __________ abroad.

5형식 – 지각동사/사역동사

A 다음 밑줄 친 부분을 어법에 맞게 고쳐 쓰시오.

1 I heard Julie <u>to sing</u> a song.

2 He told us <u>clean</u> the room.

3 They made him <u>waited</u> outside.

4 We saw them <u>to run</u> to school.

5 Please let me <u>knowing</u> your address.

B 다음 [ ] 안의 말을 알맞게 배열하여 문장을 완성하시오.

1 Did you ＿＿＿＿＿＿＿＿＿＿＿? (cry, the baby, hear)

2 I'll ＿＿＿＿＿＿＿＿＿＿ the bag. (him, carry, have)

3 Austin ＿＿＿＿＿＿＿＿＿ fast. (heart, felt, his, beating)

4 We can ＿＿＿＿＿＿＿＿＿. (find, you, seat, your, help)

5 ＿＿＿＿＿＿＿＿＿ the dishes. (washing, her, saw, she, sister)

C 다음 우리말과 같은 뜻이 되도록 [ ] 안의 말을 이용하여 문장을 완성하시오.

1 그들은 우리가 그 기계를 사용하지 못하게 했다. (let, use)

   They didn't ＿＿＿＿＿＿ ＿＿＿＿＿＿ ＿＿＿＿＿ the machine.

2 나는 내 개가 공을 가지고 노는 것을 지켜봤다. (watch, play)

   ＿＿＿＿＿＿ ＿＿＿＿＿＿ my dog ＿＿＿＿＿ with a ball.

3 그녀는 그가 그 문제를 이해하는 것을 도왔다. (help, understand)

   She ＿＿＿＿＿ ＿＿＿＿＿ ＿＿＿＿＿ ＿＿＿＿＿ the problem.

4 선생님은 우리에게 휴대폰을 끄게 하셨다. (make, turn off)

   The teacher ＿＿＿＿＿ ＿＿＿＿＿ ＿＿＿＿＿ our phones.

01-03 다음 빈칸에 들어갈 수 <u>없는</u> 말을 고르시오.

01

> She looks __________ today.

① great
② angry
③ tired
④ beautifully
⑤ like an angel

02

> My mother __________ us to go to bed.

① told
② ordered
③ asked
④ wanted
⑤ made

03

> Justin __________ a bike to me.

① bought
② gave
③ sent
④ lent
⑤ showed

04

다음 빈칸에 알맞은 말이 바르게 짝지어진 것은?

> My brother __________ a doctor. He helps sick people __________ better.

① is – gets
② is – get
③ are – to get
④ are – get
⑤ are – gets

05 서술형

다음 우리말과 같은 뜻이 되도록 주어진 말을 이용하여 문장을 완성하시오.

> 나는 Ross에게 내 사진을 보여 주었다. (show)

→ I __________ my picture __________

__________.

06-07 다음 중 문장의 형식이 나머지와 <u>다른</u> 것을 고르시오.

06

① He stood next to Laura.
② George doesn't like cake.
③ Can you open the window?
④ Students must follow these rules.
⑤ David baked a cake for his family.

07

① She is a famous artist.
② His father is very tall.
③ The soup tasted too salty.
④ They became good friends.
⑤ Alex speaks English very well.

08

다음 빈칸에 공통으로 들어갈 말은?

> • He __________ a terrible mistake.
> • Zoe __________ me a cup of coffee.
> • Our teacher __________ us stay late.

① was
② let
③ made
④ brought
⑤ fixed

09

다음 중 밑줄 친 부분의 쓰임이 나머지와 <u>다른</u> 것은?

① I heard someone <u>call</u> me.

② My uncle made me <u>a desk</u>.

③ He found the shoes <u>uncomfortable</u>.

④ Do you want me <u>to go</u> there?

⑤ People call him <u>the father of medicine</u>.

10 - 11 다음 우리말과 같은 뜻이 되도록 주어진 말을 알맞게 배열하여 문장을 완성하시오.

10

그들은 그녀가 춤추는 것을 보지 못했다.
(see, they, dancing, her, didn't)

→ ______________________________________

11

나는 네가 다음에는 더 잘할 거라 기대한다.
(expect, to, you, do, next time, I, better)

→ ______________________________________

12

다음 우리말을 영어로 바르게 옮긴 것은?

아빠는 어젯밤에 내가 TV를 보게 허락하셨다.

① My dad let me watched TV at night.

② My dad let me to watch TV at night.

③ My dad let me watch TV at night.

④ My dad allowed me watch TV at night.

⑤ My dad allowed me watching TV at night.

13 - 14 다음 중 어법상 <u>틀린</u> 것을 고르시오.

13

① His dog's name is Spot.

② The weather turns cold in fall.

③ Children should read good books.

④ I will leave for France next month.

⑤ My parents want me be home by ten.

14

① The sky grew red.

② Tim told his secret me.

③ I didn't like the idea at first.

④ They arrived at the airport in time.

⑤ She felt something touch her shoulder.

15 - 17 다음 3형식 문장은 4형식 문장으로, 4형식 문장은 3형식 문장으로 바꾸어 쓰시오.

15

He sent the photos to me.

→ He sent ______________________________ .

16

He gave me Jina's phone number.

→ He gave ______________________________ .

17

Jeremy bought his wife a ring.

→ Jeremy bought __________________________

CHAPTER 11 to부정사와 동명사

POINT 01 to부정사의 명사적 용법 - 주어 역할

A 다음 두 문장이 같은 뜻이 되도록 빈칸에 알맞은 말을 쓰시오.

1 To bake cookies is fun.

→ It is fun ＿＿＿＿＿＿ ＿＿＿＿＿＿ cookies.

2 To follow traffic rules is important.

→ ＿＿＿＿＿＿ is important ＿＿＿＿＿＿ ＿＿＿＿＿＿ traffic rules.

3 It is dangerous to touch snakes.

→ ＿＿＿＿＿＿ ＿＿＿＿＿＿ snakes ＿＿＿＿＿＿ dangerous.

4 It is difficult to write a good essay.

→ ＿＿＿＿＿＿ ＿＿＿＿＿＿ ＿＿＿＿＿＿ ＿＿＿＿＿＿ ＿＿＿＿＿＿

＿＿＿＿＿＿ difficult.

5 To watch the stars is interesting.

→ ＿＿＿＿＿＿ ＿＿＿＿＿＿ ＿＿＿＿＿＿ ＿＿＿＿＿＿ ＿＿＿＿＿＿ the stars.

B 다음 우리말과 같은 뜻이 되도록 [ ] 안의 말을 이용하여 문장을 완성하시오.

1 좋은 친구가 되는 것은 쉽지 않다. (be)

＿＿＿＿＿＿ ＿＿＿＿＿＿ a good friend is not easy.

2 피라미드를 실제로 보는 것은 놀랍다. (see)

＿＿＿＿＿＿ is amazing ＿＿＿＿＿＿ ＿＿＿＿＿＿ the Pyramids in real life.

3 아침에 일찍 일어나는 것은 힘들었다. (get up)

＿＿＿＿＿＿ ＿＿＿＿＿＿ hard ＿＿＿＿＿＿ ＿＿＿＿＿＿ ＿＿＿＿＿＿

early in the morning.

4 그녀와 이야기하는 것은 항상 나를 웃게 만든다. (talk, make)

＿＿＿＿＿＿ to her always ＿＿＿＿＿＿ me smile.

5 매일 영어 단어를 외우는 것은 도움이 된다. (helpful, memorize)

＿＿＿＿＿＿ ＿＿＿＿＿＿ ＿＿＿＿＿＿ ＿＿＿＿＿＿ ＿＿＿＿＿＿ English

words every day.

to부정사의 명사적 용법 - 보어/목적어 역할

A 다음 〈보기〉에서 알맞은 말을 골라 빈칸에 적절한 형태로 써넣으시오.

> 〈보기〉   deliver   get   start   travel

1 I expected ___________ ___________ good grades.
2 His job is ___________ ___________ packages.
3 They hope ___________ ___________ abroad next year.
4 Our plan is ___________ ___________ a new business in the city.

B 다음 [ ] 안의 말을 알맞게 배열하여 문장을 완성하시오.

1 Ann ___________________________ anything. (say, to, refused)
2 Their mission ___________________________. (children, is, teach, to)
3 We ___________________________ our house. (to, sell, not, decided)
4 ___________________________ on stage someday. (is, sing, her, to, dream)

C 다음 우리말과 같은 뜻이 되도록 [ ] 안의 말을 이용하여 문장을 완성하시오.

1 요지는 숲을 보호하는 것이다. (protect)

   The main idea ___________ ___________ ___________ the forest.

2 그들은 박물관에 가고 싶어 하지 않는다. (want, visit)

   They don't ___________ ___________ ___________ the museum.

3 내 목표는 하루에 10,000걸음을 걷는 것이다. (goal, walk)

   ___________ ___________ ___________ ___________ 10,000

   steps a day.

4 Jason은 다시 늦지 않기로 약속했다. (promise, be late)

   Jason ___________________________________

   again.

A 다음 밑줄 친 부분을 어법에 맞게 고쳐 쓰시오.

1 Tell me <u>to start when</u>.

2 He showed her <u>where sit</u> in the classroom.

3 We can't decide <u>how to buy</u> for his birthday.

B 다음 ( ) 안의 말을 알맞게 배열하여 문장을 완성하시오.

1 They learned _________________________. (last year, to, swim, how)

2 I don't know _________________________. (leave, when, my house, to)

3 Ryan asked _________________________. (to, what, the picnic, bring, to)

4 We aren't sure _________________________. (invite, the party, to, who, to)

5 She told us _________________________. (go, where, for, to, dinner)

C 다음 우리말과 같은 뜻이 되도록 〈보기〉에서 알맞은 말을 골라 문장을 완성하시오.

〈보기〉	choose	meet	park	say	turn

1 나는 그에게 뭐라고 말할지 모르겠다.

I'm not sure __________ __________ __________ to him.

2 Laura는 그 기계를 어떻게 켜는지 설명했다.

Laura explained __________ __________ __________ on the machine.

3 그들은 차를 어디에 주차해야 할지 몰랐다.

They didn't know __________________________ their car.

4 너는 친구들을 언제 만날지 정했니?

Did you decide __________________________ your friends?

5 우리는 팀에 누구를 뽑을지 논의할 것이다.

We will discuss __________________________ for the team.

to부정사의 형용사적 용법 – (대)명사 수식

A 다음 밑줄 친 부분을 어법에 맞게 고쳐 쓰시오.

1 It is a good way <u>learn</u> English.

2 We have <u>no to waste</u> time.

3 She bought a dress <u>wear</u> to the wedding.

4 There is <u>nothing eating</u> in the refrigerator.

5 I have <u>interesting something to show</u> you.

B 다음 〈보기〉에서 알맞은 말을 골라 빈칸에 적절한 형태로 써넣으시오.

〈보기〉 join	share	watch	write

1 He chose a movie _______________ _____________ tonight.

2 Did they bring any food _______________ _____________ with us?

3 We didn't find anyone _______________ _____________ the group.

4 I have several essays _______________ _____________ for homework.

C 다음 우리말과 같은 뜻이 되도록 [ ] 안의 말을 알맞게 배열하여 문장을 완성하시오.

1 이제 작별 인사를 할 때이다. (goodbye, to, time, say)

It's _______________________________.

2 이 선반에 읽기 좋은 것이 있나요? (to, anything, read, good)

Is there _______________________________ on this shelf?

3 그들은 머물 곳을 찾고 있었다. (stay, looking for, to, a place)

They were _______________________________.

4 Jack은 그의 문제에 대해 이야기할 누군가가 필요하다. (someone, talk to, needs, to)

Jack _______________________________ about his problems.

to부정사의 부사적 용법 - 목적

A 다음 두 문장이 같은 뜻이 되도록 빈칸에 알맞은 말을 쓰시오.

1 She practiced every day because she wanted to win the race.

→ She practiced every day _______________ _______________ the race.

2 We need to buy some snacks, so we'll go to the supermarket.

→ We'll go to the supermarket _______________ _______________ some snacks.

3 You can turn off the lights to save energy.

→ You can turn off the lights _______________ _______________ _______________

_______________ energy.

B 다음 [ ] 안의 말을 알맞게 배열하여 문장을 완성하시오.

1 They _______________________________ money. (earn, hard, to, work)

2 Henry _______________________________ her. (to, wrote, thank, an email)

3 My mom _______________________________ breakfast. (early, cook, to, got up)

4 I _______________________________ a job. (the city, find, to, moved, to)

C 다음 우리말과 같은 뜻이 되도록 [ ] 안의 말을 이용하여 문장을 완성하시오.

1 Sarah는 그날을 기억하기 위해 사진을 찍었다. (remember, that day)

Sarah took a photo _______________ _______________ _______________ _______________.

2 우리는 조언을 구하기 위해 선생님과 이야기했다. (ask for, advice)

We talked to the teacher _______________ _______________ _______________.

3 자원봉사자들이 그 아이들을 돕기 위해 왔다. (help, children)

The volunteers came _______________ _______________ _______________.

4 그는 근육을 키우기 위해 운동을 하고 있다. (build, muscle)

He is working out in _______________ _______________ _______________.

to부정사의 부사적 용법 - 감정의 원인 / 결과

A 다음 두 문장이 같은 뜻이 되도록 빈칸에 알맞은 말을 쓰시오.

1 Mia got a gift, so she was happy.

→ Mia was happy ________________ ________________ a gift.

2 I was so shocked. I couldn't speak.

→ I was ________________ ________________ ________________ ________________.

3 You are so late. You can't join the game.

→ You are ________________ ________________ ________________ ________________ the game.

B 다음 [ ] 안의 말을 알맞게 배열하여 문장을 완성하시오.

1 He ________________ a doctor. (to, grew up, become)

2 I was ________________ to school. (go, to, sick, too)

3 Are you ________________ it? (enough, try, to, brave)

4 We ________________ the game. (disappointed, to, were, lose)

C 다음 우리말과 같은 뜻이 되도록 [ ] 안의 말을 이용하여 문장을 완성하시오.

1 나는 너무 배가 불러서 이 케이크를 다 먹을 수 없다. (full, finish)

I'm ________________ ________________ ________________ ________________ this cake.

2 Chloe는 길에서 친구를 봐서 기뻤다. (glad, see)

Chloe was ________________ ________________ ________________ her friend on the street.

3 그는 천장에 닿을 만큼 충분히 높이 뛰었다. (high, touch)

He jumped ________________ ________________ ________________ the ceiling.

4 그들은 집에 와서 문이 열려 있는 것을 알았다. (come home, find)

They ________________ ________________ ________________ the door open.

동명사 - 주어/보어 역할

A 다음 〈보기〉에서 알맞은 말을 골라 빈칸에 적절한 형태로 써넣으시오. (단, 한 번씩만 사용할 것)

> 〈보기〉 eat   climb   plant   read   swim   watch   win

1 Her greatest achievement was ____________ the prize.

2 ____________ in deep rivers is dangerous.

3 ____________ healthy food is important for everyone.

4 The main activity is ____________ trees and flowers.

5 ____________ the mountain took a lot of energy.

6 His hobby is ____________ baseball games on TV.

7 ____________ science magazines makes us curious.

B 다음 우리말과 같은 뜻이 되도록 [ ] 안의 말을 알맞게 배열하여 문장을 완성하시오.

1 물 없이 사는 것은 불가능하다 (water, living, is, without)

____________________________________ impossible.

2 다음 단계는 도움 없이 문제를 푸는 것이었다. (solving, the problem, was)

The next step ____________________________________ without help.

3 그 에세이를 쓰는 것은 내 머리를 아프게 했다. (gave, the essay, me, writing)

____________________________________ a headache.

4 Lucy의 가장 큰 두려움은 사람들 앞에서 말하는 것이다. (is, in, speaking, front, people, of)

Lucy's biggest fear ____________________________________ .

5 다른 나라로 여행하는 것은 멋진 경험이다. (other, to, is, traveling, countries)

____________________________________ a great experience.

동명사 - 목적어 역할

A　다음 밑줄 친 부분을 어법에 맞게 고쳐 쓰시오.

1　He finished <u>read</u> the book.

2　Kate is afraid of <u>ride</u> a bike.

3　I hope <u>working</u> at NASA someday.

4　You should avoid <u>to stay</u> up late.

5　She was worried about <u>to get</u> a new job.

B　다음 〈보기〉와 같이 동명사를 이용하여 두 문장을 한 문장으로 만드시오.

> 〈보기〉　I took a guitar lesson. I enjoyed it. → I enjoyed taking a guitar lesson.

1　They talked during class. They kept doing it.

　　→ They kept ＿＿＿＿＿＿＿＿＿＿＿＿＿＿＿.

2　Abigail sings well. She is famous for it.

　　→ Abigail is famous for ＿＿＿＿＿＿＿＿＿＿＿＿＿.

3　I help my little brother. I don't mind doing it.

　　→ I don't mind ＿＿＿＿＿＿＿＿＿＿＿＿＿.

C　다음 우리말과 같은 뜻이 되도록 [ ] 안의 말을 이용하여 문장을 완성하시오.

1　그는 한밤중에 게임하는 것을 멈췄다. (stop, play)

　　He ＿＿＿＿＿＿＿ ＿＿＿＿＿＿＿ the game at midnight

2　우리는 겨울에 스키 타러 가는 것을 즐긴다. (enjoy, go skiing)

　　We ＿＿＿＿＿＿ ＿＿＿＿＿＿ ＿＿＿＿＿＿ in the winter.

3　나는 손으로 물건 만드는 것을 잘한다. (be good at, make)

　　I ＿＿＿＿＿ ＿＿＿＿＿ ＿＿＿＿＿ ＿＿＿＿＿ things with my hands.

4　Maria는 그 강아지를 찾는 것을 포기하지 않았다. (give up, look for)

　　Maria didn't ＿＿＿＿＿ ＿＿＿＿＿ ＿＿＿＿＿ the puppy.

01-02 다음 빈칸에 알맞은 말을 고르시오.

01

He called his friend ___________ sorry.

① say
② saying
③ to say
④ to saying
⑤ in order to saying

02

The girl grew up ___________ a great writer.

① was
② to be
③ be
④ what to be
⑤ in order to be

03

다음 빈칸에 알맞은 말이 바르게 짝지어진 것은?

A: Can you tell me ___________ this printer?
B: Sure. You need ___________ this button first.

① what to use – pressing
② what to use – to press
③ how to use – press
④ how to use – to press
⑤ when to use – pressing

서술형

04-05 다음 우리말과 같은 뜻이 되도록 주어진 말을 이용하여 문장을 완성하시오.

04

나는 비행 중에 읽을 책 한 권을 샀다. (read, book)

→ I bought ___________ ___________ ___________
___________ on my flight.

05

새로운 언어를 배우는 것은 어렵다.
(learn, a new language)

→ ___________ ___________ ___________ ___________
is difficult.

06-07 다음 중 〈보기〉의 밑줄 친 부분과 용법이 다른 것을 고르시오.

06

〈보기〉 He went to the market to buy eggs.

① Do I need a visa to visit China?
② He called me to ask about our trip.
③ James went to the store to get a refund.
④ We planned to leave home before 8:00 a.m.
⑤ Please visit our website in order to get more information.

07

〈보기〉 I hope to live in Europe someday.

① It is important to keep promises.
② She wants to buy a good laptop.
③ I have so many things to do now.
④ His purpose in life is to help others.
⑤ They decided to develop a new product.

08

다음 빈칸에 공통으로 들어갈 말은?

• ___________ hot milk helps you fall asleep.
• You should avoid ___________ cold water.

① Drink[drink]
② To drink[to drink]
③ Drunk[drunk]
④ Drinking[drinking]
⑤ To drinking[to drinking]

09

다음 중 짝지어진 두 문장의 의미가 같지 <u>않은</u> 것은?

① It is wrong to lie.

　→ Lying is wrong.

② Luke is too young to drive.

　→ Luke is so young. He can't drive.

③ Exercise regularly to stay healthy.

　→ Exercise regularly in order to stay healthy.

④ Her job is to manage the store on weekends.

　→ Her job is managing the store on weekends.

⑤ I was so tired that I couldn't get out of bed.

　→ I was tired enough to get out of bed.

10 - 12 다음 우리말과 같은 뜻이 되도록 주어진 말을 알맞게 배열하여 문장을 완성하시오.

10

너를 울린 것에 대해 미안해.

(for, sorry, I'm, cry, you, making)

→ ____

11

그는 그 경주에서 뛰게 되어 들떴다.

(the race, he, excited, run, was, in, to)

→ ____

12

그는 그녀에게 언제 그 진실을 말해야 할지 몰랐다.

(the truth, know, didn't, tell, he, to, her, when)

→ ____

13

다음 밑줄 친 우리말을 영어로 바르게 옮긴 것은?

A: Why don't you play the game?

B: <u>내 컴퓨터는 그것을 실행할 만큼 빠르지 않아.</u>

① My computer isn't fast too run it.

② My computer is too fast to run it.

③ My computer isn't too fast to run it.

④ My computer isn't enough fast to run it.

⑤ My computer isn't fast enough to run it.

14

다음 중 밑줄 친 부분이 어법상 <u>틀린</u> 것은?

① Ms. Kim told us <u>to be</u> quiet.

② He gave up <u>to fix</u> the old car.

③ There are a lot of books about <u>cooking</u>.

④ This question is too hard <u>to answer</u>.

⑤ How did you decide <u>whom to marry</u>?

15 - 16 다음 두 문장이 같은 뜻이 되도록 to부정사를 이용하여 빈칸에 알맞은 말을 쓰시오.

15

Bob is so lazy. He can't keep a job.

→ Bob is ________ ________ ________ ________ ________ ________ .

16

I was so full. I couldn't eat dessert.

→ I was ________ ________ ________ ________ dessert.

12 접속사

POINT 01 등위접속사 and

A 다음 [ ] 안에서 알맞은 말을 고르시오.

1 Angela works quickly and (careful / carefully).

2 He painted the wall and (fixed / fixing) the door.

3 We woke up early, and (breakfast / we made breakfast).

4 I listened to music and (read / reading) a book in the park.

B 다음 두 문장을 한 문장으로 만들 때, 빈칸에 알맞은 말을 쓰시오.

1 Mr. Jang is a writer. He is a professor, too.

→ Mr. Jang is ______________ ______________ ______________ ______________

______________.

2 I love swimming. I love watching movies, too.

→ I love ______________ ______________ ______________ ______________.

3 They can go to the museum. They can go to Namdaemun Market, too.

→ They can go to ______________ ______________ ______________ ______________

______________.

C 다음 우리말과 같은 뜻이 되도록 [ ] 안의 말을 알맞게 배열하여 문장을 완성하시오.

1 그는 이메일을 보내고 전화를 했다. (a phone call, and, made)

He sent an email ______________________________.

2 그녀는 피아노와 바이올린을 둘 다 잘 연주한다. (the violin, and, the piano, both)

She plays ______________________________ well.

3 나는 Fred를 만났고 우리는 같이 산책하기로 결정했다. (and, a walk, decided, take, to, we)

I met Fred, ______________________________ together.

POINT 02 등위접속사 but

A 다음 ( ) 안에서 의미상 가장 알맞은 말을 고르시오.

1 He is kind (and / but) friendly.

2 His problem is simple (and / but) important.

3 He tried his best, (and / but) he didn't win the race.

4 He cleaned the living room, (and / but) she cooked dinner.

B 다음 두 문장을 접속사 but을 이용하여 한 문장으로 만들 때, 빈칸에 알맞은 말을 쓰시오.

1 This book is old. It is very useful.

→ This book is ______________ ______________ ______________ ______________.

2 I didn't have lunch. I'm not hungry.

→ I didn't have lunch, ______________ ______________ ______________ ______________.

3 We wanted to go outside. It started to rain.

→ We wanted to go outside, ______________ ______________ ______________

______________ ______________.

C 다음 우리말과 같은 뜻이 되도록 ( ) 안의 말을 알맞게 배열하여 문장을 완성하시오.

1 그들은 작지만 아늑한 방에 묵었다. (but, small, room, cozy)

They stayed in a ______________________________.

2 Susan은 Mike에게 잘해 주었지만 그와 멀리 떨어져서 앉았다. (far away, she, him, sat, but, from)

Susan was nice to Mike, ______________________________.

3 그 운동화는 비싸지만 아주 편하다. (comfortable, are, but, very, expensive)

The sneakers ______________________________.

4 우리는 그 메시지를 두 번 읽었지만, 그것을 이해하지 못했다. (didn't, but, it, understand, we)

We read the message twice, ______________________________.

등위접속사 or

A 다음 [ ] 안에서 알맞은 말을 고르시오.

1 She is interested in painting (but / and) in photography.

2 (Both / Either) you or I should talk to him.

3 They ran fast, (but / or) they missed the train.

4 Which kind of food do you like better, Chinese (and / or) Italian?

B 다음 두 문장을 접속사 or를 이용하여 한 문장으로 만들 때, 빈칸에 알맞은 말을 쓰시오.

1 Can I call you after lunch? Can I call you in the evening?

→ Can I call you after lunch ______________ ______________ ______________

______________?

2 She may be lying. She may be hiding something.

→ She may be ______________ lying ______________ hiding something.

3 He will attend the meeting. He will send an email instead.

→ He will attend the meeting ______________ ______________ ______________

______________ an email instead.

C 다음 우리말과 같은 뜻이 되도록 [ ] 안의 말을 알맞게 배열하여 문장을 완성하시오.

1 오늘이 6월 25일인가요, 6월 26일인가요? (June 25, today, June 26, or)

Is ______________________________?

2 네 빨간 셔츠나 파란 셔츠 중에서 입어라. (your, or, blue one, red shirt, your)

Wear ______________________________.

3 너는 우리와 함께 가거나 여기에서 기다릴 수도 있다. (you, with us, can, come, or, wait)

You can ______________________________ here.

4 나는 졸업 후 유학을 가거나 취직을 할 것이다. (a job, study, or, get, either, abroad)

I will ______________________________ after graduation.

POINT 04 등위접속사 so

A 다음 [ ] 안에서 알맞은 말을 고르시오.

1 It is late, (or / so) you should go home now.

2 He wanted to go swimming, (but / so) the pool was closed.

3 We can watch a movie, (or / so) we can play a game.

4 I studied all night, so (tired / I was tired) during the test.

B 자연스러운 문장이 되도록 알맞게 연결하시오.

1 I missed the bus, •   • ⓐ so I ate three pieces.

2 I forgot my keys, •   • ⓑ so I watched it again.

3 The cake was delicious, •   • ⓒ so I walked to school.

4 The room smelled bad, •   • ⓓ so I can't get in the car.

5 The movie was exciting, •   • ⓔ so I opened the window.

C 다음 〈보기〉에서 알맞은 접속사를 골라 두 문장을 한 문장으로 만드시오. [단, 한 번씩만 사용할 것]

〈보기〉 and	but	or	so

1 We didn't have enough money. We couldn't buy it.

→ ____

2 She opened the book. She started to read.

→ ____

3 I knocked on the door. No one answered.

→ ____

4 You can go to the park. You can visit the zoo.

→ ____

시간을 나타내는 접속사 when / while

A 다음 〈보기〉와 같이 접속사 when을 이용하여 두 문장을 한 문장으로 만드시오.

> 〈보기〉   I have time. I draw pictures. → When I have time, I draw pictures.

1 She is cold. She drinks tea.

→ ____

2 He saw the dog. He ran away.

→ ____

3 Dad will come back. We will have dinner.

→ ____

B 다음 우리말과 같은 뜻이 되도록 접속사 when 또는 while과 〔 〕 안의 말을 이용하여 문장을 완성하시오.

1 우리는 공항에 도착했을 때 신이 났다. (arrive)

______________ ______________ ______________ at the airport, we were excited.

2 그가 요리하는 동안, 나는 상을 차렸다. (cook)

______________ ______________ ______________ ______________, I set the table.

3 그녀는 그 선물을 볼 때 미소를 지을 것이다. (see)

She will smile ______________ ______________ ______________ the gift.

4 내 남동생은 샤워를 하는 동안 보통 노래를 부른다. (take)

My brother usually sings ______________ ______________ ______________ ______________

a shower.

5 나는 호주에 갔을 때, 코알라를 보았다. (go to)

______________ ______________ ______________ ______________ Australia, I saw Koalas.

6 나는 그들을 기다리는 동안 이 사진을 찍었다. (wait for)

I took this photo ______________ ______________ ______________ ______________

______________ ______________ .

POINT 06 시간을 나타내는 접속사 before / after

A 다음 우리말과 같은 뜻이 되도록 〈보기〉에서 알맞은 접속사를 골라 문장을 완성하시오.

> 〈보기〉　before　　　after　　　when　　　while

1 네가 나아질 때, 우리는 산책을 갈 것이다.

_______________ you feel better, we will go for a walk.

2 나는 잠자리에 들기 전에 자명종을 맞춘다.

I set the alarm _______________ I go to bed.

3 그들이 공부하는 동안 집이 매우 조용해졌다.

The house became very quiet _______________ they were studying.

4 그녀는 양치질을 한 후에는 아무것도 먹지 않는다.

She doesn't eat anything _______________ she brushes her teeth.

B 다음 우리말과 같은 뜻이 되도록 접속사와 [ ] 안의 말을 이용하여 문장을 완성하시오.

1 우리가 회의를 시작하기 전에 잠깐 쉬자. (start)

_______________ _______________ _______________ the meeting, let's take a quick break.

2 비가 그친 후에, 나는 자전거를 탈 것이다. (the rain, stop)

_______________ _______________ _______________ _______________, I will ride my bike.

3 어제 우리가 만났을 때 Ben은 나에게 그의 전화번호를 줬다. (meet, yesterday)

Ben gave me his number _______________ _______________ _______________ _______________.

4 우리는 어두워지기 전에 호텔로 돌아가야 한다. (get, dark)

We should go back to the hotel _______________ _______________ _______________

_______________.

5 Emma는 그 파티가 끝난 후에 주방을 청소했다. (party, end)

Emma cleaned the kitchen _______________ _______________ _______________ _______________.

이유, 조건을 나타내는 접속사 because / if

A 다음 ( ) 안에서 알맞은 말을 고르시오.

1 You will be late (if / because) you don't leave soon.

2 Everybody knows him (if / because) he is very famous.

3 If she (gets / will get) some rest, she will be fine.

B 자연스러운 문장이 되도록 알맞게 연결하시오.

1 The road was closed   •　　　•　ⓐ they will arrive early.

2 If they take the subway,   •　　　•　ⓑ if the weather is nice.

3 They will go to the park   •　　　•　ⓒ they made some sandwiches.

4 Because they were hungry, •　　　•　ⓓ because there was an accident.

C 다음 우리말과 같은 뜻이 되도록 접속사 because 또는 if와 ( ) 안의 말을 이용하여 문장을 완성하시오.

1 너는 너무 많이 일하면 피곤해질 것이다. (work)

You'll be tired ＿＿＿＿＿＿＿ ＿＿＿＿＿＿＿ ＿＿＿＿＿＿＿ too much.

2 우리는 좋은 소식을 들었기 때문에 기뻤다. (hear)

We were happy ＿＿＿＿＿＿＿ ＿＿＿＿＿＿＿ ＿＿＿＿＿＿＿ the good news.

3 그녀는 숙제를 잊어버려서 걱정스러운 얼굴이었다. (forget)

＿＿＿＿＿＿＿ ＿＿＿＿＿＿＿ ＿＿＿＿＿＿＿ her homework, she looked worried.

4 네가 액션 영화를 좋아한다면 이 영화를 재미있게 볼 것이다. (like, action films)

＿＿＿＿＿＿＿ ＿＿＿＿＿＿＿ ＿＿＿＿＿＿＿ ＿＿＿＿＿＿＿ ＿＿＿＿＿＿＿, you will

enjoy this movie.

5 그는 그의 다리 한 쪽을 다쳐서 축구를 할 수 없었다. (hurt, leg)

He couldn't play soccer ＿＿＿＿＿＿＿ ＿＿＿＿＿＿＿ ＿＿＿＿＿＿＿ ＿＿＿＿＿＿＿

＿＿＿＿＿＿＿.

POINT 08 명사절을 이끄는 접속사 that

A 다음 밑줄 친 부분을 어법에 맞게 고쳐 쓰시오.

1 We think <u>it</u> he is a genius.

2 <u>This</u> is clear that I did nothing wrong.

3 It is <u>a fact the Earth</u> goes around the Sun.

B 다음 문장을 가주어 It을 이용한 문장으로 바꾸어 쓰시오.

1 That she speaks three languages is amazing.

→ ____

2 That he often loses things is a problem.

→ ____

3 That they missed the meeting surprised everyone.

→ ____

C 다음 우리말과 같은 뜻이 되도록 [ ] 안의 말을 알맞게 배열하여 문장을 완성하시오.

1 그녀의 생각은 우리가 다시 시도해야 한다는 것이다. (try, that, should, again, we)

Her idea is _______________________________.

2 그들이 무언가를 훔쳤다는 것은 놀랍지 않다. (they, something, that, stole)

_______________________________ is not surprising.

3 그녀가 곧바로 사과한 것은 좋았다. (that, good, was, it)

_______________________________ she apologized right away.

4 나는 그가 Amy를 위해 파티를 계획하고 있다는 것을 안다. (is planning, he, a party, that)

I know _______________________________ for Amy.

01-03 다음 빈칸에 알맞은 말을 고르시오.

01

A: Why were you late for school?
B: I didn't hear my alarm, __________ I got up late.

① but ② when ③ so
④ because ⑤ that

02

A: Do you like baseball?
B: I like watching it, __________ I don't like playing it.

① and ② but ③ or
④ after ⑤ before

03

다음 빈칸에 알맞은 말이 바르게 짝지어진 것은?

A: Do you prefer skirts __________ pants?
B: I prefer pants __________ they are comfortable.

① and – because ② or – because
③ and – if ④ or – while
⑤ but – if

서술형

04-06 다음 우리말과 같은 뜻이 되도록 접속사와 주어진 말을 이용하여 문장을 완성하시오.

04

우리는 네가 밖에 있는 동안 저녁을 먹었다. (be, out)

→ We had dinner __________ __________ __________ __________.

05

그는 그의 엄마가 집에 오기 전에 숙제를 끝냈다. (come home)

→ He finished his homework __________ __________ __________ __________ __________.

06

내일 내가 시간이 있으면 조부모님을 찾아뵐 것이다. (have time)

→ I will visit my grandparents __________ __________ __________ __________ tomorrow.

07-08 다음 중 밑줄 친 부분의 쓰임이 나머지와 다른 것을 고르시오.

07

① When she saw me, she smiled.
② When are you going back home?
③ Be careful when you cross the street.
④ He was a soccer player when he was in middle school.
⑤ When you wake up in the morning, what do you do first?

08

① I felt great after I finished the race.
② I went shopping after I got off work.
③ What are you going to do after class?
④ He became a teacher after he graduated.
⑤ She began to learn French after she read the book.

09

다음 빈칸에 공통으로 들어갈 말은?

- It was his fault ___________ she got upset.
- I heard ___________ Logan is leaving the company.

① and ② but ③ or
④ if ⑤ that

10

다음 중 밑줄 친 부분을 생략할 수 <u>없는</u> 것은?

① We think <u>that</u> he is right.
② I didn't know <u>that</u> she was your friend.
③ <u>That</u> he lied is surprising.
④ He heard <u>that</u> I passed the exam.
⑤ I believe <u>that</u> everyone is unique.

11 - 12 다음 우리말과 같은 뜻이 되도록 주어진 말을 알맞게 배열하여 문장을 완성하시오.

11

비가 오고 있었기 때문에 우리는 집에 머물렀다.
(stayed, was raining, we, because, home, it)

→ _______________________________

____

12

너는 들어올 때 신발을 벗어라. (come in, you, take off, when, your shoes)

→ _______________________________

____

13 - 14 다음 중 어법상 <u>틀린</u> 것을 고르시오.

13

① We had fun while we were there.
② Both my friend and I liked the dish.
③ Write it down before you forget it.
④ I will buy either the shirt and the skirt.
⑤ Wash your hands after you go to the bathroom.

14

① We hope that she is doing well.
② I don't think he is honest with you.
③ I will help you if you will ask me.
④ She had no money, so she walked home.
⑤ The problem is that I'm very busy now.

15 - 16 다음 문장을 우리말로 해석하시오.

15

It was lucky that no one got hurt.

→ _______________________________

16

He listens to music while he is driving.

→ _______________________________

13 전치사

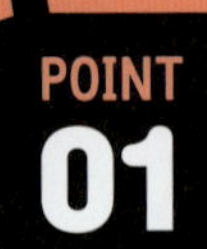

POINT 01 시간의 전치사 in / on / at

A 다음 빈칸에 들어갈 수 <u>없는</u> 것에 ✔ 표시하시오.

1 The bus arrives at __________. ☐ 8:30 ☐ midnight ☐ the afternoon

2 She moved to Seoul in __________. ☐ summer ☐ May 23 ☐ 2020

3 The school festival is on __________. ☐ July ☐ Friday ☐ October 12

B 다음 밑줄 친 부분을 어법에 맞게 고쳐 쓰시오.

1 The movie starts <u>in</u> noon.

2 We live <u>on</u> the 21st century.

3 The new restaurant opens <u>at</u> April 7.

4 Come to my office <u>on</u> five thirty.

5 He sometimes takes a short nap <u>at</u> the afternoon.

6 Did you meet your friends <u>in</u> your birthday?

C 다음 빈칸에 in, on, at 중 알맞은 전치사를 쓰시오.

1 I work ____________ night these days.

2 The store is closed ____________ Sundays.

3 Are you planning to travel ____________ the winter?

4 He didn't look very happy ____________ that time.

5 She graduated from university ____________ 2023.

6 ____________ Christmas Day, we went to my grandparents' house.

시간의 전치사
around / before / after / for / during / until / by

A 다음 우리말과 같은 뜻이 되도록 빈칸에 알맞은 전치사를 쓰시오.

1 정오 무렵에 비가 내리기 시작했다.

It started raining ＿＿＿＿＿＿ noon.

2 면접은 한 시간 동안 지속되었다.

The interview lasted ＿＿＿＿＿＿ an hour.

3 우리는 오후 5시까지는 공항에 도착할 것이다.

We will arrive at the airport ＿＿＿＿＿＿ 5:00 p.m.

4 너는 방학 동안 무엇을 했니?

What did you do ＿＿＿＿＿＿ the vacation?

5 그녀는 저녁 전에 숙제를 끝내지 않았다.

She didn't finish her homework ＿＿＿＿＿＿ dinner.

B 다음 우리말과 같은 뜻이 되도록 전치사와 [ ] 안의 말을 이용하여 문장을 완성하시오.

1 그들은 점심 식사 후 공원에 갔다. (lunch)

They went to the park ＿＿＿＿＿＿ ＿＿＿＿＿＿.

2 그는 그 회의 동안 아무 말도 하지 않았다. (meeting)

He didn't say anything ＿＿＿＿＿＿ ＿＿＿＿＿＿ ＿＿＿＿＿＿.

3 나는 다음 주말까지 기다릴 수 없어! (weekend)

I can't wait ＿＿＿＿＿＿ ＿＿＿＿＿＿ ＿＿＿＿＿＿!

4 그녀는 아침에 45분 동안 운동을 했다. (minute)

She exercised ＿＿＿＿＿＿ ＿＿＿＿＿＿ ＿＿＿＿＿＿ in the morning.

5 우리는 보통 정오 무렵에 쉬는 시간을 가진다. (noon)

We usually take a break ＿＿＿＿＿＿ ＿＿＿＿＿＿.

장소·위치의 전치사 in / on / at

A 다음 빈칸에 들어갈 수 <u>없는</u> 것에 ✔ 표시하시오.

1 I left my bag in __________.　　☐ the box　　☐ the table　　☐ their house

2 There is a fly on __________.　　☐ the air　　☐ that plate　　☐ the window

3 He is waiting at __________.　　☐ the theater　　☐ the bus stop　　☐ the ground

B 다음 빈칸에 in, on, at 중 알맞은 전치사를 쓰시오.

1 There's no bed ____________ my room.

2 Hang your picture ____________ the wall.

3 He forgot his book ____________ school.

4 They will travel ____________ Italy next summer.

5 She dropped her phone ____________ the ground.

6 We ate some delicious cake ____________ the party.

C 다음 우리말과 같은 뜻이 되도록 전치사와 [ ] 안의 말을 이용하여 문장을 완성하시오.

1 그들은 집에서 야구 경기를 보았다. (home)

They watched a baseball game ____________ ____________.

2 나는 꽃병을 저 책장 위에 놓을 것이다. (bookshelf)

I'll put the vase ____________ ____________ ____________.

3 우리나라에는 사계절이 있다. (country)

____________ ____________ ____________, we have four seasons.

4 그 식당은 이 건물의 5층에 있다. (fifth floor)

The restaurant is ____________ ____________ ____________ of

this building.

장소·위치의 전치사 near / over / under / behind / to

A 다음 우리말과 같은 뜻이 되도록 〈보기〉에서 알맞은 말을 골라 문장을 완성하시오.

〈보기〉　behind　　near　　over　　to　　under

1 열쇠는 신문 아래에 있다.

The keys are ______________ the newspaper.

2 그는 내 뒤에 줄 서 있었다.

He stood ______________ me in line.

3 이 근처에 병원이 없다.

There isn't a hospital ______________ here.

4 문 위쪽의 팻말에는 '환영'이라고 쓰여 있었다.

The sign ______________ the gate said "Welcome."

5 Mary는 과일을 사러 슈퍼마켓으로 갔다.

Mary went ______________ the supermarket to buy some fruit.

B 다음 우리말과 같은 뜻이 되도록 전치사와 [ ] 안의 말을 이용하여 문장을 완성하시오.

1 물은 그 다리 아래에 흐른다. (bridge)

The river flows ______________ ______________ ______________.

2 너희 집 근처에 은행이 있니? (house)

Is there a bank ______________ ______________ ______________?

3 나는 이 커튼 뒤에 선물을 숨겼다. (curtain)

I hid the gift ______________ ______________ ______________.

4 그 개울 위에 돌다리가 있었다. (stream)

There was a stone bridge ______________ ______________ ______________.

POINT 05 **장소·위치의 전치사 in front of / next to / across from / between A and B**

A 다음 두 문장이 같은 뜻이 되도록 빈칸에 알맞은 말을 쓰시오.

1 City Hall is opposite the department store.

→ The department store is ______________ ____________ City Hall.

2 The café beside the gym is very popular.

→ The café ______________ ____________ the gym is very popular.

3 I was sitting behind a tall man at the theater.

→ A tall man was sitting ____________ ______________ ____________ me at the theater.

4 Who is the girl in the middle of Jack and Emma?

→ Who is the girl ____________ Jack ____________ Emma?

B 다음 우리말과 같은 뜻이 되도록 전치사와 [ ] 안의 말을 이용하여 문장을 완성하시오.

1 그의 맞은편에 있는 여자아이는 책을 읽고 있었다. (he)

The girl ____________ ______________ ____________ was reading a book.

2 이 건물 앞에 차를 주차하면 안 됩니다. (building)

You can't park your car ____________ ______________ ____________ ____________

______________ .

3 그녀의 개는 그 문 옆에서 참을성 있게 기다렸다. (door)

Her dog waited patiently ____________ ______________ ____________ .

C 다음 우리말과 같은 뜻이 되도록 [ ] 안의 말을 알맞게 배열하여 문장을 완성하시오.

1 우리 집은 라디오 방송국 맞은편에 있다. (is, the radio station, from, my house, across)

____

2 그녀는 Charlie와 나 사이로 공을 던졌다. (Charlie, threw, me, and, she, the ball, between)

____

3 공연장 앞에 십 대 아이들이 서 있다. (front, some teenagers, of, the concert hall, in, are standing)

____

기타 전치사 for / with / by / about / from A to B

A 다음 우리말과 같은 뜻이 되도록 빈칸에 알맞은 전치사를 쓰시오.

1 그는 칼로 상자를 열었다.

He opened the box ______________ a knife.

2 그들은 파리에서 기차로 도착했다.

They arrived ______________ train from Paris.

3 우리는 그 프로젝트에 대해 회의를 했다.

We had a meeting ______________ the project.

4 그녀는 피아노 대회를 위해 연습하고 있다.

She is practicing ______________ the piano competition.

5 그 식당의 직원들은 3시부터 5시까지 휴식을 취한다.

The restaurant's workers take a break ______________ three ______________ five.

B 다음 우리말과 같은 뜻이 되도록 전치사와 [ ] 안의 말을 이용하여 문장을 완성하시오.

1 그 뉴스에 대해 이야기를 해 보는 게 어때? (news)

Why don't we talk ______________ ______________ ______________?

2 나는 내 친구들과 함께 보드게임을 할 것이다. (friend)

I'll play board games ______________ ______________ ______________.

3 그녀는 규칙을 어긴 것 때문에 미안했다. (break)

She was sorry ______________ ______________ the rules.

4 그는 영상 통화로 팀과 연락했다. (video call)

He contacted his team ______________ ______________ ______________.

5 공항에서 그 도시까지는 약 30km이다. (the airport, the city)

It's about 30 km ______________ ______________ ______________ ______________

______________ ______________.

01

다음 빈칸에 들어갈 수 <u>없는</u> 말은?

> A: Excuse me. Where is the national museum?
> B: It's __________ this park.

① in   ② next to   ③ near
④ between   ⑤ across from

02 - 03 다음 빈칸에 알맞은 말이 바르게 짝지어진 것을 고르시오.

02

> A: I will be in Spain __________ May 1 to May 8.
> B: Oh, really? Send me some pictures __________ text message.

① from – with   ② in – with   ③ from – by
④ in – by   ⑤ on – for

03

> A: Do you want to study together in the library __________ class?
> B: Sure! Let's meet __________ front of the library.

① around – on   ② around – at
③ after – to   ④ until – for
⑤ after – in

서술형

04 - 06 다음 우리말과 같은 뜻이 되도록 주어진 말을 이용하여 문장을 완성하시오.

04

> Amy는 프린터를 그녀의 책상 아래에 놓았다. (desk)

→ Amy put the printer __________ __________ __________.

05

> 그들은 대개 정오 무렵에 만나서 점심을 함께 먹는다. (noon)

→ They usually meet __________ __________ and have lunch together.

06

> Jacob은 그의 남동생과 함께 공원으로 갔다. (go)

→ Jacob __________ __________ the park __________ his brother.

07 - 08 다음 중 빈칸에 들어갈 말이 나머지와 <u>다른</u> 것을 고르시오.

07

① He found a $100 bill __________ the ground.
② We are going to the beach __________ Friday.
③ She woke up at seven __________ the morning.
④ Let's put the painting __________ the wall.
⑤ I always have dinner with my family __________ New Year's Day.

08

① I was __________ home today.
② Seoul is the best city __________ the world.
③ He usually goes to bed __________ midnight.
④ They can catch the train __________ the station.
⑤ She saw someone standing __________ the door.

09

- They are studying ___________ the math test.
- She worked at the restaurant ___________ ten months.

① to
③ from
⑤ about

② for
④ by

10

- Harry lived ___________ Boston for five years.
- My mother put the cake ___________ the box.

① in
③ with
⑤ under

② at
④ on

서술형

11-13 다음 우리말과 같은 뜻이 되도록 주어진 말을 알맞게 배열하여 문장을 완성하시오.

11

해가 산 위로 떠올랐다.
(rose, the, over, sun, mountain, the)

→ ___________________________________

12

한국은 중국과 일본 사이에 있다.
(and, Japan, is, Korea, between, China)

→ ___________________________________

13

너희 학교 근처에 체육관이 있니?
(there, gym, a, near, is, school, your)

→ ___________________________________

14

다음 우리말을 영어로 바르게 옮긴 것은?

나는 내일까지 집세를 내야 해.

① I should pay my rent for tomorrow.
② I should pay my rent on tomorrow.
③ I have to pay my rent during tomorrow.
④ I have to pay my rent by tomorrow.
⑤ I have to pay my rent until tomorrow.

15

다음 중 밑줄 친 부분이 어법상 틀린 것은?

① Let's finish it <u>before</u> lunch.
② I run <u>during</u> an hour every day.
③ He sat <u>on</u> a chair near the door.
④ She first met him <u>in</u> the summer of 2022.
⑤ He told me <u>about</u> the change by phone.

서술형

16-17 다음 두 문장이 같은 뜻이 되도록 문장을 완성하시오.

16

Emily sat beside me in class.

→ Emily sat ___________ ___________ me in class.

17

There is a pizza place opposite my office.

→ There is a pizza place ___________ ___________ my office.

MEMO

MEMO